A THEORY OF THE INDIVIDUAL
FOR
ECONOMIC ANALYSIS

CONTRIBUTIONS
TO
ECONOMIC ANALYSIS

114

Honorary Editor

J. TINBERGEN

Editors

D. W. JORGENSON

J. WAELBROECK

NORTH-HOLLAND PUBLISHING COMPANY
AMSTERDAM · NEW YORK · OXFORD

A THEORY
OF THE INDIVIDUAL FOR
ECONOMIC ANALYSIS

JACQUES LESOURNE

Conservatoire National des Arts et Metiers
Paris

1977

NORTH-HOLLAND PUBLISHING COMPANY
AMSTERDAM · NEW YORK · OXFORD

ISBN North-Holland for this series: 0 7204 3100 X
ISBN North-Holland for this volume: 0 7204 0702 8

Publishers:

NORTH-HOLLAND PUBLISHING COMPANY
AMSTERDAM · NEW YORK · OXFORD

Sole distributors for the U.S.A. and Canada:

ELSEVIER NORTH-HOLLAND INC.
52 VANDERBILT AVENUE
NEW YORK, N.Y. 10017

Library of Congress Cataloging in Publication Data

Lesourne, Jacques, 1928–
    A theory of the individual for economic analysis.
    (Contributions to economic analysis; v. 114)
    Bibliography: p. 385.
    Includes indexes.
    1. Economics–Psychological aspects. 2. Economics.
I. Title. II. Series.
HB74.P8L45   330.1   77-7900
ISBN 0-7204-0702-8

PRINTED IN THE NETHERLANDS

INTRODUCTION TO THE SERIES

This series consists of a number of hitherto unpublished studies, which are introduced by the editors in the belief that they represent fresh contributions to economics science.

The term 'economic analysis' as used in the title of the series has been adopted because it covers both the activities of the theoretical economist and the research worker.

Although the analytical methods used by the various contributors are not the same, they are nevertheless conditioned by the common origin of their studies, namely theoretical problems encountered in practical research. Since for this reason, business cycle research and national accounting, research work on behalf of economic policy, and problems of planning are the main sources of the subjects dealt with, they necessarily determine the manner of approach adopted by the authors. Their methods tend to be 'practical' in the sense of not being too far remote from application to actual economic conditions. In addition they are quantitative rather than qualitative.

It is the hope of the editors that the publication of these studies will help to stimulate the exchange of scientific information and to reinforce international cooperation in the field of economics.

The Editors

To Odile

Time is limitless, and successive generations travel through only a part of it. Each of them passes on to the other its own heritage, increased and enhanced. This – and not the passage of the soul into a body other than the one it used to quicken – is the true metempsychosis.

Al Biruni (Xth century)

CONTENTS

INTRODUCTION

Il est plus facile de connaître l'homme en général qu'un homme en particulier.

La Rochefoucault
Maximes

Man is at the heart of economic science. So deep at its heart that, for years, generations of economists have been traumatised by this very fact. With the motto: 'Human suffering is not a matter for equations,' they have rejected any mathematical representation which could not convey mankind's unlimited richness and, with an attitude more philosophical than scientific, have discussed schools of thought and doctrines, scorning colleagues who were not afraid to attack the human fortress.

These very colleagues, the real founders of modern economics, approached the problem in a different spirit: they proposed the simplest representation of man so as to obtain significant economic models. They divided him, therefore, into parts: consumer and worker on the one hand, entrepreneur and capital owner on the other. The second half was easy to deal with, since profit maximisation appeared as an obvious rule in the Western countries of the 19th century. For the first half, they had to create the utility theory, that admirable theory which, with very few assumptions, makes it possible to build equilibrium theory, interest theory, optimum theory and cost benefit analysis. Born one hundred years ago, this theory remains almost unchanged in economic science, except for the fact that it has been submitted to a rigorous axiomatisation and considerably extended to cover uncertainty.

Unrelated or loosely related to this theoretical core, many partial attempts to represent particular aspects of human behaviour can be found in economics: for instance, to describe the individual's attitudes towards money in inflationary periods, or to propose processes of habit-forming. At the same time, other scientists try to replace utility maximization by adaptive models of limited rationality, or by weaker structures of multiattribute utilities.[1] But, in spite of the increase in pioneering papers in the last years[2] these efforts have not as yet had any great impact on economics as a whole, because they are not integrated in a coherent set of propositions.

Consequently, in the present state of economic science, the theory of the individual used by economists has been developed almost entirely independently from other human sciences. Economists have ignored the decisive progress made by these sciences in the last half-century. During these fifty years, ethology has shown the psychological continuity from animal to man; neurophysiology has studied the phylogenetical and ontogenetical aspects of the human nervous system, described its organisation and investigated the behaviour of bigger and bigger subsystems; psychoanalysis has introduced the concept of drives, unveiled the immense realm of the Unconscious, examined the progressive elaboration of personality; psychology has been concerned with learning, perceptual and emotional processes while, in its genetical tendencies, it has established the successive levels of concept building and intelligence development; sociology has been interested simultaneously in small groups and big organisations, looking also for simple representations of human behaviour; anthropology has tried to separate in individual psychology aspects related to a given culture and those resulting from human characteristics; finally, applied sciences such as marketing, organisation and methods techniques, management science have become interested in motivations, attitudes or behaviour of workers, consumers, executives, voters, etc. But what is fascinating in this extraordinary scientific explosion is that the paths of the various sciences converge.[3] Of course, we still have a long road before us, but we can imagine a time when we shall have at our disposal a satisfactory

---

[1] For adaptive models of limited rationality, see (where an asterisk indicates reference listed in 'other human sciences' section): H.A. Simon* (1957) and C.B. McGuire and R. Radner, eds., 1972, Decision and organisation, chapter 8, Theories of bounded rationality (North-Holland, Amsterdam); R. Radner (1975); R. Radner and M. Rothschild (1975); and L. Hurwicz, R. Radner and S. Reiter (1975).

For multiattribute utilities, see: selected proceedings of a seminar on multicriteria decision making, 1973 (University of South Carolina Press, Columbia).

[2] The reader will find references to these attempts in the last part of chapter 1.

[3] The reader will find references to this research in chapter 2.

model of man, conceived as a hierarchical, self-organizing system, built up progressively through the interaction of society and environment.

Economists can no longer ignore this situation. They cannot neglect the other countries of the scientific empire and build the foundations of their science on the present utility theory – an efficient but very raw theory. They have a choice of attitudes:

– Some take vociferous advantage of the deficiencies of economics to launch a severe and radical attack against an economic science inspired by "bourgeois" ideology. They propose to abandon it entirely and to build a new one based on the Marxian message. But they forget that science itself is a self-organizing system, influenced, of course, by surrounding ideologies, but still more oriented by the challenges resulting from its own development. We should try to avoid the error of the French economist who, soon after the second world war, began his lectures for beginners with the solemn declaration that Keynes's General Theory had reduced to nothing all previous economic thinking. Such an attitude now appears totally outdated. But there is still a tendency to reject the scientific models of the past in the name of the latest new discovery, rather than to enlarge these models and integrate them into more comprehensive structures.
– Other economists – and we share their views – believe that the most rapid development of a science will result from the elaboration of more general models, the old ones being special cases, just as in physics, the theory of relativity may, given known assumptions, be reduced to classical mechanics. A development of this kind, like the progressive construction of intelligence as described by genetical psychology, preserves past results, but integrates them in a broader framework where a rich harvest of new facts may easily be interpreted.[4]

Seen in this light, the purpose of this book becomes easy to understand. It is *to build a theory of the individual*:
– *adapted to economics* (i.e. retaining, among the discoveries of other human sciences, those necessary for a better understanding of economic facts, and of economic facts alone);

[4] We have discussed this problem in: J. Lesourne (1975).

- *integrating the propositions of the various human sciences,* or at least compatible with them;
- *containing, as a special case, the conventional utility theory* (which makes possible an easy generalisation of present results of economics);
- *describing real behaviour rather than offering optimal decision rules* (which excludes any discussion of rationality or of optimal aggregation of individual choices).

However, these four conditions leave unsolved a fundamental problem concerning the type of models to be used to describe individual behaviour. There is no doubt, as we shall see, that the various sciences tend to adopt a systems view of human behaviour. According to this view, a human being is characterized, at all times, by a set of goals and by aspiration levels associated with these goals. The individual's drive for activity, and the discrepancies induced by his environment between the levels to which he aspires and those he actually experiences, generate behaviour which seeks to reduce some of the discrepancies. In the process, new actions may be discovered or learned, aspiration levels may be adapted and new goals may even be created. Such a view implies successive time periods and stochastic processes. For this reason, it is well suited to economic models in two cases:

(1) in applied economics (or in operations research) when data is available to simulate the adaptive behaviour of individuals. Such simulations have been used to describe the adoption of a new product by consumers, the choice of portfolio by an investor, the change of prices set by big department stores, etc.
(2) in theoretical economics, when studying the asymptotic properties of stochastic processes.

Unfortunately, however, it is not adapted to theoretical general models when time is restricted to one period only, or the environment is perfectly well known. For these models, the only possible representation of individual behaviour is some kind of maximisation under constraints.

But the gap between the two representations is probably not as formidable as is commonly thought, if utility maximisation is considered as a kind of limiting case of adaptive behaviour, a case in which the individual can adapt perfectly and immediately. This explains why *most of the concepts we shall introduce can be integrated in the two structures, adaptation and maximisation.*

The book being intended for economists, we shall start with assumptions concerning time and knowledge of environment which practically impose maximisation under constraints. Later, the types of hypothesis envisaged will be more compatible with the adaptive approach.

To avoid any misunderstanding, our position on the matter had to be made quite clear from the start.

To sum up, the book seeks to propose *an integrated theory of individual behaviour, constructed for economics, taking into account as much as possible the results of the other human sciences, enlarging the utility theory and adopting mathematical representations suited to the assumptions made concerning environment.*

As a direct consequence of this programme, the work has been divided into two volumes, but each of them is self-contained.

The first volume begins with two chapters devoted to an analysis of the *present state of the theory of the individual:* on the one hand, in economics (chapter 1); on the other hand, in human sciences – neurophysiology, psychoanalysis, psychology, anthropology, sociology and management sciences (chapter 2).

The six remaining chapters present the theory itself assuming *a unique time period and perfect knowledge of environment.* In such models, each economic variable is entirely determined by the decisions of economic agents. In other words, during the unique period, the economy may be in a certain number of states described by different values defining allocation of resources, levels of production, consumption patterns. At the end of the period, the economy is blown up: individuals, industries, resources, disappear. The assumptions imply that the psychology of every individual is given for the period.

Chapter 3 enlarges the fundamental concepts of economics. This is necessary in order to represent in a unified way the various aspects of individual behaviour: the notions of commodities and firms are replaced by the more general concepts of resources, organizations and processes. Individual characteristics are introduced in chapter 4, and behavioural constraints studied in chapter 5. These two chapters contain all the elements needed for the integrated model presented in chapter 6. The last two chapters are devoted to applications of this model: applications to partial fields of economic theory (chapter 7) and applications to equilibrium theory (chapter 8). A short conclusion tries to establish the prospects opened by the book for new developments in economics.

The second volume will begin by chapters replacing the assumption of perfect knowledge of environment by the assumption that there is a probability distribution of the state of the economy, once the agents have taken their decisions. But a unique time period is still assumed.

Then, the theory will be extended to multiperiod models. This problem is much more interesting than in conventional utility theory, since it is possible to take into account learning and adaptive processes and to introduce the impact of environment on individual goals. Instead of being given, utilities become partly the result of endogeneous relations in the model.

Finally, it will be possible to give a tentative answer to the question of how to use the theory to describe, in macroeconomic models, the behaviour of social groups which change progressively in attitude and volume.

It is important to understand that the book is, in many ways, tentative in character. It hopes only to promote new research fields and to contribute to freeing economic theory from a situation where efforts to improve axiomatisation and to enlarge models are hindered by narrow, ingenuous representations of individual behaviour. In that respect, it may be a modest milestone on the road leading to a more realistic economic theory.

Chapter 1

MODELS OF MAN IN PRESENT-DAY ECONOMICS

*L'élaboration de toute économie mathémati-
que est subordonnée à la possibilité de sou-
mettre les goûts des hommes au calcul.*

Maurice Allais
Traité d'économie pure[1]

Introduction

As is usual for any scientific theory, individual theory in present-day
economics is composed of a simple core based on a few approximate
axioms and described in all elementary textbooks; of a central, strictly
coherent, theoretical corpus which develops this core and is commonly
used in research; and of a myriad unrelated, challenging papers,
scattered throughout economic literature.

This chapter will follow this ternary division closely, except that, for
precise theories, a double dichotomy (one period, several periods;
certain environment, uncertain environment) will introduce additional
subdivisions. Consequently, the following paragraphs will deal with:

(1) the core of utility theory,
(2) utility theory for one period and a certain environment,
(3) utility theory for one period and an uncertain environment,
(4) utility theory for several periods,
(5) recent developments in economic models of man.

[1] Maurice Allais, 1953, Traité d'économie pure (Paris).

There is nothing original or complete in this chapter. Its purpose is simply to discuss the psychological postulates supporting today's individual theory in economics, and to explore the main lines of research suggested by certain stimulating papers.

1. The core of utility theory

Traditional economics considers an individual consuming and working in an economy where the list and the characteristics of commodities are given. If i ($i = 1, 2, \ldots, n$) denotes the ith commodity, q_i the quantity of this commodity consumed by the individual ($q_i \geqslant 0$ for a consumption, $q_i \leqslant 0$ for labour services) and q the consumption vector with the q_i's as components,[2] the individual is supposed to choose, among the possible consumptions, the preferred q (or q's).

Such a formulation imposes a double modelling: the modelling of the feasible consumption set and the modelling of the preferences.

1.1. The feasible consumption set

Most frequently, it is assumed that commodities characteristics are compatible with any consumption vector q in $Q = \prod_i \mathbf{R}^{\varepsilon_i}$ (where $\varepsilon_i = +$ for a consumption and $-$ for a labour service), which means that quantity can be biunivocally associated with real numbers (positive or negative). Among other things, it implies that consumptions are indefinitely divisible. This may be called a *Euclidian assumption*.

In addition, it is generally admitted that the only constraint limiting consumption possibilities is the income constraint. If p_i denotes the price, supposed fixed and given, of the ith commodity and r the individual income (excluding the income obtained in exchange of labour services), any feasible consumption vector must be such that:

$$\sum_i p_i q_i \leqslant r, \tag{1.1}$$

which defines a set S in $\mathbf{R}^n$. (1.1) may be called the *income constraint assumption*.

---

[2] The consumption vector will also be called a commodity bundle.

Hence, the feasible consumption set is the *budget set B:*

$$B = Q \cap S. \tag{1.2}$$

1.2. The preferences

With differences depending on the authors, individual preferences are more or less supposed to have a certain number of properties, well known to all beginners in economics (completeness, transitivity, desirability or monotonicity, convexity, continuity).

If preferences satisfy these conditions, there exists a continuous, monotone, strictly concave mapping of Q into $\mathbf{R}^+$ which defines an ordinal *utility function U(q)*.

Convexity implies another important property, the existence of which is necessary to rule out lexicographic utilities:

Substitutability: For any consumption bundle, if one consumption is slightly decreased, it is always possible to find an equivalent consumption bundle by slightly increasing the level of any other consumption, all remaining consumptions being unchanged.

Having thus introduced ordinal utility functions, classical economists have studied their properties by psychological introspection. Assuming that $U(q)$ is twice differentiable, they have considered the *marginal utilities* $\partial U/\partial q_i$ and the second derivatives $\partial^2 U/\partial q_i^2$ and examined their behaviour.[3]

The central problem of individual economics is then *to find the consumption vectors q which maximize U on the budget set B.*

Under the preceding assumptions, q is unique and satisfies the following $(n + 1)$ conditions if U is differentiable:

$$\sum_i p_i q_i = r \quad \text{(the totality of income is consumed),} \tag{1.3}$$

$$\partial U/\partial q_i - \lambda p_i = 0 \quad \text{if } q_i > 0 \text{ (for a consumption),} \tag{1.4}$$

$$q_i < 0 \text{ (for labour services),}$$

$$\partial U/\partial q_i - \lambda p_i \leqslant 0 \quad \text{if } q_i = 0, \tag{1.5}$$

the $(n + 1)$ unknowns being the q_i's and the positive Lagrange multiplier λ.

---

[3] The subject is treated in depth in Maurice Allais (1953) and P.A. Samuelson (1948).

It is important, at this stage, to list and discuss the main assumptions, implicit or explicit, which stand behind the present theory. Such an attempt will be enlightening in showing how economists may forget the considerable number of assumptions incorporated in their simplest models.

H1: *One period and a certain environment.*

H2: *Role unicity.* The individual consumes or provides labour, but all the other aspects of his life are without importance for the problem studied. This is a dangerous assumption. A human being is an entity. He cannot consume and offer labour without being a family member, a voter, a union member, without taking decisions on behalf of organizations as an executive, a foreman, a clerk, etc.

H3: *Stability of commodities*, their list and their characteristics being given. This is a very strong hypothesis since firms frequently launch new products and constantly modify the characteristics of old ones.

H4: *Euclidian consumptions.* For any commodity, all the possible consumptions can be associated with the points of a real half-line. Though it is obviously wrong, since some consumptions can only take a few integer values (like the number of automobiles used), this simplifying assumption is probably not as far-reaching as is commonly thought.

H5: *Existence of preferences.* The individual expresses given preferences among *some*, at least, of the possible consumptions offered to him. This hypothesis rules out a whole range of phenomena: there are individuals who, at times, have difficulty in choosing. For others, preferences fluctuate according to an ephemeral mood.

H6: *Independence of preferences.* The social group, other members of the family, friends, advertising cannot influence an individual's preferences. Such a concept of a personal "closed" utility prevents any analysis of habit formation in a society.

H7: *Selfishness.* The individual expresses preferences only for his consumptions. On the contrary, in real life, individual preferences often depend on other characteristics of the economy, for instance consumptions or utilities of others (the second-class railway passenger is jealous of his first-class fellow-travellers, the mother is ready to sacrifice her own consumptions to increase her children's share).

H8: *Completeness.* The individual is able to classify any two commodity bundles. This assumption is stronger than assumption 5. Frequently, an individual cannot express a preference between commodity bundles which are very different or do not correspond to an immediate possibility of choice.

H9: *Transitivity.* It is well known that some choices may not be transitive, though many examples given are not perfectly adapted to a unique period. There may be conflict situations between underlying dimensions that generate intransitivity, as for the Condorcet effect in group decision rules.

H10: *Monotonicity.* In other words, an increase in any consumption is always desirable. But satiation is a reality. When this point is reached for a commodity, the individual attaches no value to an additional consumption. He may even suffer a severe disutility if he cannot dispose freely of the useless commodity.

H11: *Substitutability.* Convexity implies that a linear combination of any two commodity bundles is preferred to the least preferred of the two, or to the two if they are equivalent. Substitutability means that it is always possible to find a commodity bundle equivalent to another by changing only two consumptions of amounts opposite in sign. But the individual may consider some consumptions as priority consumptions and take the other consumptions into account only to classify commodity bundles equivalent from the point of view of priority consumptions. Chipman, for instance, has rightly pointed out that no increase in income could have persuaded N. Khrushchev to change into a capitalist.[4]

---

[4] J.S. Chipman (1960).

H12: *Continuity.*   For the utility function to be continuous, the sets of elements preferred to *x*, or to which *x* is preferred, must be open in *Q*. One may imagine situations in which the existence of thresholds in preferences excludes this condition.

H13: *Perfect information on existing commodities.*   The individual knows the list of commodities. In fact, no individual ever knows all existing products. Good housewives spend a lot of their time in looking for new products. Fashionable women waste hours in boutiques to find the dress that suits them perfectly.

H14: *Perfect perception of possible choices.*   This assumption implies that the individual is fully aware of the real characteristics of commodities. He is not the victim of perceptual biases induced by advertising or insufficient information. As such, H14 has to be distinguished from H13, which is concerned with the knowledge of commodities existence; from H5, which states that individual have preferences on perceived choices; from H6, which rules out the possibility of influencing any individual's preferences once his perceptions are determined.

H15: *Income as the unique constraint.*   In reality, many other constraints limit the feasible consumption set. Time, ability, government or local regulations, etc. You cannot be a doctor without a degree. On the turnpike, speed is limited to 70 miles per hour. The rich bundle of constraints that bounds any individual's activity will be taken into account in a subsequent chapter.

H16: *Fixity of income and unit prices.*   But income depends on decisions taken by the individual in other roles (like the capital owner who has chosen a firm to invest his capital; the executive who has received stock options from his firm; the worker paid partly in productivity bonuses, etc.). Unit prices depend on quantities (for instance, when a fixed cost is incurred to have access to consumption).

H17: *Perfect information on prices.*   Even if the environment is certain, the individual may know only imperfectly the prices offered by producers. In everyday life, an experienced housewife has to spend time comparing the differences in prices for the same goods in various shops.

H18: *Perfect computational abilities.* Using the information at hand, the individual is able, immediately and without cost, to determine the preferred consumption bundle. How different things are in real life! The individual proceeds through trial and error. After a long period of routine, luck or necessity, he experiences a new consumption and adopts it (like the child that thought he did not like mushrooms, etc.). This fact may appear trivial, for ordinary consumptions. But how much more serious it is for marriage, choice of a career, the education of children, the strategic investments of a firm!

Obviously, the above eighteen assumptions are of unequal importance. But the fact remains: *very many essential economic phenomena are ruled out by the elementary utility theory.*

Modern abstract and precise theoretical developments have considerably improved the preceding theory; but they have not fundamentally changed the validity of the statement, since they have not really been concerned with the relaxation of assumptions 2, 3, 6 and 13 to 18. Nevertheless, they make a very good starting point for new research.

2. Utility theory for one period and a certain environment

As it has been built up in the last thirty years by numerous economists, this theory generalizes, on three points, the elementary theory of the prewar generations:

(1) It deals with a "deciding entity" – individual, committee, board, organisation – and assumes that the behaviour of this entity will respect a certain number of precise axioms. Hence, an enlargement and a danger: an enlargement, since the field of application is no longer limited to individual consumption; a danger, because it is not always clear *whether one is trying to describe real behaviour or to define norms of rational decisions.*
(2) The deciding entity expresses preferences on elements whose nature is not limited and which may be "alternatives, consequences, commodity bundles, cas flows, systems, allocations, inventory policies, strategies, and so forth." [5]

---

[5] P.C. Fishburn (1970).

(3) The presentation uses the much more convenient language of modern mathematical analysis. However, minor differences may exist from one text to another, on the wording of axioms and on the scope of proved theorems.

Our purpose here is not to present this theory, since it can be found in many textbooks, but to discuss its limitations for economics. So, we shall refer mainly to Fishburn's (1970) recent and complete synthesis, while retaining a certain number of comments due to Chipman.[6] Conditions of existence for ordinal utility functions, for cardinal utility functions and for additive utilities will be reviewed in the first three paragraphs, while the last will deal with weaker choice structures.

2.1. Conditions of existence for ordinal utility functions

Assuming that the individual expresses preferences on elements x of a given set X, we write:

$$x < y \quad \text{or} \quad x R y \quad \text{(for any } x \in X, y \in X\text{)},$$

iff y is preferred to x and not equivalent to it (strictly preferred). R is a binary relation on X.

Then, when X is uncountable,[7] the introduction of ordinal utility functions rests on two assumptions.

Assumption 1. *The individual's strict preference relation is a weak order.*[8]

If R is a weak order, it is well known that it is possible to partition X into equivalence classes x' and to introduce the set X' of these equivalence classes. On X', R induces a preference relation R' which is a *strict order.*[9]

---

[6] J.S. Chipman (1960).

[7] Assumption 2 is not needed when X is countable.

[8] By definition, R is a weak order iff: (1) it is *asymmetric:* $x R y$ implies (not $y R x$) for every $x \in X, y \in X$; (2) it is *negatively transitive:* (not $x R y$, not $y R z$) implies (not $x R z$) for every $x \in X, y \in X, z \in X$.

[9] A strict order is a weak order which is weakly connected: $x' \neq y'$ implies $x' R' y'$ or $y' R' x'$ throughout X'.

Assumption 2.   *There exists in X' a countable subset Z' which is dense with respect to R'.*

A set $Z' \subseteq X'$ is said to be dense with respect to a binary relation R' iff, for every $x' \in X'$, $x' \notin Z'$, $y' \in X'$, $y' \notin Z'$, such that $x' R' y'$, there exists $z' \in Z'$ such that $x' R' z'$ and $z' R' y'$. In other words, *there is always an element of Z' that is, as far as the preferences are concerned, "between" any two elements of X'.*

With these two assumptions, Fishburn and others have proved the following theorem.

Theorem 1.   *When X is uncountable, if assumptions 1 and 2 are valid, there exists a real-valued function u on X such that: $x < y$ implies $u(x) < u(y)$ and reciprocally.*

Unfortunately, assumption 2 has no intuitive appeal. It hides, in fact, two different concepts, so that ordinal utility theory supposes, as Chipman as shown, three basic concepts:

(1) *a concept of order* which includes the ideas of completeness and transitivity. Without assumptions of this kind, individual choices would not exist for some pairs or would be cyclical for some triples (i.e. one would have $x < y$, $y < z$, $z < x$ for some $x \in X$, $y \in X$, $z \in X$).
(2) *a concept of density of possible choices* which insures the existence of a "great number" of possibilities and excludes the existence of a choice preferred to (or less desired than) all others. In elementary theory, this concept appears in the Euclidian and in the monotonicity assumptions.
(3) *a concept of substitution* which rules out lexicographic utilities, i.e. cases where a utility function is replaced by a utility vector whose components are ordered like decimal numbers or words in a dictionary. In such cases, an element x is always preferred to another element y if it gives a higher value to the first component. If the values of the first component are equal, one considers only the second, and so on.

The concept of substitution expresses, very generally, the intuitive notion that, given a certain quantity of a commodity consumed by an individual, it is always possible to find quantities of other commodities large enough to compensate the individual for the loss of the consumption of the first commodity.

It is well known that theorem 1 and similar theorems only present necessary and sufficient conditions for the existence of ordinal utility functions labelling the equivalence classes corresponding to increasing preferences. But since the dawn of mathematical economics, economists have tried to describe the assumptions on individual preferences necessary to make utility measurable or cardinal. In that case, the utility function is *unique* up to a positive linear transformation.

2.2. Introduction of cardinal utility

A fourth concept has to be added to the three preceding ones to make utility measurable: *a concept of intensity* which postulates the individual capability to compare preference intensities among possible choices.

Thus, the preference degree of x over y can be associated with any pair of choices $x \in X$, $y \in X$.

If x, y, z, w are any four elements of X:

$$d(x, y) <^* d(z, w) \quad \text{or} \quad d(x, y) S d(z, w)$$

will mean that the individual prefers more strongly z to w than x to y, where $<^*$ and S are obviously binary relations on $X \times X$.

When $<^*$ is a weak order, it induces an equivalence relation $\sim^*$ on $X \times X$.

Whether X is countable or not, the main theorem on which cardinal theory is based has been expressed by various authors in slightly different forms (see Suppes and Winet (1955), Scott and Suppes (1958), Debreu (1960), Suppes and Zinner (1963)). The following presentation is adapted from Debreu by Fishburn (p. 84).

X is supposed to be a topological space with topology $\mathscr{C}$. The product topology is naturally attributed to $X \times X$.

Theorem 2. *If: (1) $<^*$ is a weak order on $X \times X$; (2) $d(x, y) <^* d(z, w)$ implies $d(w, z) <^* d(y, x)$; (3) (z_1, z_2, z_3) being a permutation of (x_1, x_2, x_3) and (w_1, w_2, w_3) a permutation of (y_1, y_2, y_3), the conditions: $d(x_j, y_j) <^* d(z_j, w_j)$ or $d(x_j, y_j) \sim^* d(z_j, w_j)$ for $j = 1,2$ imply $[\text{not } d(x_3, y_3) <^* d(z_3, w_3)]$; (4) With topology $\mathscr{C}$, X is connected and separable; and*

(5) *For every* $(z, w) \in X \times X$, *the sets of* $(x, y) \in X \times X$ *such that* $d(x, y) <^* d(z, w)$ *and* $d(z, w) <^* d(x, y)$ *are open in* $X \times X$; *then, there is a continuous function u defined up to a positive linear transformation such that:*

$$d(x, y) <^* d(z, w) \quad and \quad u(x) - u(y) < u(z) - u(w)$$

imply each other.

Let us consider the various assumptions of this theorem:

(1) The first one is an expression of the intensity axiom and the second one is a condition logically related to it: if the individual prefers w to z more strongly than y to x, it should be more "unpleasant" for him to pass from w to z than to pass from y to x (figure 1.1).

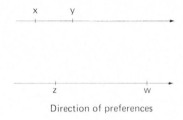

Direction of preferences

Figure 1.1

(2) The reader will recognize in assumption 3 a kind of substitutability condition, connected, however, with the existence of the intensity axiom. Examples are shown in figure 1.2, on which X is assumed to be the real half-line (2.1a) or the first orthant $\mathbf{R}^{+2}$ (2.1b). From these examples, the meaning of the assumption is clear, if it is admitted that the "distance" between consumptions is related to the degree of preferences between them.

(3) Finally, assumptions 4 and 5 concern the density of possible choices, the last one being necessary, obviously, for the continuity of u.

In his Traité d'économie pure,[10] Allais has clearly emphasized the psychological hypothesis leading to cardinal utilities (which he calls "absolute satisfactions"). He introduces:

---

[10] Maurice Allais (1953).

(1) The "*law of equivalent psychological degrees*" which is an intensity axiom: "Psychological introspection shows that, more or less consciously, any individual mentally establishes equivalences between successive increases in his consumption."

(2) The "*law of minimum perceivable thresholds*": "Experimental psychophysiology shows that, when a stimulus E is increased by ΔE, the increase is perceived only if it is greater than a value ΔE_p which may be called minimum perceivable threshold."

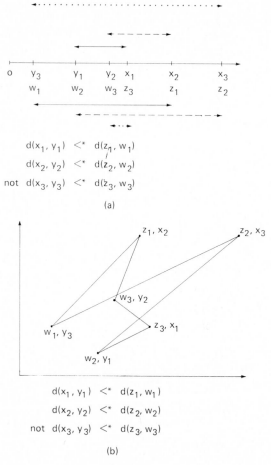

$$d(x_1, y_1) \; <^* \; d(z_1, w_1)$$
$$d(x_2, y_2) \; <^* \; d(z_2, w_2)$$
$$\text{not} \; d(x_3, y_3) \; <^* \; d(z_3, w_3)$$

(a)

$$d(x_1, y_1) \; <^* \; d(z_1, w_1)$$
$$d(x_2, y_2) \; <^* \; d(z_2, w_2)$$
$$\text{not} \; d(x_3, y_3) \; <^* \; d(z_3, w_3)$$

(b)

Figure 1.2

The first law enables him to introduce a cardinal utility as a family of functions:

$$v(x) = au(x) + b, \tag{1.6}$$

totally defined by an element of the family, a and b being two real constants ($a > 0$).

The second law determines the constant a, if the minimum perceivable threshold is taken as the unit of utility.[11]

But economists were confronted with the cardinal utility problem in another way, when they asked themselves whether the utility functions could be broken down into a sum of partial utility functions.

2.3. Additive utility theory

Sometimes, any possible choice $x \in X$ can be broken down into a sequence of elementary choices $(x_i)_{1 \leq i \leq n}$ (n finite) with $x_i \in X_i$ and $X = \prod_{i=1}^{n} X_i$.

For instance, x_1 may represent food consumption, x_2 time spent looking at television, x_3 number of square feet of the family house, etc. XIXth century economists often assumed that utility $u(x)$ could be written:

$$u(x) = \sum_{i=1}^{n} u_i(x_i). \tag{1.7}$$

Implicitly, they supposed that an increase in x_i had the same effect on $u(x)$ independently of the level of any x_j ($j \neq i$). In other words, they considered the elementary choices as *utility-independent*.

Hence, the question: under what conditions does *the structure of preferences insure the existence of functions* $u_i(x_i)$ *such that*:

$$x < y \quad \text{and} \quad \sum_{1}^{n} u_i(x_i) < \sum_{1}^{n} u_i(y_i), \quad x = (x_i)_{1 \leq i \leq n},$$

$$y = (y_i)_{1 \leq i \leq n};$$

imply each other.

---

[11] A recent and interesting application of similar ideas will be found in: Yew-Kwang Ng, 1975, Bentham or Bergson? Finite sensibility, utility function and social welfare functions, Review of Economic Studies, October.

J. Lesourne

Luce and Debreu[12] have both presented a general answer to this question. Their theorems introduce a very strong condition which implies simultaneously cardinal utility and additivity of partial utilities.[13]

We shall call it a condition of *certainty independence* to avoid any confusion with the independence condition commonly introduced in uncertain environments.

Figure 1.3 is a summary of the preceding discussion. This figure puts an end to the presentation of the "corps de bataille" of utility theory for one period and a certain environment. Its strength and weaknesses are obvious: its strength lies in the mathematical rigour of axioms and theorems and the exploration in depth of the consequences of behavioural assumptions; its weakness is that too heavy a weight is laid on rationality, rather than on the description of real behaviours in existing economic systems.

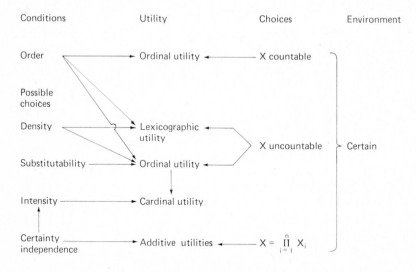

Figure 1.3

[12] G. Debreu (1960) and R.D. Luce (1966).
[13] This condition is the following: Suppose $X = \prod_{i=1}^{n} X_i$, $n \geqslant 3$, $<$ on X being a weak order, then: if, for each i, (x_i, z_i) is a permutation of (y_i, w_i), $x < y$ or $x \sim y$ imply [not $z < w$] for any $x \in X$, $y \in X$, $z \in X$, $w \in X$.

This accounts for the interest of studies made on choice structures that are weaker than the weak order.

2.4. Weaker choice structures

Utility theory presented so far rests mainly on the hypothesis that the strict preference relation is a weak order. Such a postulate assumes transitivity and admits two types of situations only for a pair of elements of X: strict preference or indifference.

In recent years, scientists have frequently had to recognize in applied studies that executives have to consider decisions whose consequences are multiple and difficult to compare: choice of an urban development plan in a historic city, allocation of research funds between scientific disciplines, etc. In such cases, it is impossible to assume completeness and transitivity from the start. Nevertheless, it is feasible to enumerate *dimensions (each dimensions corresponding to a type of consequence) and to postulate a strict order on each dimension.*

For instance, B. Roy [14] quotes some of the dimensions found in the study of a new suburban highway through a forest: the investment cost, the yearly maintenance cost, the increase in traffic capacity, the users' time savings, the surface of spoiled forests, the number of inhabitants subjected to nuisances, the degree of consistency with the urban development plan, the gain or loss of favourable votes from the surrounding districts in future elections for the politicians involved in the decision, etc.

Then, if n is the number of dimensions $(1 \leqslant i \leqslant n)$, with each $x \in X$ is associated a utility vector:

$$u(x) = [u_1(x), \ldots, u_i(x), \ldots, u_n(x)], \tag{1.8}$$

$u_i(x)$ being an evaluation of x along dimension i.

But the problem of comparing vectors $u(x)$ remains. Even if completeness and transitivity are refused, there is still, nevertheless, the possibility of exploring weaker choice structures. Obviously, these structures may be defined either on the elements u of the set of feasible utility vectors, or directly on the elements x of X. We shall adopt this second solution, which is more in line with the preceding developments.

---

[14] B. Roy has made important contributions in multicriteria decision making. See, for instance, Roy (1973).

Let us now assume that *between some* $x \in X$, there exists a strict preference relation (R or $<$) and let us consider stronger and stronger properties of that relation:

(1) R is a *suborder* iff, for every $x \in X$, not $x < x$ and for every finite sequence $x_i \in X$ ($0 \leqslant i \leqslant n$), $x_0 < x_1 < \ldots < x_n$ implies [not $x_n < x_0$]. In other words, a suborder is not *complete* and it may be impossible to compare many pairs x, y. Also, it is not *transitive* since $x_0 < x_1 < x_2$ does not imply $x_0 < x_2$ but [not $x_2 < x_0$], which means that two cases are possible: x_2 and x_0 cannot be compared, x_2 is preferred or judged equivalent to x_0.

(2) R is a *partial order* iff, for every $x \in X$, not $x < x$ and for every $x \in X$, $y \in X$, $z \in X$, $x < y$ and $y < z$ imply $x < z$. Such an order is partial since many pairs are not comparable, but strict preferences are, when they do exist, transitive. In such a case, four situations may prevail between two elements x, y of X:

(a) $x < y$,
(b) $y < x$,
(c) $x \approx y$, the relation $\approx$ meaning that, for any $z \in X$, (not $x < z$, not $z < x$) and (not $y < z$, not $z < x$) imply each other. Any element not comparable to x is not comparable to y and reciprocally. Since not $x < x$, x *and* y *are not comparable.*
(d) not $x < y$, not $y < x$, not $x \approx y$. There exists in X elements comparable to x and not to y and vice versa.

In X, the subsets of elements x, y such that $x \approx y$ are equivalence classes and *the assumption that R is a strict partial order coupled with assumption 2 of section 2.1 is sufficient to imply the existence of a utility function such that:*

$$x < y \Rightarrow u(x) < u(y),$$
$$x \approx y \Rightarrow u(x) = u(y),$$

the reciprocal being, in the two cases, untrue.

(3) R is *a semitransitive order* iff it is a partial order and satisfies the following assumption: for all

$$x \in X, \ y \in X, \ z \in X, \ w \in X : (x < y, y < z) \Rightarrow (x < w \text{ or } w < z).$$

Figure 1.4 helps to understand the assumption: if $x < y < z$, any element w is either strictly preferred to x, the least preferred element of the sequence, or less preferred than z, the most preferred element of the sequence.

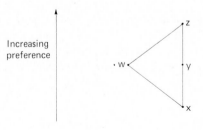

Figure 1.4

The idea of a *threshold* begins to appear, w being comparable to the farthest element.

(4) R is an *interval* iff it is a partial order and satisfies the following assumption: for all

$$x \in X, \, y \in X, \, z \in X, \, w \in X : (x < y, z < w) \Rightarrow (x < w \text{ or } z < y).$$

In other words, if one considers the two preferred elements of any two ordered pairs (y and w), one of them is necessarily preferred to the worst element of the other pair. Translation: if the individual is able to separate x from y, and z from w (and to order them), then he must be able to separate either x from w or z from y, i.e. to order the pair corresponding to the bigger interval between two elements belonging initially to different pairs. Figure 1.5 represents the four elements. One of the diagonals must correspond to a strict preference.

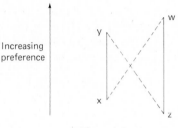

Figure 1.5

When R is an interval and when the set X' of equivalence classes induced by ≈ is countable, two real-valued functions u and σ exist on X, so that:

$$x < y \quad and \quad u(x) + \sigma(x) < u(y)$$

imply each other for any $x \in X$, $y \in X$. *For any* $x \in X$, $\sigma(x) > 0$.

$\sigma(x)$ represents a threshold: x and y are only comparable if the difference between their utilities is greater than the threshold.

(5) *R* is a *semiorder* iff it is simultaneously an interval and a semi-transitive order.

When R is a semiorder and when the set X' of equivalence classes induced by ≈ is countable, a real-valued function u exists on X, so that: x < y and u(x) + a < u(y) imply each other for any $x \in X$, $y \in X$, *a being a positive constant.*

For a semiorder, the threshold is independent from x.

A strict preference relation R may not be a semiorder, even if a constant threshold exists, when there are many underlying choice dimensions, or when dimension is unique but preferences increase and then decrease with consumption level. In this last case, two very different groups of alternatives may correspond approximately to the same level of utility. The individual may be able to compare with precision the alternatives of the same group, while there is some range of noncomparability between the two groups.

If we suppose a partial order (or a semiorder) to be complete, we define *a weak order*, which is an asymmetric and negatively transitive relation (see definition in section 2.1). This weak order becomes a strict order if for any $x \in X$, $y \in X$, $x \sim y$ implies $x = y$.

Figure 1.6 shows clearly the links between the various types of preference relations introduced so far. All these relations belong to the more general class of *outranking relations*, which recognizes that four situations may prevail between any two alternatives $x \in X$, $y \in Y$:

(a) *indifference* when the individual clearly and firmly accepts x and y as equivalent;
(b) *strict preference* when one of the two alternatives is positively preferred to the other;

(c) *weak preferencg* when one of the two alternatives is preferred to the other, both indifference and strict preference remaining conceivable;
(d) *noncomparability* when none of the three precedings situations prevails.

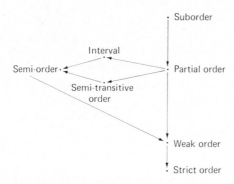

Figure 1.6

Traditional theory excludes the last two possibilities, but, faced with a choice-field X, an individual may, at a certain stage of the decision process, be unable to compare some alternatives (because the evaluations $u_i(x)$ are not yet precise enough, or because the classifications of the alternatives along the various dimensions are too antagonistic).

The definition of an outranking relation directly follows from this analysis: *a binary relation R on X is an outranking relation if, for any* $x \in X, y \in X$:

(1) ($x R y$ *and* $y R x$) *implies that the individual finds x and y equivalent;*
(2) ($x R y$ *and not* $y R x$) *implies that the individual prefers x to y, strictly or weakly;*
(3) (*not $x R y$ and not $y R x$) *means that the individual considers x and y as noncomparable.*

The types of relations studied so far are cases of outranking relations where weak preferences are excluded.

In practical problems, the introduction of weak preferences has an enormous advantage, since, as the information on the problem progresses, the individual may refer to more and more precise orderings R_i:

$$R_1 \subset R_2 \subset R_3 \subset \ldots,$$

the inclusion meaning that, if $x\ R_{i-1}\ y$, there must be $x\ R_i\ y$.

Multicriteria decision research is a fascinating field, one of the really essential fields for applied systems analysis. Its interest for economic theory will depend on the possibility of introducing some kind of deterministic or stochastic mechanism generating, as a result of environmental stimuli, adequate series of outranking relations converging on a decision, since such a condition is necessary to insert a model of the individual into a model of the economy.

But, in spite of its limitations, it is a breath of fresh air in the confined space of conventional utility theory.

3. Utility theory for one period and an uncertain environment

Created after the second world war by Morgenstern and Von Neumann (1947), Marschak (1950), Savage (1954) and many others, this theory cannot get rid of a fundamental ambiguity: does it describe real individual behaviour, at least for educated people; or does it present rationality axioms that individuals willing to behave consistently should respect?

We shall have to discuss the axioms from this point of view, bearing in mind that in this book we are essentially interested in real behaviour.

On the other hand, the introduction of uncertainty means that the elements on which preferences bear must be specified. In an environment which is certain, individual decisions generate a unique set of consequences. Hence, preferences on consequences immediately induce preferences on decisions, and either decisions or consequences may be the utility function arguments. In an uncertain world, any decision generates multiple sets of consequences and preferences must be built on decisions out of the preferences for consequences, though these are the only ones corresponding to a psychological reality.

Following an established practice, we shall call *state of the world* any environment x which is liable to occur and of concern to the individual, whether or not it results from his decisions: bad weather next Sunday, the election of Valery Giscard d'Estaing as President of France, the result of a negotiation with a partner etc., X is the set of x.

The theory can then be split into two parts, depending on the existence or otherwise of "states of the world" probabilities given externally and known by the individual.

(1) Buying National Lottery tickets; taking out insurance policies; selecting dresses for a tour in Spain in the month of May – all these are examples of decisions taken with a reasonable knowledge of "states of the world" probabilities.
(2) Choosing the politician to serve when you are an ENA alumnus;[15] guessing the result of an election in the absence of polls; deciding which chapter to prepare for an examination – these decisions correspond to the second situation, where no probabilities can be estimated from measures of frequency.

The main results obtained so far in these two cases will now be briefly presented and analysed with reference to actual behaviour.

3.1. Utility theory when "states of the world" probabilities are given externally

One of the most general theorems proved in this case rests on five structure conditions and on four preference conditions (Fishburn, p. 130).

X is now the set of the states of the world x. A σ-algebra Σ on X is assumed to be given.[16]

$\mathscr{P}$ will denote the set of probability measures on Σ, P an element of $\mathscr{P}$.

The *structure conditions* are the following:

S_1. $\{x\} \in \Sigma$ for any $x \in X$. This condition means that a probability can be attached to any state of the world of concern to the individual. Obviously, this is a basic condition in the framework of the problem studied.

---

[15] ENA: Ecole Nationale d'Administration: a post-graduate State training school which provides the majority of France's top civil servants.

[16] A σ-algebra on X is a set Σ of subsets of X having the four following properties:

(1) $X \in \Sigma$,
(2) $A \in \Sigma$ implies $C_X A \in \Sigma$,
(3) $A \in \Sigma, B \in \Sigma$ implies $A \cup B \in \Sigma$,
(4) $A_i \in \Sigma$ for $i \equiv 1, 2, \ldots$, implies $\bigcup_{i=1}^{\infty} A_i \in \Sigma$.

S$_2$. For any $y \in X$, the sets $\{x \in X; x < y\}$ and $\{x \in X, y < x\}$ are in Σ. This condition means that, for any given y, there is a probability of the occurrence of a situation preferred by the individual, or of the occurrence of a worse situation. In a different context, this condition is very similar to some of the topological conditions of Debreu's theorem.

S$_3$. For any $x \in X$, $\mathscr{P}$ contains the probability measure P_x which attaches probability one to state of the world x. In other words, any state of the world can be conceived as an event which is sure to take place.

S$_4$. $\mathscr{P}$ is such that, for any countable sequence of P_i in $\mathscr{P}$ ($i = 1, 2, \ldots$), the probability measure:

$$\sum_{i=1}^{\infty} \alpha_i P_i,$$

is in $\mathscr{P}$, for any sequence α_i such that $\alpha_i \geqslant 0$ and $\sum_{i=1}^{\infty} \alpha_i = 1$. In common language, if the P_i's are possible lottery tickets, the composite lottery which gives the P_i's as prizes with probabilities α_i is also possible.

S$_5$. $\mathscr{P}$ is such that, for any $P \in \mathscr{P}$ and any $A \in \Sigma$ with $P(A) > 0$, the conditional probability measure $P(B \cap A)/P(A)$ is in P for any $B \in \Sigma$. In other words, the probability measure which assumes as certain the appearance of a set A of consequences, to which is attached a nonzero probability, is always considered possible.

Now, to introduce the *preference conditions*:

P$_1$. The strict preference relation $<$ is a weak order on $\mathscr{P}$.

P$_2$. For any $P \in \mathscr{P}$, $Q \in \mathscr{P}$, $R \in \mathscr{P}$, the condition $\{P < Q, Q < R\}$ implies the existence of two real-numbers $\alpha \in \,]0, 1[$ and $\beta \in \,]0, 1[$ such that:

$$\alpha P + (1 - \alpha)R < Q \quad \text{and} \quad Q < \beta P + (1 - \beta)R.$$

P$_3$. For any $P \in \mathscr{P}$, $Q \in \mathscr{P}$, $R \in \mathscr{P}$, the condition $\{P < Q, 0 < \alpha < 1\}$ implies:

$$\alpha P + (1 - \alpha)R < \alpha Q + (1 - \alpha)R.$$

P$_4$.   (P(A) = 1 and $y < x$ for any $x \in A$) implies $P_y \leqslant P$.
(P(A) = 1 and $x < y$ for any $x \in A$) implies $P \leqslant P_z$.

What can be said about the fundamental meaning of these four conditions?

(1) The *first* one is an old friend, an unavoidable axiom of *order*.

(2) To understand the *second*, consider the following example: P is a distribution which makes it certain that you are going to be killed in a car accident. Q gives you the assurance of not being killed while not receiving a long-awaited big inheritance. R adds to the assurance of not being killed the certainty of the big inheritance.

Without effort, it may be assumed that: $P < Q < R$. Condition P_2 states that there is:

– a probability α, distinct from 0 or 1, such that one prefers the certainty of not being killed, even without inheritance, to a lottery ticket offering death with probability α and life and wealth with probability $(1 - \alpha)$ (quite an obvious assertion, if α is big enough);
– a probability β, distinct from 0 or 1, such that to the certainty of being alive and poor is preferred a lottery ticket offering death with probability β and a wealthy life with probability $(1 - \beta)$. (In this case, the condition is not so obvious, but economists will reply: who will refuse to take the risk of crossing a street for several million francs?)

In this example, the real nature of condition P_2 appears: it is a *substitution condition*. When it is violated (see Hausner (1954)) a lexicographic order reappears. These first two conditions do not insure the existence of a utility function of $\mathscr{P}$ to R, because, as may be shown, they do not imply the necessary density of possible choices (Fishburn, p. 110).

But it appears useless to introduce the density condition explicitly because it is a byproduct of the other conditions.

(3) As is well-known, the *third* condition is very strong and has been constantly questioned by a minority of economists. With the same regularity, it has been justified by the majority on the basis of the following reasoning.

Admit that you prefer lottery ticket Q to lottery ticket P. Consider lottery ticket S, which gives you P with probability α and any other ticket R with probability $(1 - \alpha)$; and lottery ticket T, which gives you Q with probability α and R with probability $(1 - \alpha)$. It would be irrational not to prefer T, since it offers the same result R if the chance $(1 - \alpha)$ comes out and a preferred result Q if the chance α comes out.

So this condition assumes the acceptance of a breakdown of S and T into elementary lotteries, i.e. that the choices for the two events of probability α and $(1 - \alpha)$ are considered independently. In other words, it is *a random independence axiom*.

In his famous article written in 1953, M. Allais criticized the above reasoning.[17] He showed that many executives and civil servants considered rational did not behave in accordance with this axiom.

As Fishburn writes: "My understanding of the Allais criticism lies in the assertion that, even though the above way of viewing P_3 seems appealing, an individual's preference judgment between $P + (1 - \alpha)R$ and $Q + (1 - \alpha)R$ is properly based on a comparison of these two gambles in their full perspectives and not on a comparison of separate parts such as P versus Q. If we adopt this holistic comparison point of view ... then the status of P_3 ... is not as simple as the foregoing analysis would suggest."

Discussions on this conditions clearly emphasize *the difference in perspective between a theory of the individual that tries to be an adequate model of observed behaviour and a decision theory which looks for the axioms underlying consistent choices.*

(4) The fourth and last condition P_4 states, in its first part, that if the individual prefers the certain appearance of any x in a set of events A to a probability distribution Q, he must prefer to Q any probability distribution P attributing probability 1 to A. The second part is obtained when the preference order is reversed.

P_4 is obviously another type of independence condition.

This analysis strongly suggests that a fruitful field for research remains the experimental study of effective individual behaviour in uncertain situations (see among others A. Tversky (1975)). It justifies also the theoretical developments proposed in the second volume.

---

[17] See: M. Allais (1953, 1972).

The quotation is from P.C. Fishburn (1975). The text has been slightly adapted for differences of notation.

The main theorem follows directly from the four preceding conditions:

Theorem 3.   *Under conditions* S_1 *to* S_5 *and* P_1 *to* P_4, *there is on* $\mathscr{P}$ *a real-valued function u, unique up to a positive linear transformation such that:*

$$P < Q \quad and \quad u(P) < u(Q)$$

imply each other for any $P \in \mathscr{P}$, $Q \in \mathscr{P}$. *In addition, u is bounded on* $\mathscr{P}$ *and such that:*

$$u(P) = E(u, P),$$
$$u[\alpha P + (1 - \alpha)Q] = \alpha u(P) + (1 - \alpha)u(Q),$$

for any triple $(\alpha, P, Q) \in [0, 1] \times \mathscr{P}^2$. (The symbol $E(u, P)$ denotes the mathematical expectation with the probability measure P of the function $u(x)$ on X, this function being defined by the condition $u(x) = u(P_x)$.)

It is important really to understand what the preceding theory adds to the core of consumer economics (Lesourne (1964)).

Let $k(1 \leqslant k \leqslant p)$ be used to label the states of the world. The individual has the possibility of acquiring:

– *certain rights,* the unit of certain right $i(1 \leqslant i \leqslant n)$ giving access to a unit of commodity i for any state of the world.
– *uncertain rights,* the unit of uncertain right $j(1 \leqslant j \leqslant m)$ giving access to quantities α_{ijk} of commodity i when e_k is the state of the world.

If the individual buys q_i units of certain right i and a_j units of uncertain right j, he will dispose of:

$$q_i + \sum_j \alpha_{ijk} a_j$$

units of commodity i if the state of the world k becomes reality.

Under the conditions of theorem 4, if π_k is e_k's probability, the individual utility function can be written:

$$U(q, a) = \sum_k \pi_k u(q + \alpha_k a), \tag{1.9}$$

where q and a respectively are vectors with components q_i and a_j and α_k the $n \times m$ matrix $[\alpha_{ijk}]$.

At this stage, two possibilities of describing the market are opened:

(1) In *ex ante markets*, the individual is supposed to buy rights at prices p_i and p_j with his income r. If he cannot influence the prices, the following conditions are satisfied in a situation of maximum utility where $q_i > 0$, $a_j > 0$:

$$\sum_k \pi_k u_k^i / p_i = \sum_{ki} \pi_k \alpha_{ijk} u_k^i / p_j = 1/\lambda, \tag{1.10}$$

with

$$u_k^i = \partial u / \partial q_{ik} \quad \text{and} \quad q_{ik} = q_i + \sum_j \alpha_{ijk} a_j.$$

If we define a set of elements c_{ik} through the relations:

$$\pi_k u_k^i / c_{ik} = 1/\lambda, \tag{1.11}$$

the c_{ik}'s can be interpreted as the ex ante value of one unit of commodity i in the state of the world k. As a result:

$$p_i = \sum_k c_{ik}, \tag{1.12}$$

$$p_j = \sum_{ki} \alpha_{ijk} c_{ik}. \tag{1.13}$$

The ex ante prices of the rights are equal to the sum, on the different states of the world, of the values of the commodities to which they give access.

(2) *In ex post markets*, the individual only buys commodities when the knows the state of the world. Confronted with prices p_{ik}, having at his disposal an income r_k, he chooses consumptions q_{ik} so that:

$$u_k^i / p_{ik} = 1/\lambda_k, \qquad \sum_i p_{ik} q_{ik} = r_k. \tag{1.14}$$

But, *if a perfect risk-market exists*, he can always exchange 1 franc in state k against β_k sure francs, i.e. francs available in any state of the world. He can then replace his income distribution r_k by any distribution ρ_k such that:

$$\sum_k \beta_k \rho_k = \sum_k \beta_k r_k. \tag{1.15}$$

It is possible to show that his equilibrium position is then the same as on an ex ante market with:

$$p_i = \sum_k \beta_k p_{ik}, \quad p_j = \sum_{ki} \beta_k \alpha_{ijk} p_{ik}, \quad r = \sum_k \beta_k r_k, \tag{1.16}$$

which, with $c_{ik} = \beta_k p_{ik}$, insures the consistency of ex ante and ex post models.

So, to the eighteen hypotheses of elementary theory, expected-utility theory adds *three types of assumptions:*

– assumptions on the probabilities of the states of the world and on the perfect information of the individual about them and about the decisions available to him,
– assumptions on individual preferences,
– assumptions on the risk market, defining the rights available and the way in which their prices are established.

Among these assumptions, *perhaps the most treacherous is the one which admits implicitly that the individual cannot improve his information or invent new possible decisions to release the pressure of constraints and uncertainty.* Human reaction is conceived as a kind of passive adaptation. The expected-utility maximizing individual has paid for his excess of rationality by the ablation of his creativity centers! The very nature of any behaviour in an uncertain world may have been lost.[18]

3.2. *Utility theory when states of the world probabilities are not given externally*

In this case, utility theory starts with two possible formulations:

(1) In the first, due to Savage, the set K of the states of the world k contains all the environmental aspects independent from the decision taken by the individual. In other words, the individual cannot influence the chance of appearance of a state $k \in K$.
If a decision $d \in D$ is taken and if the state $k \in K$ appears, the consequence is an element $x(k, d)$ of the set X of possible consequences, or a probability measure $P(k, d)$ defined on X.

---

[18] For a criticism of this attitude, see François Perroux's (1975) stimulating book.

The theory tries to give a meaning: (a) to a subjective probability $p(k)$, expressing the individual's belief in k's appearance, (b) to the utility of a decision, utility defined as the mathematical expectation of the utilities of its consequences, computed with the subjective probabilities.

(2) In the second formulation, each decision has direct consequences and a state of the world is a couple composed of a decision and a consequence. It is no longer necessary to introduce separately and artificially a description of the world independent from the decisions taken.

The purpose of the theory is, then, to give a meaning to the subjective probability $p(d, x)$ of appearance of consequence x if decision d is taken, and to the utility of d expressed as the mathematical expectation of the x's utilities, computed with the probabilities $p(d, x)$.

Since it has been shown that the two formulations are equivalent, only the first one will be discussed hereunder.

As is well-known, the main theorem (Savage (1954)) rests on *seven* assumptions.

D is the set of decisions, X the set of consequences, K the set of states of the world. d, e, d', e' are elements of D; x, y, x', y' elements of X; k an element of K; A, B subsets of K. d_x will denote the decision that always has consequence x, independently of the state of the world.

P1. The strict preference relation $<$ is a weak order on D.

P2. If $x(d) = x(d')$ and $x(e) = x(e')$ on A, $x(d) = x(e)$ and $x(d') = x(e')$ on $C_K A$, then $d < e$ and $d' < e'$ imply each other.

P3. If $A \neq 0$, $x(d) = x$ and $x(e) = y$ on A imply that $(d < e$ for A given$)$ and $d_x < d_y$ imply each other.

P4. If $d_x < d_y$, $x(d) = y$ on A, $x(d) = x$ on $C_K A$, $x(e) = y$ on B, $x(e) = x$ on $C_K B$ and if $d_{x'} < d_{y'}$, $x(d') = y$ on A, $x(d') = x'$ on $C_K A$, $x(e') = y'$ on B, $x(e') = x'$ on $C_K B$, then $d < e$ and $d' < e'$ imply each other.

P5. $d_x < d_y$ for one pair $x \in X$, $y \in X$ at least.

P6. If $d < e$, there exists a finite partition on K such that if A is any element in the partition, then $x(d') = x$ on A, $x(d') = x(d)$ on $C_K A$ implies $d' \leqslant e$ and $x(e') = x$ on A, $x(e') = x(e)$ on $C_K A$ implies $d \leqslant e'$.

P7. If $d_x < d_{x(k,e)}$ for A given and for any $k \in A$, then $d \leqslant e$ for A given. If $d_{x(k,e)} < d_x$ for A given and for any $k \in A$, then $e \leqslant d$ for A given.

Let us consider these conditions one by one:

(1) The *first* is the traditional weak order assumption, but here this assumption must be made on the set of decisions in order to deduce simultaneously the individual preferences on consequences and the subjective probabilities.

(2) The *second* condition means that preferences between two decisions must not depend on the states of the world for which they have identical consequences. In fact:

– If A appears, d and d' on the one hand, e and e' on the other have similar consequences.
– If $C_K A$ appears, d and e on the one hand, d' and e' on the other have similar consequences.

Consequently, the preference order between d and e must be the same as between d' and e'. Obviously, this axiom is similar to the independence axiom in section 3.1.

(3) The *third* condition considers decisions d and e, which have consequences x and y if A materializes; and decisions d_x and d_y which have these consequences independently of the state of the world. It postulates that if d_y is preferred to d_x, e then must be preferred to d when it is known that A will appear, and *reciprocally*.

This axiom is obviously debatable, since one may have $d_y > d_x$ because the context in which x is more advantageous than y is not very likely to occur. But if A is precisely this context, it is reasonable to assume $d > e$ for A given. *Condition 3 is then a kind of independence condition between the appearance of the states of the world and the ordering of consequences.*

(4) The *fourth* condition is essential to the introduction of subjective probabilities. It considers two decisions d and e, each of which has only two possible consequences: for d, the first consequence appears when external environment A occurs, the second when A does not occur; for e, the first consequence appears when external environment B occurs and the second when B does not occur. If the first consequence is preferable, the individual who prefers e to d, must necessarily consider B more "probable" than A.

Consequently, he must order as d and e two decisions (d', e') having an identical first consequence when respectively A or B occurs, an identical second consequence when neither A nor B occurs; and if the first consequence is preferable to the second. Such an axiom looks reasonable, once the preceding one has been accepted.

(5) *Condition 5* is easy to interpret: all decisions with constant consequences cannot be equivalent. This axiom is necessary for the unicity of the subjective probability measure.

(6) The *sixth* condition is a *substitution* condition. Four decisions d, e, d', e' are introduced, e being preferred to d. What can be said about these decisions?

For any x, there is a partition of the states of the world such that if A is any element of this partition, decision e is preferred or equivalent to a decision d' having the consequence x when A occurs and the consequence $x(d)$ when A does not occur. Similarly, decision d is not preferred to a decision e' having the consequence x when A occurs and the consequence $x(e)$ if A does not occur.

In plain language, there is no consequence x so desirable (or so undesirable) that the individual chooses a decision which generates it (or eliminates any decision which generates it) *even if the probability of its occurrence is very small.* No x is so important that it is given absolute priority. As usual, this condition excludes lexicographic orderings.

(7) Finally, the *seventh* condition considers a subset A of states of the world and two decisions d and e. It states that e is preferred or *equivalent* to d for A given if one prefers to d any decision which has on all the states in A one of the consequences of e.

Roughly speaking, the above conditions reproduce the traditional assumptions of utility theory, plus a brand-new one: the notion of independence between the states of the world occurrences and the ordering of consequences.

The main theorem follows directly from the conditions:

Theorem 4. *Under conditions P_1 to P_7, if a binary relation $<^*$ is introduced on the set of K so that: $A <^* B$ and $d < e$ imply each other* *whenever* $d_x < d_y$, $x(d) = y$ *on* A, $x(d) = x$ *on* $C_K A$, $x(e) = y$ *on* B, $x(e) = x$ *on* $C_K B$, *then there is:* (*i*) *a unique probability measure* P^* *defined on the set of subsets of* K *such that:* $A <^* B$ *and* $P^*(A) < P^*(B)$ *imply each other for any* $A \subseteq K$, $B \subseteq K$. P^* *is such that:* ($B \subseteq K$, $0 \leqslant \rho \leqslant 1$) *imply* $P^*(C) = \rho P^*(B)$ *for some* $C \subseteq B$. (*ii*) *with* P^* *given, a real-valued utility function* u *on* X, *bounded and unique up to a positive linear transformation such that:* $d < e$ *and* $E\{u[x(d, k), P^*\} <$ $< E\{u[x(e, k)], P^*\}$ *imply each other for any* $d \in D$, $e \in D$.

Obviously, the binary relation $A <^* B$ means that the chance of occurrence of B is greater than the chance of occurrence of A.

In fact, the theorem simultaneously introduces a subjective probability distribution $P^*(k)$ and a utility of consequences such that to any decision d is attached the utility:

$$u(d) = \sum_{k \in K} P^*(k) u[x(d, k)]. \tag{1.17}$$

Savage's theory is one of the great monuments of modern utility theory, but it is subject to the same criticisms as expected utility theory when external probabilities are given. On another level, it establishes no links between subjective probabilities and objective probabilities when these exist and are known by the individual.

This last gap has been filled by various authors (Anscombe and Aumann (1963)) who have derived utility and subjective probabilities from axioms which involve external probabilities on condition that there is a sufficient overlap among consequences which are relevant for different states.

In that case, if an individual considers a decision d which generates consequence x_i with probability $p_i(d, k)$ when state of the world k occurs, the utility attached to decision d is:

$$u(d) = \sum_{k \in K} P^*(k) \sum_i p_i u[x_i]. \tag{1.18}$$

Savage's theory is a generalization of expected-utility theory when world probabilities are externally given. Hence, any broadening of the second theory will have, as a consequence, a transformation of the first. We shall have to examine this problem in the second volume.

Figure 1.7 is a natural complement to figure 1.3. It summarizes the axiomatic skeleton of expected-utility theory.

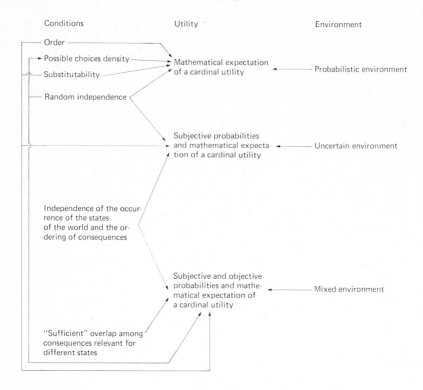

Figure 1.7

4. Utility theory for several periods

Some comments on the extension of conventional utility theory to several periods will make an ideal introduction to the presentation of the main concepts and theorems of advanced multiperiod theory.

4.1. Elementary theory

When a textbook introduces an horizon of n successive time periods $(1 \leqslant i \leqslant n)$ and considers a utility function:

$$U = U[(q_i)_{1 \leqslant i \leqslant n}], \tag{1.19}$$

of the corresponding *n* consumption vectors, maximising this utility under a discounted income constraint, it considerably strengthens the hypotheses of section 3, while adding to the list a major new assumption.

This assumption is, of course, *the acceptance of a fixed horizon* (finite or infinite), a hypothesis which imperfectly describes a world where death is in God's hands.

Among the other assumptions:

H5. *Preferences existence* is not acceptable if the possible acts of any kind offered to the individual are not introduced as arguments of the utility function, since the individual may, by his present acts, modify his future preferences on consumptions. For instance, an individual who decides to learn a foreign language will later be in a better position to appreciate the literary masterpieces in that language and will reallocate his consumptions in consequence.

H7. *Selfishness* implies that the individual is not concerned to bequeath his wealth to his children. Where is Jean de La Fontaine's "Le laboureur et ses enfants"?

H8. *Completeness* now becomes a formidable hypothesis: why should I order now two houses between which I shall have to choose in five years time? Preferences for future periods are not complete, but are progressively built by the individual as and when they correspond to an operational necessity.

H11. *Substitutability* means that it is always possible to replace a consumption decrease at one time by an increase at another time. But for some present consumption levels, you will not be alive to take advantage of this compensation in the future.

H13. *Perfect information on existing commodities* implies a great deal more than in the one-period case, since, to save information costs, the individual is satisfied, at each period, with the information necessary to enter the next period in a "satisfactory" situation. Information is looked for progressively as its usefulness increases and its cost diminishes.

H14. *Perfect perception of possible choices* rules out a whole range of behaviours which are explained only by a distorted perception of the future ("La cigale ayant chanté tout l'été...").[19]

---

[19] A famous verse from Jean de la Fontaine's poem: 'The ant and the grasshopper' where a grasshopper who has danced throughout the summer finds herself without food reserves when the winter comes.

H15. *Income as the unique constraint* is very difficult to accept, since the present markets for future commodities exist only partially and frequently make it impossible to exchange the promise of future commodities against the delivery of present ones! The same criticism can be made concerning H17 (Perfect information on prices).

H18. *Perfect computational abilities* misses the fact that the individual computes by successive approximations on limited horizons.

Unfortunately, the more serious deficiencies of elementary theory are not overcome by the new versions of utility theory. But hope, from various quarters, is at hand, as we shall see in the last part of this chapter.

4.2. *Recent concepts and theorems*

The interesting developments of modern theory generally assume that the individual is confronted with the same choice set A during any period. The combined choice $x = (x_i)_{1 \leqslant i \leqslant n}$ is then an element of $x = A^n$.

Koopmans and others (Koopmans (1960), Koopmans, Diamond and Williamson (1964)) have introduced the two essential notions of *persistence* and *impatience* for such choices. To present them briefly:

Persistence: A strict preference relation is persistent iff:

$$(x_1, \ldots, x_{i-1}, a, x_{i+1}, \ldots, x_n) < (x_1, \ldots, x_{i-1}, b, x_{i+1}, \ldots, x_n)$$

implies

$$(y_1, \ldots, y_{j-1}, a, y_{j+1}, \ldots, y_n) < (y_1, \ldots, y_{j-1}, b, y_{j+1}, \ldots, y_n)$$

for any i or j in $(1, 2, \ldots, n)$ *and for all n-tuples in* A^n.

At first sight, persistence looks very reasonable; If, in a certain context, the switch from a to b generates a preferred choice, why not accept that it also generates a preferred choice in a different context? But economists have learned to their cost that many axioms have consequences as contrary to intuition as they are appealing in themselves! Assume that the choices concern the successive countries chosen by an individual for his annual vacation. First consider the two following sequences:

Sequence 1: (Italy, ..., Italy, Italy, Italy, ..., Italy),
Sequence 2: (Italy, ..., Italy, Spain, Italy, ..., Italy).

Suppose that 2 is preferred to 1, which means that Spain is preferred to Italy for year i. Now consider the two sequences:

Sequence 3: (Spain, ..., Spain, Italy, Spain, ..., Spain),
Sequence 4: (Spain, ..., Spain, Spain, Spain, ..., Spain).

It is quite reasonable for the individual to prefer 3 to 4, since it offers some variety, as does sequence 2. Such behaviour is not persistent. This criticism is, of course, less applicable to *income streams*.

Impatience: A strict preference relation reveals impatience iff $a < b$ implies:

$$(x_1, ..., x_{i-1}, a, b, x_{i+2}, ..., x_n) < (x_1, ..., x_{i-1}, b, a, x_{i+2}, ..., x_n)$$

$a \sim b$ *implies:*

$$(x_1, ..., x_{i-1}, a, b, x_{i+2}, ..., x_n) \sim (x_1, ..., x_{i-1}, b, a, x_{i+2}, ..., x_n)$$

for any $i \in (1, 2, ..., n-1)$ and for all n-tuples in A^n.

The meaning of impatience is obvious: the individual prefers that a favourable event should occur earlier. As Fishburn writes (p. 90), "the reverse of impatience could hold in some situations for people who prefer to postpone favourable events, perhaps to increase their anticipatory pleasure...."

Persistence and impatience have strong and illuminating consequences when the utility function u is a sum of utility functions u_i attached to the successive periods and when there is just one bounded argument, for instance the one-period income r_i for each of these utility functions.

Persistence implies that u_i is an increasing function of r_i. Persistence and impatience imply that:

$$u_i(r) < u_{i-1}(r) \quad \text{for any} \quad i \in [1, ..., n] \quad \text{and any} \quad r.$$

A third and key concept, also due to Koopmans (Koopmans (1960)) is *stationarity* which makes it possible to give a remarkable expression to utility:

Stationarity: A strict preference relation is stationary on A^n, iff there is $e \in A$ such that, for any $(x_1, \ldots, x_{n-1}) \in A^{n-1}$, $(y_1, \ldots, y_{n-1}) \in A^{n-1}$:

$$(x_1, \ldots, x_{n-1}, e) < (y_1, \ldots, y_{n-1}, e) \quad and$$

$$(e, x_1, \ldots, x_{n-1}) < (e, y_1, \ldots, y_{n-1})$$

imply each other.

Stationarity means that there is a one-period situation e such that individual orderings do not change when this situation is experienced at the first period instead of the last, all other situations being postponed by one period.

Hence, the essential theorem 5.

Theorem 5.   *Under the conditions necessary and sufficient for additive one-period utilities and if $<$ is stationary on A^n, there exists a positive number λ and a real-valued function v on A, such that:*

$$x < y \qquad and \qquad \sum_{i=1}^{n} \lambda^{i-1} v(x_i) < \sum_{i=1}^{n} \lambda^{i-1} v(y_i)$$

imply each other for any $x \in A$, $y \in A$. λ is unique and v is defined up to a positive linear transformation.

This theorem shows that in order to introduce a discounted utility, at the individual level, it is necessary to add two major assumptions to the traditional ones of utility theory: *certainty independence and stationarity.* Heroic assumptions: man only infrequently accepts the independence of his situations at different times and he knows that his preferences will change in the future.

But, in spite of these defciencies, utility theory for several periods makes an excellent starting point for new developments.

Some readers may think until now we have been systematically negative. However, this is not our intention. The purpose of our criticisms is not to destroy, but to seek ways for improvement. Many economists have preceded us along this road, and it is fascinating to discover the pioneering work of some of them.

5. Recent developments of economic models of man

Let us begin with two remarks:

- It is often difficult to decide what is an economic or a noneconomic model of man. We have tried to present in this chapter the research mainly inspired by conventional economic theory, and in the next chapter the ideas which seem more in line with the concepts of other human sciences. Although arbitrary, such a division is necessary because of the immensity of the field.
- When one abandons the centre of any science to explore its outskirts, it is hard to insure that no major contribution has been forgotten. By its very nature, the search for scattered research is random. This section does not try to be exhaustive. Its purpose is rather to show that the *process of transformation of the formal central theory of individual in economics has already begun for some time* and that exist already many contributions which could be integrated in a more general theory.

Among many others, G. Katona and G.S. Becker merit special mentions, the first for his pioneering work (Katona (1951)), the second for his theoretical contributions (see references).

The substance will be divided into ten subsections, dealing respectively with:

(1) elimination of the transitivity axiom,
(2) use of special functional forms for utilities,
(3) new consumer-demand theory,
(4) introduction of additional constraints,
(5) alternatives to random independence axiom,
(6) life-cycle and human capital,
(7) consumer behaviour in a multiperiod random environment,
(8) change of utilities in time,
(9) acquisition and processing of information in time,
(10) bounded rationality models.

5.1. Elimination of the transitivity axiom

Recently, Sonnenschein (1975) has shown that the transitivity axiom is not necessary in order to prove the existence and continuity of demand correspondences. Even in such a case, individual behaviour can be interpreted as a constrained maximum problem (Shafer (1974)).

Let x and y be two consumption bundles in $E = \mathbf{R}_+^n$ and P a preference relation meaning that x is preferred or indifferent to y iff $(x, y) \in P$. Introduce the notations:

$P(x) = \{y; (y, x) \in P\}$ for the set of y's preferred or indifferent to x,

$P^{-1}(x) = \{y; (x, y) \in P\}$ for the set of y's to which x is preferred or indifferent,

$R(x) = \{y; y \in P(x) \text{ and } x \notin P(y)\}$ for the set of y's strictly preferred to x.

With these notations, the following two theorems can be proved:

Theorem 6. *Under the following axioms:*
(1) *Comparability:* For any $x \in E$, $y \in E$, either $x \in P(y)$ or $y \in P(x)$.
(2) *Strong convexity:* For any $x \in E$, $y \in E$, $z \in E$, $(x, z) \in P(y)$, $x \neq z$ implies: $ax + (1 - a)z \in R(y)$ for $0 < a < 1$.
(3) *Continuity:* For any $x \in E$, the sets $P(x)$ and $P^{-1}(x)$ are closed.
There is a real continuous mapping k from E to the real line satisfying:
 (i) $k(x, y) > 0$ *iff* $x \in R(y)$,
 (ii) $k(x, y) < 0$ *iff* $y \in R(x)$,
(iii) $k(x, y) = -k(y, x)$.

Theorem 7. *Under the conditions of theorem 6, for each positive price vector p inducing a budget set $B(p)$ there is $y^* \in B(p)$ such that: $k(y^*, x) \geqslant 0$ for any $x \in B(p)$.*

In other words, assuming comparability, strong convexity and continuity of preferences, for any budget constraint there is at least one consumption preferred or equivalent to any other feasible consumption. To prove this, the hypothesis of strong convexity of preferences, is essential.

If, for any $y \in E$, $p \in \text{int } E$, the function:

$$h(y, p) = \min_{z \in B(p)} k(y, z), \tag{1.20}$$

is considered, it may be shown that the preferred y^* can be obtained by maximizing $h(y, p)$ in $B(p)$, so that $h(y, p)$ can still be interpreted as a utility function, but as a utility function *depending on the price vector*.

Remark: For an individual with an ordinary utility function $u(x)$, the function $k(y, z)$ is equal to $u(y) - u(z)$ and:

$$h(y, p) = u(y) - \max_{z \in B(p)} u(z), \tag{1.21}$$

or

$$h(y, p) = u(y) - q(p), \tag{1.22}$$

where $q(p)$ is the indirect utility function.[20] It is obvious that the maximization of $h(y, p)$ on the budget set leads to a most preferred consumption.

The discoveries made in recent years in this already deeply ploughed field suggest that we have still a lot to learn about preference relations. Fortunately, the later developments of this book, which deal with substance rather than with the logical structure of individual behaviour, may be reshaped in looser axiomatic frameworks if new results are obtained in this direction.

5.2. Use of special functional forms for utilities

Since the birth of utility, a minority of economists has been trying constantly to build simple analytical utility functions which take into account the major observed econometric facts. In spite of the simplistic nature of these efforts, it is not without interest for what follows, to mention the last two species of this evolutionary tree[2] which have appeared.

The first, the *S-branch utility tree* assumes that the n commodities consumed are partitioned into S subsets of n_s commodities $(1 \leqslant s \leqslant S) q_{si}$ denoting the quantity consumed of the ith commodity of the sth type $(1 \leqslant i \leqslant n_s)$. The utility function U is written:

$$U = \left\{ \sum_{s=1}^{S} \alpha_s \left[\sum_{i=1}^{n_s} \beta_{si} (q_{si} - y_{si})^{\rho_s} \right]^{\rho/\rho_s} \right\}^{1/\rho}, \tag{1.23}$$

---

[20] The indirect utility function is the relation between the price vector (and the individual income) and the maximum utility feasible under such a constraint.

[21] In addition to the well-know papers of L.R. Klein and H. Rubin (1948) and of R.H. Strotz (1957), the basic articles are: M. Brown and D. Heien (1972); A. Kraft and J. Kraft (1975); A.P. Barten (1975).

where α_s, β_{si}, γ_{si}, ρ_s, ρ are constants and:

$$\beta_{si} > 0, \quad (q_{si} - \gamma_{si}) > 0, \quad \gamma_{si} \geqslant 0, \quad \alpha_s > 0, \quad \rho = 1 - (1/\sigma) < 1,$$
$$\rho_s = 1 - (1/\sigma_s) < 1.$$

Obviously, γ_{si} can be interpreted as *the minimal consumption of commodity* (*si*), so that U is equal to zero when any of the q_{si}'s is equal to its minimum. β_{si} can be considered as a "commodity-intensity" parameter, i.e. the larger β_{si} relative to β_{sj}, ceteris paribus, the more utility is yielded by $(q_{si} - \gamma_{si})$ relative to $(q_{sj} - \gamma_{sj})$. σ_s is an intragroup partial elasticity of substitution while σ is an interbranch elasticity of substitution. If one calls:

$$m_s = \sum_1^{n_s} p_{si}\gamma_{si}, \qquad \text{the minimum income spent on goods of subset } s \text{ for the price system } p_{si},$$

$$m = \sum_s m_s, \qquad \text{the minimum income spent on all goods for the price system } p_{si},$$

$$y_s = \sum_1^{n_s} p_{si}q_{si}, \qquad \text{the income spent on goods of subset } s \text{ for the price system } p_{si},$$

$$y = \sum_s y_s, \qquad \text{the income spent on all goods for the price system } p_{si},$$

the maximization of U, subject to the conventional income-constraint, can be carried out as a two-stage process. In the first stage, one maximizes the utility associated with the s group for y_s constant, which leads to the demand equations:

$$q_{si} = \gamma_{si} + \left(\frac{\beta_{si}}{p_{si}}\right)^{\sigma_s} \left[\sum_{j=1}^{n_s} \left(\frac{\beta_{sj}}{p_{sj}}\right)^{\sigma_s} p_{sj}\right]^{-1} \left[y_s - m_s\right]. \tag{1.24}$$

In the second stage, the utility obtained is maximised by inserting (1.24) into (1.23) for y constant, which leads to the demand equations:

$$q_{si} = \gamma_{si} + \left(\frac{\beta_{si}}{p_{si}}\right)^{\sigma_s} \left[\alpha_s^\sigma X_s^{((\sigma-1)/(\sigma_s-1))-1}\right]$$

$$\times \left[\sum_{r=1}^{S} \alpha_r^\sigma X_r^{((\sigma-1)/(\sigma_r-1))}\right]^{-1} (y - m), \tag{1.25}$$

where

$$X_s = \sum_{j=1}^{n_s} \left(\frac{\beta_{sj}}{p_{sj}}\right)^{\sigma_s} p_j. \tag{1.26}$$

For the S-branch utility tree, the Allen partial elasticities of substitution ($\sigma_{si,rj}$) between ($q_{si} - \gamma_{si}$) and ($q_{rj} - \gamma_{rj}$) are

$$\sigma_{si,rj} = \begin{cases} \sigma, & \text{for } s \neq r, \\[2ex] \sigma + \dfrac{1}{w_s}(\sigma_s - \sigma), & \text{for } s = r, \end{cases} \tag{1.27}$$

with

$$w_s = \frac{y_s - m_s}{y - m} \tag{1.28}$$

denoting the fraction of the disposable income spent on subset s.

"For the S-branch, the elasticity of substitution is the same at all points on an indifference surface independent of the level of utility. However, one should expect the elasticity of substitution to change as the quantity of commodities consumed changes, since its value is a measure of the ease with which one commodity is substituted for another utility remains constant. The *V-branch utility function* has all the properties of the S-branch system and also allows the elasticity of substitution to vary depending on the quantities of the commodities involved in the substitution ratio."[22]

Notations being identical, except for β_{si}, U is written:

$$U = \left\{ \sum_{s=1}^{S} \alpha_s \left[\sum_{i=1}^{n_s} \beta_{sii}(q_{si} - \gamma_{si})^{2\rho_s} + \right. \right.$$

$$\left. \left. + 2 \sum_{i<j} \beta_{sij}(q_{si} - \gamma_{si})^{\rho_s}(q_{sj} - \gamma_{sj})^{\rho_s} \right]^{\rho/2\rho_s} \right\}^{1/\rho}, \tag{1.29}$$

where

$$\beta_{sii} \geqslant 0, \quad \beta_{sij} \geqslant 0, \quad \sum_{i=1}^{n_s} \beta_{sii} + 2 \sum_{i<j} \beta_{sij} = 1.$$

[22] A. Kraft and J. Kraft (1975).

Obviously, the V-branch utility function is reduced to the S-branch function if $\beta_{sij} = 0$ for all i, j's.

For the V-branch utility tree, the Allen partial elasticities of substitution become:

$$\sigma_{si,rj} = \begin{cases} 1/(1 - \rho_s - v_s), & \text{for } s = r, \\ 1/(1 - \rho - v_{sr}), & \text{for } s \neq r, \end{cases} \tag{1.30}$$

where v_s is a function of ρ_s and of all β_{sii}, β_{sij}, q_{si}/q_{sj} within group s, and v_{sr} is a function of ρ and of all β_{sii}, β_{rii}, β_{sij}, β_{rij}, q_{si}/q_{sj}, q_{ri}/q_{rj} within groups s and r.

Interesting estimations of the S-branch and the V-branch utility systems have been made on the basis of econometric data, but this line of research cannot really enlarge the scope of representation of individual behaviour in economics.

Much more promising, of course, is the new consumer demand theory.

5.3. New consumer-demand theory

K. Lancaster (1971) is the best exponent of this theory in the English language; but similar thoughts have been expressed independently by French economists (Ph. d'Iribarne (1969, 1972), J.P. Dupuy (1974a) J. Lesourne (1975b)) and have certainly been latent in economic literature for some time.

We shall briefly sketch Lancaster's ideas here, pointing out some ambiguities in his work which will be avoided in the construction of chapter 4. In spite of these criticisms, new consumer demand theory represents a major step forward towards a more satisfactory theory of individual behaviour for economics.

Lancaster's book is based on two fundamental propositions:

"(1) All goods possess objective characteristics relevant to the choices which people make among different collections of goods. The relationship between a given quantity of a good (or a collection of goods) and the characteristics which it possesses is essentially a technical relationship, depending on the objective properties of the goods and, sometimes, a content of technological 'know-how' as to what the goods can do, and how."

"(2) Individuals differ in their *reactions to* different characteristics rather than in their assessment of the characteristics content of various goods collections. It is the *characteristics* in which consumers are interested. They possess preferences for collections of characteristics, and preferences for goods are *indirect* or derived in the sense that goods are required only in order to produce characteristics. The view of some economists of an earlier generation that goods were desired in order to satisfy 'wants' was somewhat along the (same) general line... the various characteristics can be viewed ... as each helping to satisfy some kind of 'want'."[23]

The structure of the model is directly deduced from this analysis. If $(q_i)(1 \leqslant i \leqslant n)$ represents the consumption vector, a_{ij} the quantity of characteristic $j(1 \leqslant j \leqslant m)$ in a unit of commodity i, z_j the amount of characteristic i consumed, p_i the price vector and r the income, one assumes that the individual maximizes his utility:

$$U = U[(z_j)_{1 \leqslant i \leqslant m}]$$ (1.31)

subject to the constraints:

$$\begin{cases} \sum_i p_i q_i = r, & (1.32) \\ z_j = \sum_i a_{ij} q_i. & (1.33) \end{cases}$$

The last relation supposes that the transformation of a commodity vector into a characteristic vector is linear, but nothing fundamental would be changed if such a simplifying hypothesis was not made.

In the model, the marginal utility of commodity i becomes:

$$\sum_j \frac{\partial u}{\partial z_j} a_{ij}.$$

The meaning of the theory would be more precise if three stages were considered instead of two. Let us suppose, for instance, that I want to go to Bordeaux to visit my parents. I can take the train or the plane. The first level is represented by the airplane trip or the train trip from Paris to Bordeaux. Each of these trips has certain characteristics: speed, comfort, safety and the fact that they bring me to Bordeaux.

[23] K. Lancaster (1971).

This is the second level introduced by Lancaster. But why do I want these characteristics? To satisfy a certain number of motivations: love for my parents, search for prestige, need for safety, etc. These motivations constitute a third level, a level of "wants" totally different from the second. And finally, utility is derived from an aggregation of the motivation degrees experienced.

With these adjunctions, new consumer demand theory will be integrated in the theory proposed in subsequent chapters of this book.

5.4. Introduction of additional constraints

Traditional individual behaviour theory assumes that the consumer maximizes his utility subject to one constraint only: the budget constraint. But, about ten years ago, the study of transportation investments led Lesourne (1964) and Becker (1965) to introduce a *time constraint*. More recently, S.B. Linder has made an extensive use of this constraint in "The harried leisure class" (1970).

In the simplest formulation, it is supposed that a length of time T is available to the individual and that the consumption of a unit of commodity i uses a time t_i. Then, with the notations introduced in present elementary theory, the individual maximizes his utility $u((q_i)_{1 \leqslant i \leqslant n})$ subject to the two constraints:

$$\sum_i p_i q_i = r, \tag{1.34}$$

$$\sum_i t_i q_i = T. \tag{1.35}$$

Under the assumptions of section 2, λ and μ being two positive Lagrange multipliers associated with (34) and (35), the preferred consumption vector q satisfies the conditions:

$$
\begin{cases}
\partial u/\partial q_i - \lambda\left(p_i + \dfrac{\mu}{\lambda} t_i\right) = 0 \quad \text{if } q_i > 0 \text{ (for a consumption),} \quad (1.36) \\
\qquad\qquad\qquad\qquad\qquad\qquad q_i < 0 \text{ (for labour services),}[24] \\
\partial u/\partial q_i - \lambda\left(p_i + \dfrac{\mu}{\lambda} t_i\right) \leqslant 0 \quad \text{if } q_i = 0. \quad (1.37)
\end{cases}
$$

[24] For these services, $q_i \leqslant 0$ and t_i must be given a negative value.

It is well-known that μ/λ can then be interpreted as the implicit value for the individual of a unit time. As we shall see later, the same ideas can, of course, be introduced for a variety of constraints.

Interesting contributions by F. Hahn (1971), M. Kurz (1974a) and Heller and Starr (1976) correspond to a different way of making the constraints on individual behaviour more realistic. These authors try to study in depth *the technology of exchange*. Let us follow Kurz's presentation:

R_+^k being the nonnegative orthant of the k-dimensional Euclidean space and n the number of commodities, five vectors in R_+^n are associated to the behaviour of a given individual:

w = vector of initial endowments,
x = vector of purchases,
y = vector of sales,
g = vector of resources used in exchange,
c = final consumption bundle.

An exchange vector (x, y, g) in R_+^{3n} is then said to be *technologically feasible* if:

$$(x, y, g) \in Z,$$

where Z is a set in R_+^{3n} which states all the technologically feasible transactions. Z is called the transaction set. It is assumed that:

(1) Z is a closed convex set,
(2) if $(x, y, g) \in Z$ then $x' \leqq x$ and $y' \leqq y$ and $g' \geqq g \Rightarrow (x', y', g') \in Z$,
(3) $(0, 0, 0) \in Z$,
(4) there is $\hat{x} \geqslant 0$, $\hat{y}$ and $\hat{g}$ such that $\hat{y} - \hat{g} \gg 0$ and $(\hat{x}, \hat{y}, \hat{g}) \in Z$.

(1) is a traditional assumption of equilibrium theory which may be questionable here, (2) says that, if g are resources sufficient to carry out a given set of transactions, then any $g' \geqslant g$ will suffice to carry out transactions of smaller or equal volume, (3) allows inaction and (4) allows some positive action.

Obviously:

$$c = w + x - y, \tag{1.38}$$

and, if p is the price vector,

$$px \leqslant py - pg, \tag{1.39}$$

so that the *budget set* is the set:

$$B(p) = \left\{ (x, y, g) \in \mathbf{R}_+^{3n} \; \middle| \; \begin{array}{l} \text{(a)} \;\; (x, y, g) \in Z \\ \text{(b)} \;\; px \leqslant py - pg \\ \text{(c)} \;\; w + x - y \geqslant 0 \end{array} \right\} \tag{1.40}$$

the individual maximizing a utility $u(w + x - y)$.

We shall try to develop similar ideas in chapter 5.

5.5. *Alternatives to random independence axiom*

As early as 1953 (a and b), M. Allais suggested that the mathematical expectation of utility be replaced by a utility function showing the global characteristics of the probability distribution of prizes. Such a formulation does not imply the random independence axiom. For instance, if prizes are income levels, and if m and σ are respectively the average income and the standard deviation, utility is written:

$$u = u(m, \sigma), \tag{1.41}$$

with (assuming that u is differentiable) the inequalities:

$$\partial u / \partial m \geqslant 0, \tag{1.42}$$

$$\partial u / \partial \sigma \gtrless 0, \tag{1.43}$$

The sign of the last one depending on individual attitude towards risk. The idea can be extended to situations where the prizes are quantities of certain commodities.

Unfortunately, though simple and appealing, the formulation runs into difficulties when the probability distributions of prizes may be asymmetric.

In his book on decision theory, W. Krelle (1968), following a proposal made by G. Bernard in 1964, tried to enlarge the scope of the expected utility function. He introduces the set X of certain events x and a real-valued function $u(x)$, defined on X, which represents the utility of certain events. Then any probability measure P on X induces a probability measure Q on R which is the probability distribution of utilities $u(x)$. W. Krelle then associates to outcome x *when it appears in the context Q* a subjective valuation $\phi(Q, x)$, so that the utility of P is:

$$U(P) = E[\phi(Q, x)]. \tag{1.44}$$

Krelle calls the function ϕ the "risk-preference" function. It changes with the amount of information on uncertainty. It is not the utility function of certain values, "but a representation of the behaviour of the person in the simultaneous presence of value and uncertainty."[25]

Lately, G. Bernard has proposed for ϕ the special form:

$$\phi(Q, x) = x^a p^{c-1}, \tag{1.45}$$

where p is the probability of x, a and c two constants ($a \geqslant 0$, $c \geqslant 1$), which implies:

$$U(P) = \sum_i p_i^c x_i^a, \tag{1.46}$$

but, though the consequences of (1.46) look pretty reasonable, it is difficult to accept that only the probability of x, and not the entire distribution, appears in the valuation of x.

Another interpretation will be proposed in the second volume.

5.6. Life-cycle and human capital

In subsequent chapters, we shall stress the importance of the concept of individual capability, but similar notions already exist in the literature, though all their implications have not really been considered.

For instance, Mirrlees's model of optimum fiscal policy assumes that each individual is characterizes by a *skill* measured by the output per working hour (Mirrlees (1971)). Similarly, the theory of the life cycle (Becker (1964), Ghez and Becker (1975), Blinder and Weiss (1976)) introduces a *human capital* which changes endogenously over time.

As an example, Blinder and Weiss consider the following model. Time t is continuous. The individual derives his utility from three sources: the stream of lifetime real consumption, $c(t)$; the fraction of time devoted to leisure, $l(t)$; and the bequest of real assets $A(T)$, where T is the (certain) date of death. In other words, the individual maximizes:

$$V = \int_0^T U(c, l)\,e^{-\rho t} + B[A(T)], \tag{1.47}$$

where $U(c, l)$ and $B[A(T)]$ are assumed to be twice-differentiable,

[25] G. Bernard (1974).

strictly concave functions of their arguments, and ρ a positive discounting coefficient.

Letting $h(t)$ denote the fraction of time devoted to work and education, the time budget requires:

$$\begin{cases} h(t) + l(t) = A, \\ h(t) \geqslant 0. \end{cases}$$

$$(1.48)$$
$$(1.49)$$

$x(t)$ will be an index characterizing the nature of the job performed by the individual at time t. The different jobs may have a different effect on the increase of "human capital." A job will be assigned an index $x (0 \leqslant x \leqslant 1)$ such that the effect of spending 1 hour on this job will be equivalent to x hours of schooling. A number $K(t) \in \mathbf{R}^+$ will represent the value of human capital at time t. Human capital will be generated by the production function:

$$\dot{K} = (axh - \delta)K, \tag{1.50}$$

where $a > 0, \delta > 0$. Such a function implies that, in absence of activity $(h = 0)$, human capital deteriorates at the constant rate δ, but that performing h hours on job x increases the human capital in the amount $axhK$.

Nonhuman capital $A(t) \in \mathbf{R}^+$ is generated by the differential equation:

$$\dot{A} = rA + g(x)hK - c, \tag{1.51}$$

where r is the real rate of interest and $g(x)$ the wage-rate of job x per unit of human capital for one hour of work.

The analysis of this maximization problem shows that four qualitatively distinct phases may occur in an individual's life cycle:

Phase I : schooling: $x = 1, h > 0$,
Phase II : on the job training (OJT): $0 < x < 1, h > 0$,
Phase III: work: $x = 0, h > 0$,
Phase IV : retirement: $h = 0$.

It may be shown "that if the life plan includes schooling and has no cycles, the only possibility is that schooling comes first, followed by OJT, work and then retirement" (Blinder and Weiss), the human capital and the total wages received passing by a maximum in the course of life.

Such models present an extreme interest and could be usefully coupled with the study of consumption streams on random futures.

5.7. Consumer behaviour in a multiperiod random environment

Since the pioneering papers of Phelps and Samuelson which appeared respectively in 1962 and 1969, many economists (D. Levhari and T.N. Srinivasan (1969), F. Hahn (1970), N.H. Hakansson (1970), Sandmo (1970), B.L. Miller (1974), H.E. Leland (1974), A. Anastasopoulos and S. Kounias (1975)) have studied the optimal strategy of a consumer whose behaviour has random effects and who wants to maximize his expected utility over time.

In spite of their differences, the models used are quite similar. All of them assume that the individual maximizes the expected discounted value of a flow of utilities on an infinite horizon ($t = 0, 1, \ldots, \infty$) or on a finite horizon ($t = 0, \ldots, T$) with fixed or open-ended conditions.

Then, a central part of the maximized function is always:

$$U = \sum_{t=0}^{T} \rho^t u(c_t), \tag{1.52}$$

where $\rho < 1$ is the discounting factor and c_t the consumption of period t.

Let us denote wealth at time t by w_t (w_0 is given). The assumptions made on the generation of wealth differ according to the paper. They can be sketched as follows for some of the models:

Phelps: $w_{t+1} = (w_t - c_t)r_t + y, \qquad w_t \geqslant 0. \tag{1.53}$

The individual receives a sure income y during each period. He cannot borrow. The r_t's are independent random variables which define the amount received at the end of period t per franc invested at the beginning of the period.

Samuelson: $w_{t+1} = (w_t - c_t)[\alpha_t z_t + (1 - \alpha_t)\beta], \qquad w_t \geqslant 0, \tag{1.54}$
$$0 \leqslant \alpha_t \leqslant 1.$$

Each time, the individual splits his investment into a fraction $(1 - \alpha_t)$ which gives a sure income β per unit invested; and a fraction α_t, which gives a random income z_t per unit invested. The probability distribution of z_t is given. The individual cannot borrow.

Miller: $w_{t+1} = (w_t - c_t)\beta + y_t. \tag{1.55}$

Here $w_t \gtrless 0$, and the individual is entitled to borrow. $(\beta - 1)$ is the certain rate of interest obtained on investments or paid on debts. y_t is a *positive* random income received at the end of period t. The y_t's are independently distributed and their discounted value is bounded.

y_t is supposed divided between a certain income a_t and a random positive or zero income b_t, and at no time may the individual have a debt bigger than the discounted value of his future certain income. In other words:

$$w_t \geqslant - \sum_{t}^{\infty} \beta^{-(\tau - t)} a_{\tau + t - 1} \qquad (1.56)$$

Hakansson:
$$\begin{cases} w_{t+1} = \beta \alpha_{1t} + \sum_{i=2}^{M} r_i \alpha_{it} + y, & (1.57) \\[2mm] \sum_{i=1}^{M} \alpha_{it} = w_t - c_t. & (1.58) \end{cases}$$

In this model, the wealth available after consumption can be invested into M different assets in amounts α_{it} $(1 \leqslant i \leqslant M)$. The first one gives a certain income β per franc invested, the $(M - 1)$ other ones an uncertain income, r_i being a random variable with a probability distribution which is known and independent of time. y is a certain income derived from other services. The author rules out any strategy for which at any one time the probability of having a wealth level smaller than the discounted future certain income would be positive.

A different path has been followed by other authors, such as Epstein (1975). They limit the analysis to two periods, but they do not aggregate the various consumptions.

Let x and p be respectively the first period consumption and price vectors. Let I and Q be random variables representing respectively the discounted income of the two periods and the price vector of the second period. Then Y, the consumption vector of the second period, is a random variable. The values taken by these random variables depend upon the state of the world w that appears in the second period.

At the end of the first period, the individual receives full information on the state of the world w for the second period. Then, for x given, he chooses $Y(w)$, maximizing $u(x, Y)$ under the constraint:

$$Q(w)Y(w) \leqslant I(w) - px,$$

x being limited to the values making the right hand term positive or zero. The optimal Y is a function $Y^*(w, x)$.

The utility $u[x, Y^*(w, x)]$ then becomes a random variable function of x alone and the individual chooses x to maximize his expected utility.

Such a formulation has proved especially fruitful for temporary equilibrium theory. Its key contribution is the introduction of *individual expectations about the future through the probability distributions of the states of the world.*

These models combine, in an interesting way, two sections of utility theory: the one with a sequence of periods and the one with a random environment. They are useful to clarify some aspects of individual behaviour such as portfolio selection, but they only take into account the minor characteristics of risks, since they regularly eliminate *any possibility of ruin*, i.e. any fundamental change in the situation of the individual.

Nevertheless, they open the way towards a more realistic formulation.

5.8. *Changes of utility in time*

Individual preferences do change in time, and partly as a consequence of the operation of the economic system itself. So there is nothing more dangerous than the attitude of some economists who claim that tastes are given exogenously. Of the utmost importance, on the other hand, are the contributions of Peston (1967), Gorman (1967), Krelle (1968), Pollak (1970), Von Weizsäcker (1971), Lluch (1974) and Hammond (1976) on endogenous change of tastes.

Gorman considers an individual whose utility function:

$$u = u(x, \alpha), \tag{1.59}$$

depends on a commodity bundle $x = (x_i)_{1 \leqslant i \leqslant n}(x \in X)$ and on a taste parameter $\alpha = (\alpha_j)_{1 \leqslant j \leqslant m}(\alpha \in A)$. He assumes that u is differentiable in in (x, α), is strictly increasing and strictly quasi-concave in x on $X \times A$. In any given state of taste $\alpha \in A$, then an $x \in X$ is chosen at prices p and income r. It is defined by:

$$\frac{\partial u}{\partial x_i}(x, \alpha) = \lambda p_i \tag{1.55}$$

$$\sum_i p_i x_i = r \tag{1.60}$$

But, in the long run, tastes depend on past behaviour, so that:

$$\alpha_j = \alpha_j(x). \tag{1.61}$$

If these functions are differentiable in X and map X into A or a subset of it, the *long-run equilibria* are defined by (1.59), (1.60) and (1.61).

Pollak introduces time explicitly as a discrete variable ($t = 0, 1, \ldots$), but specifies the utility function $u_t(x_t)$ of period t:

$$\left. \begin{array}{l} u_t(x_t) = \sum_{i}^{n} a_i \log(x_{it} - b_{it}), \\ a_i > 0, \quad b_{it} > 0, \quad (x_{it} - b_{it}) > 0, \quad \sum_i a_i = 1. \end{array} \right\} \tag{1.62}$$

b_{it}, the quantity of commodity i considered as necessary by the individual at period t, is supposed to be a function of the consumption of the last period:

$$b_{it} = b_i + \beta_i x_{i,t-1}, \qquad 0 \leqslant \beta_i < 1. \tag{1.63}$$

For Von Weizsäcker, demand at period t is a function of existing prices and income and of consumptions of the preceding period. Such a demand is deduced from a short-run or instantaneous utility function. But one can prove the existence of a long-run utility function corresponding to individual preferences when the demand for given prices and income is constant throughout time.

Lluch makes real progress when he formulates the individual problem as follows:

Choose $q(t)$, $0 \leqslant t \leqslant \infty$, so that:

$$U(q(t), s(t)) = \int_0^\infty e^{-\delta t} u(q(t), s(t)) \, dt,$$

is maximized, subject to:

$$\dot{w}(t) = \rho w(t) + y(t) - pq(t), \quad w(0) = w,$$
$$\dot{s}(t) = q(t) - \alpha s(t), \qquad s(0) = s,$$

given $(\rho, \delta, y(t), p)$.

where:

$q(t)$ is a n-vector of commodity flows;
$s(t)$ a n-vector of stocks of habits;
p a n-vector of prices of commodities in terms of the numeraire stock, $w(t)$;

$w(t)$ wealth;
$y(t)$ an exogenous flow of labour income;
ρ a rate of reproduction of wealth;
α a rate of memory loss;
δ the subjective rate of discount;
$u(.)$ the instantaneous utility function.

In all these models, utility changes as a consequence of a learning process where the stimulus is consumption. Other authors have referred to other stimuli, such as the amount of education received.

More ambitious, but more difficult to interpret is the work of Krelle. Time being a continuous variable, on the real line, he takes three different notions into account:

– an instantaneous utility $u(t)$,
– a basic welfare level $\overline{w}(t)$ depending on social and individual characteristics,
– a welfare level $w(t)$ (Befriedigungsniveau).

These notions are linked by the relation:

$$w(t) = \overline{w}(t) + \int_{-\infty}^{t} \frac{\dot{u}(\tau)}{u(\tau)} e^{-\delta(t-\tau)} \, d\tau + \int_{t}^{\infty} \frac{\dot{u}_E(\tau)}{u_E(\tau)} e^{-\rho(\tau-t)} \, d\tau, \qquad (1.64)$$

which can be interpreted in the following way:

– At time τ in the past, the individual has experienced an impulse $\dot{u}(\tau)/u(\tau)$[26] of relative increase in utility. The memory of this event, damped at rate δ increases the difference between his present welfare and his basic welfare.
– At time τ in the future, the individual *expects* an impulse $\dot{u}_E(\tau)/u_E(\tau)$ of relative increase in utility and experiences it now, damped at rate ρ, in the difference between his present welfare and his basic welfare.

Figure 1.8, borrowed from Krelle's book explains how an increase in instantaneous utility from t_1 to t_2 is reflected in $w(t)$ for a constant basic welfare level $\overline{w}(t)$.

---

[26] $\dot{u}(\tau) = du/d\tau$.

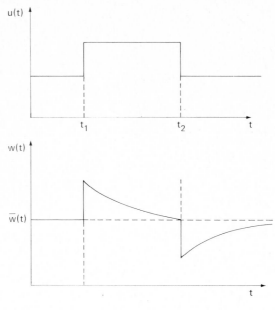

Figure 1.8

For Krelle, the instantaneous utility level depends on the economic situation of the individual, on his positions in the various social hierarchies and on his relations with other individuals.

The basic welfare level also depends on the same variables, but in a different way, since $\overline{w}(t)$ is insensitive to the variables as soon as a "normal" situation is reached.

The discussion of Krelle's ideas, which are stimulating but need clarification, will be postponed to the second volume, but it is essential to realise that the study of such problems is necessary in order to establish a bridge between economic theory and any interpretation of long-term social evolutions.

5.9. Acquisition and processing of information in time

The black and white separation between a certain environment and an uncertain one with given objective or subjective probabilities, is, of course, a violation of reality since it is always possible to increase information in exchange for consumption of scarce resources.

Following Murphy (1965) and others, we shall consider an individual who lives T periods $(t = 1, \ldots, T)$. During each period, an uncertain event i occurs among n possibilities, the probabilities of which are unknown but constant from one period to another. At the beginning of each period t, the individual takes two decisions:

- a decision of action a_t, which determines his utility level for the period if event i appears: $u(a_t, i)$;
- a decision of information I_t, which transforms his evaluation of the subjective probability distribution. If this evaluation is $\hat{P}_t$ at the beginning of the period, the evaluation will become:

$$\hat{P}_{t+1} = f[\hat{P}_t, I_t, i_t], \tag{1.65}$$

at the beginning of period $(T + 1)$, i_t being the event which effectively appeared in period t. The decision (a_t, I_t) must be in a feasible set D (for instance, the individual can divide his income into consumption expenditures and buying of information).

At the beginning of the last period, the individual will choose (a_T, I_T) so that: $\sum_n \hat{P}_{it}u(a_T, i)$ is maximized, $\hat{P}_{it}$ being the subjective probability of event i for the period. Let us call:

$$U_T(\hat{P}_T) = \max_{(a_T, I_T) \in D} \sum_n \hat{P}_{iT}u(a_t, i). \tag{1.66}$$

At the beginning of period $(T - 1)$, the individual will choose (a_{T-1}, I_{T-1}) so that:

$$\sum_n \hat{P}_{i,T-1} [u(a_{T-1}, i) + \rho U_T(\hat{P}_T)] \tag{1.67}$$

is maximized, assuming that he discounts at rate ρ the utility of subsequent periods. Notice that $U_T(\hat{P}_T)$ is, through $\hat{P}_T$, a function of I_{T-1} and of the event i_{T-1} appearing in period $(T - 1)$.

Let us call:

$$U_{T-1}(\hat{P}_{T-1}) = \max_{(a_{T-1}, I_{T-1})} \sum_n \hat{P}_{i,T-1} [u(a_{T-1}, i) + \rho U_T(\hat{P}_T)]. \tag{1.68}$$

This process can obviously go on until the first period, at the beginning of which the subjective probability distribution $\hat{P}_1$ is assumed given.

In such an adaptive process, the individual always has the choice of spending more on current expenditures, but at the risk of adapting them badly to the uncertain environment; or of buying more information in order to improve his future behaviour in exchange for an immediate situation which will, on the average, be worse.

But with formulations of this type, we are obviously demanding enormous capabilities of the individual. This explains why some economists are ready totally to abandon the roads explored so far for models of bounded rationality.

5.10. Bounded rationality models

In his papers and books ("Models of man" (1957), "Administrative behavior" (1958), "Organizations" [27] (1958)), H.A. Simon has been the brightest advocate of models which demand from the individual less than the perfect maximization of a utility function under constraints. Simon suggests building individual behavioural models on the following assumptions:

(i) Any decision d has consequences which can be judged along n different dimensions $(1 \leqslant i \leqslant n)$. The n marks obtained by a decision are not aggregated by the individual into a single utility level.

(ii) On each dimension, the "pay-off function" is very simple, since satisfaction can take only two values (satisfactory: 1 or unsatisfactory: 0) or three values (win: 1, draw: 0 or lose: -1).

Hence, with each decision d, the individual associates a vector $s = (s_i)_{1 \leqslant i \leqslant n}$ of consequences in a set S. For each i, in the case of two values, there is a consequence level σ_i such that the satisfaction index $U_i(s_i)$ is equal to zero if $s_i < \sigma_i$ and to one if $s_i \geqslant \sigma_i$.

(iii) The individual considers only a small subset D of decisions at any time. If, in this subset, there is a "satisfactory" decision, i.e. a decision d such that $U_i[s_i(d)] = 1$ for every $i(1 \leqslant i \leqslant n)$, the decision is chosen. If there is no such decision, the individual starts a process of information-gathering with a time limit in mind.

[27] In collaboration with J.G. March.

If, before the time limit, a "satisfactory" decision is found, this decision is chosen and the process stops.

If the search-period ends without success, the individual decreases the levels σ_i which have proved too high for the decisions available. Then two possibilities again appear: a "satisfactory" decision is found and the process stops; no "satisfactory" decision exists and a new search begins.

In the next chapter, we shall consider the utilization of these ideas in organization theory, but it is essential to study here how they have been developed in economics by R. Radner (1975), R. Radner and M. Rothschild (1975), L. Hurwicz, R. Radner and S. Reiter (1975).

For instance, Radner presents a fascinating model with a single utility index and with multidimensional utilities.

5.10.1. A single utility index

In this case, R. Radner adopts the following formulation: let (X, F, P) be a basic probability space, "where F is a σ-field of subsets of X, and P a probability measure on F. Let (F_t), $t = 0, 1, 2, \ldots$, be an increasing sequence of subfields of F; F_t is to be interpreted as the set of observable events through date t. Let $\{U(t)\}$ be a corresponding sequence of integer-valued random variables on X, such that $U(t)$ is F_t-measurable." $U(t)$ will be the *utility level* at t. "Finally, let (T_n), $n = 0, 1, 2, \ldots$, be a nondecreasing sequence of random times, possibly taking on the value $+\infty$, so that $T_n < T_{n+1}$ if T_n is finite; for n odd, T_n is to be interpreted as a date at which a period of search for improvement begins, and T_{n+1} as the date at which that period ends (a random time T is an integer-valued random variable possibly equal to $+\infty$, so that the event $(T = t)$ is F_t-measurable). Take $T_0 = 0$".[28]

Then an interval $(T_n \leqslant t \leqslant T_{n+1})$ is a *search period* if n is odd and a *rest period* if n is even.

Now introduce the aspiration level or the "satisfactory level of performance" $S(t)$ at date t. $\{S(t)\}$ will be a sequence of random variables such that $S(t)$ is F_t-measurable.

The random times T_n are determined by conditions (for n even):

[28] R. Radner (1975).

$$\begin{cases} T_{n+1} \text{ is the first } t > T_n \quad \text{so that } U(t) < S(t), \\ T_{n+2} \text{ is the first } t > T_{n+1} \text{ so that } U(t) \geqslant S(t). \end{cases} \qquad (1.69)$$

Let $Z(t)$ be the successive increments of the process:[29]

$$Z(t + 1) = U(t + 1) - U(t), \qquad (1.70)$$

and ξ, η and β three given positive numbers. For $T_n \leqslant t < T_{n+1}$, it is assumed that:

(i) *for n even* (rest) that the increments $Z(t + 1)$ are independent and identically distributed with:

$$E[Z(t + 1) | F_t] = -\xi, \qquad (1.71)$$

$$S(t) = U(T_n) - \beta; \qquad (1.72)$$

(ii) *for n odd* (search) that the increments $Z(t + 1)$ are independent and identically distributed with:

$$E[Z(t + 1) | F_t] = \eta, \qquad (1.73)$$

$$S(t) = U(T_{n-1}). \qquad (1.74)$$

In other words, if a search period ends with a utility $U(T_n)$, the next search period begins as soon as the utility reaches or falls below $U(T_n) - \beta$. On the contrary, during a search period, the aspiration level remains fixed.

From (1.71) and (1.73), it is evident that, during rest, the performance process is a random walk with negative drift; and during search, a random walk with positive drift. To minimize technical complications, Radner has further assumed that these random walks were integer-valued and aperiodic.

Let $a(t) = 1$ during search, and 0 during rest. The process $\{a(t - 1), U(t), S(t)\}$ is a Markov chain with countably many states and a single class.

For any n, the $U(T_{2n})$'s are the performance levels at which successive search periods end, and each $U(T_{2n})$ is the aspiration level for the next search period.

---

[29] For technical reasons, the existence of $b > 0$ so that $[Z(t)] \leqslant b$ for all t is assumed.

The process will be called *strictly favourable* if there is a strictly positive number v such that for every n:

$$E[U(T_{2n+2})\,|\,F_{2n}] \geqslant U(T_{2n}) + v. \tag{1.75}$$

With these assumptions, Radner has shown that:

(a) *The process* $\{a(t - 1), \ U(t) - S(t)\}$ *is Markovian and positive recurrent.*

(b) *The long-run frequency* $\bar{a}$ *with which* $a(t) = 1$ *exists.*

(c) *The process is strictly favourable iff:* $\bar{\zeta} = \bar{a}\eta - (1 - \bar{a})\xi$ *is strictly positive.*

(d) *If* $\bar{\zeta} > 0$, *then almost certainly:*

$$\lim_{t \to \infty} \frac{U(t)}{t} = \bar{\zeta}. \tag{1.76}$$

(e) *If* $\bar{\zeta} > 0$, *then positive numbers* H, K *exist such that, if* $U(0) \equiv u > \beta + b$, *then:*

$$\text{prob}\,\{U(t) \leqslant 0 \text{ for some } t\,|\,F_0\} \leqslant H\,e^{-Ku}. \tag{1.77}$$

If $\bar{\zeta} = 0$, *the above probability is one.*

It may be said that the individual *survives* if the utility $U(t)$ remains positive for all t. Hence, for strictly favourable processes, with random-walk rest and search, utility increases in the long run at a positive average rate per unit time and the probability of survival approaches unity exponentially, or faster as a function of the initial utility level $U(0)$.

5.10.2. Multidimensional utilities

Frequently, however, utility has to be considered as a vector $(U_i(t))_{1 \leqslant i \leqslant I}$, $U_i(t)$ being the utility index on dimension i.

Symmetrically, instead of searching for $(a(t) = 1)$, or being at rest $(a(t) = 0)$, the individual allocates his efforts during each period between different activities liable to improve his performances along the various dimensions. Assume, for instance, that there is exactly one activity corresponding to each dimension. An *allocation behaviour* is a sequence $\{a(t)\}$, where $a(t)$ is an F_t-measurable random vector with coordinates

$a_i(t)$ $(i = 1, \ldots, I)$, such that, for any date t, exactly one coordinate of $a(t)$ is 1 and the other are 0. If $a_i(t) = 1$, there is a search for improvement in activity i at date t.

With obvious notations, (1.71) and (1.73) can be replaced by:

$$E[Z_i(t + 1) \,|\, F_t] = a_i(t)\eta_i - [1 - a_i(t)]\xi_i, \qquad (1.78)$$

where η_i and ξ_i are given positive numbers. One assumes also:

$$\mathrm{var}\,[Z_i(t + 1) \,|\, F_t] = s_i[a_i(t)], \qquad (1.79)$$

where $s_i(0)$ and $s_i(1)$ are given positive numbers. The coordinates of $Z(t + 1)$ are supposed mutually independent, integer-valued, uniformly bounded by $b > 0$ and aperiodic.

Radner studies the *policy of putting out fires* which consists of devoting all efforts to the dimension with the worst performance. Formally, if:

$$M(t) = \min_i U_i(t). \qquad (1.80)$$

This policy is defined by the three rules:

(i) if $U_i(t) > M(t)$ then $a_i(t) = 0$,
(ii) if $U_i(t) = M(t)$ and $a_i(t - 1) = 1$, then $a_i(t) = 1$,
(iii) if neither (i) nor (ii) holds, then $a_i(t) = 1$ for i equal to the smallest j such that $U_j(t) = M(t)$.

Radner introduces the coefficients:

$$\bar{\zeta} = \left(1 - \sum_i \frac{\xi_i}{\eta_i + \xi_i}\right)\bigg/\left(\sum_i \frac{1}{\eta_i + \xi_i}\right), \qquad \bar{a}_i = \frac{\bar{\zeta} + \xi_i}{\eta_i + \xi_i}, \qquad (1.81)$$

and proves the following propositions:

If $\bar{\zeta} > 0$ and if the probabilities $P\{Z_i(t + 1) = 0 \,|\, a_i(t)\}$, $P\{Z_i(t + 1) = 1 \,|\, a_i(t) = 1\}$, $P\{Z_i(t + 1) = -1 \,|\, a_i(t) = 0\}$ are strictly positive:

(a) *The long-run frequency with which $a_i(t) = 1$ is almost certainly equal to $\bar{a}_i$.*
(b) *The rate of growth of $U_i(t)$ is for any i almost certainly $\bar{\zeta}$.*
(c) *If $M(0) > 0$, the probability of survival is positive.*

Moreover, "survival is possible with positive probability if it is possible with putting out fires."

What a breath of fresh air! An immense new field is opened for economic research and significant progress should be possible if a synthesis is made between this formulation and conventional utility theory.

The study of a stochastic decentralized resource allocation process by L. Hurwicz, R. Radner and S. Reiter (1975) is already a step in that direction. In this process, every individual has a utility function, but, at each step of the process, makes a *bid*, defined in the following way in the case of pure exchange:

- *If the commodities are indivisible,* the individual selects a probability distribution over all the exchanges which would leave him as well off as he is, and uses a randomized device, governed by this distribution, to make a bid to trade given amounts of goods with other participants.
- *If the commodities are divisible,* the individual, still according to an appropriate probability distribution, picks a trade, the *central bid*, among those generating a utility not inferior to his present one; but he is also ready to accept all trades within a specified "distance" from the central bid which do not lead to a smaller utility.

Then a referee enters the picture and checks whether individual bids are compatible. If there is one, any individual receives the results of this bid and the process goes on from a better or equivalent situation for any individual. If not, the individuals are requested to make new bids.

It is clear that in such a model, *it would be easy to introduce the quality of the search activity of the individuals and to choose aspiration levels different from the existing utility levels.* A merger between Arrow–Debreu equilibrium theory and Simon's proposals seems to be at hand, fulfilling Perroux's expectations of "equilibrations" with active agents.[30]

This short description of certain recent developments is undoubtedly unfair to the contribution of many economists; but it does prove that around the Temple of present theory, the search is going on actively in every possible direction.

[30] See F. Perroux (1975).

Part of this research begins to fill the gap between economics and other human sciences; but the discrepancy remains wide. Economists are too wrapped up in their own problems. They must be more conscious of what sciences like neurophysiology, psychology, psychoanalysis and sociology could bring to their discipline. The impossible task of the next chapter will be to mention a few of the possible contributions of these sciences to an improved theory of the individual for economics.

Chapter 2

A FEW CONTRIBUTIONS OF OTHER HUMAN SCIENCES

Economics and the behavioral sciences: A desert frontier?

K.E. Boulding[1]

Introduction

Within the limits of a short chapter, it is an impossible task to try to extract from the various human sciences a few of their possible contributions to a theory of the individual adapted to the needs of economics. How can one choose the meaningful elements in this immensity of knowledge and ignorance? In many ways, it would have been more satisfactory – and safer – to refuse the challenge and drop this chapter. But such cautious strategy would have weakened our double claim:

(*i*) that a theory of the individual in economics should be *compatible* with the results of other human sciences, and should even be able to absorb them whenever they are relevant for economics;

(*ii*) that economic science should build *bridges* across to the other human sciences in order to deal more adequately with a multitude of economic problems which have psychological, political or social dimensions.

In view of the difficulties, *this chapter is not a survey*. It has selected only *a few topics* to show how, in spite of heterogeneity of concepts,

[1] Boulding* (1956).

imprecision of vocabulary, challenges of ignorance, the development of the different human sciences may contribute to the progressive construction of a model of man, compatible, at one end, with neurophysiological mechanisms and, at the other, with the most creative types of sociopsychological behaviours. (Of course, we are still far from the goal.) The topics selected do not cover the whole field. They may not even be the most important. But they should help economists to form a different view of what a suitable theory of the individual for economics could be.

Two important fields which cannot be used for immediate applications have been excluded from our list, though they may be of great help to a general understanding of the landscape:

(1) *ethology*, the science of animal behaviour, in which there have been tremendous developments in the last fifty years, stressing *the biological, psychological and sociological continuity from animal to man*, proving certain animals' ability to manipulate abstract ideas, to master simple languages, to anticipate and forecast, to possess self-consciousness, to accept and modify social orders and even, to a modest degree, to innovate.[2]

(2) *human paleontology*, which, at a crossroads of sciences, has begun to establish the way in which our present species evolved from a first ancestor who probably lived in tropical forests, this evolution giving probably rise not only to a succession of species, but to several contemporaneous species with some hominian features, the last chromosomic mutation being completed in less than eighty years through the marriage of a mutant father with his mutated daughter. Paleontology suggests that our ability to self-organization comes from the fact that we are a foetalized species, in which, because of neoteny, development goes on after birth; it stresses the importance, in our progress, of the freeing of the hand through vertical stance, a key step in the rise of intelligence; it studies fundamental questions concerning the emergence of fathers, the constitution of the family, the prohibition of incest and leads us to the borders of history and anthropology.

The various human sciences scarcely describe behaviour in terms of functional maximization. The language of systems theory is, on the

[2] See, for instance: I. Eibl-Eibesfeldt* (1972) (published in German in 1967).

contrary, widely used, implicitly or explicitly. Since we have discussed briefly, in the introduction, the links between these two formulations, the case will not be reopened here.

We assume that readers are familiar with the fundamental elements of general systems theory. For our purpose, it is sufficient to have mastered the few notions which explain how it is possible to pass progressively from the simplest to the most elaborate systems capable of learning, self-organization and interference:

- At a first level, the *systems with states* only transform in a deterministic, stochastic or uncertain way, inputs into outputs. Their evolution can be interpreted in terms of gain, loss and transformation of information.
- These systems may be *controlled by man,* which raises some important questions: What are the goals of the controller? How does he get the information? How does he compute his decisions out of the information? Is his control deterministic, stochastic, imperfect or through learning? Is he able to control the system, i.e. to bring it on the target within the admissible time limits?
- At a second level, the *goal-oriented systems* integrate the controller, since they include at least one internal regulation modifying the behaviour of the system as a result of the discrepancy observed between the value of the goal and the value of the output. But frequently such systems incorporate a huge number of amplifying or stabilizing regulations frequently organized into hierarchies. This considerably increases the scope of homeostasis, the reliability of the system and the possibility of building complex systems out of simple ones. Such systems often exhibit multiple goals. With respect to these goals, the state of the system is characterized by the values of essential variables which have to stay within certain bounds for the system to survive.
- At a third level, the *learning systems* appear. These, with the help of the information stored in a memory, progressively adapt their answer to the stimuli received from the environment. At a fourth level, the *self-organizing systems* generate, at random, possible behavioral structures and rules and exhibit not only greater possibilities of adaptation, but also creativity. These systems have an essentially hierarchical structure. Each additional hierarchical level corresponds to a new step in the more and more abstract analysis of the invariants

imbedded in the evolutions of the system and of the environment, and permits the adjunction to the behaviour of new and more complex programmed sequences.

These systems may be made more complex in a double way. First, the search activity of the imagination center, instead of appearing as a response to the environment, may be conceived as autonomous and existing even in the absence of external stimuli. Second, the storage center of the objectives, instead of being independent of the other parts of the system, may be under the influence of the memory or of the imagination center. The system becomes capable of elaborating its own objectives itself.

Different self-organizing systems may be coupled, creating game structures, or hierarchical organizations, or societies in which partial hierarchies exist between the componing systems, depending on the nature of the activities. Then new types of regulations appear with the creation of institutions, the elaboration of languages, the permanent existence of internal tensions, etc. Nevertheless, it must never be forgotten that systems theory is only a conceptual framework, and that its usefulness depends entirely on the substantive propositions of the various scientific disciplines.

With these considerations in the background, a natural division of the chapter is to consider first a few topics in psychological sciences, and to examine later some contributions of sociology and anthropology. But the picture would be biased without a preliminary presentation of some essential concepts of neurophysiology, the key discipline in the field, the only one which may lead to ultimate explanations.[3,4]

[3] The interested reader will find at the end of the volume a separate bibliography corresponding to the content of this chapter. Nevertheless, it may be useful to mention a few key publications: UNESCO* (1970), P. Fraisse and J. Piaget* (1968), R.D. Luce, R.R. Bush and E. Galanter* (1963), R.D. Luce, R.R. Bush, E. Galanter* (1965), G. Palmade* (1967), J.C. Eccles* (1966), C. Kayser* (1969) and Centre de Royaumont* (1974).

[4] We have developed related topics in a totally different context in 'Les systèmes du destin', Dalloz, Paris, 1976.

1. The hierarchy of nervous structures

What is essential for the economist, in the wonderful achievements of modern neurophysiology, is its conception of the human nervous system:

– as a system which has progressively acquired complexity in the process of *phylogenetic* evolution, new structures appearing at different stages and inducing a reallocation of the tasks between the older structures;
– as a system exhibiting self-organization in the course of the *onto-genetic* development of the individual, all the complexity being embedded in a set of *neurons* organized in a hierarchy of structures, from the spinal cord at one end to the neocortex at the other, with the various encephalic structures in between.

Seen from the *spinal cord*, all the other elements of the nervous system appear only as additional and successive improvements which the evolution of the vertebrates has superimposed. With its three types of inputs and its two types of outputs, a segment of the spinal cord is almost a prototype *of an elementary goal-oriented system*, whose goals are partly controlled by upper centers. Even at this level, interconnections between segments ensure some coordination between the responses.

But the spinal cord is also a kind of transmission cable common to numerous information lines with different entries and exits.

Just above, the *cerebral trunk* is a complex tissue of intermingled regulations, a primitive organization ensuring the basic activities of the nervous system. These networks of regulations are far from being totally known. For instance, the importance of one of them, the reticulated system of the cerebral trunk, with its activating and inhibiting influences has only been recognized since the second world war. This system coordinates mastication, respiration, deglutition. . . and plays a central part in the control of sleep.

Behind the cerebral trunk, the *cerebellum* operates like a process control computer, regulating the position of the head, postural and voluntary motility.

The economist is not very much interested in these structures, which play no significant role in economic behaviour. But the situation changes entirely with the three brains of our nervous system: the paleoencephalon, the limbic system and the neocortex.

We still possess, with the *paleoencephalon* (thalamus, hypothalamus, metathalamus, corpus striatum) an old reptilian brain, which emerged two hundred million years ago. This primitive brain regulates stereotyped behaviours, programmed through ancestral learning. It coordinates the water circulation, the heart movements, the sexual behaviour, the endocrinal system. It dominates in certain primitive behaviours, such as choice of territory, hunting, creation of social hierarchies, hunger and thirst, struggle and flight. It is an instrument totally inadapted to the learning of new-behaviours in response to new and unexpected situations.

In this brain, the hypothalamus has been recognized as an aggressivity center (Bard (1928)) which generates a behaviour of sham rage when its influence is not counterbalanced by the messages of cortical centers.

Later on, in the course of the evolution, the first brain has been covered over by other nervous structures. These had been believed, at first, to be connected only to the olfactive apparatus; but since Papez (1937) it has been realized that they really constitute a second brain: the *limbic system*. This plays an important part in the appearance of emotions such as fear, anger, love, joy, in the creation of attitudes towards food and sex and in the long-term storage of information. Its action counteracts the aggressive influence of the hypothalamus, since cats, deprived of their neo-cortex, but with an intact limbic system, are subject to absolute placidity.

Finally, in a third stage of evolution, a third brain appeared, enveloping the two others. The more it develops, the more the species is able to find original adaptations to the environment. Many of its centers have been progressively identified: receptive centers, motor centers, language centers. But the most interesting part of this *neo-cortex* is the associative zone of the orbito-frontal lobe, permitting the emergence of new and original behavioural solutions. Here must lie the imagination able to create new functional structures and to generate complex nervous activities largely independent of the environment.

As H. Laborit, a French systems analyst and physiologist, writes: "Cerebral trunk and limbic system, guided by the pleasant and unpleasant quality of the information received, make it possible to seek immediate survival, or, in other words, the protection of the hierarchical structure of the (individual) organization. We only become conscious of their unconscious operations through the accompanying vegetative phenomena: vasoconstriction (cold generated by fear), acceleration of heartbeat (the heart pounding in the chest), change in the rhythm of respiration (breathlessness or gasping), perspiration (cold sweat), or through the pleasure: vasodilatation (penetrating heat), muscular relaxation, etc. But, even, when we are conscious of these emotional reactions, we remain unconscious of their phylogenetic meaning, of the deep and ancestral finality which directs them; for, if they express a state of functional activity between certain neurons, this state is located at a hierarchical level of central nervous structures too primitive to be expressed in a logico-mathematical language of the type we use in exchanges with our contemporaries. We are unable to express the obscure anxiety of the phylum, when human beings were not yet able to speak. Yet this is exactly what we have done: we have interpreted, with our brand-new language, our neo-cortex language, our logico-mathematical language, our language of relational structures with the environment, our primitive drives." [5]

So, the message of neurophysiology underlines, on the one hand, the importance of fundamental drives, poorly controlled by our modern brain, and, on the other, the crucial role of our possibilities of association, imagination and forecasting which, in their turn, partly – but partly only – escape the influence of our primitive motivations.

Such a message is, by many aspects, compatible with the numerous propositions of contemporaneous psychological sciences.

2. Some propositions of psychology

Modern psychology? A kind of monster with multiple faces, sending out tentacles in many directions with no apparent consistency. A monster which includes, at the same time, the empirism of Skinner, unceasingly registering the behaviour of rats in his boxes; the psychoanalysis of Freud's followers, accumulating clinical observations and theoretical interpretations; the constructivism of Piaget, studying how intellectual structures are progressively built during the child's development, and many other tendencies.

In this huge amount of knowledge, we shall select only certain topics

[5] H. Laborit* (1971).

which, *in psychoanalysis* and *in experimental psychology*, seem to be among those which have to be taken into account in a theory of the individual for economics.

2.1. The metapsychology of psychoanalysis

Because of the lack of precision and the evolution through time of the concepts; because, too of the diversity of the theoretical schools, the aspects of psychoanalysis which are important for economics cannot easily be extracted. To try to do so implies a certain heroism. To make things easier, we shall refer essentially to Freud's contribution, though we shall also mention the works of M. Klein and, more recently, Bowlby.

The theory of self-organizing systems provides a guide which may render many psychoanalytic notions more accessible to economics. The authority for this comes from Freud himself in a key sentence of "Beyond the pleasure principle":[6] "We believe... that the course (of mental events) is invariably set in motion by an unpleasure tension, and that it takes a direction such that its final outcome coincides with a lowering of that tension – that is, with an avoidance of unpleasure or a production of pleasure."

But where does this tension come from? Naturally, from the fact that an essential variable – i.e. one which has been built as such in phylogenesis – tends to get out of its equilibrium range during the evolution of the organism. The impression of being insufficiently loved generates psychical reactions just as a deficit of water in the body induces a search for drink.

The psychoanalytic *drive* is nothing more than the process which ensures, for the permanence of the organism, the presence of an essential variable in its range. Such a definition does not imply an individual who merely reacts, since some of the essential variables may correspond to a *positive activity level of the individual.*

Freud considers that the action of the drive is stimulated by a *source*, either external (for instance, excitement of an erogenous zone) or internal (psychical phenomenon). In the language of systems theory, the source simply results from the fact that the evolution of the organism

[6] S. Freud* (1950) (first edition in German, 1920).

or of the environment generates a change in a variable inducing, in its turn, a movement of the essential variable.

According to Freud, the drive has *an aim* "which is to suppress the state of tension prevailing at the source of the drive." In fact, systems theory does not need this concept, which is implicit in the very definition of the drive. This theory uses the word aim (or goal) with a different meaning, since the goal is the equilibrium value of an essential variable. Let us go on: Each drive generates a *pressure*, "variable quantitative element, which accounts for the action initiated to get the satisfaction; even when the satisfaction is passive (to be seen, to be beaten), the drive, since it exerts a pressure, is active." [7] This force redistributes a kind of quantifiable *energy* (the energy of the drive), which may increase or decrease. But the vocabulary should not lead us astray. The word energy does not imply a physical energy. An economic comparison would be more suitable, since Freud perceives rather the redistribution of the energy of the drive as a reallocation of a monetary stock between the various elements of the psychical system, as kinds of short or long-term investments. He speaks of *free energy* and bound *energy*. Free energy is immediately available. It is the predominant form at the start of the psychological development: on the contrary, bound energy is related to a *cathexis* attached to a representation, a group of representations, a part of the body, an object.[8] When the organism is highly developed, the operations of the drives imply changes in the distribution of bound energy, i.e. withdrawals of cathexis much more difficult to perform than the simple use of free energy. Like invested sums of money, bound energy is at the disposal of given elements of the psychical system and consequently may generate tensions in the course of ontogenesis. Hence the use of other sums of energy to counterbalance its effects: *The anticathexis* of psychoanalysis.

A last step: in a self-organizing system there is a whole hierarchy of goals progressively built through the interaction of the system and the environment. To use another vocabulary, psychoanalysis has some intuition of this situation: according to the history of the subject, a tension may be reduced in different ways, through the use of different objects (let us translate "objects" by "elementary goals"): Starting from

---

[7] J. Laplanche and J.P. Pontalis* (1967).

[8] It is highly meaningful that the work cathexis is rendered in French by the word 'investissement' (in German: Besetzung).

a study of perversions and of the characteristics of infant sexuality, Freud criticizes the popular conception which attributes a specific object to the sexual drive, and locates this drive in the stimulation and operation of the genital apparatus. On the contrary, he shows how the object is variable and contingent and how, finally, it is chosen as a result of the vicissitudes of the subject's history." [7]

The meaning of several psychoanalytical concepts may be directly derived from what has just been said:

– *The pleasure principle* is nothing else but an equilibrium principle, the individual reacting and organizing himself to suppress the tensions that start the drive actions.
– In this equilibrium situation, there is, at the same time, what psychoanalysis calls an *economic* equilibrium, since there is no tendency to a reallocation of energy between the elements of the system; or an equilibrium in terms of *dynamics*, since the effects of the forces constituted by the pressures of the drives neutralize themselves.
– *The reality principle*, on the contrary, results from the learning of the system. Inasmuch as external reality is taken into account, the search for satisfaction no longer uses the shortest ways, but is prepared to delay results in relation with the conditions imposed by the external world. It is obvious, then, that the emergence of the reality principle should accompany the transformation of free energy into bound energy.

But what, according to psychoanalysis, is the *nature of drives* or, in other words, the list of the essential variables of an individual? It is well known that Freud changed his views in the course of his life:

– At the start, he introduced the *sexual drives* and the *self-preservation drives*, the first covering a much broader field than that of sexual activities in the daily meaning of the word; the second denoting the set of needs which, like hunger, are related to the functions necessary to individual survival.
– In a second theory, he merges in one group – the group of *life drives* (Eros) – the set of sexual drives and self-preservation drives, and opposing them to *death drives* (Thanatos), whose existence he constantly argued until the end of his life. For Freud, the death drives tend to bring the individual back to an inorganic state. Directed first internally, and tending to self-destruction, they are later

orientated externally, taking, then, the shape of an aggressive or destructive drive.

The concept of a death drive has never been unanimously accepted by psychoanalysts, but it plays a central part in the work of Mélanie Klein:

The immature ego of the infant is, immediately after birth, exposed to the anxiety generated by the innate polarisation of the drives, i.e. by the immediate conflict between the life drive and the death drive. He is also immediately exposed to the shock of an external reality, which is simultaneously a source of anxiety like the birth traumatism and a source of life like the warmth, the love and the food received from the mother. Confronted with the anxiety generated by the death drive, the Ego puts it aside. This deviation of the death drive, as described by Freud, consists, for Mélanie Klein, partly in a projection and partly in the transformation of the death drive into aggressivity. The Ego splits itself and projects outside, on the initial external object, the body of the mother, the part of itself containing the death drive... In this way, the initial fear of the death drive is changed into the fear of a persecutor.[9]

On the contrary, the observation of infants' behaviour has led J. Bowlby, in "Attachment and Loss,"[10] to a rather different theory of drives which recognizes "*attachment*," i.e. the need for relations with another person, normally the mother, as a primary drive. Bowlby has tried to explain, with an explicit reference to systems theory, how the attachment processes organize themselves during the first two years of life. Five behavioral patterns (suckling, hugging, crying, smiling, act of following) seem to contribute to attachment and tend to constitute a system of regulation which maintains the child near the mother. The similarity between attachment and imprinting in ethology is an important feature of the theory. As very well-observed by R. Spitz,[11] a *loss* situation, which means that the attachment level is out of its equilibrium range, induces serious damage to the child's development.

To economists, psychoanalysis presents a theory of drives which is

---

[9] H. Segal* (1964). The quotation is not from the original text, but is a translation of the French edition.

[10] J. Bowlby* (1970). See also R. Zazzo (1974).

[11] See, for instance: R.A. Spitz* (1962, 1968).

far from satisfactory, but which nevertheless has to be considered as a background to the introduction of motivations.

That hypercomplex system, the individual Psyche, has been broken down by Freud – in a double way – into subsystems. In the first breakdown, the major split is between the *Unconscious* on the one hand, the *Preconscious* and the *Conscious* on the other.

For systems theory, conscience is associated to the existence of an information center which collects data on the internal state of the system and on the conditions of environment. But these data are only fragmentary; the state of whole sectors may be unknown; some information may be transmitted only in exceptional situations. The Unconscious is that part of the psychical system on which the center of conscience has no information, but which nevertheless stores information and is the locus of psychical energy transfers.

One of Freud's great discoveries is the double nature of the information stored in the Unconscious: a fraction of this information has never had access to the Conscious. It probably corresponds to the innate releasive mechanisms of the ethologists and to the paleo-structures of neurophysiology. Another fraction, on the contrary, has been conscious in the past, but has been submitted to repression, i.e. to "an operation through which the subject has tried to repulse or to maintain in the unconscious ideational representatives (thoughts, images, memories) related to a drive. The repression occurred in cases in which the satisfaction of a drive – liable to be, in itself, a source of pleasure – might generate impleasure with respect to other requirements" (Laplanche and Pontalis (1967)). This repressed information, strongly associated to cathectic energy has a permanent tendency to become conscious again, but this can happen only after censorship and compromises.

As for energy movements, Freud has opposed the *primary* processes of the Unconscious to the *secondary processes* of the Conscious and Preconscious:

"The way of operating (of the primary process), which the dream puts clearly into evidence is characterized, not by an absence of meaning, as claimed in classical psychology, but by an incessant slide of the meaning. The existing mechanisms are, on the one hand, the displacement through which an ideational representative, which may seem trivial, may be attributed the whole psychical value, the meaning, the intensity, originally attributed to another, on the other hand, the condensation, all the meanings supported by several associative chains becoming liable to be integrated into a unique representative. The over determination of the symptom is another example, of the way of operating characterizing the Unconscious" (Laplanche and Pontalis* (1967)).

On the contrary, the secondary processes correspond to the classical mechanisms of conscious thinking.

With the exception of repression, the psychoanalytical concepts introduced so far correspond rather to a synchronic situation than to a diachronic development. A different situation occurs with the trinity introduced in the second breakdown.

This second breakdown results from a progressive differentiation of the psychical system in the course of its self-organization.

Initially, conscience does not exist; the various processes, to which the drives correspond, operate independently; the available psychical energy is free, since it has not yet been subjected to cathexis. But it is not the chaos described by Freud, since neurophysiology shows how high is the organisation level implied by the life of the infant-born. We are rather, in the presence of a basic organization resulting from the operation of the drives.

Development will not destroy this organization. It will only be progressively and partially controlled by superior centers, which, through learning, will be changed from potential regulators into real ones.

To the subsystem constituted by this basic organization – which is totally unconscious – Freud has given the name of *Id*. Psychoanalysis cannot define its limits precisely, but neurophysiology suggests that it covers, for a great part, the activities of the cerebral trunk, of the paleoencephalon and of a fraction of the limbic system.

But self-organization will induce strict coordination between the superior regulation centers. These centers will act together to ensure integrated answers to tensions born internally or externally. A sufficient number of these centers being related to the center of conscience, this last center will be able to materialize the individual's unity. In other words, self organization creates a new subsystem, mainly conscious, but partly unconscious, which coordinates responses and operates the defence mechanisms. This system is the second personality agency, the *Ego* of psychoanalysis.

A child's development is not only the result of a hierarchical integration of the organization, the drives and the goals being given. Environmental contacts also induce the learning of new goals, permitting the
individual, progressively, to interiorize society's values. For instance,
there is the psychological process of *identification*, through which a
subject assimilates a feature, a property, an attribute of the other and
transforms himself accordingly – totally or partially. So the third
personality agency appears, the *Superego*, whole role may be compared
to that of a judge or censor of the Ego. Freud considers that ethical
conscience, self-observation, the creation of ideals, are functions of the
Superego. Of course, the borders between Ego and Superego are not
clear. The two may correspond to the activity of the neocortex and the
limbic system. But does it matter? Obviously, the breakdown of the
psychical system into three agencies can only be a very rough approxi-
mation, interesting because it permits a better analysis of the psychical
conflicts which are a permanent characteristic of the human being.
To the conflicts resulting from the contacts between the organism and
the environment (the constraints of the principle of reality), and those
between the various drives, must be added the conflicts between the
different personality agencies, especially the Id and the Ego, the Superego and the Ego. The organism, through the Ego, will try to limit these,
with the help of defence mechanisms depending on the type of conflict,
its developmental phase, its genetical stage. Anna Freud has attached
her name to a description of the variety, complexity and importance of
these defence mechanisms.

A better knowledge of psychoanalysis could help economists towards
a more profound interpretation, not only of the psychological background of certain consumptions, but also of attitudes towards labour,
saving, money, inflation, unemployment, etc. But though they may
suggest meaningful formulations, psychoanalytical interpretations
cannot be directly introduced in theoretical models, since the language
of psychoanalysis is not adapted to model-building. Naturally, there is
less difficulty with experimental psychology.

2.2. The many messages of experimental psychology

Almost all the subfields of experimental psychology have some relevance for economic theory.

What headlines do we find if we open, for instance, two handbooks as different as: "The handbook of mathematical psychology," published in three volumes by Luce, Bush and Balanter* in 1963, on the one hand, and the "Traité de psychologie expériementale," published in nine volumes by Fraisse and Piaget* in 1970?

The 21 chapters of the former are entitled:

(*i*) Basic measurement theory; characterization and classification of choice experiments; detection and recognition, discrimination; psychophysical scaling; stochastic latency mechanisms; computers in psychology; estimation and evaluation;

(*ii*) Stochastic learning theory; stimulus sampling theory; introduction to the analysis of natural languages; formal properties of grammars; finitary models of language users; mathematical models of social interactions;

(*iii*) Analysis of certain auditory characteristics; theoretical treatments of selected visual problems; identification learning; concept utilisation; preference utility and subjective probability; stochastic processes; functional equations.

The nine volumes of the second deal with: history and method; sensation and motricity; behavioral psychophysiology; learning and memory; motivation, emotion and personality; perception; intelligence; logic, communication and decision; social psychology.

All these topics have some impact on economics. The selection made will be somewhat arbitrary, though partly guided by a dual purpose:

– to choose the fields which are closest to the conventional economic theory of chapter 1,
– to give preference to topics directly related to the developments of this book.

We shall therefore examine hereunder the five following themes:

(1) psychological analysis of preferences;
(2) motivation and personality;
(3) learning processes;
(4) intelligence;
(5) social interactions.

2.3. Psychological analysis of preferences

The conventional utility theories presented in chapter 1 belong, of course, to a common field of economics and mathematical psychology. Following R.D. Luce and P. Suppes* (1965), we shall call these theories *algebraic*. They were first studied, and have been constantly used, in economics and statistics.

Parallel to these, have emerged *probabilistic theories* which are largely the product of psychological thought as a consequence of the need of interpret laboratory results. Many of the ideas and most of the results in this field are due to J. Marschak and his collaborators (Becker, de Groot, Marschak* (1963a), Black and Marschak* (1960), Marschak* 1960)).

It would be of a great interest to combine this approach with some of the proposals of this book. Hence, we shall try, in a few lines, to describe its essential characteristics. At the start, it considers a subset X of the set A of all outcomes used or potentially available in an experiment. This subset is repeatedly presented to a subject who, however, does not constantly choose the same element $x \in X$, since his choice is probabilistic. The proportion of times that x is chosen when X is presented is taken as the estimate of the choice probability of x in X: $p_X(x)$.

When X is only a pair (x, y) of elements, the above probability is a binary probability $p(x, y)$.

"Basically, there are only two approaches to how response probabilities and utility scales relate. In the approach characterized by the constant utility models discussed here, the utility function is a fixed numerical function over the outcomes, and the response probabilities are some function of the scale values of the relevant outcomes. The choices are assumed to be governed directly by these response probabilities. In the other approach, defined by the random utility models, the utility function is assumed to be randomly determined on each presentation, but once selected, the subject's decision is unequivocally determined by the relevant utilities, just as in the algebraic models. Probabilistic behaviour arises from the randomness of the utility function, not from the decision rule" (Luce-and Suppes* (1965)).

The reader will easily recognize these two approaches in the following analysis, which describes how sets of conditions on the probabilities induce various types of utility functions.

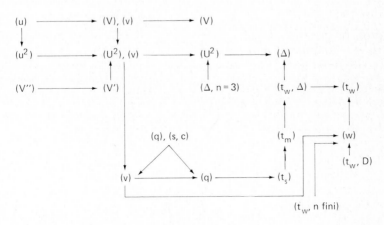

Figure 2.1

The most general condition is *condition* (U), which claims that the probabilities $P_X(x)$ are such that, for any $X \subseteq A$ (A being finite), there exists a random-valued vector U defined on A,[12] such that:

$$\mathrm{pr}\,\{\,U(x) \geqslant U(y),\, y \in X\,\} \,=\, P_X(x). \tag{2.1}$$

A *random utility model* is a set of preferences satisfying condition (U). If the random vector U consists of components which are independent random variables, the model is an *independent random utility model*.

A more restrictive condition is *condition* (U^2), which restricts the binary probabilities $p(x, y)$ to be such that there exists on A a random real-valued vector U^2 such that, for any $x \in A$, $y \in A$:

$$\mathrm{pr}\,\{\,U^2(x) \geqslant U^2(y)\,\} \,=\, p(x, y). \tag{2.2}$$

In other words, the individual has a utility, as in conventional theory, but this utility is subject to random fluctuations.

It is obvious that condition (U) implies condition (U^2).

---

[12] U is a random vector on A, if U is a function defined on A such that for each $x \in A$, $U(x)$ is a random variable.

J. Marschak has also introduced condition (Δ). This condition implies that for $\forall x \in A$, $\forall y \in A$, $\forall z \in A$:

$$p(x, y) + p(y, z) \geqslant p(x, z). \tag{2.3}$$

Condition (Δ), also known as the triangle condition, means that the probability of preferring x to z through any arbitrary intermediate choice y is greater than in a direct comparison, because of the additional uncertainties introduced by the double operation. Condition (U^2) implies (Δ) and Δ implies (U^2), but for *three alternatives* only.

Conditions (U) and (U^2) correspond to the random utility approach. The following conditions, on the contrary, are related to the introduction of constant utilities.

The strong transitivity condition (condition (t_s)) is expressed thus:

$$\min\left[p(x, y), p(y, z)\right] \geqslant \tfrac{1}{2} \Rightarrow p(x, z) \geqslant \max\left[p(x, y), p(y, z)\right]. \tag{2.4}$$

In ordinary language, if we adopt the convention to say that x is stochastically preferred or equivalent to y iff $p(x, y) \geqslant \tfrac{1}{2}$, the preferences show strong transitivity when, x being stochastically preferred or equivalent to y, and y being stochastically preferred or equivalent to z, then the probability to prefer x to z is at least equal to the *greater* of the two successive binary probabilities.

The *moderate transitivity condition* (condition (t_m)) is expressed by:

$$\min\left[p(x, y), p(y, z)\right] \geqslant \tfrac{1}{2} \Rightarrow p(x, z) \geqslant \min\left[p(x, y), p(y, z)\right]. \tag{2.5}$$

Then, the probability to prefer x to z is at least equal to the *smaller* of the two successive binary probabilities.

The *weak transitivity condition* (condition (t_w)) is expressed by:

$$\min\left[p(x, y), p(y, z)\right] \geqslant \tfrac{1}{2} \Rightarrow p(x, y) \geqslant \tfrac{1}{2}. \tag{2.6}$$

Here, it is possible only to assert that x is stochastically preferred or equivalent to z. (t_w) and (Δ) do not imply each other; but (t_m) simultaneously implies (t_w) and (Δ). It is also obvious that (t_s) implies (t_m).

Condition (w) implies that the binary probabilities are such that, for any $x \in A$, $y \in A$, there exists a real-valued function on A such that:

$$p(x, y) \geqslant \tfrac{1}{2} \Leftrightarrow w(x) > w(y). \tag{2.7}$$

Marschak has shown that if the number n of alternatives is finite, t_w implies (w). If n is infinite, (t_w) and a new condition (D) jointly imply (t_w). D is the following condition: D must contain a countable and dense subset, and for any $a \in A$, the sets $(x \mid p(x,a) \geqslant \frac{1}{2})$ and $(x \mid p(x,a) \leqslant \frac{1}{2})$ must be closed. It is easy, on the contrary to prove, that (w) always implies (t_w).

Condition (v) implies that the binary propabilities are such that there exists for any $x, y \in A$ a real-valued function v on A and a strictly increasing function $\phi(v)$ on R such that:

$$\phi[v(x) - v(y)] = p(x, y), \qquad \phi[0] = \tfrac{1}{2}. \tag{2.8}$$

The function v is called a *strong utility function*.

Condition (q), which is also called *the quadruple condition*, introduces four alternatives x, y, z, t in A and claims that:

$$p(x, y) \geqslant p(z, t) \Rightarrow p(x, z) \geqslant p(y, t). \tag{2.9}$$

It has been proved that (v) implies (q) and (t_s) on the one hand, (w) and hence (t_w) on the other hand. On the contrary, (q) only implies (v) if a *condition* $(s.c.)$ of *stochastic continuity* is simultaneously satisfied.

$(s.c.)$ is the following: for any real number q such that $p(x, y) < q < < p(x, z)$, there exists $t \in A$ such that $p(x, t) = q$.

When conditions (U^2) and (v) are simultaneously satisfied, it is possible to define a random real valued function $V(x)$ on A such that:

$$U^2(x) = v(x) + V(x) \quad \text{with} \quad EV(x) = 0 \tag{2.10}$$

In other words, the function v measures the "sensation", while V is a random error which is the cause of the stochastic choices observed.

Assuming the existence of function V, two more specific conditions may be introduced:

(1) *Condition* (V') implies that, for any $x \in A$, $y \in A$, there exist three functions on A: a real-valued function v, a random function V and a real-valued function ϕ from R to $[0, 1]$, such that:

$$p(x, y) = \phi[v(x) - v(y)],$$

$$\text{pr} \{(V(y) - V(x)) \leqslant \lambda\} = \phi(\lambda). \tag{2.11}$$

(2) *Condition* (V'') assumes, in addition, that function V's multiple probability distribution is symmetrical with respect to its arguments, i.e. for any real numbers α, β,

$$\text{pr} \{V(x) \leqslant \alpha, V(y) \leqslant \beta\} = \text{pr} \{V(x) \leqslant \beta, V(y) \leqslant \alpha\} \tag{2.12}$$

(V') implies (U^2) and (v).

Finally, in the upper left-hand part of figure 2.1, two conditions appear:

(i) *Condition* (u^2) supposes that the binary probabilities $p(x, y)$ are such that there exists a positive real-valued function u^2 on A such that for any $x \in A$, $y \in A$:

$$p(x, y) = \frac{u^2(x)}{u^2(x) + u^2(y)}. \tag{2.13}$$

u^2 is a *binary strict utility function*.

J. Marschak has shown that condition (u^2) implies condition (v), and at least when A is finite, (U^2). On the contrary, (U^2) and (v) together do not imply (u^2), which is a stricter condition.

(ii) *Condition* (u) supposes that the probabilities $p_X(x)$ are such that there exists a positive real-valued function on A such that for any finite subset $M \subseteq A$:

$$p_M(x_i) = \frac{u(x_i)}{\sum\limits_{j \in M} u(x_j)}. \tag{2.14}$$

u is a *multiple strict utility function*.

Obviously, condition (u) implies (u^2) and, when A is finite, $[(V), (v)]$.

A set of preference probabilities defined for all the subsets of a finite A is said to satisfy the *choice axiom* if, for all x, M and X such that $x \in M \subseteq X \subseteq A$:

$$p_M(x) = p_X(x \mid M),$$

whenever the conditional probability exists. It has been proved that if the choice axiom holds and A is finite, then there exists a multiple strict utility function satisfying (2.14) for any $p_M(x) \neq 0,1$.

An interesting example of a *constant utility model* is the *model of elimination by aspects* (Tversky* (1972a, b)): "According to this model, each alternative consists of a set of aspects, each of which possesses a scale value. The selection of an aspect eliminates all the alternatives that do not include the selected aspect, and the process continues until only one alternative remains. Consider the choice of a new car, for example. The first aspect selected may be automatic transmission: this will eliminate all cars that do not have this feature. Given the remaining alternatives, another aspect, say a $ 4,000 price limit, is selected, and all cars whose price exceeds this limit are excluded. The process continues until all cars but one are eliminated. This model differs from the lexicographic model in that here no fixed prior ordering of the aspects (or attributes) is assumed, and the choice process is inherently probabilistic" (Sattah and Tversky* (1976)).

More precisely, let us consider a mapping which associates to each $x \in A$ a finite nonempty set $x' = \{\alpha, \beta, \ldots\}$ of elements called aspects of x. For any $M \subseteq A$, let us denote:

$$M' = \{\alpha \mid \alpha \in x' \text{ for some } x \in M\}, \qquad (2.15)$$

$$M^0 = \{\alpha \mid \alpha \in x' \text{ for all } \quad x \in M\}, \qquad (2.16)$$

$$M_\alpha = \{x \mid x \in M \text{ and } \quad \alpha \in x'\}. \qquad (2.17)$$

Then, a structure of choice probability satisfies the *elimination by aspects model*, iff there exists a positive real-valued function u on $A'-A^0$ such that for all $x \subseteq M \subseteq A$:

$$p_M(x) = \frac{\displaystyle\sum_{\alpha \in x' - M^0} u(\alpha)\, p_{M_\alpha}(x)}{\displaystyle\sum_{\beta \in M' - M^0} u(\beta)}. \qquad (2.18)$$

Aspects which are common to all the alternatives under consideration do not affect the elimination process and are excluded from the sums above.

When all pairs of alternatives are aspect-wise disjoints, that is $x' \cap y' = \emptyset$ for all $x \in A$, $y \in A$, the above model is nothing more than the strict utility model of (2.14).

However, in many cases, it shows much more satisfactory properties. For instance, let $A = \{x, y, z\}$ where x and y are two recordings of the same symphony and z the recording of a piano sonata. Suppose the individual to be indifferent to all pairs of records, so that all binary probabilities are $\frac{1}{2}$. The choice axiom (which is related to the strict utility model) implies that all ternary choice probabilities are $\frac{1}{3}$. On the contrary, the elimination by aspects model is compatible with the values $p_A(x) = \frac{1}{4}$, $p_A(y) = \frac{1}{4}$, $p_A(z) = \frac{1}{2}$ which are more in agreement with experience and intuition.

This model could obviously be adapted to the introduction of the concept of motivational satisfactions introduced in chapter 4.

Similar models have been built for probabilistic choices between uncertain outcomes.

On the borders of economics, probabilistic choice theories constitute an interesting section of the theory of the individual which, in spite of the work of Hildenbrand* (1971), Bhattacharya and Majumdar* (1973), Georgescu Roegen* (1936), Quandt* (1956), Mossin* (1968), has not yet found its appropriate position in theoretical economics, but could have a more important impact in the future.

2.4. Motivation and personality

Psychologists are far from agreed on the part played by motivation in the study of behaviour.

Under this heading, some experimental psychologists seem interested only in physiological needs such as hunger, thirst, sexuality, sleep, etc. Others tend to consider behaviour only as a response to a stimulus. Others use the concept of motivation only to study why the living organism moves to a state of general activity. But these attitudes hide the real problem of motivation, and the following essential fact:

"The individual has selective or preferential relations with regard to the surrounding objects or situations. Among the present objects, some are desired or preferred; others are, on the contrary, avoided; in case of absence, some objects and situations are asked for and sought, others are feared. This orientation is expressed by the fact that the behaviour is maintained till an object of a given category is reached... This selective orientation towards the preferred and sought for object gives to the behaviour its intrinsic direction and organization. Sometimes, the object demanded by the organization is unknown to the individual, while in other cases an innate or learned behavioural relation leads him directly towards a desired object. For man, the more or less sustained search of an object still absent or nonexistent acquires an essential importance. His cognitive and imaginative functions enable him to construct in anticipation the absent object. Hence, the importance of the constructions of imagination in some researches on human motivation" (Nuttin* (1968) in Piaget, Fraisse).

Many debates have taken place between psychologists on the motivational mechanisms. The first explanation was that a need created a tension, and that the purpose of the behaviour was to reduce and eliminate this tension. But such a view does not take into account the constant need for activity of any individual. It corresponds to the economic model of the individual who, having maximized his utility, does not try to do better through an action on the environment. Nuttin's conclusion (Nuttin* (1968)) is more satisfactory:

"We do not believe it is presently possible to formulate *the* unique dynamic pattern according to which a motivation influences behaviour. For the mechanism of tension reduction to be useful, it should be completed by other processes incorporating the fact that the individual does not tend to a complete rest but to an optimum of tension, the motivation increasing when the goal is nearer and an essential phase of the motivational process consisting in the active construction of new tensions."

The links between the motivations and the psychoanalytical drives is obvious, but the motivations may be considered as the result of the processes which build an individual's personality out of the basic drives through ontogenesis. In other words, the social environment and the history of the individual have a major impact on the relative strengths of the various motivations.

In spite of its deficiencies the concept of motivation has proved useful in at least three different fields: experimental psychology, in close connection with the analysis of personality structures; market research; and work studies:

(1) *Experimental psychology* has brought into evidence the importance of *cognitive motivations* such as the tendency to explore, to perceive and to interpret constantly the perceptions. It has also underlined the major part of *social motivations* such as the search for social relations, the lust for power and prestige, *etc.*, the results of many experiments being consistent with the observations of psychoanalysts like Spitz* (1968) and Bowlby* (1970) on young children.

The conflicts between motivations have been a constant subject of experiment. Lewin, for instance, considered three types of conflicts:

- the conflict "approach–approach", in which the subject cannot decide which of two desired objects to choose;
- the conflict "avoidance–avoidance", in which the subject would like to avoid Charybdis and Scylla;

– the conflict "avoidance–approach", in which the subject is simultaneously attracted and repulsed by an object.

He has stressed that external and internal barriers preventing the normal operation of a motivation generate a frustration which liberates aggressivity or induces regressive behaviours. This impossibility of reaching a goal may also result in a change of action, with a displacement or a substitution of the object. Experimental psychology and psychoanalysis find common ground here. As common sense indicates, motivation has been found to be the most important parameter, with capability, for the efficiency of behaviour. Economics obviously has to take this fact into account.

The study of personality has introduced motivations as a result of factorial analysis. Although some aspects of the research of R.B. Cattell, J.B. Guilford and J.H. Eysenck are highly debatable, it is of real interest in connection with our subject. Factorial analysis aims at discovering all the variables necessary to describe individual differences. Among these, some should characterize motivations, if their importance changes from one individual to another. But how can we establish the list of variables? The idea is, in principle, simple: let us study all men's acts, all the goals they pursue, and let us determine the correlations between them. The goals and the acts between which relations exist must depend on common motivations. But in practice, it is more difficult: In addition to motivations, other factors such as capabilities, or temperament, or environmental influences may induce correlations between the facts observed. The words used in questionnaires to define interests, preference lists, attitudes, scales; ... the environment in which the information is obtained, all influence the results. For these reasons, the list of motivations proposed differs from one author to another.

According to J.B. Guilford, motivational factors could be the following:

(A) *Factors corresponding to organic needs:* (1) hunger (not found in factorial research), (2) male sexual drive, (3) general activity;
(B) *Needs related to environmental conditions:* (4) need for pleasant and comfortable surroundings, (5) need for order and cleanliness, (6) need to be considered and respected;
(C) *Needs related to working conditions:* (7) general ambition, (8) perseverance, (9) constancy of effort;

(D) *Needs related to the subject's position:* (10) need for freedom, (11) self-reliance, (12) conformism, (13) honesty;

(E) *Social needs:* (14) need for the company of others, (15) need to be agreable, (16) need for discipline, (17) aggressivity;

(F) *General interests:* (18) needs for exploration or, on the contrary, security, (19) need for amusement and entertainment.

Cattell, on the contrary, proposes the following shorter list, which contains many of the above factors:

(1) Sexual needs,
(2) Need for the company of others,
(3) Need to protect,
(4) Need to explore, curiosity,
(5) Need for security,
(6) Need for self-assertion and recognition by others,
(7) Narcissistic need (search for welfare by opposition to the Superego).

In addition to motivational factors, factorial analysis introduces also temperamental factors which obviously have a very important impact on individual behaviour and on the respective strengths of the various motivations. Cattell suggests six factors of this kind:

(1) Extroversion–introversion,
(2) Anxiety–Good integration,
(3) Affective lability,
(4) Constant success–maturity through frustration,
(5) Constitutional capability to adaptation,
(6) Tendency to catatonia,

while Eysenck builds his whole system around two essential factors:

(1) Extroversion–introversion;
(2) Degree of neurosis (individuals being classified from one extreme: unstable, poorly-adapted people suffering from neurosis, to the other: hyperstable, well adapted, highly mature people).

This line of research will probably never lead to indisputable conclusions; but it is interesting in that it deals with a problem of direct concern to economics.

(2) After the second world war, the study of motivations proved to be an important part of *market research*. For practically all classes of products: automobiles, refrigerators, houses, wool, cotton, tobacco, coffee, perfumes, candies, holidays, airtravel, detergents, oil, wine, etc., research has been undertaken to determine the main motivations at work. In spite of the absence of any theoretical background or of preestablished lists of motivations, motivations similar to those proposed by Guilford and Cattell have constantly been detected, though under different names: the search for power, for prestige; altruism; the need to explore, to exert curiosity, the desire for security... Types of consumers have been defined according to the configuration of the relative importance of the motivations at work, and market segmentations have been based on these types.

Let us take as an example a study made by E. Deutsch* (1963) on the psychology of retailers. The author groups the motivations into three categories:

– The search for *efficiency* corresponds, in fact, to two different interests: on the one hand, the retailer, like any manager, wants to succeed, and considers the *profit level* as an essential criterion for efficiency. However, due to the lack of precise information and to the empirical methods used to take business decisions, he frequently reduces the maximization of profit to an increase in earnings by comparison with the preceding month or year, or to a higher margin on each sale... On the other hand, the retailer is constantly preoccupied by *security;* he must not lose his customers, he must not run out of cash, he must not miss sales through lack of inventories.

– The search for *prestige* is obviously closely related to efficiency and profit, but prestige may be found in other aspects of the retailer's activity. The retailer may attach value to the fact that he is a good salesman, that he is an honest trader, that his customers belong to an elite, that he is a real specialist, that he is considered by his customers as a valuable adviser, that he is the independent boss of his own business...

– The search for *comfort* leads the retailer to avoid all effort, whether physical, intellectual or psychological. For instance, he may try to limit repairs, or the handling of goods; he may refuse to learn new management methods, or the conditions of use of a new product; he may eliminate any course of action liable to create additional problems with customers or suppliers.

Obviously, conflicts may exist between these motivations. Comfort and efficiency are frequently contradictory; prestige is rarely compatible with comfort; average profit and security do not imply the same behaviour. Depending on the strength of the various motivations and on the solutions of the conflicts, several classes of retailers may be defined, the main division being between dynamic retailers, for whom profit and prestige are predominant, and static retailers influenced essentially by the search for security and comfort.

Economic theory cannot avoid integrating into its models the results obtained by motivation research in the description of consumers' attitudes towards different products or in the analysis of the psychological dimensions of business decisions. Such topics are of key interest to economics.

(3) The field of *work studies* is probably the first in which the human sciences have been applied to the needs of business; but for many years attention was concentrated on the psychophysiological properties of bluecollar jobs. On the other hand, in the last twenty years, more general research programs have been centered on the choice of work role, on the determinants of job satisfaction and on the conditions of effective job performance (see, for instance, Vroom* (1964). Among the motivational bases of work, five factors have been stressed by Vroom as meaningful. The work roles:

"(1) provide *wages* to the role occupant in return for his services,
(2) require from the role occupant the *expenditure of mental or physical energy*,
(3) permit the role occupant to contribute to the *production of goods or services*,
(4) permit or require of the role occupant *social interactions* with other persons,
(5) define, at least in part, the *social status* of the role occupant."

The first factor is obvious. It is the direct expression of the income constraint familiar to economists. The motivational content of the second factor is more complex. As Vroom writes, "the problem of the affective consequences of energy expenditure is central to the relationship between work and motivation but its solution appears rather complex and probably entails both innate and learned mechanisms. It does seem safe to conclude that the physical and mental effort which is involved in work is not solely a source of negative effect. There are probably conditions, e.g. continued inactivity and certain early socialization conditions, under which people derive satisfaction from energy expenditure." The third factor, which corresponds, to efficiency, is clearly related to motivations like the search for power, prestige, or interest in protecting others: "The physician reduces the pain and prolongs the life of his patients; the teacher broadens the intellectual horizons of his students; the policeman protects members of the community against those who would break its laws; and the minister enriches the spiritual life of his congregation." Some similar motivations may be at work behind the fourth factor, but in direct relation to the members of the working group. Of course, different persons will find in their job role different sources of satisfactions of this kind: "having influence over other people, being liked by other people, being cared for by other people, etc." Finally, the firth factor recalls that a person's occupation greatly influences the way in which others behave with respect to him outside his work situation.

Hence, motivation analysis has proved to be a useful tool for the understanding of attitudes towards work. It is useless to argue that economics should be able to introduce these results in its theoretical models.

But, even endowed with all the possible drives and motivations, the "homo oeconomicus" will remain a stubborn being, if he is not able to change his behaviour through time as a result of learning.

Hence, it is easy to explain the growing importance of learning models in economics, which justifies a brief review of the main learning models developed in experimental psychology.

2.5. Learning processes

The essentially stochastic character of learning must be kept in mind, though economics has not yet completely introduced learning as a deterministic process.

All learning models consider a sequence of trials ($1 \leqslant n \leqslant N$), a set of response alternatives $(A_j)_{1 \leqslant j \leqslant r}$, available to the subject on every trial, and a set of equivalent events $(E_k)_{1 \leqslant k \leqslant m}$, each event being an equivalence class of combinations of responses and outcomes.

For instance, when there are two possible responses A_1 and A_2, a learning model will generally be defined by a relation of the type:

$$p_n = F\{n, X_{n-1}, \ldots, X_1\}, \qquad (2.19)$$

where

$$p_n = \mathrm{pr}\{A_1 \text{ on trial } n\}, \qquad (2.20)$$

and where X_n is a row vector random variable with m elements corresponding to the n possible events (X_n can take on the values $(1, 0, \ldots, 0)$, $(0, 1, \ldots, 0), \ldots, (0, 0, \ldots, 1)$, which correspond to the occurrence on trial n of $E_1, \ldots, E_m$).

If, in addition, path-independence is assumed, i.e. if it is supposed that only the event at trial n transforms the existing probability p_n into a new probability p_{n+1}, relation (2.19) is simplified into:

$$p_{n+1} = f\{p_n, X_n\}. \qquad (2.21)$$

If, on the contrary, the order of appearance of events in the sequence of trials is indifferent, (2.19) may be given the expression:

$$p_{n+1} = F(W_n), \qquad (2.22)$$

where

$$W_n = \sum_1^n X_j.$$

But, since the above relations have proved far too general to lead to operational models, economics could use a certain number of models based on additional assumptions:

(a) *Combining classes condition.* This condition asserts that any set of actions by the subject can be combined and treated as one alternative.

Together with the path-independence assumption, the combining classes condition leads to the well-known linear models defined by the relation:

$$p_{n+1} = \alpha_k p_n + (1 - \alpha_k)\lambda_k \,\forall\, 1 \leqslant k \leqslant m, \qquad (2.23)$$

with the constraints $0 \leqslant \alpha_k \leqslant 1$ and $0 \leqslant \lambda_k \leqslant 1$. While α_k may be interpreted as a learning-rate parameter, λ_k is the limit point of the learning process.

(b) *Independence from irrelevant alternatives.* Path-independence of the sequence of response strengths is still assumed, but in addition it is supposed that a *response strength* $v(j)$ is associated to each response and that the probability of a response i is:

$$\text{pr}\,\{A_i\} = \frac{v(i)}{\sum\limits_j v(j)}. \tag{2.24}$$

Learning corresponds to a transformation of response strengths, but it is observed that:

– the unit of response strengths is arbitrary;
– the scale of response strengths is unbounded;
– the response strength is positive.

The combination of these remarks leads to the powerful condition that learning multiplies a response-strength by a constant.

In the case of two possible responses only, when E_k occurs, $v(1)$ and $v(2)$ will be transformed into $a_k v(1)$ and $b_k v(2)$ or:

$$\text{pr}\,\{A_1\} = \frac{a_k v(1)}{a_k v(1) + b_k v(2)} = \frac{\beta_k v}{1 + \beta_k v}, \tag{2.25}$$

with $\beta_k = a_k/b_k, \quad v = v(1)/v(2)$.

Hence the corresponding formulae for this model (known as Luce's Beta model (Luce* 1959)), are:

$$p_{n+1} = \beta_k v_n/(1 + \beta_k v_n), \tag{2.26}$$

$$p_n = v_n/(1 + v_n), \tag{2.27}$$

or:

$$p_{n+1} = \beta_k p_n/[(1 - p_n) + \beta_k p_n]. \tag{2.28}$$

(c) *Urn schemes.* The models derived from urn schemes are designed for experiments with two subject-controlled events.

On trial 1, an urn contains w_1 white balls and r_1 red balls. A ball is selected at random. If it is white, event E_1 occurs ($x_1 = 0$). The ball is replaced and the content of the urn changed into $w_1 + w$ white balls and $r_1 + r$ red balls. If the ball chosen is red, event E_2 occurs ($x_1 = 1$) and the content becomes $w_1 + w'$ white balls and $r_1 + r'$ red balls.

If:

$$t_n = \sum_{j=1}^{n-1} (1 - x_j) \tag{2.29}$$

is the number of occurrence of E_1 and:

$$s_n = \sum_{j=1}^{n-1} x_j \tag{2.30}$$

the number of occurrences of E_2, it is obvious that:

$$p_n = \text{pr}\{E_2 \text{ on trial } n\} = \frac{r_1 + rt_n + r's_n}{(r_1 + w_1) + (r + w)t_n + (r' + w')s_n}. \tag{2.31}$$

Special cases are:

$$r + w = r' + w' = 0,$$
$$r = r' = 0 \quad \text{or} \quad w = w' = 0.$$

(d) *Linear models for sequential dependences.* Sometimes, it is important to represent the autocorrelation of responses or the correlation of responses with outcomes. As an example the one trial perseverance model which applies to an experiment with a certain reward. Its mathematical expression is the following:

$$p_n = \text{pr}\{x_n = 1\} = (1 - \beta)\alpha^{n-1}p_1 + \beta x_{n-1}, \tag{2.32}$$

where $0 \leqslant \alpha \leqslant 1; 0 \leqslant \beta \leqslant 1$.

To understand relation (2.32), notice that:

– if $\beta = 1$, $p_n = x_{n-1}$ the answer at trial n is totally conditioned by the event on trial $n - 1$;
– if $\beta = 0$, $p_n = \alpha^{n-1}p_1$, p_1 being the probability of selection of 1 on trial 1, the answer is totally conditioned by the initial attitude. (2.32) is equivalent to:

$$p_{n+1} = \alpha p_n + \beta x_n - \alpha \beta_{n-1}, \qquad n \geqslant 2, \tag{2.33}$$

which clearly shows the path-dependent feature of the model.

(e) *Logistic models.* In many learning models, the problem of containing p_n in the unit interval arises. It is solved by restrictions on the parameter values; but another solution may be to replace p_n by a function of p_n such that p_n will remain in the $[0, 1]$ interval.

Such a transformation is given by the well-known logistics function, logit p_n given by:

$$\text{logit } p_n = \log \left[p_n/(1 - p_n) \right]. \tag{2.34}$$

For instance, an old but interesting learning model, due to Hull (1943), is intended to describe the change in probability of reactions of the all-or-none type: "If we assume that incentive and drive conditions are constant from trial to trial, then the model involves the assumptions that: (1) reaction potential $(_sE_r)$ is a growth function of the number of reinforcements; and (2) reaction probability (q) is a (normal) ogival function of the difference between the reaction potential and its threshold $(_sL_R)$ when this difference is positive; otherwise the probability is zero" (Sternberg (1963)). These assumptions may be mathematically translated into:

(1) $_sE_R = u(1 - e^{-v\tau})$, $(u, v > 0)$,

τ being the number of *reinforcements*. Unrewarded trials do not change $_sE_R$.

(2) $\text{logit } q = \begin{cases} \alpha + \beta \left(_sE_R - {_sL_R}\right) \left(_sE_R > {_sL_R}\right), \\ -\infty, \quad \left(_sE_R \leqslant {_sL_R}\right) \end{cases}$

(the logistic function being substituted to the normal ogive for the sake of simplicity).

Combining (1) and (2), the probability p of not performing the response is given by:

$$\log \left[\text{logit } p + c \right] = \begin{cases} -(a + b\tau), & (\tau > k), \\ -\infty, & (\tau \leqslant k). \end{cases}$$

The use of these various models in the economic theory of individual behaviour might be a matter of convenience, but it should also depend on the underlying structure of the economic situation.

The same remark especially applies to the important branch of learning theory known as *stimulus sampling theory*. The basic notion here is "the conceptualization of the totality of stimulus conditions that may be effective during the course of an experiment in terms of a mathematical set" (Atkinson and Estes in Luce, Bush, Galanter*, (1963)).

The simplest model of this type is the *one-element model*, which considers a situation where a single stimulus pattern S is presented on each of a series of trials, and each trial is terminated by the reinforcement of a given response – the correct one – and which is based on the following assumptions:

"(1) If the correct response is not originally conditioned to ('connected to') S, then, until learning occurs, the probability of the correct response is zero.

(2) There is a fixed probability c that the reinforced response will become conditioned to S on any trial.

(3) Once conditioned to S, the correct response occurs with probability 1 on every subsequent trial."

As is well-known, the same ideas may be enbedded in the *multielement pattern model*, which supposes the existence of N patterns, the subject selecting at random, with equal likelihood, one pattern at each trial:

Assume that the possible responses are $(A_j)_{1 \leqslant j \leqslant r}$ and the events $(E_i)_{0 \leqslant i \leqslant r}$, the event E_i $(i \neq 0)$ indicating that response A_i is reinforced and E_0 representing any outcome with a neutral effect.

The axioms become the following:

(1) Exactly one pattern is sampled on each trial.

(2) Given the set of N patterns available for sampling on a trial, the probability of sampling a given pattern is $1/N$, independent of the trial number and of the preceding events.

(3) On any trial, the response to which the sampled pattern is conditioned is made.

(4) On every trial, each pattern is conditioned to exactly one response.

(5) If a pattern is sampled on a trial, it becomes conditioned with probability c to the response (if any) that is reinforced on the trial; if it is already conditioned to that response, it remains so.

(6) If no reinforcement occurs on a trial (i.e. E_0 occurs), there is no change in conditioning on that trial.

(7) Patterns that are not sampled on a trial do not change their conditioning on that trial.

(8) The probability c that a sampled pattern will be conditioned to a reinforced response is independent of the trial number and of the preceding events.

The multielement pattern model supposes that all the patterns involved in an experiment are disjoint and that generalization effects from one pattern to another are negligible. Other models, the *component models*, take these aspects into account.

With the models of stimulus sampling, a structure in the learning mechanisms begins to emerge. The existence of such structures may prove to be an essential feature of learning in economics.

As an example, the economists could usefully meditate on the description given by J. Piaget of the construction of intellectual concepts.

2.6. The ontogenesis of intelligence

One of the great merits of genetic psychology is that it has shown that the development of intelligence, under the combined influences of the process of nervous maturity, social relations and experience, presents a sequential character, each level implying a *reconstruction of the elements obtained at the preceding level* and *an integration of new elements into the framework of a structure with an internal equillibrium.* The existence of surrounding objects, the concept of number, the propositions of logics, are all the result of this progressive elaboration.

The conservation of size through space and time, which is essential for the subsequent development of intelligence, is only slowly acquired. Even the concept of the permanence of an object – in the traditional meaning of the word – is the product of multiple steps; from the second month when, if a rattle is shaken, the infant tries to look for the origin of the noise, up to the second year when he becomes able to imagine invisible displacements of the object. And this permanence of the object is just a first level in the constitution of the invariants necessary to intelligence, since, for a long time, the child will conceive any transformation of the object as a simultaneous change of all its features, without any construction of the principal physical properties. Only around 8 years will he acquire the notion of the conservation of substance; around 9–10 the notion of weight; around 11 the notion of volume.

There are many steps, too, which lead to the concept of number. At the start, children only make collections where the objects are associated for the most varied reasons; then they build sets of similar objects; and finally, they constitute classes corresponding to precise hierarchical *classifications.* Only latter, do they become able to quantify inclusion, i.e. to admit that one set (the set of blue marbles) is included in another set (the set of marbles).

Seriation, which groups objects according to their differences, corresponds to classification, which groups them according to equivalences.

Towards 7–8 years, classification and seriation are the two most important operational structures at the child's disposal. They are primitive structures, *grouping* structures which do not yet permit the child to assimilate more general logical notions.

Number implies a new synthesis, all of whose elements are borrowed from these groupings:

(1) It requires the inclusion of classes (1 included in 2, 2 in 3, ...);
(2) But since it neglects qualities in order to transform objects into units, it also assumes a serial order, the only way to distinguish one unit from the next one: 1 then 1, then 1, ...

The combination of this serial order with the inclusion of the sets resulting from their union (1 included in $1 + 1$; $1 + 1$ included in $1 + 1 + 1$, ...) enables to discover what the number is.

Similar processes have been found for space, time and hazard.

At 11–12 years and till 14–15 years, the last phase of the construction of logical operations begins. The child becomes able to deduce operationally from simple hypotheses (logic of propositions). First, through a generalization of the operations of classification, he succeeds in conceiving classifications of all possible classifications. This means that he has access to combinatory logic. Then, using groupings, he discovers the group $INRC$, whose importance was first realized in genetic psychology.

This group combines four possible transformations I, N, R, C of a given proposition. If we denote m a proposition asserting that property p implies property q, I is the identical transformation ($Im = m$), N the inversion (Nm meaning that it is not true that p implies q), R the reciprocal (Rm meaning that q implies p) and C the correlative transformation (Cm meaning that it is not true that q implies p). Naturally, any proposition m may be transformed by several of the above operators in a given order.

What Piaget has shown is that the four operators have remarkable characteristics, since $NR = C$, $CN = R$, $RC = N$, $NRC = I$ and that, while the notion of inversion exists in the "groupings" of classes (classifications) and the notion of reciprocity in the "groupings" of relations (seriations), these two groupings remain heterogeneous at the level of concrete operations till the child becomes able to use *simul-*

taneously inversion and reciprocity, which means that he implicitly uses the *INRC* group and has access to the logic of propositions.

The studies on intelligence offer the brightest example of successive synchronic equilibria of a self-organized system and of the way in which these equilibria transform themselves into a diachronic process. Therefore, though they cannot immediately be transposed into economics, they suggest a direction for research which could prove to be essential and would consist of the description of the successive levels of economic behaviours of the individuals which appear along the process of economic development, each level being compatible with the equilibrium of the associated economic system, and being integrated, later, into the upper level.

2.7. Social interactions

This field of experimental psychology is worth mentioning, since it may have a much greater impact on economics as soon as individual utilities are no longer independent of the situation of others and it is admitted that they change progressively under the influence of the environment.

As can be expected, the variety of approaches is immense. Only a few paths will be recalled here:

(1) Numerous models examine *interactions in large well-mixed populations.* "The occasional explosive spreads of rumours, facts, and panics attest to the underlying similarity between social diffusion and other diffusion and chain reaction processes, such as epidemics, the spread of solvents through solutes, crystallization, dissemination of genes through an interbreeding population..." (Rapoport* 1963). In the same category may be introduced the predator-prey models, describing the evolution through time of two populations experiencing the type of conflict which result from the fact that one population is the food necessary to the other. The diffusion of new products in a population of consumers is an important part of the analysis of managerial capitalism by R. Marris (1964), and many marketing models introduce similar mechanisms; but until now, and to the great disadvantage of economics, the link with the theory of utility maximization under constraints has not really been made yet.

(2) Other models replace the assumption of well-mixedness by the explicit representation of the contacts between each individual and his "neighbours", the probability of a contact depending on the nature of the relations between two individuals. It is then possible to study *the statistical aspects of net structures*... Similar ideas could be used to represent the way in which mergers occur between firms having different mutual relations and led by executives with more or less compatible psychologies.

(3) One totally different approach is concerned with the *structure of small groups*. Sometimes, the psychological content is very poor, as in the application of graph theory to the analysis of subgroups and cliques in a given group (Harary and Norman* (1953)). But the content becomes more interesting when the number of types of relations between individuals is increased, and when the structure of certain relations has an influence on others:

- For instance, in a sociogram in which a relation between the members of a pair can be interpreted as "liking," "disliking" or "indifference," the hypothesis has been made (Newcomb* (1953, 1956)) that two persons' attitudes towards each other are influenced by their attitude towards a third individual. Hence, the pattern of relations would tend towards a balanced configuration.

- In de Backer's* (1974) theory of conflicts each individual is characterized by his preferences, his status and his role (the role being the status as it is perceived by other members of the organization). A proximity between individuals may be due to similarity in goals, to similarity in status (maintenance engineers) or to similarity in roles. Three different types of cliques may then exist, but the assumption is made that a strong proximity in one dimension will tend to narrow the distances in the others. For instance, a similarity in status induces a similarity in goals... Such ideas could obviously be used in economics to represent the formation of social groups as a result of the operation of the economic system. An attempt in this direction will be made in the second volume.

(4) Much deeper, though less immediately useful for economics, is the *double-bind theory* developed by Gregory Bateson and the Palo Alto

School to interpret schizophrenia (P. Watzlawick, J. Helmick-Beavin, D.D. Jackson* (1967)). In this theory, two individuals cannot avoid communicating, but every communication presents two dimensions: a *content* and a *relation*, this second dimension being in fact a communication *on* the communication. In addition, human beings constantly use two channels of communication: ordinary language, which is a *digital* language; and the language of gestures, postures, eye movements, etc., which is an *analogical* language. The first has a complex and convenient logical syntax, but lacks semantics adapted to the transmission of relation. The second has the semantics, but not the syntax suitable for an unequivocal definition of the message on the relation.

A double-bind situation may then happen in the following context:
- Two or several persons experience a very intense relation of great value for them (between parents and children within a family, for instance).
- In such a context, a message is sent, through the two communications channels, which has a structure such that: (a) it asserts a proposition, (b) it asserts something on this proposition, (c) the two assertions are mutually exclusive.
- The receiver of the message cannot escape from the framework imposed by the message. "Caught in a double-bind situation, an individual may be punished (or at least feel himself guilty) when he perceives things properly, and be called 'wicked or crazy' for having insinuated that, maybe, there is a discrepancy between what he sees and what he 'should' see" (P. Watlawick et al.* (1967).

When an individual constantly experiences such a situation, he will come to consider it as normal and will, logically, adopt one of three behaviours well-known in psychiatry: he will look unceasingly for a hidden meaning; he will obey any message indiscriminately; he will get out of the game (paranoïd, hebephrenic and catatonic schizophrenia).

The interest of this analysis for economics is to stress *the interdependence between the goals of an individual, as they may be expressed at a given time of his life and the environmental relations with other individuals which he has experienced in the past.*

(5) *Experiments in gaming* illustrate another approach to social relations which just deserves a mention since it is well-known to economists, and almost belongs to economic science.

(6) Finally, *group dynamics* "is a branch of social psychology in which the small (face to face) human group (e.g. a work group, a friendship circle, a family) is the object of study" (Rapoport* (1963)). Such research constantly leads to an analysis which could be used to represent economic situations.[13]

These examples are ample proof that economics may benefit from psychological theory in three different ways:

— to gain a deeper understanding of human behaviour. This is useful in order to build models adapted to economics, even if no transposition is conceivable at this stage (as is the case, for instance, for Freud's metapsychology);
— to adopt general concepts, which may directly become parts of suitable economic models (as is the case, as we shall see, for the concept of motivation);
— to introduce directly psychological models adequately representing individual or interindividual situations usually considered as pertaining to economics (as may be the case for certain learning models).

3. Two topics in sociology

Sociology has a great deal more to bring to a theory of the individual in economics than the aspects which will be discussed here; but the two topics selected undoubtedly raise key issues for economists:

— The work of Simon and others (H.A. Simon* (1957) and H.A. Simon and J.G. March* (1958)) has contributed to a considerable extension of the model of man. It has not only stressed the importance of

---

[13] See, for instance, the mathematical treatment by Simon* (1957) of Festinger's model of small group evolution. The five parameters are: D, perceived discrepancy of opinions among the members on an issue; P, pressure to communicate with each other; C, group cohesiveness; U, pressure to achieve uniformity of opinion; R, relevance of the issue to the group.

adaptive behaviour, but also introduced a variety of variables which deeply change the meaning of the consumption set.

Nevertheless, in this approach, the time span considered limits severely the possibilities of society in influencing individual goals.

– On the contrary, in anthropology, one of the main debates of the last half-century has concerned the influence of the environmental culture on the selection of leaders and on the construction of individual personalities. As a background, this debate is of importance to economists, once they accept that utility functions, rather than being given exogenously are partly conditioned by the past history at the individual, and also at the social levels.

3.1. Adaptive behaviour within organizations

The model which results from Simon's adjunctions is considerably richer than the initial utility model. The individual no longer has only to compare the consequences of his decisions with respect to a goal. He has to inform himself, to imagine, to compute. He may experience internal conflicts expressing a difficulty in deciding. This difficulty may arise from three different sources:

– the "best" decision may appear unacceptable to the individual;
– there may be several decisions which the individual feels unable to compare, although he is able to evaluate their various consequences;
– the uncertainty of the future may be such that it is practically impossible to form an opinion on the consequences of the various decisions.

The solution found by the individual to solve this conflict will depend on its very nature:

If the conflict comes from unacceptability, the individual will look for possible new decisions. Repeated failures in the discovery of acceptable decisions will lead him to reduce his acceptibility thresholds.

If the conflict results from noncomparability – several decisions being acceptable – the individual may base his choice on secondary features, such as the order of presentation.

If the conflict is a consequence of uncertainty, the individual will first look for additional information on the consequences of his decisions. If this does not make the choice easier, he will look for possible new decisions liable to generate more certain consequences.

In this process of adaptive behaviour, many characteristics of self-organizing systems will appear:

- the search for possible decisions will be in the *neighbourhood* of known solutions;
- the comparison of solutions will rely greatly on *partial models* of reality, whose nature is conditioned by the individual's history and motivations;
- the individual will frequently use *behavioural rules*, which correspond to a delegation of the decisions to lower levels of the nervous system, thus eliminating conscious conflicts and decreasing anxiety.

This new model of the individual (see figure 2.2) completes, without any contradiction, the psychoanalytical model of personality. Far more complex than the utility model, it will be a constant reference in the course of this book.

As an example, let us review briefly the way in which Simon and March* (1958) describe the influence of an organization on individual behaviour within the organization at the three consecutive steps of a decision process:

- The evocation of behaviour possibilities (i.e. the imagination step);
- The perception of the consequences of these possibilities (i.e. the "computation" step);
- The evaluation with respect to individual goals (i.e. the comparison of utility values).

First aspect: *the evocation of behaviour possibilities:* during working hours, the decision possibilities conceived may or may not be compatible with the objectives of the organization. Certain environmental characteristics will reinforce or prevent the evocation of possibilities undesired by the organization:

- the greater the number of possibilities of work outside the organization, the greater will be the probability of evoking undesired possibilities;
- the more favourable the type and level of compensation, the harder will the individual's imagination search in the direction desired by the organization;
- the nature of the work to be performed will have effects depending simultaneously on the task's complexity, on the individual's capa-

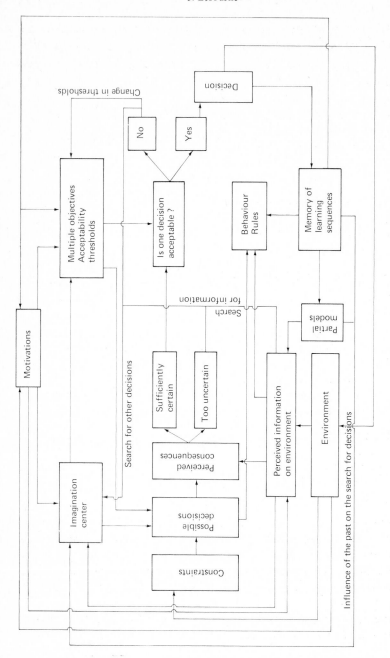

Figure 2.2 (reproduced from Lesourne* (1976))

bility, on intensity of supervision. For instance, if the task is easy with respect to the individual's capability, too strict a supervision will encourage the evocation of possibilities undesirable for the organization;
- the individual adjusts his evocations to the attitudes and behaviour of his neighbours within the group;
- finally, the higher the perceived individual participation in the decision taken by the organization, the better the organization's control over the evocations, and the lower the perception level of the power relations within the organization.

For the second aspect, the *perceived consequences of decision possibilities*, these depend simultaneously on environment, on group pressures and on group rewards:

- Environment has the same effect as for the evocation of possibilities: the individual with good job prospects outside considers it less important to take actions whose consequences are in accordance with the goals of the organization.
- Group pressures generate conformity, the level of which increases with the extent of the group's control over environment; with the uniformity of opinion within the group; with the degree of the individual's identification to the group.
- In the rewards of the organization should be included, as well as the conditions of compensation and training, the specific criteria used to evaluate the individual. The smaller the size of the group, the higher his personal position in the hierarchy, the more precisely defined the nature of his activities, the more operational will these appear to him.

Third and last aspect: the organization influences *the individual goals*. The more the individual identifies himself to the group, the more will the organization succeed in making these individual goals more compatible with its objectives. When the prestige of the group is high; when its objectives seem to be adopted by the other members within the group; when the interactions between the individual and the other members are frequent; when the proportion of the individual's needs satisfied by the group is high; when competition between the individual and the other members of the group is unimportant; then identification will reach a maximum and will tend to mould individual objectives into a common set of goals. The organization will be very close to a team.

This analysis is a good example of a broadening of the elements taken into account in the representation of individual behaviour. Its relevance to economics is obvious. Nevertheless, within an organization, the way in which individual goals may be distorted is limited, since the individual's personality is already constructed when he joins the organization. The relations between society and values have to be examined at the deeper level of what, in anthropology, is called culture.

3.2. Cultural differentiation

The first essential teaching of anthropology is that each culture is a system in synchronic equilibrium, progressively built in the course of evolution, and with all its subsystems strongly related. Through historical filiations and diffusions frequently ignored, this system conditions, to a large extent, the individuals taking part in it.

This specificity of each culture has immediate consequences on the way in which it privileges the types of personalities liable to have access to various roles; but it also raises the fundamental question of interaction between the society and the individual in the process of the double construction of individual personalities and of the culture itself. This question has been, for sixty years, at the heart of many debates between sociology and psychoanalysis.

3.3. The selection of leaders

First of all, it seems that each culture facilitates the arrival at the leading positions of the individuals whose personality presents the features it values. For instance, in Western culture, megalomania is considered to be an abnormal characteristics. The study of the Kwakitls shows, on the contrary, that it is, in this culture, the ideal imposed by the group on individuals. And precisely, among the Kwakitls, the leaders are individuals who present these very tendencies in their own nature. Catalepsy, considered in our society as a morbid symptom, is in the shamanic societies an ideal state to be reached, and the persons exhibiting it occupy leading positions in the social hierarchy.

Fifty years ago, Lasswell* (1930) examined the relations existing in our own culture between individual psychoanalytical history and types of political behaviour.

So, even if the psychoanalytical process of the construction of a personality is the same from one culture to another, each culture generates an economic system which selects certain types of individuals and gives them the possibility of influencing the whole of society through their own goals.

When economists have tried to extend to other cultures the Western model of a development induced by competition between individuals, they have grossly under estimated this fact. For this prime reason, many of their theoloretical models cannot adequately represent other than Western economies in a given historical period. To avoid this, we shall have to propose, later in this book, a theory of the individual which takes into account these cultural biases in selection processes. But for many anthropologists the influence of culture goes deeper: it directly affects the mechanisms of construction of personality.

3.4. The dialectics between the elaboration of culture and the elaboration of individual personality

Durckheim and his collective conscience, Freud and his hereditary memory of the murder of the father by the sons, have contributed to obscure the process of the relations between the individual and society, a process which may be, simultaneously, at the level of the innate and of the learned:

- On the one hand, nervous structures, programmes, part of the content of the unconscious, are progressively acquired through a genetic and chromosomic evolution which may select mutations privileging certain unconscious structures.
- On the other hand, there exists a cultural transmission with simple mechanisms: An individual is not born just anywhere, but into a family belonging to a given collectivity with its culture, its values, its parental system. Through an interaction with this very family, the individual's psychoanalytical personality is built. In his turn, through his behaviour, this individual will slightly modify the culture to which he belongs; but this change, under the influence of individuals and of the environment, will be slow. So when, at the next generation, a new individual is born, the social constraints conditioning the

formation of his personality will be almost identical. Except for local variations, the psychological history of the new individual will be similar – but not quite the same as – that of his predecessor. In spite of the absence of any heredity of acquired characteristics, the second individual almost reproduce the type of personality of the first.

He will reproduce it at the level of *conscious relations* and at the level *of the repressed fixed by the permanent structures of the unconscious:*

– At the *conscious* level, the child will learn a language. He will acquire a religious, historical, technical, scientific knowledge. He will become accustomed to many rules, covering fields as different as bodily cleanliness and politeness. He will adopt the values of his social group – those of the conservative peasant whose life is dominated by the yearly cycle of the seasons, and who knows that innovations may prove disastrous in the long run; or those of the 19th century worker who lives from day to day, and knows that only a slowly and hard-won solidarity may help him to find protection against unemployment and illness.
– But at the same time, the child, in his family, will reproduce the *repression in the unconscious* of the preceding generation, under the influence of socio-cultural institutions, i.e. the behaviours, customs, uses, legends, myths, religious rules, written documents, pedagogical principles, artistic creations, political systems, of the society in which he lives.

Hence the great question: what, in the construction of individual personalities, is a feature of mankind. What belongs only to a given culture? Geza Roheim was one of the first to prove convincingly that psychoanalytical processes are universal, though, in the framework of different cultural constraints, they generate different personalities. After Malinowski, Ruth Benedict, Margaret Mead, the work of Kardiner represents a step forward in the understanding of this problem, in spite of the defects of some of his concepts:

– Kardiner accepts from the start the existence, at the individual psychophysiological level, of a plurality of needs, among which self-conservation wants (food and safety) and sexual wants. Depending on the society and on the value it attaches to status, wealth, prestige, . . . some of these needs may generate various frustrations of a social nature.

- He then recognizes the constant interaction of the social and the psychological. In other words, an individual and a society are two self-organizing coupled systems. The first, in a rapid evolution, builds itself out of its own structure and under the influence of society. The second is submitted, generation after generation, to the action of these individual sub-systems which it has contributed to shape. Hence the difference, for Kardiner, between *primary* and *secondary* institutions: The primary institutions, such as rules of infant education, family organization, basic disciplines of oral, anal or genital tendencies, collective sets of values, induce in early life a certain type of behaviour and a certain psychological structure. Reciprocally, the individual, satisfied or frustrated in his deep tendencies, will react to these institutions to change them or create new ones, and may find a solution to his anxiety through the creation of spirits or the elaboration of myths... These are the secondary institutions.
- Kardiner deduces from this – and here the defect appears – that in each individual there coexists the character which differentiates one person from another, and the basic personality which is common to all the members of the same culture. Environmental conditions (such as lack of food) and certain aspects of the social organization (such as sexual prohibitions, various disciplines, ...), which correspond to the primary institutions, cannot be controlled by the individual. His only possibility of adaptation is to elaborate a certain basic personality.

But the self-organizing process must be more complex. Character is not superimposed on basic personality. Personality is built as a whole from psychological substratum, individual and universal, in the context of a given culture.

Hence, anthropology offers an essential regulation level in the self-organization of collectivities. Because of the universality of psychoanalytical mechanisms, mechanisms created in the process of man's evolution, each culture transfers to each individual, during his infancy, some learned unconscious. Through the interactions between drives and environment, under collective constraint, the individual personality agencies are built. Reciprocally, these basic characteristics of individual psychological patterns change social systems in a way which we are just beginning to suspect.

Of course, in this secondary repression, the individual is submitted, through the social groups to which he belongs, to the influence of the various collectivities of which he is a member: French collectivity, Catholic collectivity, bourgeois collectivity; Puritanism and Jesuit Catholicism, Western or Hindu civilization, working-class or bourgeois families do not, because of the differences in the mother's behaviour, on the father's part, in the type of education, transmit the same learned unconscious. To inform on these links, in order to understand the impact of political and social systems on individual psychologies, might be an essential task for psychoanalysis.

These links probably explain certain essential attitudes in Western civilization, such as the intensity of the need to explore and to know; the will to dominate and act; the propensity to invest for the future. Similar mechanisms generate, in other cultures, resignation, submission to the rules, indifference to tomorrow. The number of candidates wanting to become scientists, military chiefs, civil servants, entrepreneurs or monks is a direct result.

For the economist of the last quarter of this century, confronted with the huge problem of the underdevelopment of the Third World, the lesson of anthropology is essential: utility functions cannot, any longer, always be given exogenously. Behaviours such as profit maximization cannot always be considered as obvious. It appears necessary, either to study the economic system within the borders of a given culture, the choice of the exogenous utility functions being conditioned by this culture; or to explore the links between the economic system and the various types of change in individual behaviour. Contrary to the claims of many superficial papers, these changes may be of several natures. They may concern only information; or perception of the environment; or the association between motivations and resources, or the relative strengths of the various motivations; or the motivations themselves. We shall have to explore these relations in the second volume.

The two topics which have been explored point to the interest of a growing interdependence between sociology and economics. There is no doubt that exchanges will become more and more intense in the next decade.

4. Conclusion

At the present level of the respective development of economics and of other human sciences, economics has a lot to learn from psychology, psychoanalysis, sociology, political sciences, etc., not to borrow, mechanically, concepts elaborated in other contexts for other purposes; but to take advantage of observed facts, established relations and theoretical constructions generated by scientific research in other fields, and to use these messages to elaborate an adequate response to the present endogenous demands of economic science itself.

Chapter 3

A BROADENING OF BASIC ECONOMIC CONCEPTS

> *The basic functional classification under-lying the whole scheme involves the dis-crimination of four primary categories: pattern maintenance, integration, goal-attainment and adaptation... But, on another axis, it has been necessary to discriminate the structural components of such systems... The structural classification is organized about the concepts of system values, insti-tutionalized norms, collectivities and roles. It will also be necessary to categorize and classify the resources involved in the inter-change processes not only between a society and its environing systems, but between subsystems within the society.*
>
> Talcott Parsons
> *An outline of the social system*

Introduction

The time has probably come for economics to proceed, in full daylight, without any renunciation of its past elaborations, to a broadening of its basic concepts, finding inspiration in sociological research and especially in Talcott Parsons' work.[1]

---

[1] See, for instance, T. Parsons* (1961).

Present economic theory – as formulated, for instance, in micro-economics – rests on four essential concepts:

– *goods and services* liable to be produced, exchanged and consumed,
– *individuals* consuming goods and services, offering labour services and owning goods and services,
– *firms* transforming goods and services and performing production and exchange functions,
– *feasibility constraints* limiting the field of action of individuals and firms (firms' production constraints, consumers' income constraints, equations expressing conservation of goods and services through markets,...).

This chapter suggests the insertion of these concepts in five broader ones: *resource, individual, organization, process* and *constraint:*

(*i*) The word *resource* will denote any parameter through which an individual or an organization will be liable to influence another individual or organization. The usual goods and services of economics belong, of course, to the set of resources; but physical strength, the right to vote, the possibility of bestowing a university diploma, the privilege of inflicting penalties, are also resources, and their use may alter the course of any economy.

(*ii*) To the concept of a consuming-labouring-owning individual, which takes into account only a "slice" of individual, will be substituted the concept of a complete *individual* perceived in the sociological reality of the multiple roles he assumes simultaneously: father, voter, business, manager, member of the Catholic church.

(*iii*) Economics recognizes the existence of firms, of public utilities and sometimes of the State; but we shall start here from the broader concept of *organization*, an organization gathering individuals (for a fraction of their time) and resources, to achieve tasks which may well change as time goes on. A business firm is, of course, an organization; but a University, a church, a political party, a hospital, a medical laboratory, the army, the police, a national assembly, are also organizations which take part in the activities of the collectivity.[2]

(*iv*) To introduce the *process* concept, it will be necessary to charac-

---

[2] The word 'agent' will be used to denote individuals and organizations.

terize all the ways of transforming a set of resources into another set. To the traditional production processes which transform equipment, raw materials, labour hours... into manufactured goods, will be added other processes such as, for instance, electoral processes which "produce" members of Parliament out of candidates, votes and offices.

(v) As far as the *constraint* concept is concerned, what is essential is to perceive its diversity and generality: constraints may be attached to individuals, to organizations or to processes; constraints may be social or technological; constraints may be violated or not.

A study in depth of these concepts, and the analysis of the consequences of their use for economics, would be far beyond our present ambition, and this chapter will only consider the developments necessary for the formulation, in an adequate framework, of a theory of the individual.

1. Resources

When Lionel Robbins defined economics as the science concerned by the utilization of scarce means with multiple uses,[3] he implicitly introduced a resource concept, considerably broader than the usual concept of commodity, since a citizen may use his unique voting right (a scarce resource) to vote for one or another candidate (alternative uses); he may take advantage of his influence on his political friends (a scarce resource) to recommend for a job one or another person he knows (alternative uses). Hence, there is no essential difference between the definition of an economist like Robbins and the definition proposed by Dahl in political science.

For Dahl, a resource is any parameter giving an individual or an organization the possibility of influencing another individual or another organization. Such a parameter will almost always be unequally distributed among collectivity members, and hence scarce for many, while the fortunate owners will be free to use it. In fact, Dahl writes that, in politics, resources include money, information, food, strength, friendship, social status, the right to make laws, voting rights, ...[4]

---

[3] See Robbins (1947).
[4] R.A. Dahl* (1963–1970).

Such a list is in line with Robbins' definition, as well as with his own.

Hence, it is essentially common practice which eliminates from economics a lot of resources and which concentrates attention on traditional commodities such as labour time, consumer goods, raw materials, intermediary goods, equipment, money.

Here, we shall only stress the generality of the resource concept and examine its fundamental properties.

1.1. The generality of resource concept

To sketch what resources are is fairly easy if one starts from the point of view of an individual, a firm or an organization.

Let us consider an *individual*. He is interested in the resources with which he can influence his environment – including himself – and in the resources with which others can influence his own behaviour:

- Naturally, he controls the traditional commodities he owns or consumes, but also those commodities that economics has only recently introduced (his time, his trips, the information at his disposal and, to a certain extent, his health and his life); then the rights given him by the collectivity (the right to vote, the right to marry, the right to recruit or fire the members of his staff); then his physical strength (to beat his little brother or to get rid of pursuers), and, more generally, all his physical or intellectual capabilities, learned or innate (his knowledge of languages, his ability to drive a car...); finally (but the list is not exhaustive), his friendship, his help which he refuses or gives according to his own will.
- Reciprocally, he constantly suffers from the use made of their rights by other individuals or other organizations (he is not promoted to the desired job; the candidate elected is not the one he prefers); he is influenced by the advice and the feelings of his friends, by advertising messages, by newspaper comments; he may fear physical violence threatening his property, his health or his life.

The *firm*, too, is concerned with a set of resources far greater than the one implied by the traditional image of inputs:

- Here are some of the resources it more or less controls: the staff with its knowledge, its abilities, its values, its inter-individual relations; the internal documents concerning organizational procedures, training methods, marketing studies, research reports; the information networks with other agents, civil servants, retailers, consumers, bankers, ...; the rights given by the law of the country; the cash available and the usual inputs implied by investment or by current operations.

– Reciprocally, the firm is submitted to the influence that other agents draw from the resources they control: tax agents check its accounts; various public departments define the rules of the profession or pass orders; other firms try to conquer its market with their products, their distribution network, their advertisements; banks offer or limit an overdraft; individuals it needs agree or refuse to work for it.

Let us take, finally, an *organization* of a different type, such as the Catholic church. It uses a lot of specific resources. For instance, men only have the right to become priests; priests only can celebrate Mass, baptize children, give absolution; bishops only can confirm... Simultaneously, the Church imposes rules on believers (obligation to attend Mass every Sunday, impossibility of divorce...). But, in addition to these purely religious resources, the Church uses resources similar to the ones with which the firm operates: knowledge and abilities of clergymen; oral and written traditions; communication networks with believers and non-believers; church equipment; cash availabilities...

The variety of resources existing in a developed society is almost infinite. No model can dream of taking all their riches into account, but it must nevertheless claim to introduce in each case the resources that are essential. For this, the properties of this concept have to be understood.

1.2. The resource concept properties

Resources may be considered from four different viewpoints: in their relations with society; in their scarcity and multiplicity of uses; in the definition of their levels; and in their interrelations.

1.2.1. Relations with society

Our definition implies that the set of possible resources directly depends on the society considered. What would it mean to give the Légion d'Honneur to a Pueblo Indian, to excommunicate an atheist, to teach a Central Asian cameleer to drive a car where there are no roads?

The possibility of transforming one resource into another through production or exchange is also governed by the global society. If this is obvious for production, because of the necessary technical knowledge, it is also true for exchange.

Different societies classify conceivable exchanges differently in the three following groups:

- Forbidden exchanges: no gift nor money can be offered in exchange for the violation of a taboo, of a religious rule or of a code of honour. In our society, it is no longer possible to buy indulgences, slaves or substitutes for military service.
- The exchanges authorized, but without the use of money: the advantages given to the supporters of a party after an electoral victory, the help that two professors each bring to the candidate of the other, love between two beings, gifts in thanks for a favour.
- The exchange authorized through money. In France, one can buy cars, labour, paintings, but not coal mines or railway lines. In the Middle Ages, the church forbade loans with interest. In 18th century England, to buy a seat in Parliament was a possibility.

1.2.2. Scarcity and multiplicity of uses

Robbins' definition has to be made more precise on two points:

- The *scarcity* concept must include not only the usual scarcity notion (for instance, a limit on the land surface available) but also the fact that a *resource cannot be created or developed without the use of others*. When announced, a scientific discovery is freely available (it is no longer scarce in the traditional meaning of the word), but equipment and effort have been necessary to arrive at it; to give a voting right to all citizens, the voting rights of Parliament members or revolutionary efforts may have been required.
- One must consider as *alternative uses* the utilization of the same resource at *different levels:* Person A can bestow more or less love on person B; a confessor can inflict on a sinner a milder or a harder penitence, etc.

1.2.3. Definition of resource levels

The scope of the resource concept frequently precludes simple formulation. Some special cases will enable us to define the problem better:

- Economists' education has acquainted them with *purely private consumptions* where total consumption of a resource i is the sum of all individual consumptions q_i^k $(1 \leqslant k \leqslant m)$:

$$q_i = \sum_k q_i^k. \tag{3.1}$$

As suggested by S.Ch. Kolm (1970), total consumption may be represented in this case by a graph composed of a series of arrows, each arrow representing one individual consumption and the consumptions being added from one arrow to the other (figure 3.1).

Figure 3.1

- In the last twenty years, economists' attention has been attracted by *purely collective consumptions* where the level is the same for all individuals (for instance the level of national defence). In this case:

$$q_i = q_i^k \; \forall k, \quad 1 \leqslant k \leqslant m, \tag{3.2}$$

which corresponds to parallel arrows with the same origin and the same end and associated to the same consumption (figure 3.2).

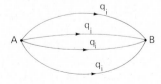

Figure 3.2

– But there are also *collective consumptions privately divided between groups.* Such a case is quite frequent since it concerns households as well as political, religious, or cultural associations... If there are m groups j $(1 \leqslant j \leqslant m)$ of size K_j $(1 \leqslant k \leqslant K_j$ for group $j)$, one can write:

$$q_i^{k,j} = q_i^j \quad \forall k, \quad 1 \leqslant k \leqslant \tag{3.3}$$

$$q_i = \sum_j q_i^j, \quad 1 \leqslant j \leqslant m, \tag{3.4}$$

q_i^j being the collective consumption of group j and $q_i^{k,j}$ the consumption of individual k in group j. The corresponding graph corresponds to figure 3.3.

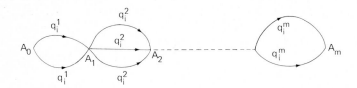

Figure 3.3

– Finally, there are *private uses of a collective consumption* in cases like the following: a firm determines a production parameter q_i (for instance, a motorway capacity), offering then a *variety* of economic services j differing by date, place, state of the world $(1 \leqslant j \leqslant h)$. If we also call j the group of individuals of size K_j $(1 \leqslant k \leqslant K_j)$ consuming j, we can write:

$$q_i = \sum_{k=1}^{K_j} q_{ij}^k \quad \forall k, \quad 1 \leqslant k \leqslant m, \tag{3.5}$$

q_{ij}^k being the consumption of individual k of group j. Such a situation is represented in figure 3.4, in which each type of service is associated to a series of K_j successive arrows between origin and end.

Obviously, all combinations of the preceding cases are possible. But there are also resources spcifically attached to individuals and organizations, so that it is meaningless to aggregate their levels when the agents are different:

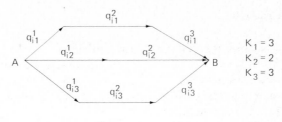

Figure 3.4

— the state of health of an individual k can be represented by a variable or a vector but it is impossible to combine these on the set of individuals.

— The voting right of an individual k in a restricted electoral system can be associated to a variable equal to 1 or 0 (1 if the individual is entitled to vote, 0 if he is not), but the sum of these variables on the population (the number of voters) has not the same meaning as for a normal commodity.

What is essential is to introduce, for each resource, the adequate formalization of the conservation relations on the set of agents.

1.2.4. Interrelations between resources

Due to the generality of the resource concept, several resources are often transmitted *simultaneously* in one exchange.

If I offer my wife a gift, she receives an economic commodity but also a testimony of my love. Examples of similar situations are frequent: the same product associated to two brand names of different prestige (Philips and Radiola); the national anthem; a drug prescribed by a doctor having expressed sympathy or not, etc. The whole symbolism of social life rests on such relations between resources.

A broad resource concept lowers barriers between economics, sociology and political science. It will prove useful to analyse numerous aspects related to education, information, organization, etc. but its usefulness will be reinforced by the broadening of other basic concepts.

2. *Individuals*

Paradoxically, the concept of the individual is absent from today's economics. Only the consumer, the labourer, the entrepreneur, the commodity owner exist – i.e. *slices* of individuals or portions of behaviour corresponding to roles. This makes it very much easier to introduce man in economic models:

- as business executive, he maximizes profit, independently of his personality;
- as consumer and labourer, he maximizes a utility function on the budget set, which reduces human diversity to shades in preferences for oranges or pears.

This modelling transforms all individuals into strangely similar beings, but in an abstract way, since it has nothing to do with similarity within a homogeneous social group.

In addition, these individual slices have exogenous characteristics which are immutable parameters, not modified by the exercise of any job or profession, nor by education, training or social and economic evolution. With such assumptions, it is impossible to describe anything more than the consequences of interactions between these rigid and partial behaviours. No feedback can be taken into account. It is impossible to understand how a new product is adopted, how consumption habits are progressively modified, how new values prevail: growth theory is even more handicapped than equilibrium theory.

Finally, capability differences are totally neglected: illiterates and Nobel prize winners are identical, except for a vague discrepancy between the qualities of their labour services. In mathematical models, it becomes difficult to see why developing countries do not create industry based on advanced research or why nations devote to education such a proportion of their *GNP*. On the contrary, individual capability is a notion as important as utility.

The individual of this book will differ from the traditional *homo economicus* in three important aspects:

(1) He will be considered in the diversity of his roles: consumer, father, engineer, member of a political party, etc. The models will try to explain the distinctions made between the roles and the decisions taken within each role.

(2) He will be represented with all the variety of his tastes and abilities

and with the wealth of the constraints on income, health, time, information, etc. that limit his possibilities.

(3) Interacting with society, he will change in the course of time.

This reintroduction of the individual concept should also make possible a better insertion into the models of groups of individuals. Between micro- and macroeconomics, economic science should build models with social groups of homogeneous individuals progressively differentiated under the influence of various environments and re-distributed in new groups. Such models of medioeconomics[5] would bring in the evolutions of values and the social migrations induced by economic development.

3. Organizations

In our structurally complex societies, economics would be well advised not to adopt, as a basic notion, the firm producing commodities out of other commodities, but the organization, permanent gathering of individuals who devote part of their time to it and use its resources to fulfil common tasks. The firm is then nothing more than a special case.

3.1. The generality of the organization concept

It is useless to build a complete typology of organizations. For our purpose, it is sufficient to enumerate the main ones:

– For an individual, the first organization to which he belongs is his *household*. Unless he is a bachelor, he is not its only member, and the decisions he takes for the organization are numerous. The mother in shopping, the father in deciding about his children's education, the couple in choosing jointly a new house, act for all the organization members.

This example shows that, rather than considering isolated individuals, as does economic theory, it is more satisfactory to assume that an individual takes two kinds of decisions:

[5] See J. Lesourne (1954).

- decisions to fulfil given roles in given organizations,
- decisions chosen within roles.

Thus, there is no difference between a man's buying cigars – a decision that his wife may seriously question – and writing a report in the office – a decision that may be criticised by his boss. In both cases, these decisions are taken within a role. On the contrary, there is a huge difference between buying cigars (an act within a role) and becoming a member of Communist party (to accept a role).

It is because a household is an organization that aggregating household decisions is as formidable for the theoretician as studying business choices.

- Business *firms* represent a second type of organization. They may be private or State firms. They may be involved in production, transport, carrying inventories, research or information, etc. In all cases, other organizations are generally free to consume or otherwise the resources generated by these firms.
- The situation is different for the third type, that of *administrative organizations* such as the army, the police, the judiciary, whose service levels are frequently fixed for the whole economy.
- *Political organizations* come next: governments, municipal councils, local or national legislative assemblies, etc. Political science is devoted to the study of these organizations, but economics cannot forget them, since parliamentary laws and government decrees regulate the whole economic life.
- In a fifth group will be gathered *political and economic associations:* political parties, trade unions, etc. These have never been properly taken into account by economists obsessed as they were by the interaction on markets of independent agents.
- Finally, a last group would be composed of *cultural and religious associations*, from the Catholic church to the Econometric Society, from a famous orchestra to an association for the defence of the Corsican language.

The above list is neither thorough nor exhaustive, but it will help to understand organizational properties.

3.2. Organizational properties

Since the notion of process has not yet been introduced, only three aspects of organizations will be considered here.

3.2.1. Organizational evolution in time

In the course of time, an organization may change much more profoundly than an individual. The Suez Canal Company, a French firm, remains formally the same organization before the nationalization of the Canal and after this nationalization, when it received compensatory contributions. Turkey is the same State in 1910 and 1920. Beyond the men involved and the tasks fulfilled, forms of organizational death and continuity are various: individuals are replaced, tasks are modified, the organization develops or declines, prospers or disappears, absorbs other organizations or is absorbed by another.

3.2.2. Relations between organizations and individuals

The most important fact is that an organization is never reduced to *a unique decision center*, with one individual deciding – for instance, to maximize profit – while all others are purely passive workers. Any role within an organization implies responsibility and initiative, and any organization has to insure in one way or another the consistency of decisions of all its members.

3.2.3. Relations between organizations

Apart from Siamese twins, individuals are neatly defined entities. But organizations are a different matter:
- Frequently, an organization can be broken down into more elementary organizations, a firm into divisions and departments, a church into parishes, an army into corps, divisions and brigades, ...
- Reciprocally, an organization may be only a fraction of a bigger one, such as a firm which belongs to an industrial holding.

– Organizations may fulfil roles in other organizations, as nations do within UNO or as parent-companies do for a common subsidiary.

For these reasons, the organizational concept is complex, but its introduction is necessary in order to represent the network of relationships within which the individual moves.

4. Processes

The process concept makes it possible to broaden, simultaneously, the notions of production and exchange. It is important to show how general this concept is and how it is linked to the notion of organization.

4.1. The generality of the process concept

A process transforms a set of resources into another set. For instance:

– classical production processes transform equipment, raw materials, labour, etc., into finished or half-finished industrial products;
– transportation processes substitute a commodity available at the point of arrival for one available at the place of origin;
– exchange processes transfer resources from one organization to another;
– training processes consume equipment and labour to improve individual capabilities;
– information search processes use inputs to improve knowledge of an environment;
– information diffusion processes change inputs into emission;
– judicial processes consume equipment and work, require knowledge of law and factual information in order to inflict penalties for breach of rules;
– administrative processes produce outputs such as decrees or rules which must be obeyed by individuals or organizations;
– electoral processes "manufacture" congressmen out of candidates, equipment and votes.

The list could be made longer, but as it stands it should be convincing enough.

Any process has *inputs* and *outputs*, but economics, because of its narrow notion of a commodity, has underestimated the variety of outputs. Even the simplest economic process not only generates an economic good, but also brings cash-flow, develops the firm's image, transforms the men involved in its operation.

4.2. Relations between processes and agents

Two aspects are important here: there are *internal* and *external* processes, and the relation between agents and internal processes is not a one-to-one mapping.

4.2.1. Internal and external processes

A process is *internal* when it is totally operated within the same organization. Coal extraction up to the loading on cars, the elaboration of a decree up to publication, preparation of an advertisement up to reception by the media, are internal processes. Thus, the internal characteristic of a process is not specific. It depends on the distribution of activities between organizations. On the contrary, a process is *external* when it is associated to the transfer of resources from certain agents to other agents, as in the exchange of labour time for a salary, of a loan for interest. Obviously, there are also *complex* processes which can be broken down into a sequence of internal and external processes, such as car production out of raw materials.

4.2.2. Relations between internal processes and agents

The relation between the set of internal processes and the set of agents is not a one-to-one mapping. In other words: the same process is frequently operated by several agents. Even electricity production is not, in France, an Electricité de France monopoly, since some firms have their own power stations.

In political science, G. Almond underlines the multiplicity of organizations which insure the same function of demand articulation, demand aggregation or rule-making. For instance, in Western countries,

Parliament, Government, administration and even courts are involved in rule making.[6] Reciprocally, an agent generally operates several processes. A firm produces several resources, transports them, sends information, carries out research, trains people. The Catholic church recruits members through baptism, develops the religious training of believers, prays for world peace, performs the usual ceremonies of current religious life.

The purpose of these rather elementary remarks is to help us not to think only in terms of the classical production functions so as to be ready to examine the last concept, the concept of constraint.

5. Constraints

Constraints limiting economic agents' possibilities of choice are permanently attached to resources, individuals, organizations and processes. Here are a few examples showing their incredible variety:

- Constraints attached to *resources:* in different forms, where location in space and time, information level, smaller or bigger divisibility, reproductibility degree, intervene, these are essentially quantity constraints.
- Constraints attached to *individuals:* apart from income and time constraints, an individual is limited by his health and survival possibilities, by his information, his imagination, his abilities, etc. He cannot rob, spy, desert, etc. at least not without risk.
- Constraints attached to *organizations:* a firm, independently of the processes it operates, must obey legal rules, must have board meetings and shareholders' assemblies, must comply with accounting regulations. It cannot violate labour laws concerning recruitment, dismissal, unions. To avoid bankruptcy, it has to retain customers, bankers, staff and cash.
- Constraints attached to *processes:* these are probably the most familiar to economists, who deal constantly with production functions and commodity conservation equations. But the broadening of the process concept multiplies the constraints of this type, since they now include electoral rules as well as penal law.

[6] See: Almond and Powell* (1966).

All these constraints can be split into two classes. *They are liable to be violated or not:*

– Some constraints are not *violable:* the existence of only one true Mona Lisa, the scientific laws of physics, chemistry and biology, the technical limits associated with a certain level of knowledge, etc.
– But there are also violable constraints: an individual can commit suicide, pay with false banknotes, throw Molotov cocktails at police cars. An administrative department may, willingly or otherwise, issue decrees in contradiction with the law. A firm may breach business regulations. The dead may vote, as in Corsica. When such a barrier is crossed, the *mode of operation changes.* On the one hand, the agents' possibilities are enlarged; on the other hand, the agent runs the risk of a fine, a prohibition of activity, a time in jail... The study of controls and fraud, and, more generally, of all abnormal modes of operations, should normally be one of the most interesting parts of a broadened economic science.

With the introduction of these five concepts, the preliminary part of this book ends. The field is now prepared for the tentative elaboration of a theory of the individual, integrating the contribution of various human sciences, while accepting, as a special case, the present theory used in economics.

Chapter 4

INDIVIDUAL CHARACTERISTICS

> *Chaque agent est une unité énergétique.*
> *Il est porteur d'une énergie de changement*
> *du milieu dans lequel il se trouve: choses et*
> *autres agents. Il reçoit, il transforme et il*
> *émet des messages; il est un centre de*
> *condensation et de diffusion de l'informa-*
> *tion. Il attire à soi des biens dont il dispose*
> *plus ou moins durablement et auxquels il*
> *impose un arrangement.*
>
> François Perroux
> *Unités actives et mathématiques nouvelles*

Introduction

Many people believe that the gap between utility theory and models
of man proposed by other human sciences cannot be filled. The next
three chapters will try to prove that this is not true. They sketch,
for the needs of economics, a theory of the individual taking into account
the points of view of the surrounding sciences.

To make the analysis as simple as possible, three hypotheses are
constantly assumed. They will be abandoned one after the other in the
following parts of the book:

– *Individual psychology is assumed given* independently of economic
  and social environment. This hypothesis, traditional in pure econom-

ics, and which excludes fluctuations of fashion as well as slow changes in values, or outbursts of revolutionary passions, will be eliminated in the second volume, with the help of the concepts which are going to be introduced.

- *The future is limited to one period*, the individual taking only one series of decisions to modify the environment. This hypothesis sometimes means that events which are in reality successive have to be made simultaneous.
- *The future is supposed certain*, even if some tricks make it possible for the individual to improve his information. Uncertainty will be reintroduced in the second volume.

This chapter is devoted to a presentation of the five categories of concepts which will be used to describe the psychological characteristics of an individual: *motivations and satisfactions, real and perceived social states, acts (roles and allocations), individual capability* and *correspondence between acts and social states.*

(1) Contributions in other human sciences clearly show that there is no hope of progress in economic individual theory if utility is introduced at the level of preferences between commodities. What would be the interest of keeping utility functions which have to be changed – and we do not known how – as soon as the smallest producer puts a new gadget on the market? With such a utility notion, the economist who stands beside God's throne to keep the book of poor mortals' utilities, would have to spend his time writing a new edition every day – not because psychologies change, but because environment is transformed. The first section of this chapter will propose the introduction of *utility* at a more fundamental level, the level of *motivation satisfactions.*

(2) For some time, many authors have emphasised that to relate utility levels to individual consumptions only is an unacceptable restriction, since any individual takes into account in his choice the *social state* of the collectivity. To analyse this notion, and to separate individual *perception* from objective reality, will be the purpose of the second section.

(3) Any individual tries, through his behaviour, to modify the social state (or his own image of it) so as better to satisfy his various needs.

But, in traditional theory, a correspondence is established between social states and decisions, without any investigation of the sociological content of decisions. The third section tries to suppress this deficiency. It defines behaviour as a set of *acts*, but separates these into *role-choices* and acts within roles or *allocations*. It also introduces *explicitly the search for information*.

(4) Individuals do not differ only in preferences or income. Curiously economics – at least in its mathematical developments – has neglected the diversity of abilities, although, from this point of view, individuals are far from equivalent. They cannot be simply jet pilots, country clergymen, sociologists or coal miners. Even if they have access to the same role, they will perform it with varying *efficiency*. The fourth section introduces the concept of *capability*, which will play a role as important as utility.

(5) The fifth and last section examines the *correspondence between acts and real or perceived social states*, taking into account all the aspects liable to be described in the above concepts.

In all sections (except the last), simple models follow theoretical presentation. Illustrating new notions, they are only sketches – some may say caricatures. However, we believe they may show the model-building possibilities offered by the proposed theory, either for the study of a specific theoretical point without a complete description of reality; or for the establishment of a link between economic science and an applied study in town planning, management or marketing, using quantified representations of real behaviour.

1. Motivations, satisfactions and utility

Market research, work studies, analysis of personality structure[1] propose the base on which, through *motivation satisfactions*, a new *utility* theory will be built. But such a theory cannot be understood without reference to psychoanalysis. After this confrontation, we shall present a few models showing the possibilities opened up by these notions.

[1] See chapter 2.

1.1. Motivations and satisfactions

We have seen that, in the thousands of marketing studies devoted in the Western world to hundreds of products, the same motivations always appear, under names that may differ according to the author: conscious or unconscious wants which guide attitudes and behaviour: safety, comfort, prestige, power, exploration, altruism, narcissism, etc. Simultaneously, statistical studies on personality structure have, through factorial analysis, discovered *motivational factors* which can be interpreted. Even if the list changes from one study to another, a common core exists, quite consistent with the results of marketing research. For instance, Cattell suggests:[2]

(1) sexual urge,
(2) gregarious instinct,
(3) urge to protect,
(4) exploration and curiosity urge,
(5) self-assertion urge,
(6) narcissic urge (welfare search by opposition to superego).

This enumeration includes in narcissic urge other physiological urges (eating and drinking needs, protection against cold) and the search for safety. It does not, although this is sometimes necessary, separate the self-assertion urge into the search for prestige and the search for power. But to quarrel about the ideal list is useless: Motivations have a lattice structure. Their nature and number depend on the cut line.[3]

What is important, on the contrary, is whether we can or cannot postulate the existence of the same set of motivational dimensions in a vast cultural field. The success – in marketing, psychosociology, political science – of clinical studies made on small samples suggests that all *motivational dimensions are present in all individuals*, though, of course, with very different intensities. One individual will attach a high value to safety, while another will look for adventure; but in the heart of the boldest explorer some safeguard instinct will remain.

Hence, the first assumption of this chapter:

---

[2] See: P. Fraisse and J. Piaget* (1968) and R.B. Cattell* (1946, 1957).

[3] Cattell's list is nevertheless preferable to that of d'Iribarne, which separates an evasion motivation, a utilitarian motivation, a poetical motivation and the gratifying character of relations with others (Ph. d'Iribarne (1972)).

Assumption 1: *similarity of psychological structures. Motivational dimensions are identical for the individuals of the same cultural field.*

The words "of the same cultural field" have been introduced to avoid any discussion with anthropologists. Such a discussion would be useless, since economic models generally concern economic evolution within an homogeneous cultural field.

Assuming that the number n of motivations is finite – which is not a real loss of generality – each motivation can be represented by an index i $(1 \leqslant i \leqslant n)$.

To go further, it is necessary to suppose that one can associate to any motivational dimension i a set Σ_i of possible motivational states σ_i and that some kind of order exists between $\leqslant$otivational states from the point of view of motivation fulfilment. To avoid useless difficulties, we shall make assumption 2:

Assumption 2: *ordering of motivational states. To each motivational dimension $(1 \leqslant i \leqslant n)$ is associated a set Σ_i of possible motivational states $\sigma_i \in \Sigma_i$ and a strict order P_i on Σ_i.*[4]

We shall represent P_i by $<_i$ meaning "less preferred than" from the point of view of motivation i.

Two remarks:

(1) The theory could be developed with the weaker hypothesis of the existence of a weak order on Σ_i; but a stronger hypothesis shortens the presentation. Also, there is nothing to prevent the introduction of thresholds on the Σ_i's; but, in spite of the importance of this possibility for measurement, its theoretical interest is not very high for the economist, who must first take account of many other aspects.

(2) To assume that ordering on Σ_i between *motivational states* is complete does not imply that the individual will be able to put *the social states* completely in order from the point of view of motivation i. He may be unable or unwilling to associate a motivational state to a given social state.

---

[4] A strict order P on a set Y is a binary relation which is asymmetric $(x\,P\,y \Rightarrow$ not $y\,P\,x$ for every $x, y \in Y)$, negatively transitive (not $x\,P\,y$, not $y\,P\,z \Rightarrow$ not $x\,P\,z$ for every $x, y, z \in Y)$, weakly convected $[x \neq y \Rightarrow (x\,P\,y$ or $y\,P\,x)$ throughout $Y]$.

The above two assumptions make it possible to state:

Theorem 1. *Under assumptions 1 and 2 there exists a real-valued function S_i on Σ_i, such that:*

$$\sigma_i P_i \sigma_i' \Leftrightarrow S_i(\sigma_i) < S_i(\sigma_i'), \qquad for\ every\ \sigma_i \in \Sigma_i,\ \sigma_i' \in \Sigma_i$$

The function S_i will be called the *satisfaction of motivation i* or the *i-satisfaction.*

Hence, under assumptions 1 and 2, an individual situation can be represented in $\mathbf{R}^n$ by a vector S, the n coordinates of it being the satisfaction levels:

$$S = (S_i)_{1 \leqslant i \leqslant n}, \qquad S \in \mathbf{R}^n. \tag{4.1}$$

It is obvious that the S_i's are ordinal satisfactions and that if ϕ is a strictly increasing function from $\mathbf{R}$ to $\mathbf{R}$, $\phi(S_i)$ is also an *i*-satisfaction.

1.2. Utility

This multidimensional representation of psychological preferences again opens up, but in a different context, the three well-known possibilities of utility theory.

The *first* is to adopt a *multicriteria* attitude, to reject any permanent aggregation of satisfactions and to study how a specific aggregation is built in a precise choice situation. Though we are convinced of the fruitfulness of this attitude, we shall not accept it, since a satisfaction vector is not conveniently introduced in general economic models.

The *second possibility* postulates an order axiom and a density of possible choices axiom on $\mathbf{R}^n$ but rejects any substitution axiom. It leads to a vectorial utility, the components of which, $U_1, \dots, U_j \dots, U_m$ are lexicographically ordered on a Euclidian space $\mathbf{R}^m$:

$$U = \{ U_j[(S_i)_{1 \leqslant i \leqslant n}]_{1 \leqslant j \leqslant m} \}. \tag{4.2}$$

Nevertheless this second possibility is not very interesting since *practically* all the *psychologically* important aspects emphasized by it are present in the third alternative.

The *third possibility* postulates in addition a substitution axiom. More precisely, we shall consider the space $\Sigma = \prod_{i=1}^{n} \Sigma_i$ and make two additional hypotheses. For this, break down any $\sigma = (\sigma_i)_{1 \leqslant i \leqslant n}$ in Σ into its ith element σ_i and the other $(n - 1)$ element:

$\tau_i = (\sigma_1, \ldots, \sigma_{i-1}, \sigma_{i+1}, \ldots, \sigma_n)$, $\tau_i \in T_i$ with
$T_i = \Sigma_i \times \ldots \times \Sigma_{i-1} \times \Sigma_{i+1} \times \ldots \times \Sigma_n$.

Assumption 3. *There is on Σ a weak order R^5 such that for any $i(1 \leqslant i \leqslant n)$, any σ_i, $\sigma_i' \in \Sigma_i$ and any $\tau_i \in T_i$:*

$$(\sigma_i, \tau_i)\, R(\sigma_i', \tau_i) \Leftrightarrow \sigma_i P_i \sigma_i',$$

R induces on Σ a set Σ' of equivalence classes and a strict order R' on Σ'.

Assumption 4. *There is a countable subset of Σ' that is R' – order dense in Σ'.*

The above assumptions make it possible to state:

Theorem 2. *Under assumptions 1 to 4, there exists, for any satisfaction vector $(S_i)_{1 \leqslant i \leqslant n}$ in $\mathbf{R}^n$, a real-valued function U from $\mathbf{R}^n$ to $\mathbf{R}$ such that:*

$$\sigma R \sigma' \Leftrightarrow U[(S_i(\sigma_i))_{1 \leqslant i \leqslant n}] < U[(S_i(\sigma_i'))_{1 \leqslant i \leqslant n}]. \tag{4.3}$$

Assumptions 3 and 4 here apply to motivational states and not to social states. Some social states may not be comparable. The set of social states may not have the required properties. The axioms of order and density of possible choices no longer correspond to a psycho-economic hypothesis but to a purely psychological assumption.

As is well known, the functional form of U depends on the specific set of i-satisfactions chosen to obtain U.[6] Since U is defined as an ordinal function, for any function ψ from $\mathbf{R}$ to $\mathbf{R}$ strictly increasing, $\psi(U)$ is also a utility function.

This third possibility will be adopted throughout the book, but a few remarks will justify this choice. Nevertheless, in order to present them more easily, we shall make two additional assumptions:

(a) We shall introduce a topology $\mathscr{C}_i$ on each Σ_i and suppose that P_i is such that there is one S_i continuous on Σ_i in the topology $\mathscr{C}_i$.

---

[5] A weak order R on a set Y is an asymmetric and negatively transitive binary relation.
[6] As for a collective utility function U expressed in terms of individual utilities.

(See Fishburn (1970, p. 36.)) Then, any point of an interval $]a_i, b_i[$ on $\mathbf{R}$ (perhaps with a_i and/or $b_i = \pm\infty$) is associated to a motivational state σ_i.

(b) We shall introduce on $\mathbf{R}^n$ the topology $\mathscr{C}$ induced by all open rectangles and suppose that the ordering $\mathbf{R}$ is such that there is one U continuous on $\mathbf{R}^n$ in topology $\mathscr{C}$.

Then U is a continuous function of S, S a continuous function of σ, and U a continuous function of σ.

This being assumed:

Let us consider first the effect on U of a change in S_i, *all other satisfactions being constant*: U is an increasing function of S_i, the shape of the graph depending on two factors:

– There is or is not a maximum level of i-satisfaction corresponding to an i-bliss state σ_i^*. Such a state should exist for hunger or thirst, not necessarily for lust for power.

– There is or is not a minimum level of i-satisfaction, in other words a threshold such that, if the individual reaches it, his personality is changed, as in René Thom's catastrophes:[7] he dies of hunger; he commits suicide; he becomes an outcast or a psychotic. Remember Spitz's babies who let themselves die from lack of maternal love.[8] Consequently, U decreases sharply when S_i approaches the level corresponding to the catastrophe state σ_{i*}.

With a different meaning for the threshold, one can adopt Simon's ideas and retain for U the graph of figure 4.1:

– Any satisfaction level lower than S_i^* is considered unacceptable.
– Any satisfaction level equal to or greater than S_i^* is equivalent.*

But, in this case, S_i^* must change progressively as a result of the possibilities.

Let us consider next the varieties associated to *given utility levels*. Their shape depends on the existence or otherwise, for each satisfaction of a maximum and a minimum level. When a satisfaction has a minimum level, *the corresponding motivation becomes essential near this threshold*.

[7] See R. Thom (1972).
[8] See R. Spitz* (1968).

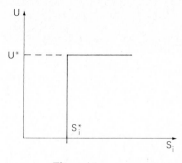

Figure 4.1

If I am dying of hunger, what do prestige or altruism mean? Hence it is not necessary to introduce a lexicographic order, since substitutability of satisfactions does not imply the same property for social states. When Chipman argues in favour of lexicographic order[9] based on the fact that there is no amount of money big enough to persuade N. Khruhschev to become an American capitalist, he has missed the following point: if money is associated to utilitarian needs, and the preference for socialism to self-respect, it is conceivable that to become an American capitalist generates a satisfaction below the minimum threshold for the second motivation; it is then rejected, independently of the amount of money offered. This does not exclude a certain substitutability between the satisfaction levels of these two motivations above the thresholds.

In exchange for a real lack of mathematical convenience, lexicographic order does not offer enough advantages for the introduction of utility function to be rejected.

With Simon's ideas, there is in $\mathbf{R}^n$ a threshold variety (T) which separates $\mathbf{R}^n$ into two subsets in which $U = U^*$ and $U = -\infty$ respectively (see figure 4.2 when $n = 2$).

The above theory has been built on motivation studies, but is it compatible with psychoanalysis which, more than any other branch of psychology, has tried to describe how the human Psyche operates?

[9] John Chipman (1960).

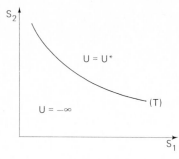

Figure 4.2

1.3. Psychoanalysis and utility

As we have seen, some psychoanalytic schools conceive personality
as a self-organizing system, where drives function as essential variables,
and which progressively builds out of the Id coordinating regulators
such as the Ego and Superego.

Hence, we have to examine here the relations between psychoanalysis
and utility theory from three angles: the correspondence between drives
and motivations, the influence of personality agencies; the difference
between a system equilibrium and a functional maximization.

Though we have no solid scientific evidence, it is not unreasonable
to suppose that the differentiation of motivations develops out of
drives in the course of the integrative process of the psychological
system. For instance, when, in the second part of his life, Freud separates
drives into two classes: *life drives*, with a broadly conceived sexual
component and a self-conservation component; and *death drives*,
with their double aspect of self-destruction and aggressivity towards the
outside world, he suggests direct links: Sexual urge, urge to protect,
gregarious instinct and narcissistic urge are related to life drives. On
the contrary, exploration, curiosity, self-assertion wants have some
connections with death drives. Of course, there is no such things as a
complete correspondence. Motivations are the product of a secondary
elaboration where all drives intervene, and only ontogenesis specificities
give the motivation satisfactions their respective importance: sexual
drive may be redirected towards narcissism and associated with great
intellectual curiosity; self-destruction drive may appear as a need to

sacrifice oneself for others; the search for evasion may express a narcissistic drive finding its way out of reality. The same analysis could be
made of Bowlby's concepts of attachment and loss.[10] What matters
here is that the world of drives described by psychoanalysis and the set
of motivations used in the new utility theory are compatible.

The personality agencies of Freudian metapsychology, Id, Ego and
Superego may be considered as parameters influencing the utility
function.

Close to fundamental drives, the Id constantly reinforces the motivations which express these drives most directly, fighting against the
constraints of Superego and breaking motivations substitutability near
the minimum thresholds.

The Ego, on the contrary, is a regulator. Built up through interaction
between the constraints of reality and the psychological system, it
coordinates the actions of the system, and its importance grows as the
substitutability of satisfactions progresses. "Not everything is possible,"
says reality. "Drives exigencies may have to be compensated, derived
or belated." Hence, if the Id is essential to the existence of motivational
dimensions, the Ego gives birth to utility. For instance, in some cases
of schizophrenia, the patient seems to have several Egos, each corresponding to different preferences or different utilities.

Created later, at the time of Oedipian conflict resolution, the Superego will modify the utility function, changing the respective importance
of the various satisfactions, some motivations being magnified and
others refused.

Hence, one could formally write utility:

$$U = U[(S_i)_{1 \leqslant i \leqslant n}, P], \tag{4.4}$$

P denoting the characteristic parameters of personality structure.
In this way the *temperamental factors* found in personality factorial
analysis would also be introduced, since these factors obviously depend
on psychoanalytic elements.

For instance, Cattell has isolated the following dimensions:[11]

(1) extroversion–introversion,
(2) anxiety–integration or adjustment,
(3) affective liability,

[10] J. Bowlby* (1970).
[11] See note 2 of this chapter.

(4) constant success–maturity through frustration,
(5) constitutional adaptive capacity,
(6) disposition to catatony,

and Eysenck has built his theory entirely on the first two dimensions (extroversion and anxiety).[12]

One cannot consider P as constant throughout life, since individual basic psychology is influenced by physiological factors and by the effects of environment – though the latter are operative mainly during early infancy.

In addition, it is highly probable that the correspondence between P and U is under the influence of psychocultural factors K which, at a rather superficial level, reinforce certain motivations and weaken others. This cultural influence bears, of course, no relation with two other mechanisms:

– the impact of society on the process of Ego's and Superego's construction, a question which has caused controversies between anthropologists and psychoanalysts,[13]
– the effect of environment on phylogenesis through an orientation of natural selection.

From now on the set of parameters P and K will be represented by a psychological factor $\bar{\omega}$ (an element of the set π of all feasible personalities in a given cultural field), which means that utility will be written:

$$U = U[S_i)_{1 \leqslant i \leqslant n}, \bar{\omega}]. \tag{4.5}$$

It will be seen that, when $\bar{\omega}$, as well as the satisfaction levels, is considered a variable, the utility function is the same for all individuals and can be identified with the *total utility function* introduced by S.Ch. Kolm (1972) and used by him to compare utility levels.

From the point of view of personality agencies, there is consistency between utility and psychoanalysis. But what about the third problem?

Psychoanalysis represents behaviour as a permanent adaptation and self-organization of the Psyche, while utility theory considers it as the result of a maximization under constraints. Nevertheless, for anyone who has understood the profound meaning of these formalizations,

[12] H.J. Eysenck (1960).
[13] See, for instance, Roger Bastide* (1972).

there is no real divorce: utility maximum is nothing other than an equilibrium of drives within a certain environment. We shall only have to be careful, when uncertainty and several periods are introduced, to avoid falling into the trap of a utility defined once and for all.

Other relations between psychoanalysis and the theory proposed in this book will appear later, but it was important at this stage to be sure that a utility based on motivations does not contradict psychoanalytic contribution to knowledge.

1.4. Some examples

Four simple models will illustrate the above notions. They concern tourists' attitudes to air-trips, housewives' behaviour with respect to soluble coffee, problems raised by supersonic transportation, psychology of management. More general economic applications will be presented in chapters 7 and 8.

1.4.1. Tourists attitudes to air-trips

Approximately ten years ago, an airline interested in the development of air transport for tourism studied, like many others, tourists' attitudes to air-trips, and found that this attitude was governed by the interaction of four factors. In comparison with other means of transport, the plane:

– induced additional satisfaction due to *prestige*, since it was a modern means of transport, using advanced techniques and reserved to an elite;
– fulfilled the need for *evasion*, offering unusual transport conditions and giving access to distant countries;
– was associated with the fear of accidents, i.e. generated a decrease in *safety* satisfaction;
– was handicapped by its high *cost*.

This qualitative analysis can be formalized with the above concepts:
Let x be the number of air-trips made by an individual and p the price of a trip; y the index of quantities of other commodities consumed (including numbers of trips made by other means of transport) and q the price index of these commodities; r the individual income.

The utility function can be expressed in terms of four motivations: (1) prestige, (2) evasion, (3) safety, (4) other motivations, and be written:

$$U = U[S_1(x, y), S_2(x, y), S_3(x, y), S_4(y)]. \tag{4.6}$$

With an obvious notation for partial derivatives, individual behaviour will be at equilibrium, *under normal regularity conditions*[14] in agreement with the following relations:

$$(U_1S_{1x} + U_2S_{2x} + U_3S_{3x})/p = U_y/q, \tag{4.7}$$

$$px + qy = r. \tag{4.8}$$

It is clear that the behaviour – and hence the attitudes – of a given individual will depend on:

– the monetary factor (r and p),
– the relative strength of marginal utilities resulting from prestige (U_1S_{1x}), evasion (U_2S_{2x}) and fear (U_3S_{3x} with $S_{3x} \leqslant 0$) in case of an increase in the number of air-trips.

Taking into account the level of the four factors for different individuals, it will be possible to build a typology of possible clients (eight principal types if two levels are considered for each factor); to measure the quantitative importance of each type; to order the types from the point of view of their interest for the airline and, finally, to adopt a marketing strategy.

1.4.2. Housewives' behaviour with respect to soluble coffee

This example is extracted from a rather old study devoted to the definition of a marketing policy for soluble coffee.

Individual consumption is represented by three products: (1) soluble coffee (quantity consumed x, price u), (2) ordinary coffee (quantity consumed y, price v), (3) other commodities (quantity index z, price index w). There are two possible uses for ordinary coffee and soluble coffee: (1) at breakfast (use 1), (2) after lunch (use 2).

---

[14] *Important:* we shall frequently use the words '*under normal regularity conditions*' in the context of maximization of a function under one or several constraints, the variables being all positive or zero. These words mean that the function and the constraints are such: that there is one maximum and one only, that for this maximum all the variables are *strictly positive*, that, in the vicinity of the maximum, the Hamiltonian is differentiable.

But the psychological context of these two consumptions is totally different:

– At breakfast, consumption has only a utilitarian character (satisfaction S_1).
– After lunch, in contrast, to prepare good coffee is, for the housewife, a way of expressing love of her family and of being acknowledged as a good cook (satisfaction S_2).

Denoting other satisfactions by S_3 and labelling each coffee consumption with the proper use-index, individual utility is written:

$$U = U[S_1(x_1, y_1, z), S_2(x_2, y_2, z), S_3(z)]. \tag{4.9}$$

With an obvious notation and appropriate assumptions on functions U, S_1, S_2, S_3, the following conditions are met in equilibrium:

$$u(x_1 + x_2) + v(y_1 + y_2) + wz = r \tag{4.10}$$

$$U_1 S_{1x} - \lambda u = 0 \quad \text{if } x_1 > 0, \qquad U_1 S_{1x} - \lambda u \leqslant 0 \quad \text{if } x_1 = 0, \tag{4.11}$$

$$U_2 S_{2x} - \lambda u = 0 \quad \text{if } x_2 > 0, \qquad U_2 S_{2x} - \lambda u \leqslant 0 \quad \text{if } x_2 = 0, \tag{4.12}$$

$$U_1 S_{1y} - \lambda v = 0 \quad \text{if } y_1 > 0, \qquad U_1 S_{1y} - \lambda v \leqslant 0 \quad \text{if } y_1 = 0, \tag{4.13}$$

$$U_2 S_{2y} - \lambda v = 0 \quad \text{if } y_2 > 0, \qquad U_2 S_{2y} - \lambda v \leqslant 0 \quad \text{if } y_2 = 0. \tag{4.14}$$

$U_1 S_{1z} + U_2 S_{2z} + U_3 S_{3z} - \lambda w = 0$ since the nature of z implies $z > 0$.

But: $u < v$ if one introduces in the price of ordinary coffee the value of preparation time, S_{2x} is small and perhaps even negative, S_{2y} is big, $S_{1x} = S_{1y}$ since the two coffees are judged equivalent at breakfast.

It is deduced: from (4.12): $x_2 = 0$, soluble coffee is not consumed after lunch; from (4.11) and (4.13): $y_1 = 0$, ordinary coffee is not consumed at breakfast.

Naturally, reality is less extreme. All individuals do not behave in the same way. But it was reasonable, at that time, to advise the firm producing soluble coffee to concentrate its advertising on use at breakfast and not to hurt satisfactions S_2.

1.4.3. Problems raised by supersonic transport

The work of Ph. d'Iribarne and J.P. Dupuy[15] on consequences of supersonic transport is immediately interpreted in terms of satisfaction.

Let us express an individual utility through two motivations only: (1) a utilitarian motivation represented by a satisfaction S_1, (2) a prestige motivation represented by a satisfaction S_2; and let us assume that, for this individual, the social state is defined by:

- the number x of miles in air-trips, independently of the type of airplane,
- the quality q of air-trips (q being measured, for instance, by cruise speed),
- the maximum possible quality $\bar{q}$ for these trips ($\bar{q}$ sharply increases when Concord is put into operation),
- the quantity index y of other commodities consumed.

Psychologically, it is reasonable to assume that the level of utilitarian satisfaction depends upon the quantities consumed (x, y) and upon the quality of the air trips experienced (q); while the level of prestige satisfaction is a function of the ratio between the quality consumed and the maximum possible quality $(q/\bar{q})$:

$$U = U[S_1(x, y, q), S_2(q/\bar{q})]. \tag{4.15}$$

It is then perfectly understandable that the introduction of a technological innovation like Concord and its impact on $\bar{q}$ may induce *a decrease in an individual utility, even if his consumption is not changed and Concord is not used.* An individual having a strong urge for prestige will go on consuming maximum quality, even if he has to reduce his consumptions x and y, his utilitarian satisfaction S_1 and his utility U (since S_2 is constant).

1.4.4. Psychology of management

Numerous authors, among them R. Marris (1964) have questioned the assumption of profit maximization by managers. They have stressed

---

[15] These authors have coined the word: 'Obselescence psychologique' for the phenomenon they describe. See: J.P. Dupuy (1973). See chapter 8, section 3.2, for a more complete presentation.

that, in addition to the search for a high income r, five main motivations appeared in the behaviours observed (Lesourne (1973)):

- power S_1: (to command a big staff, to increase the size of the firm, ...);
- prestige S_2: (to be the head of a reputable and well-known firm);
- independence S_3: (not to risk a take-over, not to fall into the clutches of a bank);
- safety S_4: (to keep one's job, to avoid bankrupcy);
- comfort S_5: (to avoid heavy duties).

The most commonly quoted variables influencing these satisfactions have been:

- dividends d,
- profits p,
- stock value coefficient v, ratio of the value of the stock to the value of firm's own funds;
- borrowing ratio e, or its inverse k, equal to the fraction of assets represented by firm's own funds,
- size x,
- rate of growth $\dot{x}$.

If q is the quantity index of other commodities consumed and u their price index, a manager's income constraint can be written:

$$uq = r(p, x), \tag{4.16}$$

since an executive's compensation maintely depends on the size of the firm he manages and on the profits made. Utility can be expressed by:

$$U = U\left[q, S_1(p - d, k, x, \dot{x}), S_2\left(\frac{p}{x}, x, \dot{x}\right), S_3(p, v, k), \right.$$

$$\left. S_4(d, p, v, k), S_5\left(\frac{p}{x}, x, \dot{x}\right) \right], \tag{4.17}$$

if observed or supposed relations are taken into account. For instance:

- power increases with self-financing possibilities, with the fraction of assets covered by firm's own funds, with size and rate of growth;
- prestige is a function of *rate* of profit to size, size and rate of growth;
- independence requires sufficient profits, a stock value coefficient unfavourable to takeovers, a modest borrowing ratio;

– safety is reinforced by good dividends, good profits, a high stock
  value coefficient, a small borrowing ratio;
– comfort needs sufficient rates of profit, but is more compatible with
  modest size and a small rate of growth ($S_{5x} < 0$, $S_{5\dot{x}} < 0$).

Taking into account the links between the different variables,
simpler representations can be obtained, for instance the one which
attaches to managers utilities:

$$U = U(v, \dot{x}),   \tag{4.18}$$

where the rate of growth and the stock value coefficient appear.

This broader representation of managers' behaviour has already
given rise to new developments in business economics.

The modifications introduced in utility theory may be far-reaching,
since *the bulk of motivation studies* in marketing, sociology, political
science, organizational science *can now be interpreted in an economic
science, the form of which is no longer void of real content.*

But it is only the foundation stone of the building.

2. Social states and perceptions

Upon what do satisfactions depend? It is necessary, before any analysis
of the *relations between social states and satisfactions,* to introduce
precise *definitions of social states.* Some examples will illustrate the
possible use of the proposals made. They will be followed by a first
enumeration of parameters influencing satisfactions.

2.1. Social states

During the period under study, the situation of the economy can be
described globally by a set of parameters, including:

– the list of individuals, with their characteristics;
– the organizations, with the individuals involved and the processes
  operated;
– the resources, with their amounts and their distribution between
  individuals and organizations;

– the processes, with the associated social and technical constraints and with the prices possibly attached to exchange processes;
– the constraints concerning individuals, organizations, resources and processes.

Any set of "positions" for these parameters defines a *social state E* for the economy, E being an element of the set $\mathscr{E}$ of all possible social states:

$$E \in \mathscr{E}. \tag{4.19}$$

But utility of the individual k does not depend on all the parameters necessary to describe the economy and is generally a function of a smaller number of variables, the positions of which define an *individual social state* for the individual k, e_k which is an element of the set $\mathscr{E}_k$ of all possible individual social states for k:

$$e_k \in \mathscr{E}_k. \tag{4.20}$$

Assume for instance that m parameters ($1 \leqslant i \leqslant m$; $M = \{1, 2, \ldots, m\}$) are necessary to describe the whole economy and that x_i and X_i respectively denote a position of i and the set of all positions for i:

$$x_i \in X_i, \quad E = (x_i)_{1 \leqslant i \leqslant m}, \quad \mathscr{E} \subset X_1 \times \ldots \times X_m. \tag{4.21}$$

The individual k is only concerned by a subset $M_k \subset M$, so that:

$$e_k = (x_i)_{i \in M_k}, \quad \mathscr{E}_k \subset \prod_{i \in M_k} X_i. \tag{4.22}$$

Nevertheless, the individual is not directly sensitive to the real individual social state e_k, but to the *image* he has of it, through the distorting filters of perception. In other words, there is a set $\mathscr{E}'_k$ of possible perceived individual social states for individual k, the image e'_k being an element of this set:

$$e'_k \in \mathscr{E}'_k. \tag{4.23}$$

To avoid any confusion between reality and image, the symbol x' will consequently always denote the image for an individual of a social state x.

We shall suppose that the perception process is such that there is a mapping α from $\mathscr{E}_k$ on $\mathscr{E}'_k$, i.e. to each individual social state e_k corresponds, for given individual characteristics, an image e'_k,

$$\mathscr{E}_k \xrightarrow[\alpha_k]{} \mathscr{E}'_k. \tag{4.24}$$

How can Lancaster's ideas be interpreted in this framework? Assume the existence of M and M_k. Lancaster considers two subsets M_{1k} and M_{2k} of M_k:

(1) M_{1k} is the set of consumption parameters, so that $x_i \in X_i$ for $i \in M_{1k}$, represents the quantity consumed of a certain commodity, $e_k^1 = (x_i)_{i \in M_{1k}}$ being a consumption bundle.

(2) M_{2k} is the set of objective commodity characteristics, so that $x_i \in X_i$ for $i \in M_{2k}$ represents the level of a characteristic in which the individual is interested, $e_k^2 = (x_i)_{i \in M2k}$ being a characteristic vector.

Lancaster introduces a mapping β of $\mathscr{E}_{1k} = \prod_{i \in M_{1k}} x_i$ on $\mathscr{E}_{2k} = \prod_{i \in M_{2k}} x_i$:

$$\mathscr{E}_{1k} \xrightarrow{\ \beta\ } \mathscr{E}_{2k}. \tag{4.25}$$

Consequently, *the mapping α will associate the same image to any individual social state e_k corresponding to an identical e_k^2.*

Of course, the perceptive process may associate the same e_k' to different e_k's.

But there is another way of analyzing social states: to start from an individual's possibilities of action. Suppose the existence of M, and consider an individual k and a parameter i. Call:

$$E_{-i} = \{x_1, \ldots, x_{i-1}, x_{i+1}, \ldots, x_m\}, \tag{4.26}$$

the social state defined by the position of all parameters, except i. In the *context E_{-i}*, the parameter i is in a *context-constrained feasibility set $X_i(E_{-i})$*, which is in fact the projection of $\mathscr{E}$ on X_i. With respect to this parameter, the individual can, roughly, be in two situations:[16]

– He has no action whatsoever on the position x_i of the parameter i. The tax-payer, with respect to his taxes; or the theater fan, with respect to the price of his seat, knows this situation perfectly.

– He can choose freely x_i within $X_i(E_{-i})$. We may say that he *controls* it. The manager who fixes the price of a product, the father of a family who decides the location of his house, experience such a situation.

---

[16] More complicated situations could be introduced, but it would lengthen the analysis without much profit.

Naturally, such a division only rests on *direct* individual actions, since through interdependence within the economy, any individual can have an *indirect* action, small as it may be, on any other parameter.

More generally, through his actions, an individual can compel the social state E to be in a set $\mathscr{C}_k$ which is a subset of all the possible social states $\mathscr{E}$,

$$\mathscr{C}_k \subset \mathscr{E}. \qquad (4.27)$$

Correspondingly, he can compel his individual social state to be in a set $\mathscr{D}_k$, which is a subset of all the possible individual states $\mathscr{E}_k$:

$$\mathscr{D}_k \subset \mathscr{E}_k. \qquad (4.28)$$

This implies that the image will be in a subset $\mathscr{D}'_k$ which is the set of images of all $e_k \in \mathscr{D}_k$ (the image of $\mathscr{D}_k$ through the mapping α).

Naturally, the individual could be the victim of a perception bias and believe wrongly that his span of control of the image is a set $\mathscr{D}''_k$ instead of $\mathscr{D}'_k$.

The above concepts are important in order to understand, later, the influence of the environment on an individual, perception distortions and power relations. But they can be used immediately to examine the relations between individual social states and satisfactions.

2.2. Relations between individual social states and satisfactions

These relations are generated by two simultaneous and closely linked processes, which the modelization adopted separates: the mapping of individual social states into their images; the mapping of these images into satisfaction levels. These relations are progressively built, through a permanent adaptation, during the life of the individual. To express them in a one-period model is, then, to a large extent arbitrary.

2.2.1. The mapping of individual social states into their images

The image may be poorer or richer than reality: where the lover of operas perceives every single note, is sensitive to the smallest changes of tempi, appreciates subtleties in stage direction, the beginner who attends for the first time a performance of Mozart's "Le Nozze di Figaro" selects only a few arias and retains only the main elements of the plot. The civil servant who prepares a government decision on pensions has a very simplified image of the way in which 60 year-old French people imagine their future. On the other hand, the man who discovers in a cupboard the watch which belonged to his father, dead for many years, will associate with this object all the emotions of his childhood memories. For him, the watch image is considerably richer than reality.

During one period, the mapping α_k which transforms e_k into e'_k seems to depend on a certain number of endogenous factors:

- *the satisfaction situation* S_k^0 at the beginning of the period, since the more a motivation is frustrated, the more sensitive an individual will be to the aspects of the environment liable to satisfy this motivation, except in the case of an interdiction by the personality agencies: a hungry man will see an object only as a food possibility; a vain man will see in others people's speeches only flattery or criticism,
- *the psychological factor* $\bar{\omega}_k$, since the Superego may prevent some image components being consciously perceived (e.g. the puritan may be insensitive to the beauty of women); or since the Id may give birth to preconscious associations; or since the Ego may transform the image through defence mechanisms,
- progressive *learning* in the past, the cycle being: image of a social state; individual decision to make this state appear; experience of resulting satisfaction levels; adaptation of the image; this learning tends to bring image and reality nearer when satisfaction come mainly from objective characteristics of the state, but it remains compatible with a permanent dissociation when satisfactions proceed from other image components,
- finally, *capability:* architects do not see a building, doctors do not examine patients, as other humans do.

However, in addition to these endogenous factors, the image is influenced by *exogenous factors:* The advertisement of a product, the opinion of retailers and consumption leaders about it, the attitude adopted by family and friends, all condition to a large extent the image of a product built by the individual.

Denoting past learning by t_k, capability by c_k and external actions by b (all these notations will be more precisely defined later),[17] the

---

[17] Later on, b will be denoted by $e_{k,1}$ but this notation cannot be justified at this stage.

preceding discussion, which conciseness makes superficial, will be embedded into the relation:

$$e'_k = \alpha_k[e_k, S^0_k, \bar{\omega}_k, t_k, c_k, b]. \tag{4.29}$$

2.2.2. The mapping of images into satisfaction levels

Assume now that an individual starts from a satisfaction situation S^0_k at the beginning of the period.

At this time, the individual *forecasts*, for any possible image, the satisfaction situation that will result from it. This corresponds to a *first mapping* s_k from $\mathscr{E}'_k$ into $\mathbf{R}^n$:

$$\mathscr{E}'_k \xrightarrow{\quad s_k \quad} \mathbf{R}^n. \tag{4.30}$$

At the end of the period, if the individual has been confronted with a given image, he realizes that he has experienced a certain satisfaction situation S_k, corresponding to a *second mapping* σ_k from $\mathscr{E}'_k$ into $\mathbf{R}^n$:

$$\mathscr{E}'_k \xrightarrow{\quad \sigma_k \quad} \mathbf{R}^n. \tag{4.31}$$

These mappings will generally be different. We shall study here only the second, leaving the analysis of the first to the last section of the chapter.

The same factors appear as in the α_k mapping, but here the main role seems to be played by the associations learned during past development, when the psychic energy generated by the various drives has been attached to presentations, groups of presentations, body parts, objects, etc., what Freud calls cathexis of bound energy. On this are superimposed the influences of exogenous environment. In other words:

$$S_k = \sigma_k[e'_k, \bar{\omega}_k, t_k, b], \qquad S_k \in \mathbf{R}^n. \tag{4.32}$$

The theory developed until now makes it possible, to a certain extent, to introduce psychic conflicts into economic science:

– conflicts between the individual and his environment (principle of reality and pleasure principle) are present in the constraints limiting individual behaviour, in the fact that the individual only partially controls his individual social state and in the progressive adaptation of image to reality.

– As for the internal conflicts between drives and personality agencies, they appear in triple form: (1) compromises between motivations satisfactions at the level of utility function,[18] (2) distortions imposed on reality by perception, (3) associations between images of social states and satisfaction of motivations.

Defence mechanisms emphasized by Anna Freud[19] frequently incorporate the three aspects. For instance, in projection, the individual throws out of himself and attributes to a person or to a thing qualities, feelings, desires which he refuses in himself; there is then simultaneously an alteration of reality perception and a change in the relative weights of motivations in utility. In sublimation, the individual substitutes socially highly valued objects for the ones that should normally satisfy a motivation; or a motivation is replaced by another and the images of objects are simultaneously transformed. In reaction-formation, the individual adopts an attitude totally in opposition with the repressed desire.

To be quite clear; it would be childish to try to build a model of man incorporating as such psychoanalytical results. But we may ask that an economic theory be compatible with other human sciences.

2.3. Some examples

After a very simple model, only presented here to give the reader some practice in the notions of this section, we shall sketch some aspects of the theory of advertising proposed in chapter 7.

2.3.1. A model for a tale

Durand and Dupont are two bachelors who have known each other for a long time. Durand, who enjoys a rather high standard of living, does not attach too much importance to Dupont, with whom he does not

---

[18] For instance, if there are two satisfactions and if, in a given situation the best possible utility level is reached with a very high and a very low satisfaction, the individual may act in the short-run in agreement with utility maximization, but, immediately after, he starts looking for other external conditions which could not impose such an internal conflict upon him.

[19] Anna Freud* (1949).

feel he is in competition. His consumptions are composed of his current consumptions x, the use of a house y, and the use of a car z. (x, y, z are elements of the sets X, Y, Z of possible current consumptions, services of possible houses, services of possible cars.) Durand is matter-of-fact. His perception is not very different from reality. He does not especially value either his car or his house.

On the contrary, Dupont is extremely jealous of Durand, who has been more successful. He does not know of his colleague's house, but the perception he has of Durand's car is strongly influenced by advertisements which present this car as prestigious. Dupont also overestimates his neighbour's utility. As far as his own consumptions w are concerned, he despises them, for jealousy prevents him from sleeping (w is an element of the set W of all possible consumptions for Durand). Only consolation: he has the right $d(d \in D)$ to prevent Durand from crossing his fields, and thus compels him frequently to lose time in longer trips.

With an obvious notation, utilities of our bachelors are:

$$U = U(x, y, z, d), \qquad \text{for Durand,} \qquad (4.33)$$

$$V = V(U'_v, w'_v, z'_v, d), \qquad \text{for Dupont.} \qquad (4.34)$$

If the world is limited to just what has been said:

– the *social state* is the element: $E = (x, y, z, w, d, U, V)$ of a set $\mathscr{E} \subset X \times Y \times Z \times W \times D \times R^2$;
– the *individual social state* for Durand is: $e_u = (x, y, z, d)$ an element of a set $\mathscr{E}_u \subset X \times Y \times Z \times D$;
– the *individual social state* for Dupont is: $e_v = (U, w, z, d)$, an element of a set $\mathscr{E}_v \subset R \times W \times Z \times D$.

If, for Durand, the image of the individual social state is identical to reality (so that we can assume: $\mathscr{E}'_u = \mathscr{E}_u$ and $e'_u = e_u$), for Dupont:

– *the image of the individual state* is: $e'_v = (U'_v, w'_v, z'_v, d)$, an element of a set $\mathscr{E}'_v \subset R \times W' \times Z' \times D$, where we suppose no perception distortion on d.

In his individual social state, Durand *controls* $f_u = (x, y, z)$ an element of $X \times Y \times Z$, (the corresponding image being identical); *he does not control* $g_u = d$, which has also an identical image.

On his side, Dupont *controls* $f_v = (w, d)$ an element of $W \times D$, the image of which being: $f_v' = (w_v', d)$ an element of $W' \times D$, and *does not control* $g_v = (U, z)$, an element of $R \times Z$, the image of which being $g_v' = (U_v', z_v')$, an element of $R \times Z'$.

Remark. With these definitions, perceptions are excluded from social states. In fact, they are a part of them: I am happy to see my 8-year old daughter taking pleasure in a false ring she finds magnificent. In other words, in my utility function, a parameter is my perception of her perception of the ring.[20]

2.3.2. A partial theory of advertising

Advertising has two main functions: to spread knowledge of a product and of its characteristics; to modify the image the potential customers have of it. Only the second aspect will be examined here.

Therefore, consider an individual reduced to his consuming role. His utility is $U[(S_i)_{1 \leqslant i \leqslant n}]$; he consumes commodities $j(1 \leqslant j \leqslant m)$ of price $p_j \in \mathbf{R}^+$ in quantity $q_j \in \mathbf{R}^+$ (in vectorial notation $p \in \mathbf{R}^{m+}$ and $q \in \mathbf{R}^{m+}$). Each firm carries out a volume $v_j \in \mathbf{R}^+$ of advertising, its message being an element m_j of the set M of possible messages and its distribution between p media being characterized by a vector $s_j \in \mathbf{R}^{p+}$, the components s_{jh} of which $\sum_{h=1}^{p} s_{jh} = 1$ are the fractions of the advertising volume passing through the different media (in vectorial notation $v \in \mathbf{R}^{m+}$, $m \in M^m$ and $s \in \mathbf{R}^{(p+m)+}$). Advertising influences the image a_j' which the individual has of his consumption q_j. As for a_j', it is an element of a set A_j' which obviously cannot be identified to $\mathbf{R}^+$. The global image $a' = (a_j')_{1 \leqslant j \leqslant m}$ is an element of $A' = \prod_{1 \leqslant j \leqslant m} A_j'$.

The mapping from q to a' depends on the advertising policies. So we can write:

$$a' = a'[q, v, m, s, \bar{\omega}]. \tag{4.35}$$

Assuming that he can forecast perfectly the image of a consumption, the individual will try to maximize:

$$U = U\{(S_i(a'))_{1 \leqslant i \leqslant n}, \bar{\omega}\}, \tag{4.36}$$

---

[20] G. Bateson and the Palo Alto school have emphasized this aspect in their analysis of interindividual communication.

under the constraint:

$$pq \leqslant r, \tag{4.37}$$

where r is the income.

If we assume, for convenience, that the sets M and A' are spaces on which we can define norms; that U is a jointly differentiable function of the S_i's; that each S_i is a differentiable function of a'; that a' is a jointly differentiable function of its arguments in (4.35); and finally, that U is a strictly concave increasing function of the q's through the S_i's and the a_j''s, a necessary and sufficient condition for U to be maximum is that:

$$f_j = \sum_{\substack{0 \leqslant i \leqslant n \\ 0 \leqslant 1 \leqslant m}} U_i \frac{\partial S_i}{\partial a_i'} \frac{\partial a_i'}{\partial q_j} - \lambda p_j = 0 \quad \text{if } q_j > 0, \qquad f_j \leqslant 0 \quad \text{if } q_j = 0,$$

λ being a positive Lagrange multiplier and $U_i = \partial U/\partial S_i$ the marginal utility of satisfaction i. Relations (4.35), (4.37) and (4.38) are sufficient to define the individual demand functions:

$$q = q[p, r, v, m, s, \bar{\omega}], \tag{4.39}$$

and, through aggregation on the set of individuals, for given incomes and psychologies, the total demand function $Q(Q \in \mathbf{R}^{m+})$:

$$Q = Q[p, v, m, s]. \tag{4.40}$$

As for the firm producing j, its profit is:

$$R = p_j Q_j - D_1(Q_j) - D_2(v_j, s_j), \tag{4.41}$$

$D_1(Q_j)$ denoting the total production cost and $D_2(v_j, s_j)$ the advertising cost which only depends a priori on the advertising volume and on its distribution between media. Assuming normal condition on the demand and cost functions, the maximization of firms' profits will imply, since normally $Q_j > 0 \,\forall j$:

$$p_j + Q_j \bigg/ \frac{\partial Q_j}{\partial p_j} = \frac{dD_1}{dQ_j}, \tag{4.42}$$

$$[p_j - dD_1/dQ_j]\partial Q_j/\partial v_j = \partial D_2/\partial v_j, \tag{4.43}$$

$$\partial Q_j/\partial m_j = 0, \tag{4.44}$$

$$[p_j - dD_1/dQ_j]\partial Q_j/\partial s_{jh} = \mu \partial D_2/\partial s_{jh}. \tag{4.45}$$

These four relations are easily interpreted: translating equality between marginal proceeds and marginal cost, the first is an elementary result of monopoly theory. The second – already discovered by various authors – is much more interesting. This states that the cost of an additional unit of advertising must be equal to the product of the additional quantity sold and the marginal profit. The last one is basically identical, except that the variables are the fraction passing through the different media, and that a positive Lagrange multiplier μ appears, due to the fact that the sum of these fractions is necessarily equal to 1. As for the third, it simply underlines that the message chosen maximizes production sold.

These relations stress that, in a perfect competitive market (in which price and marginal cost are equal) advertising has no interest at all. So pricing and advertising policies, these two means of action of the firm on the consumer, appear to be closely related.

But the model is consistent with several features of reality:
- The advertising of firm j influences the demand for other products in several ways: creating a favourable image for a whole class of products, it increases the demand for this class; modifying only the perception of product j, it directs demand towards this firm; consequently it stimulates the demand for complementary products; reducing the income available for other expenditures, it decreases all other demands. These facts are well-known by advertising agencies: when a firm dominates its market, its advertising must be directed towards a broadening of the total market even if competitors take advantage of it. On the contrary, a firm, with only a minor share, must do its best to create a specific brand image.
- However, contrary to some opinions,[21] advertising cannot do everything. It cannot associate any product to a motivational satisfaction. In other words, the influence of q_j on a'_j remains dominant. The doctrine of total manipulation of individuals through big firms' marketing is convenient for those who contest the consumers' society, but it grossly distorts reality.

After these two examples, which show how to use social states and their images, it becomes necessary to try to enumerate the parameters involved in an individual social state.

---

[21] See for instance, J.F.K. Galbraith, The new Industrial State.

2.4. The parameters of individual social states

This highly complex question cannot receive any really satisfactory answer, since any parameter characterizing one aspect of society is liable to concern, at one time or another, any individual. The essential purpose of the attempt made here is to stimulate reflection. It is based on an analysis we have presented elsewhere [22] and which suggests six dimensions for the political aims of a society: efficiency, liberty, participation, equality, adaptability and safety. Two of these dimensions (adaptability and safety) being eliminated at this stage by the certain future and one period assumptions, the key parameters of an individual social state can be grouped under four headings:

(1) individual consumptions (related to efficiency dimension),
(2) freedom parameters,
(3) participation parameters,
(4) parameters expressing relations with others (hence including equality dimension).

2.4.1. Individual consumptions

These are, if one may say so, the daily bread of economists: food, clothing, housing, housing equipment, tourism and trips, cultural consumptions, etc. are usual chapters in family budgets. But there are other important individual consumptions: health, silence, sun, the beauties of monuments and landscape.

Economists have not stressed sufficiently the double nature, *direct* and *instrumental*, of these consumptions:

– The first have a direct effect on the satisfaction of motivations and generally on several simultaneously. In Lancaster's terms (1971), a direct consumption is such that we can postulate a natural one-to-one mapping between the quantity consumed in the commodity space and the level of a corresponding characteristic in the characteristics space.
– The instrumental consumptions have no value in themselves; they

[22] J. Lesourne* (1976, chapter II).

indirectly make possible other consumptions. I take the underground to pay a visit to an exhibition, not to have the pleasure of the trip. Most patients take drugs to improve their health, not for the pleasure of swallowing pills. Obviously, it is for instrumental consumptions that Lancaster's introduction of the characteristics space is of the utmost interest.

– Nevertheless, for some individuals, the same consumption may be simultaneously direct and instrumental: some people do like to take drugs to satisfy narcissism or to calm anxiety. This means has been interiorized and leads to motivation satisfaction in a double way: directly and through the consumption process of the transformation of drugs into health ("health" being a component of the characteristic space). Many social rules have passed through this interiorization mechanism. They appear among the individual consumptions, and to respect them becomes, for the individual, a source of satisfaction. For some people, to be fined induces a double dissatisfaction: indirectly, through the decline of disposable income; and directly, through the breach of a rule.

2.4.2. Freedom parameters

When stripped of its philosophical gangue and conceived as an organizational property, freedom becomes closely related to decentralization. For an individual, freedom is then defined by the list of the decisions he is entitled to take *alone* for each of the roles he holds in society, and by the list of constraints that may limit these decisions.

The decisions of the individual may concern his own consumptions, as well as the consumptions of others; definitions of rules that others must obey, as well as creations of new organizations, but the limiting constraints depend on the role in whose name the decision is taken. Even in the worst period of the Revolutionary Court, Fouquier-Tinville could send a person to death only as President of this Court and on its premises, not as an ordinary citizen in the evening at home.

It must be underlined that what appears as the freedom parameter in the utility function *is not the consequence of a decision, but the possibility of taking it.* In other words, it is not the same thing to see somebody else take for you the decision you prefer as to take it yourself.

To represent this phenomenon is a delicate matter since there is not, as we shall see in the next chapter, a set D of decisions to be taken by a collectivity and which can be partitioned in various ways between individuals. The set D depends upon social organization: when, in a firm where the managing director had a decision monopoly, two deputies' positions are created, it is not sufficient to divide the old decision set between three persons, since the new division generates new types of decisions: appointment of deputies, arbitration between them, information rules between the three managers.

Only one certainty: among the parameters of almost all utility functions should appear the list of authorized decisions and the description of the borders imposed on these decisions.

2.4.3. Participation parameters

The notion of participation is useful to express the influence that an individual may exert on a decision he cannot take alone. The voting citizen does not elect the MP, the voting senator does not pass the bill. However, both belong to a set of individuals which, through a certain process, according to given rules, generates a certain decision; and they are not indifferent to the fact that they belong or do not belong to this set.

Of course, it is difficult to introduce, into utility, parameters which describe participation possibilities of an individual:

- As is well known, an individual's power in a participation process depends upon the attitudes of others; upon the structure of winning coalitions; upon the probabilities of their creation; upon the possibility, for the individual, to belong to them.
- Participation processes with strict or with much more informal rules exist simultaneously. It would be a pity to neglect the second, since numerous individuals get more satisfaction from their hidden roles than from their official rights.

But none of these difficulties should make us give up. Participation is one of the essential forms of exchange between an individual and the surrounding collectivity.

2.4.4. Parameters expressing relations with others[23]

First, an individual may be sensitive to others' *existence* as individuals (desire to have a son, repressed hope of the death of a hated parent) or as groups (indifference or interest for Chinese children, hate for clergymen or for Jews, etc.).

Then, he may be sensitive to others' *individual consumptions, freedom, participation* or *characteristics*, and this in a double way:

– in a cardinal way: then utility functions of other persons, or parameters of these utilities or various characteristics, appear in his utility function, individually (his wife's utility, the university diploma of his children) or anonymously (farmers' standard of living, the retirement age of post-office clerks, the number of blonde women in the population);
– in an ordinal way: then the *rank of the individual*, by comparison with others in each of the hierarchies in which he is interested, appears in utility.

Therefore, W. Krelle was right to isolate the following groups of parameters among the arguments of an individual utility function:

– the consumptions w_h of other individuals ($1 \leqslant h \leqslant p$, $w_h \in \mathbf{R}^{p+}$);
– the vector ρ of the individual hierarchical ranks (if there are m hierarchies, ρ may be considered as a vector in $\mathbf{R}^{m+}$) and the vectors ρ_h of others hierarchical ranks ($\rho_h \in \mathbf{R}^{m+}$, $\forall h$);
– the variables r describing individual relations with others, neutral with respect to the ranks.

Consequently, he writes:

$$U = U[(w_h)_{1 \leqslant h \leqslant p}, \rho, (\rho_h)_{1 \leqslant h \leqslant p}, r], \tag{4.46}$$

and assumes (with the necessary differentiability hypothesis) that:

$$\partial U/\partial w_h \leqslant 0, \tag{4.47}$$

$$\partial^2 U/\partial w_h^2 \leqslant 0, \tag{4.48}$$

(4.47) is debatable, since it postulates jealousy towards anybody, including family or friends.

---

[23] See Gary S. Becker (1974).

$$\partial U/\partial\rho \geqslant 0, \tag{4.49}$$

$$\partial^2 U/\partial\rho^2 \leqslant 0, \tag{4.50}$$

(4.49) is reasonable but (4.50) forgets that power may generate a greater thirst for power.

$$\partial U/\partial\rho_h \leqslant 0, \tag{4.51}$$

$$\partial^2 U/\partial\rho_h^2 \leqslant 0,$$

$$\partial U/\partial r \geqslant 0, \tag{4.53}$$

$$\partial^2 U/\partial r^2 \leqslant 0, \tag{4.54}$$

(4.53) means that the individual appreciates human relations which do not threaten his power and (4.54) insures, with some reason, that the interest for them decreases if they become too intense.

In spite of its deficiencies, this short description of the parameters appearing in individual social states shows the variety and complexity of these parameters. It suggests that we should look with prudence at the results of economics which assume that these states are defined only by current consumption. It shows the need, in any specific problem, to study carefully the characteristics of the individual's social states in order to select, each time, the essential variables.

But what can an individual do to obtain a social state favourable to him?

3. Acts, roles and allocations

Response to external stimuli or result of his own initiative, it is his *behaviour* which enables an individual to solve his conflicts with environment. This behaviour is the collection of all the *acts* carried out by the individual during the period. It contributes, together with the behaviour of other individuals, to the modification of the social state of the economy.

The separation of acts into *role-choices* and *allocations* within roles is the main point analyzed in this section and clarified by some examples. The meaning of this dichotomy should be easily apparent:
- To eat an apple is an allocation in a role of consumer.
- To give a degree after an examination is an allocation in a role of professor.

– To recruit a new staff member is an allocation in a role of manger.
– To vote U.D.R. or Socialist is an allocation in a role of elector.

3.1. Role-choices

Consumer, student, writer, Minister, father of a family, elector, union delegate, finance inspector are examples of the innumerable roles that exist in our society.

A role is defined by the possibility, explicitly or implicitly recognized by an organization for an individual to take certain decisions concerning processes operated by the organization.

Such a definition implies:

– an organization (which may be composed of the individual only as concerns the role of consumer or the role of individual entrepreneur),
– processes,
– a decision set, the set of all authorized decisions concerning the above processes,
– constraints which these decisions must respect.

So, for a student, the organization is a university; a process may be to obtain a master's degree; the decisions associated to the role are, among others, to attend the lectures and to pass the examination; the constraints include discipline, regular attendance, knowledge thresholds. For the father of a family, the organization is the family and the process is child-raising; the father has the right to decide about housing, clothing, food, education, but there are constraints: it is compulsory to send the children to school till they are 16; children cannot be abandoned nor severely beaten.

Descriptions of processes, of decision sets and of constraints often makes it necessary to divide the role into two separate components:[24]

– the formal component or *status* which derives from the organization's written rules (the Constitution for the main bodies of the State, laws or decrees for administrative services, internal "bibles" for big corporations, describe organizational charts, enumerate authorized decisions and constraints to respect);

[24] P. de Backer* (1974).

- the informal component or *role deviation* which corresponds to the
difference which practice introduces with respect to status. (This
deviation often stems from the fact that the environment expects
a certain behaviour from the holder of the role. This expectation
may arise from contradictory status, from the inefficiency of the
holders of other roles, or from the image left by the effective behaviour
of the previous holder.)

To enumerate the various roles in an economy raises problems
similar to the listing of commodities: on the one hand, it may be more
or less necessary to make precise divisions (a role may be: chairman of
a corporation, chairman of a corporation manufacturing cars, chairman
of Citroen). On the other hand, as for a product, does a role remain
the same when its characteristics are modified? To one chairman or
another, a board will delegate quite different powers. For commodities,
it has been necessary to introduce notions of quality and variety
(Kolm (1971)); nothing prevents associating decision sets and constraints to roles.

But where does the great importance of this concept for economics
come from? As in the case of investment – a closely related concept –
from two main characteristics:

(1) *The choice of a role is a decision with a flavour of irreversibility:*
to accept or to quit a role implies specific costs (applications to be
recruited, period without a salary when one leaves a firm, length
and difficulty of divorce proceedings, obstacle of an electoral campaign for a candidate to Parliament). The individual will bear these
costs only if he expects a sufficient increase of his utility. Secondly,
whoever holds a role becomes specialised, increases his ability in
this role and finds his interest for a change decrease. Finally, to
hold the role may be more and more associated with the satisfaction
of certain motivations and, as for the newly retired, a break is a
source of suffering.

(2) *The role is a framework for many other decisions,* which have a
meaning only with respect to it. These decisions, with respect to
role, have the same relation as operating decisions with respect to
investment. Besides, the separation of role from allocation simpli-
fies matters, since intermediary situations may exist, some kind of
"subroles" chosen within roles and more reversible (if to be a colonel
is a role, to be in command of a given regiment is a subrole).

So, at a given time, for a given economy, with a given organization, there exist types of roles r_h ($1 \leqslant h \leqslant p$), the set of all r_h's constituting the set of roles available in the collectivity.

To each role type r_h corresponds the number n_h of individuals having the role. This number may be equal to one (Président de la République), to one or two dozens (Bank chairmen), to hundreds of thousands (schoolmasters), to millions (electors).

The situation of an individual k is totally described by a sequence R_k of p numbers i_{kh} equal to 1 or 0 according to whether the individual has or has not role h:

$$R_k = \{ i_{k1}, \ldots, i_{kh}, \ldots, i_{kp} \}. \tag{4.55}$$

Naturally, for the whole economy:

$$\sum_k i_{kh} = n_h. \tag{4.56}$$

But an individual chooses his roles among those he knows. From the peasant of the old days who married a girl of his village, to the student of today who learns economics because he does not feel gifted for mathematics, the examples of this restriction of role-choices to the known universe are countless. Nevertheless, "known" does not mean "given once for all," since the individual may broaden his field of knowledge in a double way:

- Thanks to his *imagination*, he may invent possible roles or discover a new combination of several roles. This is one of the aspects of his capability which will be introduced in the next section.
- Through a *search and information* effort, he may obtain pieces of intelligence on the variety of existing roles.

To take this last feature into account, it is necessary to introduce among the individual's acts, a specific one: *his intensity of search for information on roles*. This act may be represented by the time I_k lost by the individual to obtain information on the various roles. According to the value of I_k, the individual will be aware of a greater or a smaller number of roles among which he will choose the ones he wants to hold.

Naturally, intensity I_k may be a parameter of utility function since, because of curiosity and comfort motivations, an individual may extract out of any search effort a specific satisfaction or dissatisfaction. Think of the bachelor who multiplies experiments to make himself a perfect marriage!

In a one-period model, to introduce simultaneously the choices of I_k and R_k obviously distorts reality, since the two operations are sequential; but as we shall see, this boldness is not logically inconsistent. The same remark can be applied to allocations.

3.2. Allocations

Once the roles have been chosen, an individual selects, *within each of them*, acts which generally consist in imposing constraints on or in allocating resources to a process operated by the organization (organization which may be reduced to the individual). These acts, as different as the various resources, will be called *allocations:* to give a piece of information you have to a member of your staff; to baptize a new Christian; to forbid traffic in some streets; to place a bomb if you belong to anarchist group, are all examples of allocations.

To associate allocations to roles avoids the difficult problem which would be raised by the notion of acts of an organization. If, as Chairman of a corporation, I sign a contract, I select an allocation within a role, allocation which will be, by law, a constraint for any individual at present having or liable to have in the future a role within the organization. I may be replaced as Chairman, the contract will remain valid.

As for roles, the chosen allocations depend upon the scope of individual knowledge. Here again, imagination and the search for information will play an essential part. We then have to introduce explicitly *intensities of search for information on allocations* to take into account the comparison made by a housewife between the products in different shops, the enumeration made by a manager of all possible investment projects, the reading by the elector of the programs of all candidates, the bibliographical search made by the professor before his lecture...

An individual's behaviour is then represented, in the proposed model, by four groups of variables:

I_k : intensity of search for information on roles,
R_k : role situation of an individual (sequence of 0 and 1),
J_{kh}: intensity of search for information within role h ($J_{kh} = 0$ if $i_{kh} = 0$),
a_{kh}: allocations within role h.

I_k and J_{kh} will normally be considered as time lengths. They are then elements of $\mathbf{R}^+$. a_{kh} will be an element of a set A_{kh} of feasible allocations ($A_{kh} = \emptyset$ if $i_{kh} = 0$).

Later, we shall introduce a last group of variables characterizing behaviour, *efforts*, but to present it at this stage is not very convenient because of its links with capability.

To understand better the notions of this section, let us consider for a while the example of a married man, father and business manager. The *smallest* number of his roles is four: consumer, father, manager, elector. But he could have other roles.

As an *elector*, his allocations are simple:

– to obtain information;
– to vote, or not, for one candidate or another.

As a business *manager*, the scope of his allocations is very much broader:
– to obtain information before choosing any other allocation;
– to distribute decisions among his deputies and himself;
– to impose rules for staff members;
– to appoint and dismiss the holders of some roles;
– to transfer information to staff members;
– to control their acts;
– to take himself decisions he has not decentralized (for instance: to define wages, fix selling prices, choose input and output quantities, select clients and contractors, allocate machines and surfaces to processes, etc.).

As a *father*, in cooperation with his wife, he will have:
– to obtain information;
– to choose the house, its equipment, and more generally, to fix the level of collective household consumptions;
– to decide whether or not to have an additional child;
– to determine the consumption level of the junior members of the family;
– to define programs for holidays.

Finally, as a *consumer*, the set of his possibilities is considerably richer than day-to-day economics assumes:

– to obtain information;
– to choose his consumption pattern;
– to decide about the use of his time;
– to fix the amounts of saving or borrowing;

- to settle the program of his trips with the corresponding means of transport;
- to broaden his culture.

This list shows the importance of allocations not directly related to production or consumption. It reminds us that it may sometimes be necessary to introduce hierarchies between allocations (to appoint a staff member is less reversible than to bring him into a meeting), while proving that the representation adopted for acts is flexible enough to be incorporated in very different socioeconomic models. Two examples will confirm this.

3.3. Two models as examples

A simplified version of a theory of job selection (chapter 7) and a problem of *housewife's information* will put an end to this analysis of individual acts.

3.3.1. Job selection

Let us consider an individual with only two roles, that of consumer and that of a job-holder.

In his first role, his allocations are his consumptions q ($q \in \mathbf{R}^{m+}$ if m is the number of resources) with unit prices p ($p \in \mathbf{R}^{m+}$, $p \gg 0$).

As for the jobs, they can be represented by elements h of a finite s-dimensional Banach space $\mathcal{H}$, each dimension corresponding to a *type of activity*, and the norm along a dimension to the *level of this activity* (measured for instance in points as is sometimes usual in industry). The jobs to which an individual has access belong to a subset $H \subset \mathcal{H}$.

We define on H:

- a differentiable mapping $\rho(h)$ from H to $\mathbf{R}^+$ giving the income obtained from job h,
- a differentiable mapping $h'(h)$ from H to a finite s'-dimensional Banach space H' defining the image of job h for the individual,
- a differentiable mapping $a(h)$ from H to a finite n-dimensional Banach space A defining the vector of allocations chosen by the individual when he has job h.

In this very simple presentation, we eliminate the intensities of his search for information, his capability (which has not yet been introduced) and the mechanisms of choices of allocations (studied in the next chapter).

Under these conditions, the behaviour of the individual will result from the maximization of:

$$U = U\{[S_i(\hat{q}, h'(h).\, a(h)]_{1 \leqslant i \leqslant n}\}, \tag{4.57}$$

under the constraint:

$$pq \leqslant \rho(h). \tag{4.58}$$

With an obvious notation,[25] U being assumed differentiable and strictly concave in q and h through S_i, h' and a, and λ being a positive Lagrange multiplier associated to (4.57), the job selected will be such that:

$$\alpha_j = 0 \text{ if } q_j > 0, \quad \alpha_j \leqslant 0 \text{ if } q_j = 0 \text{ with } 1 \leqslant j \leqslant m \text{ and } \alpha = DU_q - \lambda p, \tag{4.59}$$

$$\beta_k = 0 \text{ if } h_k > 0, \quad \beta_k \leqslant 0 \text{ if } h_k = 0 \text{ with } 1 \leqslant k \leqslant s$$

$$\text{and } \beta = DU_h.Dh'_h + DU_a Da_h - \lambda D\rho_h. \tag{4.60}$$

So the choice of a job in the set H of all known and possible jobs will depend on three factors:

– The *job image* which more or less satisfies the individual's desires for prestige, power, security, evasion, etc. and is strongly influenced by cultural environment. For instance, in France, as in many developing countries, the culture values the civil servant, on whom is bestowed the prestigious halo of service to the nation and a portion of the power of the State, and who enjoys exceptional conditions of security $(DU_{h'} Dh'_h)$.
– The *interest in the decisions to be taken in the job*, decisions which will demand more or less imagination, creativity, regularity or perseverance and which are important for the satisfaction of curiosity, power or comfort needs $(DU_a Da_h)$.
– The *income* generated by the job $(D\rho_h)$.

---

[25] $DU_q = (\partial U/\partial q_j)_{1 \leqslant j \leqslant m}$; $DU_{h'} = (\partial U/\partial h'_k)_{1 \leqslant k' \leqslant s'}$; $Dh'_h = (\partial h'_k/\partial h_k)_{1 \leqslant k \leqslant s, 1 \leqslant k' \leqslant s'}$ $DU_a = (\partial U/\partial a_l)_{1 \leqslant l \leqslant u}$; $Da_h = (\partial a_l/\partial h_k)_{1 \leqslant k \leqslant s, 1 \leqslant l \leqslant u}$; $D\rho_h = (\partial \rho/\partial h_k)_{1 \leqslant k \leqslant s}$.

Relation (4.60) only expresses the equilibrium between the forces corresponding to these three factors.

3.3.2. Housewife's information

This model features one aspect of the search for information within a role. A housewife spends time J in getting information on prices $p_j (1 \leqslant j \leqslant m)$ of her consumption quantities q_j (in vectorial notation $p \in \mathbf{R}^{m+}$, $q \in \mathbf{R}^{m+}$, $p \gg 0$). She is not indifferent to this search effort, whether she dislikes it strongly or obtains some satisfaction of her curiosity. So her utility function is:

$$U = U[q, J]. \tag{4.61}$$

But the minimum prices she discovers for the various commodities are decreasing functions $p_j(J)$ of the search effort, and the income constraint can be written:

$$p(J)q + cJ = r, \tag{4.62}$$

r being the income and c the constant cost of a unit of time spent on information. With usual assumptions on U, the housewife adopts the behaviour defined by:

$$\alpha_j = U_{q_j} - \lambda p_j(J), \qquad \alpha_j = 0 \text{ if } q_j > 0, \quad \alpha_j \leqslant 0 \text{ if } q_j = 0, \tag{4.63}$$

$$\beta = U_J - \lambda \left[c + \sum_j q_j \frac{\partial p_j}{\partial J} \right], \qquad \beta = 0 \text{ if } J > 0, \quad \beta \leqslant 0 \text{ if } J = 0, \tag{4.64}$$

λ being the Lagrange multiplier associated to (4.62).

If the housewife is indifferent to the search effort ($U_J = 0$), she develops information to the point where the saving $-\sum q_j \partial p_j/\partial J$ made thanks to information is exactly balanced by its marginal cost c.

If she likes to search ($U_J > 0$), she looks for information more than would be necessary. Who does not know housewives who continually explore in the name of saving but in fact for the sheer pleasure of it?

If she dislikes visiting new shops ($U_J < 0$), her search effort is smaller than good management of her budget would require.

Less elementary models will be presented in chapter 7, but they need the introduction of behaviour constraints and of other important notions, for instance capability.

4. Individual capability

Individuals cannot be appointed to roles indifferently. Their capabilities differ, and one of the most important functions of any collectivity is, at the same time, to improve the capabilities of its members and to take the best advantage of the present levels of these capabilities.

Because of the limitation of the present treatment of this subject in economic literature, a *new concept* will have to be introduced here.[26] We shall evaluate its meaning for a *collectivity*, and examine, through some *examples*, its interest for a theory of the individual.

4.1. A definition of capability

If utility expresses individual preferences, capability must describe their ability to invent solutions, perform tasks, succeed in roles, etc. However, one unquestionable result of psychophysiological studies and of research on intelligence is the muldidimensional character of this phenomenon. Obviously, the ability to perform a task depends upon a whole range of psychophysiological, psychological, intellectual and cognitive factors:

Psychophysiological factors such as ability to see, speed and precision of nervous reflexes, reistance to fatigue, rhythm of activity, psychological factors such as curiosity, constancy in effort, ability to support stress, need for selfrecognition, ability to command obedience; intellectual factors such as imagination, learning capacity, use of logic; cognitive factors described by the level of technical, scientific, linguistic knowledge.

We shall assume the existence of *capability dimensions* and, using them, build a hypothesis similar to assumption 1 on psychological structure:

Assumption 5. *similarity of capability structures. Capability dimensions are identical for all individuals of the same cultural field.*

---

[26] The concept of capability is obviously related to two other concepts: the concept of *skill* used in optimal taxation models (Mirrlees (1971)); the concept of *human capital* developed by several authors, among them G.S. Becker (1964, 1975). It may be considered a generalization of these concepts.

Naturally, it is as difficult to list these dimensions as to list motivations, and for similar reasons, since capability dimensions may be divided or grouped in many ways. But, in spite of these deficiencies, the concept remains fruitful.

To compare the various capabilities along a dimension, a second assumption will be introduced. This supposes that the number u of capability dimensions is finite and that the capability of any individual is described by a sequence of u states corresponding to the various dimensions:

Assumption 6. *ordering of capability states. To any capability dimension ($1 \leqslant j \leqslant u$) is associated a set D_j of possible capability states $d_j \in D_j$ and a strict order R_j on D_j.*

The above two assumptions make it possible to state:

Theorem 3. *Under assumptions 5 and 6, there exists a real-valued function c_j on D_j such that: $d_j R_j d'_j \Leftrightarrow c_j(d_j) < c_j(d'_j)$ for every $d_j \in D_j$, $d'_j \in D_j$.*

The function c_j will be called the *capability level* on dimension j. Marks obtained at intelligence or psychotechnical tests are examples of such functions. It is well-known that these marks have no meaning outside a culturally homogeneous group.

Consequently, *an individual capability* may be represented in $\mathbf{R}^u$ by a vector c, whose components are the capability levels c_j along the various dimensions:

$$c = (c_j)_{1 \leqslant j \leqslant u}, \qquad c \in \mathbf{R}^u. \tag{4.65}$$

But here one has to put an end to the analogy with utility, since the aggregation problem is totally different for capability. On the contrary, it is important to consider: (1) the elements which influence capability, (2) the efficiency of acts.

4.1.1. Elements influencing capability

For a given period, an individual capability c_k is the result of a long process during which the following have intervened:

- a first group of variables representing the *genetical situation* inherited by the individual (for instance, this may be represented by a vector c_{0k} in a space $\mathscr{C}_{0k}$);
- the various characteristics of the psychological structure, which may have played or play an inhibiting or stimulating role (we have already represented these by an element $\bar{\omega}_k \in \Pi$);
- the *learning* history, during which the individual has interacted with the environment (for the mapping of individual social states into their image, we shall represent this factor by t_k).

To these three sets of variables must be added *the satisfaction level* at the beginning of the period (good or bad health situation, adequate or inadequate nutrition, stimulating or depressing environment) and *certain parameters of the social state* which do not influence utility but have an impact on capability (for instance, an unknown health situation which impairs mental abilities).

Omitting this final feature, it is possible to write:

$$c_k = c[c_{0k}, \bar{\omega}_k, t_k, S_k^0], \qquad c_k \in \mathbf{R}^u. \tag{4.66}$$

4.1.2. Efficiency of acts

Let us consider an act $a_k \in A$ of an individual and neglect, to simplify matters, the difference between perceived and objective individual states. Assume that the social state is defined by the position of m parameters $x_i \in X_i$:

$$E = \{x_1, \ldots, x_i, \ldots, x_m\}, \tag{4.67}$$

the parameters being ordered in such a way that, through a_k, the individual has an action on the first m_k parameters, and is concerned by the first m_k' parameters ($m_k' \geqslant m_k$). Then, any social state may be partitioned in two different ways:

$$E = \{e_k, e_{-k}\}, \tag{4.68}$$

$$E = \{e_{1k}, e_{2k}, e_{-k}\}, \tag{4.69}$$

where e_k is the individual social state, e_{-k} the sequence of elements of the social state which do not concern individual k, $e_{1k}(e_{2k})$, the sequence of elements of the individual social state which the individual can (cannot) influence.

Denote:

$$e_{-k,1} = \{e_{2k}, e_{-k}\}. \tag{4.70}$$

In the presence of $e_{-k,1}$, when a_k describes A, e_{1k} describes a certain subset $\mathscr{D}_{1k}(e_{-k,1})$ of $\prod_{1 \leqslant i \leqslant m_k} X_i$; but this subset does not depend only on the environment, but also *on individual capability*. Roughly speaking, the higher the individual capability, the broader will be the set $\mathscr{D}_{1k}$. In other words, the mapping of A into $\prod_{1 \leqslant i \leqslant m_k} X_i$, representing the impact of individual behaviour on the individual social state, is a function of individual capability.

Since the utility U is a real-valued function of $\{e_{1k}, e_{2k}\}$, *the level of utility which can be associated to a_k in the context $e_{-k,1}$, is a function of c_k.* Reciprocally, for U given, there is a class of capabilities in $\mathbf{R}^u$ which for the same a_k make it possible to reach this utility level in the context $e_{-k,1}$. We shall say that *these capabilities have the same efficiency with respect to act a_k in the context $e_{-k,1}$.*

Obviously, the concept of $(a_k, e_{-k,1})$ efficiency generates equivalence classes on $\mathbf{R}^u$, and these equivalence classes can be strictly ordered.

But an act a_k (for instance, to enter a 440 yard race) can be performed at different levels of *effort*. It is well-known that pupils equally gifted will have different results if they work differently. If capability is a fairly stable individual characteristic, effort is a short-term component of behaviour. So it is frequently necessary to associate to each act $a_k \in A$, the effort $d_{ak} \in D_A$ allocated by the individual to this act. But d_{ak} is not only an element of behaviour, it is also an element of e_{1k}, the controlled part of individual social state, so that one can write, for instance:

$$e_{1k} = \{e_{1k}^+, d_{ak}\}, \tag{4.71}$$

e_{1k}^+ being what remains of the controlled part of individual social state, when levels of effort are eliminated.

Hence, the utility level $U(e_{1k}^+, d_{a_k}, e_{2k})$ appears as a function of a_k, c_k, d_{a_k} and $e_{-k,1}$. The effort d_{a_k} may, by itself, have a decreasing effect on utility, while through the e_{1k}^+ reached it has an increasing indirect effect.

When effort levels are introduced, it is possible to generalize the efficiency concept, but one obviously has to separate *global efficiency*, which takes into account direct and indirect effects, and *pure efficiency*, which neglects the *direct* effect.

From now on, we shall add the *efforts* to the description of individual behaviour (see chapter 6).

4.2. The meaning of individual capabilities for a collectivity

The concept of individual capability is undoubtedly useful for economics as a few straightforward remarks will show. To begin with, we neglect the influence of e'_k on c_k (relation 4.66) and the impact of d_{a_k} on e_{1k} (the pure situation).

4.2.1. The pure situation

Generally, it is possible to choose the direction of ordering of capabilities on each dimension in such a way that U_k is a nondecreasing function of any c^k_j. Then, for an act a_k and an environment $e_{-1,k}$, two dominance notions can be introduced:

Weak dominance: Capability c_k weakly dominates capability c'_k for act a_k in the context $e_{-1,k}$ iff:

$$U_k(c_k) > U_k(c'_k) \tag{4.72}$$

$U_k(c_k)$ and $U_k(c'_k)$ being the levels of utility respectively reached by individual k when he has capability c_k or c'_k.

Strong dominance: Capability c_k strongly dominates capability c'_k iff:

$$c^k_j \geqslant c'^k_j, \tag{4.73}$$

for any j ($1 \leqslant j \leqslant u$), the strict inequality being verified for one j at least.

If, on each dimension, the direction of ordering of capabilities increasing utility is independent of the utility function, of the act chosen and of the context, the concept of strong dominance can be used to compare individuals. An individual k will be said to be *superior* to an individual k', iff:

$$c^k_j \geqslant c^{k'}_j, \tag{4.74}$$

for any j, the strict inequality being verified for one j at least.

Let us consider now the space $\mathbf{R}^u$ of individual capabilities: at a given time in the history of a society, the set of all points representing individuals of the society is a subset $\mathscr{C}^* \subset \mathbf{R}^u$. In this set, there is a subset $\mathscr{C}_M^*$ of maximal possible capabilities defined in the following way: *An element $c \in \mathscr{C}^*$ is in C_M^* iff there is not $c' \in \mathscr{C}^*$ such that $c' \geqslant c$ ($\geqslant$ meaning that there is a strict inequality for one component at least).*

The nature of $\mathscr{C}_M^*$ is obviously a product of the past: if a population is deprived from food, its physical strength diminishes. Athletic performances depend on training techniques. Technical and scientific knowledge depend on the state of science (before Newton and Leibnitz, there was no capability in differential calculus among XVIIth century Europeans) (see figure 4.3).

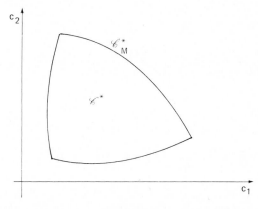

Figure 4.3

From the capability point of view, society is characterized by the distribution of individual points in the set $\mathscr{C}^*$.

Consider now a task a and a real-valued criterion V (for which the direction of ordering of capabilities is adequate); it is possible to consider in $\mathbf{R}^u$ the *efficiency equivalence classes* $C(V)$ for which V is given.

Three of these classes are of interest:

– *the maximal class* $C(V_{\max})$ which corresponds to the unconstrained maximum of V;

– *the limit-class* $C(V_{\lim})$ for a given society. This class is such that for any $V > V_{\lim}$:

$$C(V) \cap \mathscr{C}^* = 0; \tag{4.75}$$

– *the minimal class* $C(V_{\min})$ such that for $V < V_{\min}$, the task is considered not performed at all (the race is not finished, the bridge collapses).

Figure 4.4 illustrates the above notions.

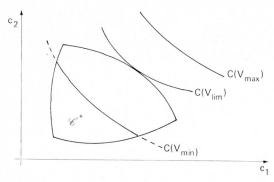

Figure 4.4

4.2.2. Complex situation

But the individual capability is not independent of the individual's social state at the beginning of the period (which depresses or stimulates him); and efficiency depends on the effort applied by the individual to the performance of the act.

To represent this situation easily, we shall make, from now on, *simplifying assumptions:*

We shall assume that the individual chooses simultaneously all the acts defining his behaviour, the effort levels being represented by an element d_k of a set D. This means that we shall neglect relations between acts and efforts. In addition, we shall suppose that, *independently of the context* $e_{k,1}$, the *indirect* effect of efforts d_k ($d_k \in D$) can be represented by assuming that the individual has a capability γ_k instead of c_k:

$$\gamma_k = \gamma_k(c_k, d_k), \qquad \gamma_k \in \mathbf{R}^u. \tag{4.76}$$

In other words:

$$e_{1k}^{+}[a_k, c_k, d_k, e_{-k,1}] = e_{1k}^{+}[a_k, \gamma_k, e_{-k,1}], \qquad (4.77)$$

for any a_k and any $e_{-k,1}$.

γ_k will be called the *effective capability of individual* k.

Obviously, for social community, the set $T^* \subset \mathbf{R}^u$ of effective capabilities of its individuals (this set corresponds to $\mathscr{C}^*$ when efforts are neglected) do *depend now on the social state* E. According to this state, there are now in the social community more or less individuals able to perform a task with a given efficiency for a chosen criterion.

We are convinced that the introduction of individual capabilities is essential to economics. Let us take, for instance, the following well-known problem: an economy produces two commodities A and B out of two production factors (land in given quantity and hours of work fixed for each individual). Let us examine three different situations which all correspond to an optimal organization:

(1) All individuals have capabilities ensuring the maximum efficiency of their work in the two productive sectors. The maximal production curve is P_1, the economic state depending only on individual preferences between A and B and on the distribution of land between individuals (since individual hours of work are fixed).

(2) Individuals apply to their job the maximum effort, but have differential efficiencies, not only between themselves, but also for the same individual between the two sectors. As a result, the maximal production curve moves towards the origin and has a different shape P_2 (for instance, the maximum production of A decreases more than the maximum production of B if the capabilities needed for A are relatively scarcer than those needed for B). The distribution of income and the relative prices of A and B are also changed.

(3) Let us imagine now that the individuals have an attraction or a repulsion towards the two tasks. The distribution of this attitude among them may be very different from the distribution of capabilities. As a result, the new maximal production curve P_3 will again move towards the origin.

The abundance of psychologists in our societies, and the difficulty in finding workers to perform certain manual tasts, proves that the above problem deserves a closer attention from economic theory. But,

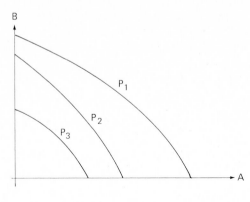

Figure 4.5

as with many other economic problems, how can it be formalised without using the concept of individual capability?

The capability vector plays, in some ways, a part symmetrical to the one of the satisfaction vector or of the utility function. It represents the *means* at the individual's disposal to obtain a certain utility: Other things being equal, for given utility U^*, there exists in $\mathbf{R}^u$ a set $c(U^*)$ of the minimum capability needed to reach this utility (figure 6a).

Reciprocally, for c^* given there exists a maximum utility $U(c^*)$ that the individual can reach (other things, naturally being equal) (figure 6b).

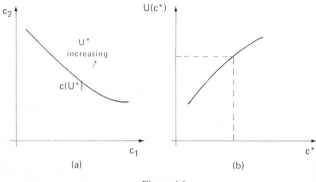

Figure 4.6

4.3. Some examples of the use of capability concept

An *individual's attitude towards training* and *managerial decisions* will serve as the basis for two examples illustrating possible uses of the capability concept.

4.3.1. An individual's attitude towards training

An individual's utility will be supposed to depend on his consumptions $q = (q_i)_{1 \leqslant j \leqslant n}(q \in \mathbf{R}^{n+})$, on this capability c $(c \in \mathbf{R}^+)$ (since an increased capability gives him access to cultural consumptions which otherwise would have no interest at all for him) and on the amount of effort d he spends on training $(d \in \mathbf{R}^+)$:

$$U = U(q, c, d). \tag{4.78}$$

U is assumed jointly differentiable in q, c, d.

Individual consumption is bounded by an income constraint, the income r obtained depending on capability and on the working time $u = T - \tau$. As for the remaining time τ, it is spent on training and defines, jointly with d, the capability level which is reached:

$$pq = r(c, T - \tau), \qquad (p \gg 0, p \in \mathbf{R}^{n+}), \tag{4.79}$$

$$c = c(\tau, d), \tag{4.80}$$

r and c are assumed jointly differentiable in their arguments.

λ being a positive Lagrange multiplier associated to (4.79) and c being replaced by its value (4.80), the individual choices q, τ and d are such that:

$$\alpha_j = \partial U/\partial q_j - p_j, \qquad\qquad \alpha_j = 0 \text{ if } q_j > 0, \alpha_j \leqslant 0 \text{ if } q_j = 0, \tag{4.81}$$

$$\beta = \frac{\partial U}{\partial c} \cdot \frac{\partial c}{\partial \tau} + \lambda\left(\frac{\partial r}{\partial c} \cdot \frac{\partial c}{\partial \tau} - \frac{\partial r}{\partial u}\right), \quad \beta = 0 \text{ if } \tau > 0, \beta \leqslant 0 \text{ if } \tau = 0, \tag{4.82}$$

$$\gamma = \frac{\partial U}{\partial d} + \frac{\partial U}{\partial c} \cdot \frac{\partial c}{\partial d} - \lambda \frac{\partial r}{\partial c} \cdot \frac{\partial c}{\partial d}, \quad \gamma = 0 \text{ if } d > 0, \gamma \leqslant 0 \text{ if } d = 0. \tag{4.83}$$

Hence, when the equilibrium is not at boundaries, the individual will choose the length of his training in such a way that the sum of the direct marginal utility he receives from an increase in his culture, and of the value of the corresponding marginal increase of his income, is exactly compensated by the value of the decrease in income resulting from the shorter length of his working time (4.82). As for his efforts, their direct marginal disutility is compensated by their double effect on capability and income (4.83).

The real mechanism is not so simple. It operates on several periods. Family constraints are frequently essential, and absence of information plays a major part.

4.3.2. Managerial decisions

We plan to examine here some of the reasons for which the profit of a firm is not at the maximum. It is assumed that the firm has only one decision center, its managing director. This managing director possesses a utility function, the arguments of which are:

- the profit of the firm r $(r \in \mathbf{R}^+)$,
- other factors x, such as the size of the firm or its rate of growth (we assume that x is an element of an Euclidian orthant $\mathbf{R}^{m+}$, the utility being an increasing function of any component of x),
- the effort d he devotes to his job $(d \in \mathbf{R}^+)$.

Then:

$$U = U(r, x, d). \tag{4.84}$$

The manager has an effective capability:

$$\gamma = \gamma(c, d), \qquad (c \in \mathbf{R}^+, \gamma \in \mathbf{R}^+). \tag{4.85}$$

The manager takes decisions a, but the set of the decisions he considers possible depends on his effective capability and on his information level J $(J \in \mathbf{R}^+, J$ given). Hence:

$$a \in A(\gamma, J). \tag{4.86}$$

Finally, the managing director associates to any decision a, forecasts:

$$r^* = r^*(a, \gamma), \qquad (r^* \in \mathbf{R}^+), \tag{4.87}$$

$$x^* = x^*(a, \gamma), \qquad (x^* \in \mathbf{R}^{m+}), \tag{4.88}$$

which are different from the real values $r(a, \gamma)$ and $x(a, \gamma)$ induced by a, but which come closer and closer to these values as γ increases.

It is then possible to enumerate the reasons for which the decisions taken are not those which would maximize profit:

- The individual has personal objectives other than pure profit maximization. He is sensitive to other variables and, for instance, limits his efforts.
- His effective capability is bounded by his own capability or by his level of effort.
- The acts he is able to imagine are restricted by his information and by his effective capability. He may be unable to discover the best solutions.
- Because of capability deficiencies, he does not forecast adequately the effects of his decisions.

On the contrary, elementary economic theory assumes:

- U independent of x and d; U increasing function of r: the individual is only interested in profit.
- d, J and c maximum. The individual field of action is not limited by effort, capability or information. The set $A(\gamma_{max}, J_{max})$ is identical to the feasible set and since $r^*(a, \gamma_{max}) = r(a, \gamma_{max})$, there are no forecasting errors.

This example leads us directly to the subject of the last section: the correspondence between acts and real or perceived social states.

5. Correspondence between acts and real or perceived social states

Some definitions on the *nature* of these correspondences will be useful before any analysis of the intervening *factors*. No example will be presented in this section.

5.1. The nature of the correspondences

Let us neglect levels of effort, to simplify analysis, and let us consider an act a_k which has to be, in the context $e_{-k,1}$, in the feasible set:

$$a_k \in A_k(e_{-k,1}).\tag{4.89}$$

As for the consequences of this act on utility, we have to consider three different mappings:

(1) *The real effect of the act on the controlled part of the individual social state* corresponds to a mapping of $A_k(e_{-k,1})$ on $\mathscr{D}_{1k}(e_{-k,1})$:

$$e_{1k} = e_{1k}(a_k), \tag{4.90}$$

and generates the individual social state:

$$e_k = \{e_{1k}, e_{2k}\}, \tag{4.91}$$

with:

$$e_{-k,1} = \{e_{2k}, e_{-k}\}.$$

(2) *The image of this real effect,* as it will be perceived by the individual when the real effect appears. The mapping:

$$e'_k = e'_k(e_k), \tag{4.92}$$

from $\mathscr{D}_{1k}(e_{-k,1})$ on $\mathscr{E}'_k$ has already been studied in the second section of the chapter.

(3) *The forecasted image of the effect of the act,* used by the individual when he takes his decision. The context $e_{-k,1}$ being assumed given, this corresponds to a mapping of $\mathscr{D}_{1k}(e_{-k,1})$ on $\mathscr{E}'_k$:

$$e'^*_k = e'^*_k(a_k), \tag{4.93}$$

but this image may not be the image of a possible real state and *be the result of contradictory expectations.* It is, nevertheless, the image through which the individual will appreciate the utility generated by any behaviour.

Hence, several hypotheses are possible as to the relations between acts and individual social states:

No perception distortion and no forecasting error. This is the traditional assumption. $\mathscr{E}'_k$ can be identified with $\mathscr{E}_k$ and for any $a_k \in A_k(e_{-k,1})$:

$$e_k \equiv e'_k \equiv e'^*_k. \tag{4.94}$$

No forecasting error but a perception distortion. This leads to the identity:

$$e'_k \equiv e'^*_k.$$

It means that the individual does not make any error on the state generated by his behaviour, but evaluates this state through his own perception.

Forecasting errors and perception distortions. e_k, e'_k and e'^*_k are different elements. Such a hypothesis may be debatable in a model with certain future; but here again, as for information search, logic tolerates such a formalization.

5.2. Influence factors

For the above analysis to be complete, it is necessary:
- to consider that a_k is not only one act, but total individual behaviour, including all roles and all allocations performed, as well as levels of search for information,
- to replace c_k by γ_k and to introduce explicitly levels of effort among the effects of behaviour (in e_k, e'_k and e'^*_k).

Then:

$$e_k = e_k(a_k, \gamma_k, e_{-k,1}), \tag{4.96}$$

$$e'_k = \alpha_k[e_k, \gamma_k, e_{-k,1}, S^0_k, \bar{\omega}_k, t_k]. \tag{4.97}$$

Relation (4.97) is relation (4.29), where c_k has been replaced by γ_k, and where external actions have received the more precise expression $e_{-k,1}$ instead of b.

As for e'^*_k, many assumptions can be made. One of the simplest is to assume that *an individual's image of the effect of his behaviour comes closer to the image of the real effect when effective capability increases.* In other words, when capability improves, the forecasting error decreases. We write:

$$e'^*_k = e'^*_k[e'_k, \gamma_k], \tag{4.98}$$

where e'_k is given by (4.97) and (4.96). If $\mathscr{E}'_k$ is a metric space, there is a distance $\varepsilon(e'^*_k, e'_k)$, which is a real-valued function of γ_k for e'_k given. This distance decreases (or at least non-increases) when any of the components of $\gamma_k \in \mathbf{R}^u$ increase.

Another simple assumption is to write directly:

$$e'^*_k = e'^*_k[a_k, \gamma_k, e_{-k,1}, S^0_k, \bar{\omega}_k, t_k], \tag{4.99}$$

e'^*_k and e'_k being then *independently generated.*

Relations (4.80–4.82) reproduce the essential characteristics of the correspondences between acts and social states:

(1) Any individual chooses his acts from the image attributed to their effects.

(2) When building this image, he superimposes on the real effect (which depends on the effective capability with which acts are performed) a double error:

- a perception bias, result of his past, his psychology, his previous satisfaction levels, his capability, and of the surrounding context,
- a forecasting error, due to the limits of his effective capability.

(3) Once the behaviour is chosen, the satisfactions he will obtain will depend on an expost image of the real social state.

To borrow a comparison from the theatre, the study of relations between acts and social states puts an end to the presentation of the actors in the play and their interactions. We now have to define the place and present the set, i.e. to describe the constraints limiting individual behaviour. This will be the purpose of the next chapter.

Chapter 5

BEHAVIOURAL CONSTRAINTS

> ... *At this point, is suggested the interesting and important related problem of placing constraints upon the consumer in addition to that imposed by fixed total income.*
>
> P.A. Samuelson
> *Foundations of Economic Analysis*

Introduction

As the science concerned with the use of scarce resources – according to some definitions – economics has constantly dealt with maximization under constraints. But this tool has been rather unevenly used and, while OR men felt proud of the thousands of constraints needed to describe the operations of a petroleum refinery, the unfortunate individual sketched by the theory had to be content with an environment reduced to one constraint on income.

This chapter will attempt to express, within the limits of a model which remains practicable, the real constraints with which individual behaviour is confronted. It thus has to go beyond the classification difficulties generated by the variety of constraints in the diversity of roles.

(1) Even if its translation is often more delicate than it appears at first, the simplest of all constraints is the *time* constraint (Lesourne (1963); Becker (1965)). Attached to the individual as such, concerning

all the roles, it is indifferent to the nature of economic systems, and cannot be isolated. Nevertheless, it has never been more important than for the inhabitants of the big modern metropolis, bedevilled by traffic jams and commuting trips and compelled to use every moment of time with maximum efficiency. Totally absent from economics a quarter of a century ago, this constraint has now been introduced under the pressure of transport economics; but its generality has barely been taken into account. The first section of the chapter will be devoted to this.

(2) Less precise, but not less important, are the health constraints which have to express, simultaneously, three types of phenomena:

– First, some of the individual's acts may provoke his death[1] (suicide, smokers' cancer, dangerous driving habits, etc.) or serious deterioration of his health (coal-miners' silicosis, liver diseases of alcoholics);
– Secondly, his survival and his health are under the influence of the socio-economic and physical environment (existence of crazy drivers, drought in the Sahel countries, situation of the health system, state of medical science, etc.) and of the biological internal environment (hypotension, arthritis, etc.).
– Finally, the two main characteristics of an individual, his utility and his capability, will depend upon his state of health, death giving to these two elements a rather specific mathematical form.

(3) After health constraints, analyzed in the second section, it is necessary to introduce roles explicitly, since all other constraints have a meaning in relation to one or several roles. The first series of these constraints concerns the very *structure* of these roles, since social habits make some roles compatible and others not (for instance managing director and union representative).

(4) Next come *capability* constraints. Not introduced explicitly in economics, omnipresent in everyday life, they make some roles impossible (e.g. how can I be recruited as an interpreter by UNO if I do not speak any of the official languages of the Organization?) and limit the possible allocations within these roles (e.g. if I do not read English, to read Shakespeare in the original text will give me little satisfaction in my role of consumer).

[1] or increase the probability of his death at a given age.

(5) Capability also has an impact on ability to imagine new solutions to avoid environmental pressure and is therefore one of the parameters of the fifth series of constraints: *information* constraints. These constraints, which the individual can, of course, lessen through his action, define the set of roles which are known and, for each role, the set of allocations which are known. (The woman in her forties, who wants to work again, but is not aware of any possible job, perceives this barrier intensely; so does the new managing director who is not familiar with the various ways of merging comporations.)

(6) Next, logically, we have to consider constraints which are normally attached to each of the roles, and which the nature of our society separates into three different groups:

– *Income* constraints, on which traditional consumer theory is based, but which is not a unique characteristic of this role (think of the manager haunted by the risk of a liquidity crisis; or of the civil servant struggling against budgetary restrictions).
– *Regulation* constraints, imposed upon the numerous organizations with which the individual has contacts (procedures to be followed within a firm, obligation to comply with the law of the country where one lives). May be included here the constraints resulting from the use of money for exchanges (see chapter 8, section 2.4.3).
– *Technique* constraints, limiting the possibility of operating a process, such constraints not being specific to production roles.

As in the preceding chapter, within each section, we shall present, successively, a formal analysis of the class of constraints and a simple model illustrating the notion.

This description of the panoply of constraints does not claim to be exhaustive, nor does it imply that any model anywhere, at any time, should introduce them all. Our only concern, in struggling against the unicity of income constraint, is to enable the introduction into economics of richer and more realistic models.

1. *Time constraints*

"Time is money." A misleading maxim, since time cannot be stolen and only in a famous Marcel Aymé short story, can time tickets be bought.

Every individual lives "24 hours out of 24," neither more nor less, and all his acts take time, even if he is able to read his paper and to take his breakfast simultaneously. He is a prisoner of time, but the nature of this captivity is more complex than at first appears and justifies a few lines of comment:

Let us consider a slice T of the life of an individual and all the acts he may wish to perform during this period. We realize, first, that there is, in fact, a constraint for each time-interval of infinitesimal length, since the individual has to use his time at each moment. We notice next that there are acts which cannot be performed simultaneously (I cannot dictate a report to my secretary and sleep) and acts which have to be finished before the beginning of others (I have to arrive at the office before reading my business mail). We also observe that some acts are only possible in some time intervals (on some beaches, you can only bathe at high tide). We discover, finally, that the length of an act is not fixed, but can be controlled by the individual to a certain extent. Scheduling models in industry have tried to represent this variety of time constraints. At the individual level, the structure of the constraints is almost the same. Like the plant manager, the individual is probably not indifferent to a choice between two schedules giving him the possibility of performing the same acts within a period T; to lunch in a few minutes only, or to be obliged to do two things at a time, are seldom sources of satisfaction.

But for the sake of simplicity we are often obliged to admit that every act has a fixed length; that it can be performed at any time within the period; and that during this performance, no other act is possible. Time constraints can then be expressed by a few equalities or inequalities. Let us describe them with the classification of acts already presented:

To intensity of search for information on roles is attached a time spent on this search; and this time I_k can often be used to measure this intensity, for individual k ($1 \leqslant k \leqslant m$).

Once a role h has been chosen ($1 \leqslant h \leqslant p$), it is possible to introduce, on the one hand, the time t_{kh} necessary to obtain it (time to be registered in a University, ...) and the time T_{kh} during which the allocations of role h have to be performed (the number of hours of lectures attended by a student, ...). According to roles, T_{kh} will be variable or fixed, generally variable for leisure time, but imposed by an organization for work time.[2]

Some roles, such as professional ones, imply a commuting time from house to office, which individuals control through the choice of the location u_k ($u_k \in \mathbf{R}^2$) of their house and of the roles h implying to be present in u_h ($u_h \in \mathbf{R}^2$).

Within the time interval devoted totally or partially to a role (the secretary who writes to her boy-friend during working hours), a new breakdown is possible with:

- the time J_{kh} measuring the intensity of the search for information within role h,
- the time corresponding to trips imposed by allocations (the consumer going to the grocer's),
- the time necessary for the allocations themselves, which depend upon the individual's capability and efforts.

Under these conditions, the time constraints imposed on an individual k can be expressed through the relations (5.1), (5.2) and (5.3) hereunder, relations followed by the definition of notation:

$$I_k + \sum_h i_{kh}\left[t_{kh} + \tau(u_k, u_h) + T_{kh}\right] = T_0, \tag{5.1}$$

$$T_{kh} = J_{kh} + \tau(a_{kh}) + t(a_{kh}, c_k, d_{kh}) + L_{kh}, \tag{5.2}$$

$$T_{kh} \geqslant T_{kh}^* \quad \text{for} \quad h \in H^*, \tag{5.3}$$

where:

T_0	: total time available ($T_0 \in \mathbf{R}^+$),
I_k	: time spent on the search for information on roles ($I_k \in \mathbf{R}^+$),
i_{kh}	: variable equal to 1 if the role is chosen and to 0 if the role is not chosen ($1 \leqslant h \leqslant p$),
t_{kh}	: "access" time to role h ($t_{kh} \in \mathbf{R}^+$),
u_k, u_h	: locations of house and of role h ($u_k \in \mathbf{R}^2$, $u_h \in \mathbf{R}^2$),
$\tau(u_k, u_h)$	: commuting time for role h,
T_{kh}	: time devoted to role h ($T_{kh} \in \mathbf{R}^+$),
T_{kh}^*	: minimum time imposed for the roles of a subset H^* of $H = (1, \ldots, p)$. ($T_{kh}^* \in \mathbf{R}^+$),

---

[2] In a one-period model, it is impossible to avoid such a "contraction" of reality.

J_{kh} :   time spent on search for information within role h $(J_{kh} \in \mathbf{R}^+)$,

$\tau(a_{kh})$:   transportation time imposed by allocation a_{kh} $(a_{kh} \in A_{kh})$,

c_k :   capability $(c_k \in \mathbf{R}^u)$,

d_{kh} :   effort intensity within role h $(d_{kh} \in D_k)$,

$t(a_{kh}, c_k, d_{kh})$: time necessary for completing allocation a_{kh},

L_{kh} :   leisure time in role h $(L_{kh} \in \mathbf{R}^+)$.

Naturally, some of these times are parameters of the individual's social state, and influence the level of utility, either because they are valued, like leisure time, or because they generate inconveniences, like transportation times. Sometimes, it is not the time length itself, but qualities associated with it, such as the comfort of a trip or the beauty of a touristic circuit, which appear in utility.

Symbolically, equations (5.1) and (5.2) can be replaced by the shorter expression:

$$a_k \in A_T(c_k), \tag{5.4}$$

where a_k describes the behaviour of individual k in all its aspects, a_k is an element of the set A_k of all possible behaviours. Time constraints limit a_k to a subset $A_T(c_k) \subset A_k$ depending upon the individual's capability.

Urban economics provides innumerable examples of the influence of time constraints. A simple model will demonstrate this.

An individual has two roles: father and consumer on the one hand, employee on the other. In the city where he lives, he has to choose the location u $(u \in \mathbf{R}^2)$ and the area s $(s \in \mathbf{R}^+)$ of his house, his consumption bundle q $(q \in \mathbf{R}^{n+})$ and his job which, to simplify matters, one assumes is defined only by his place of work u' $(u' \in \mathbf{R}^2)$. To each u' is associated a working time $T(u')$, a commuting time $t'(u, u')$, the corresponding transport cost $c'(u, u')$, a leisure time during office hours $L'(u')$ and an income $r(u')$. The rent is a function $l(s, u)$ of location and area. Consumptions q are paid at prices p $(p \in \mathbf{R}^{n+})$; they imply a transport time $t(u)$ and a transport cost $c(u)$ depending only on the house-location and need a time tq where $(t \in \mathbf{R}^{n+})$ is a vector describing the time necessary for unit consumptions. Finally, T_0 is the total time available and L the leisure time at home.

If the individual is not sensitive to the discomfort of the journeys and if we bypass the satisfaction levels, his utility function can be written:

$$U = U[u, s, q, u', L, L'(u')]. \tag{5.5}$$

As for the environment, this takes the double shape of an income constraint and a time constraint:

$$pq + l(s, u) + c(u) + c'(u, u') \leqslant r(u'), \tag{5.6}$$

$$tq + t(u) + t'(u, u') + L + T(u') = T_0, \tag{5.7}$$

$r(u')$ being the income brought by job u'. Generally, U is not a continuous function of u and u'. Similarly, $L'(u')$, $l(., u)$, $c(u)$, $c'(u, u')$, $r(u')$, $t(u)$, $t'(u, u')$, $T(u')$ are not continuous functions of their arguments. But, since we just want to show how the various elements interplay, we shall make the heroic assumption that all these functions are jointly continuous and differentiable. Hence, at a local maximum of utility, where none of the variables is equal to zero, one has, with an obvious notation:

$$U_q = \mu t + p, \tag{5.8}$$

$$U_L = \mu, \tag{5.9}$$

$$U_u = \lambda \frac{\partial l}{\partial u} + \mu \left(\frac{\partial t}{\partial u} + \frac{\partial t'}{\partial u} \right) + \lambda \left(\frac{dc}{du} + \frac{\partial c'}{\partial u} \right), \tag{5.10}$$

$$U_s = \lambda \frac{\partial l}{\partial s}, \tag{5.11}$$

$$U_{u'} + U_{L'} \frac{dL'}{du'} + \lambda \frac{dr}{du'} = \mu \left(\frac{\partial t'}{\partial u'} + \frac{dT'}{du'} \right) + \lambda \frac{\partial c'}{\partial u'}. \tag{5.12}$$

λ and μ are positive Lagrange multipliers respectively associated to income and time constraints. μ/λ can be interpreted as the individual value of a unit of time. λ is marginal utility of income.

Relations (5.8) to (5.12) have a direct economic meaning:

– (5.8) The marginal utility of a consumption is proportional to the sum of its price and of the value of the consumption time.
– (5.9) The marginal utility of leisure time is proportional to the value of time.
– (5.10) The marginal utility of a variation in house location is proportional to the sum of the additional rent (area remaining constant),

of the marginal cost of transport and of the marginal value of transport times (for a given job location).

– (5.11) The marginal utility of an increase in the area (or the "size") of the house is proportional, for a given location, to the renting price of an additional square foot.

– (5.12) The sum of the value of the marginal utility due to a preferred job,[3] of the value attached marginally to an increase of leisure time during working hours, and of the additional income generated by a variation of the job, is equal to the sum of the marginal costs of the house-office commuting trips and of the value of the additional time spent at work or on these trips (for a given house location).

With such a model, crude as it is, it is possible to build a satisfactory theory of locations, traffic flows and land prices in a town. The economist has to use, on the one hand, the results of surveys on incomes and family budgets, on travel and time-budgets, on traffic flows between zones; and on the other hand, conclusions of motivation studies on attitudes towards housing, work and transport.[4]

In economic theory, existence of time constraints introduces some change in demand theory and in supply of labour services theory, since one has to add to the prices (or to subtract from compensation) the value of the time lost and the marginal cost of transport. These elements are not always independent of prices (or of compensation).

2. Health constraints

Popular wisdom does not underestimate their importance: "Quand on a la santé...;" but medical knowledge makes it possible to postulate the existence of a list of m essential variables[5] $(1 \leqslant j \leqslant m)$, the situation of each variable v_j being an element of a set V_j, in such a way that the *state of health* can be characterized by an element: $v = (v_j)_{1 \leqslant j \leqslant m}$ of the product set $V = \prod_j V_j$. For an individual to be alive, v must be in a subset W of V:

$$v \in W, \qquad W \subset V. \tag{5.13}$$

[3] Here the job is described by its location $u' \in \mathbf{R}^2$. $U_{u'}$ is a vector of $\mathbf{R}^2$, as are dL/du', dr/du', $\partial t/\partial u'$, dT'/du', $\partial c'/\partial u'$.

[4] See J. Lesourne, R. Loué (1977). Etudes de planification régionale et urbaine and J. Lesourne (1964).

[5] With vocabulary of General Systems theory.

But what are the factors influencing v? We are only interested here in parameters related to the individual's present socio-economic behaviour. Other parameters will be supposed to be represented by the variable t_k ($t_k \in \mathbf{R}^+$) already used in the preceding chapter to sum up the individual's past.

We shall isolate:

– the structure R_k ($R_k \in P$) of the roles performed, with the corresponding number of working hours, if this number has an effect on health (so we shall take into account occupational diseases, accidents at work, . . .),

– the allocations a_{kh} within roles ($a_{kh} \in A_{kh}$) (this covers the use of opium by a consumer, as well as the accomplishment of a dangerous mission by a soldier during a war),

– some characteristics of the social state E imposed by the environment and conditioning the individual state of health (the fact that the individual is automatically sent to hospital if he is injured in a car accident; the fact that he lives in a town where there is an epidemic disease; the level of medical knowledge; the availability of drugs, . . .). Some of these characteristics restrict the feasible allocations. They may or may not belong to the individual's social state.

Finally, we shall write:

$$v_k = v_k[R_k, (a_{kh})_{h \in R_k}, E, t_k]. \tag{5.14}$$

Reciprocally, the state of health conditions the individual *capability* and limits the *effort* he is able to deploy:

$$c_k = c_k[v_k, \ldots]. \tag{5.15}$$

(5.15) represents a mapping of W into $\mathbf{R}^{u+}$, the dots recalling that the nature of the mapping depends upon other variables studied in the preceding chapter,

$$d_{kh} \in D_{kh}(v_k, \ldots). \tag{5.16}$$

(5.16) expresses the fact that there is a correspondence between $v \subset W$ and the set $D_{kh} \subset \mathbf{R}^+$ of possible efforts in role h. Here also, the dots recall that the nature of this correspondence may depend upon other variables.

Finally, because of the importance of self-conservation, the state of health is a characteristic of the individual's social state and hence influences, through satisfaction levels, his *utility*.

Nevertheless, we have to admit that information on health is incomplete and that, in this field, the perceived image may be very far from reality. Frequently, the individual behaves under a false impression of his real state of health, and with wrong assumptions concerning the influence of his behaviour on his health.

The development of health economics and of psychological studies on attitudes towards drugs (J.P. Dupuy (1975)) makes it possible to build operational models with health constraints. Here is a simple one.

An individual has just two roles, family and professional. The professional role is assumed to be represented by a variable r ($r \in \mathbf{R}^+$).[6] The consumptions are broken down into current consumptions q ($q \in \mathbf{R}^{n+}$) of prices p ($p \gg 0, p \in \mathbf{R}^{n+}$); and medical consumptions z ($z \in \mathbf{R}^{m+}$) of prices y ($y \gg 0, y \in \mathbf{R}^{m+}$). v represents the individual's health ($v \in V$); and $v' \in V$ the image he has of it. Role r generates an income $\rho(r, v)$ when the individual is in a state of health v (this assumption is a simplified way of expressing the influence of health on capability).

Since most individuals do not have a neutral attitude towards the consumption of drugs, utility must be written:

$$U = U(q, z, r, v'). \tag{5.17}$$

The individual will try to maximize it under the income constraint:

$$pq + yz \leqslant \rho(r, v). \tag{5.18}$$

and under two conditions related to health:

$$v = v[r, q, z], \tag{5.19}$$

$$v' = v'(v), \tag{5.20}$$

the last condition expressing the mapping $V \to V$ of real health into perceived health. Here again, just to explore the interactions between variables, we shall make heroic assumptions on the nature of the various sets and on the continuity and differentiability of the various mappings, sufficient to write that – with an obvious notation – at a local utility

---

[6] $r \in \mathbf{R}^+$ is obviously a strong assumption, but we are less interested here in mathematical rigour than in the substance of interactions. We could equally well assume that r is a vector in a finite dimensional Banach space, the dimensions representing role characteristics. The basic nature of the problem also remains unchanged, if r is in a finite set.

maximum (λ being the positive Lagrange multiplier associated to the income constraint):

$$\left[U_v \cdot \frac{dv'}{dv} + \lambda \frac{\partial \rho}{\partial v} \right] \frac{\partial v}{\partial z} + U_z = \lambda y, \tag{5.21}$$

$$\left[U_v \cdot \frac{dv'}{dv} + \lambda \frac{\partial \rho}{\partial v} \right] \frac{\partial v}{\partial q} + U_q = \lambda p, \tag{5.22}$$

$$\left[U_v \cdot \frac{dv'}{dv} + \lambda \frac{\partial \rho}{\partial v} \right] \frac{\partial v}{\partial r} + \frac{\partial \rho}{\partial r} + U_r = 0. \tag{5.23}$$

The term between brackets common to the three relations can easily be interpreted. It is the value s_v with which an individual rates an improvement of his health. If V is an α-dimensional Banach space, s_v is a vector in $\mathbf{R}^{\alpha+}$. s_v is the sum of two vectors:

– the first is the marginal utility vector of *perceived* health improvements,
– the second is the value vector of the marginal incomes generated by the induced increases in efficiency within a role.

Hence:

(1) The *first* of the three relations means that, for each drug, its price is proportional to the sum of its direct marginal utility U_z, and of the value attached by the individual to its effects on health.

For the consumption of a drug to be chosen optimally by the individual from the health point of view, it is necessary at the same time to live in a society where drug prices are zero ($y = 0$); to have an individual indifferent to drugs ($U_z = 0$); and to have an individual attaching a positive value $s_v \gg 0$ to any medical improvement of his health. (This notion implies that a complete weak ordering of health states from a medical point of view exists in V, and that any increase in a component of v corresponds to an improvement in health.)

To simplify the discussion, we shall assume from now on: $v \in \mathbf{R}^+$.

The first proposition is obvious: the price of drugs limits their consumption. If $U_z = 0$ and $s_v > 0 : s_v(\partial v/\partial z) > 0$ and $\partial v/\partial z$ cannot be equal to zero. Drugs are underemployed medically (but not necessarily from a social point of view).

The second is more interesting. All of us know of individuals who, to stress their independence or their lust for power, or for other psycho-analytical reasons, are against all drugs. For these individuals, $U_z < 0$. At the same time, they underestimate the improvement of their health $(\mathrm{d}v'/\mathrm{d}v < 1)$. Their consumption of drugs is well below the medical optimum. Only one factor has a different effect: a high marginal utility of income λ induces a higher consumption of drugs in order to work better (the perfect example is the managing director who finally agrees to look after himself). Other individuals, in order to be reassured, attach a positive value to medicines $(U_z > 0)$ and consume drugs far beyond the medical optimum.

As for the third proposal, its meaning is quite clear when the term $\lambda \partial \rho / \partial v$ is neglected. It corresponds to two psychological situations: a man in a depressive state is no longer interested in life, and finds some satisfaction in the deterioration of his health $(U_v < 0)$; an optimist wrongly believes that his health is improving $(\mathrm{d}v'/\mathrm{d}v < 0)$. Neither should any longer consume any medicine.

(2) The *second* relation concerns consumptions. Their marginal utilities are proportional to their prices, but they are the sum of the direct marginal utility U_q and of an indirect utility $s_v \, \partial v / \partial q$.

So the man who drinks because of a need for evasion has a high U_q and consumes in spite of a negative $\partial v / \partial q$.

On the contrary, the businessman who, because he is ambitious, wants to be in good shape, will restrict his food consumption, because s_v is high, which limits q, even for a great U_q. And the reader will easily appreciate the case of the woman who wants to remain slim.

(3) Finally, the *last* relation concerns the choice of job. Three elements are involved: the perceived effect of a change of job on health $s_v \partial v / \partial r$; the corresponding improvement of income $\lambda \partial \rho / \partial r$; and the marginal preference for the job U_r. An individual who selects a job dangerous for his health or his life may do it for three reasons: A high valued profession ("To serve the Nation", "A man's job"), where U_r high; a well-paid job ("Le salaire de la peur") where $\partial \rho / \partial r$ is high; an individual to whom is health or his life are indifferent (a desperado) or who believes in his star $(\mathrm{d}v'/\mathrm{d}v < 1$ or $< 0)$; in these two cases, s_v is small.

The remarks of this section may be useful in different realms of economics: economics of health, naturally; but also economics of transport (because of road accidents); economics of insurance; and what might be called economics of violence, including war, riots, terrorism and criminality.

3. Role constraints

In a given society, the sequence $R_k = (i_{kh})_{1 \leqslant h \leqslant p}$ with $i_{kh} = 0$ or 1 describing the roles of an individual is not of any kind indiscriminately:

- Some roles are forbidden, such as being a Protestant at the end the reign of Louis the XIVth; or a member of the Communist Party today in certain countries (they can be performed only clandestinely).
- Numerous other roles are not compatible: until recently, an airhostess could not be married. In many countries, it is impossible to be lawfully a bigamist. Frequently, a member of Parliament cannot exercise certain professions, ...

These facts can be translated in ascribing to the sequence R_k to be in a set P of *feasible individual role structures*:

$$R_k \in P. \tag{5.24}$$

Three remarks have to be made about P:

(1) P differs from one society to another and, for a given society, changes in time. With social development, new roles are created, others disappear; some interdicts vanish, others are established; but the general trend corresponds to an increase in the number and specificity of roles. A diachronic analysis of economic evolution should be able to account for role transformations.

(2) The structure of P is rather special, since the list of the p existing roles can be approximately partitioned by type (family role: bachelor, married without children, married with children; professional role: manager, engineer, clerk; religious role: Catholic, Protestant clergy man; political role: Socialist Member of Parliament, UDR voter).

P is such that:

– within one type it is generally impossible to exert more than one role,
– from one type to another, the conditions of exclusion are less strict, plurality often being possible except in special cases.

In passing from a one-period to a multiperiod model, new conditions appear between roles of the same type: anteriority conditions, which express the fact that a role cannot be held (Ingénieur Général des Ponts et Chaussées, for instance) if another role has not been held previously (Ingénieur en Chef). These conditions correspond to "trees" of possible roles, well-known in all big organizations. At the start of a channel, the individual has had to pass through a selection filter (examination, initiation rite, . . .), the success of the test depending on – among other things – his capability.

(3) Some role constraints can be embedded either in the structure of P or in capability constraints. As an example, let us take the constraint: "It is forbidden to marry before the age of sixteen." This can be represented by defining classes of individuals of different age, sex, nationality, religion and so on, and by associating with each class a different set of feasible individual role structures. It is also possible to consider age as a dimension of individual capability and to write that age must be above a minimum for the roles of married man or woman. Each of these two solutions has advantages, but also drawbacks.

In any case, close relations exist between role constraints and capability constraints.

4. Capability constraints

The individual capability vector has, at the same time, an impact on the roles available to an individual and on the allocations he may choose within these roles:

The *first* phenomenon can be expressed through a constraint such as:

$$R_k \in R_c(\gamma_k), \tag{5.25}$$

$R_c(\gamma_k)$ being a subset of the set R of all conceivable role sequences.

Since:

$$\gamma_k = \gamma_k(c_k, d_k),$$

relation (5.25) translates at the same time:

- the limits which, for a given effort d_k, capability c_k imposes on roles and combinations of roles,
- the weakening of these limits when the effort is increased for a given capability c_k.

The subsets $R_c(\gamma_k)$ probably verify the following assumption:
An increase in effective capability cannot eliminate a role sequence from the possibility set.
In other words, if $\gamma_j^k \geqslant \gamma_j'^k$ (with inequality for one j at least):

$$R_c(\gamma_k') \subseteq R_c(\gamma_k). \tag{5.26}$$

To simplify the influence of capability on possible roles, it is frequently acceptable to postulate *role independence with respect to effective capability*. Relation (5.25) can then be replaced for each role h ($1 \leqslant h \leqslant p$) by the condition:

$$F_h(\gamma_k) \geqslant 0, \tag{5.27}$$

F_h being a mapping from $\mathbf{R}^u$ to the real line. If, through γ_k, F_h is assumed to be an increasing and jointly continuous and differentiable function of all the c_j^k's, there exists in $\mathbf{R}^u$, for d_k given, a *minimal surface* $\sigma_h(d_k)$ of individual capability necessary to hold a role. If the set D of possible efforts is a Euclidean orthant $\mathbf{R}^{v+}$ such that any component of γ_k does not decrease when a component of d_k increases, there exists amond the $\sigma_h(d_k)$ an *extremal surface* which represents the limit to which effort can replace capability in holding a role (figure 5.1).

What has just been said about roles can, almost word for word, be transposed to the *second* phenomenon, i.e. to the capability constraints on allocations. Assuming role independence with respect to effective capability and supposing (5.27) true for a role h, the capability constraint on allocations within role h can be written:

$$f_h(a_{kh}, \gamma_k) \geqslant 0, \tag{5.28}$$

f_h being a mapping from A_{kh} to the real line. It defines in A_{kh} a subset $A_{khc}(\gamma_k) \subseteq A_{kh}$ of feasible allocations, but it is much more difficult here

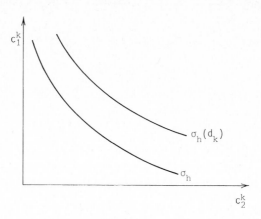

Figure 5.1

to postulate allocation independence with respect to effective capability.

Constraints (28) are not theoretical at all: In the case of production, they have been studied for quite a time by industrial engineers who have, empirically, found compatibilities and incompatibilities between tasks, necessary capability levels and psychophysiological factors influencing task performance.

An example will help us better to understand the importance of capability constraints, though it is already possible to look at the models in chapter 4, section 4.3. The example will be devoted to the *compensation policy* of many firms.

To begin with, these firms define separately:
– *jobs* (production engineer, sales manager, head of a research unit) i.e. in our vocabulary, roles h,
– *capability dimensions* j (technical knowledge in the job technique, ability to find new solutions to problems, capacity to command), with a scale for each of these dimensions.

Depending on the possible impact on the firm of the decisions taken by an individual holding job h, they determine for each job and each capability dimension a *normal capability level* c_{jh}. Any job h then receives a profile π_h which is a vector in $\mathbf{R}^u$:

$$\pi_h = (c_{jh})_{1 \leqslant j \leqslant u}. \tag{5.29}$$

The firms transform this profile into a *figure in points* n_h attached to the job, using for this purpose various relations which may be simple weighted sums or much more sophisticated formulae:

$$n_h = n_h(\pi_h), \tag{5.30}$$

n_h being a mapping from $\mathbf{R}^u$ to the set of positive integers N.

Finally, they observe, through surveys, the labour market, and learn the salary level $s(n)$ paid *on the average* to holders of jobs n, and even the statistical distribution of this salary for n given. Having defined independently their compensation policy with respect to the market (they want to pay more or less, according to the various categories), they can deduce the *normal* salary $\sigma(n)$ they are going to pay for a figure in points n.

The interest of such a method is that, for a given job, n is stable even though the $s(n)$ distribution may change rather quickly. The lengthy determination of the n_h's does not need to be done frequently.

Scale n_h and the function $\sigma(n)$ do not depend on effective job holders. To determine the *compensation of a precise individual k having a job h,* the firm often combines two different approaches:

– on the one hand, it evaluates the profile p_k of the individual capability levels c_j^k. This profile enables the firm to estimate the individual's adaptability to the job and his career potential. It then offers a salary:

$$\sigma_k = \sigma(n_h) \cdot \delta_{kh}, \tag{5.31}$$

δ_{kh} being a coefficient depending on the discrepancy between p_k and π_k and on personal individual characteristics such as age, average effort intensity... (δ_{kh} is frequently between 0.8 and 1.2),
– on the other hand, the firm defines evolution criteria and yearly objectives (so that it becomes a posteriori possible to assess the individual's efficiency during the year) and it adds to the fixed salary a premium σ_k^+ increasing with any positive difference between effective results and objectives.

To take capability constraint explicitly into account would improve economic theory in at least two essential fields: education or training and salary determination on employment market.

5. Information constraints

"Un homme averti en vaut deux" says the proverb.[7] Obviously, economics cannot accept this elementary arithmetic, but it must recognize that capability is not a sufficient condition to choose roles and decide allocations, since the individual will only select *a solution he has invented or learned to know.*

So, inspite of the crude way in which they are expressed in order to remain within the fremework of a certain future, information constraints express essential aspects of individual behaviour:

- They represent, first, the opportunity an individual has *to get informed on existing possibilities* in exchange for a given intensity of search for information.
- They account, in the second place, for the possibility he has *to invent new solutions* enabling him to use the environment to get rid, at least partially, of external constraints.

Hence, information constraints have not the same meaning as time or health constraints, which are physical or biological constraints; or as income or role constraints, which are rather social constraints. They are similar to capability constraints, since they also express individual characteristics.

Information constraints can be studied at the levels of roles and allocations:

At the level of *roles*, depending on his search intensity $I_k \in \mathbf{R}^+$ and on his effective capability $\gamma_k \in \mathbf{R}^{u+}$ (which takes into account the quality of his imagination), the individual perceives as possible roles R_k such that:

$$R_k \in R_I(I_k, \gamma_k), \tag{5.32}$$

$R_I(I_k, \gamma_k)$ being a subset of the set R of all conceivable role sequences or such that:

$$g_k(R_k, I_k, \gamma_k) \geqslant 0, \tag{5.33}$$

g_k being a mapping of $P \times \mathbf{R}^{(u+1)+}$ to the real line. For instance, a young woman may have enough capabilities to be a librarian, but not know it. Nevertheless, if she looks for information, she will probably learn that

---

[7] "A man warned is worth two."

such a career is a possibility for her. Similarly a bright and hard-working young scientist (γ_k and I_k high) may invent a new product or a new process and create his own firm, thus making possible a new role.

At the level of *allocations* within a role h held by an individual, the same phenomenon appears again: the higher the individual's capability or the harder his search for information (including imaginative efforts), the greater the set of allocations considered as possible:

$$a_{kh} \in A_{kh}(J_{kh}, \gamma_k), \quad \text{with } A_{kh}(J_{kh}, \gamma_k) \subseteq A_{kh}, J_{kh}, \in \mathbf{R}^+, \tag{5.34}$$

or:

$$g_{kh}(a_{kh}, J_{kh}, \gamma_k) \geq 0, \tag{5.35}$$

g_{kh} being a mapping of $A_{kh} \times \mathbf{R}^{(u+1)+}$ to the real line.

For instance, before launching a new product, a sales manager will look for information on prices of competitive products in order to estimate the range of possible prices. Depending on his capability, he may or may not also invent a new type of distribution. . .

To appreciate properly how creation and information efforts are introduced in the present theory, one must not forget that variables I_k and J_{kh} also appear in two other important ways:

– *They influence the levels of some satisfactions* through motivations of curiosity and exploration.
– *They have an impact on the individual's evaluation of surrounding constraints.* For example, according to his information level, for the *time* constraint, the individual will allow a larger or smaller margin to reach the airport; for the *income* constraint, he will know, more or less, the prices of various commodities or the income generated by different jobs (see the model of housewife's information in chapter 4, section 3.3). Similar remarks can be applied to any constraints. Naturally, through lack of information, an individual may unwillingly violate a constraint. But to avoid uncertainty, we assume here that deficiency of information results in the acceptance *of constraints which are too strong.*

Two crude models, one on roles, the other on allocations, will make the preceding development clearer.

5.1. Information and job selection

An individual, who is naturally also a consumer, looks for a job. To make things easier, the possible jobs are represented by points r on the closed interval $[0, \bar{r}]$ of the positive half-line. His current consumptions $q \in \mathbf{R}^{n+}$ are bought at a price $p \in \mathbf{R}^{n+}$ ($p \gg 0$). He accepts an intensity $I \in \mathbf{R}^+$ of search for information and has to pay for that πI (π is a positive scalar). His capability is $\gamma \in \mathbf{R}^+$.

The individual utility can be written:

$$U = U(q, I, \gamma, r). \tag{5.36}$$

It depends on γ since the individual has to make efforts to increase his capability level. We assume that the labelling of jobs is such that U is an increasing function of r.

The income constraint is:

$$pq + \pi I = \rho(r, I), \tag{5.37}$$

$\rho(r, I)$ being the highest income found by the individual – in a state of information I – for a job r. We shall assume that ρ is an increasing continuous differentiable function of r and a continuous differentiable function of I.

If the jobs become more and more difficult as r increases, the capability constraint is an inequality:

$$r \leqslant r_1(\gamma), \tag{5.38}$$

and the information constraint an inequality:

$$r \leqslant r_2(\gamma, I), \tag{5.39}$$

$r_2(I, \gamma)$, denoting the job of maximum income which is conceived when the individual makes search effort I and has capability γ. r_2 is an increasing function of I and of γ, which will be supposed jointly continuous and differentiable in I and γ.

If U is a jointly continuous and differentiable function of its arguments, its constrained maximum can be studied through the differential of the Lagrangian L:

$$dL = U_q \, dq + U_I \, dI + U_\gamma \, d\gamma + U_r \, dr] -$$

$$\lambda \left[p \, dq + \pi \, dI - \frac{\partial \rho}{\partial r} \, dr - \frac{\partial \rho}{\partial I} \, dI \right] +$$

$$\mu \left[\frac{dr_1}{d\gamma} \, d\gamma - dr \right] + v \left[\frac{\partial r_2}{\partial I} \, dI + \frac{\partial r_2}{\partial \gamma} \, d\gamma - dr \right], \qquad (5.40)$$

μ and v being positive or zero Lagrange multipliers associated to constraints (5.38) and (5.39) and λ a positive Lagrange multiplier associated to (5.37).

The two constraints (5.38) and (5.39) cannot both be equalities in a situation of maximum utility (except in the improbable case where $r_1(c) = r_2(c, I)$). Hence, one of the two multipliers μ and v has to be equal to zero and two extremal possibilities exist:

First regime: $v = 0$, $\mu > 0$. Relation (5.39) is a strict inequality. An additional search for information would induce a better evaluation of ρ, but would not make it possible to discover feasible new jobs. Under this regime, necessary conditions for a maximum, where $q \gg 0$, $r > 0$, $\gamma > 0$, $I > 0$, are:

$$U_q - \lambda p = 0, \qquad (5.41)$$

$$U_I + \lambda \frac{\partial \rho}{\partial I} = \lambda \pi, \qquad (5.42)$$

$$U_\gamma + \left[U_r + \lambda \frac{\partial \rho}{\partial r} \right] \frac{dr_1}{d\gamma} = 0. \qquad (5.43)$$

(5.41) is obvious. (5.42) expresses that the marginal cost γ of search for information is equal to the sum of the value of the direct marginal utility generated by information search and of the additional income resulting marginally from information search. (5.43) tells us that the marginal disutility resulting from efforts made to improve capability is compensated by the marginal direct utility of the job chosen and by the additional income obtained.

The respective values and even the signs of U_I, U_γ and U_r may vary from one individual to another. The reader will easily adapt the above analysis.

Second regime: $\mu = 0$, $v > 0$. Relation (5.38) is a strict inequality. Lack of information prevents the individual from finding the best job his capability would make possible. Under this regime, necessary conditions for a maximum, where $q \gg 0$, $r > 0$, $\gamma > 0$, $I > 0$ are:

$$U_q - \lambda_p = 0, \tag{5.44}$$

$$U_I + \lambda \frac{\partial \rho}{\partial I} + v \frac{\partial r_2}{\partial I} = \pi, \tag{5.45}$$

$$U_\gamma + v \frac{\partial r_2}{\partial \gamma} = 0, \tag{5.46}$$

$$U_r + \lambda \frac{\partial \rho}{\partial r} = v. \tag{5.47}$$

Let us consider only differences: (5.46) shows that v can be interpreted as the marginal value for the individual of the job chosen, value which is the sum of a direct marginal utility and of the value of the marginal income. (5.45) then expresses that the marginal cost of information search is equal to the two terms of the left-hand side of (5.42) plus the *value of the marginal improvement of job made possible by additional information.* As for (5.46), it means that marginal disutility of capability $(-U_\gamma)$ is equal to *the value of the marginal improvement of job made possible by a better ability to search.*

Obviously, the part played by ability is *totally different under the two regimes.*

5.2. Information and consumption

A housewife's utility is supposed to depend on her current consumptions $q \in \mathbf{R}^{n+}$ bought at price $p \in \mathbf{R}^{n+}$ ($p \gg 0$) and on her intensity of search for information $I \in \mathbf{R}^+$ which costs $\pi \in \mathbf{R}^+$ per unit. Her income ρ is given. For a level of search I, the housewife has access to a consumption set defined by:

$$g(q, I) \geqslant 0. \tag{5.48}$$

Such an expression for the information constraint is not very satisfactory, since the housewife does not really need information on quantities but on product types. A more satisfactory model will be built later, but this one is enough to capture the essence of the matter. Utility is written:

$$U = U(q, I), \tag{5.49}$$

and the income constraint:

$$pq + \pi I = r. \tag{5.50}$$

If U and g are jointly continuous and differentiable functions of their arguments and if λ is the positive Lagrange multiplier attached to (5.50), a maximum of utility for which $q \geqslant 0$ may correspond:

- to a zero level of search for information: $I = 0$, $g(q, I) > 0$ and $U_q - \lambda p = 0$,
- to a nonzero level of search for information: $I > 0$, $g(q, I) = 0$ and:

$$U_q - \lambda p - (U_I - \lambda\pi) \frac{\partial g/\partial q}{\partial g/\partial I} = 0. \tag{5.51}$$

The last relation means that the marginal value of a consumption is proportional to the sum of its price and of the marginal cost of the information needed to get it. This cost is the product of $(\pi - U_I/\lambda)$ – the difference between the unit cost of information and the monetary equivalent of the search marginal utility – and of $(-\partial g/\partial q)/(\partial g/\partial I)$ – the increase in information needed for a unit increase in consumption.

So, with distortions that some may find severe, but which we consider admissible at this very general level, the meaning of information constraints can be fully understood, even with a certain future. A rough design seems preferable to a blank sheet.

6. Income constraints

In our society and in many others, most roles impose income constraints on the individuals who fulfil them:

- In a firm, the managing director must prevent its cash situation from becoming negative. He must have a positive profit and loss account.
- These global constraints at the corporation level are frequently transformed into specific constraints attached to each role in the hierarchy. These constraints become stricter and stricter when the

roles approach the base of the pyramid. They may be expressed in terms of the volume of clients' accounts, the size of investment budget, the level of current result. At the bottom, the constraints are generally so strong that they practically exclude any choice between different resources.

- The same situation occurs for all roles within the State, since the government, caught in the net of a budget voted by Parliament, with authorized ceilings chapter by chapter, distributes these global constraints among its civil servants.
- But a scientific association, a political party, a parish, a terrorist organization also have budget problems and must also define rules to obtain income and decide expenditures.

These examples underline two important features of these constraints:

(1) The income – or rather the proceeds – is not given, but depends on individual behaviour. So, in his role of consumer, an individual has an income which results from the other roles he holds (dividends of a shareholder, wages of a clerk, . . .) and from his efficiency within these roles (productivity premium, profit of an individual entrepreneur). Similarly, a political party is liable to influence the volume of resources it will devote to an electoral campaign through a promotional action directed towards its members. It is necessary to stress these rather obvious remarks because the elementary theory of the consumer has frequently been interpreted as a description of an adaptation of consumption to an income passively accepted.

(2) The structure of income constraints is much more complex than is usually thought. Let us try to understand why, starting first from the point of view of a consumer or of a global organization. For the one as for the other, the essential constraints is a *cash constraint*, which has to be met at any time and corresponds, in fact, to a series of constraints. The decision centre is then compelled to look for an admissible schedule of its receipts and its payments; but since there is always a lag (certain or random, which may or may not be modified) between the act generating the operation and the monetary operation itself, it must forecast the consequences of the act on the cash situation as soon as the decision is taken. Hence, the interest of having operating accounts which make it possible to

appreciate – within each period of time – whether one is getting richer or poorer; and the introduction, at the level of these accounts, of *derived constraints*. Finally, the decision centre may regulate its input and output money flows through lending or borrowing; but it is submitted to the constraints imposed by lenders who evaluate its capability to reimburse out of its operating accounts. This second reason will reinforce the importance of derived constraints for any decision centre with complex operations.

If we now abandon the level of the organization as a whole and consider a specific role within this organization, we observe the substitution of *partial constraints* attached to each role to the global constraints studied above. These partial constraints are chosen to express, as well as possible, the global ones.

All these constraints also differ by the penalties incurred when they are not obeyed. Even if prison for debt no longer exists, penalties are always serious when cash constraints are violated. For other income constraints, the range of penalties is wide; decrease of a premium, compulsory change of role within the organization, exclusion from the organization...

Hence, it is not totally devoid of interest for economics to improve the way in which income constraints are represented.

Within the narrow possibilities offered by a unique period, we shall suggest here, as examples, two simple models on the income constraints of a head of family and of a managing director.

6.1. Income constraints of a head of family

The head of a family has, at the beginning of the period, resources in amount A ($A \in \mathbf{R}^+$) liable to give him some utility if he keeps them at his disposal; but he may renounce a fraction A' of A, and obtain in exchange an income iA'. Similarly, he may borrow resources K ($K \in \mathbf{R}^+$) at a cost iK; but the lenders will not generally agree to lend more than a fraction kA of the individual's personal resources. Current consumptions are represented by $q \in \mathbf{R}^{n+}$, role by $r \in \mathbf{R}^+$. Finally, $d \in \mathbf{R}^+$ is the effort developed by the individual and $\rho(r, d)$ the income generated by role r with effort d. ρ is assumed to be an increasing continuous and differentiable function of its arguments.

The individual has to choose r, d, K, A', q in order to maximize:

$$U = U[r, d, K, A - A', q], \tag{5.52}$$

under the constraints:

$$0 \leqslant K \leqslant kA, \tag{5.53}$$

$$0 \leqslant A' \leqslant A, \tag{5.54}$$

$$pq = \rho(r, d) - iK + i'A'. \tag{5.55}$$

U will be supposed jointly continuous and differentiable in its arguments. Hence, necessary conditions for U to be maximum (with $q \gg 0$, $d > 0$, $r > 0$) are first the obvious relations:

$$U_q - \lambda p = 0, \tag{5.56}$$

$$U_d - \lambda \frac{\partial \rho}{\partial d} = 0, \tag{5.57}$$

$$U_r - \lambda \frac{\partial \rho}{\partial r} = 0, \tag{5.58}$$

and then the two groups of three exclusive relations:

$$\{U_A > \lambda i' \text{ and } A' = 0\} \text{ or } \{U_A < \lambda i' \text{ and } A' = A\}$$
$$\text{or } \{U_A = \lambda i' \text{ and } 0 \leqslant A' \leqslant A\}, \tag{5.59}$$

$$\{U_K < \lambda i \text{ and } K = 0\} \text{ or } \{U_K > \lambda i \text{ and } K = kA\}$$
$$\text{or } \{U_K = \lambda i \text{ and } 0 \leqslant K \leqslant kA\}. \tag{5.60}$$

6.2. Income constraints of a corporation managing director

The managing director – who, as a consumer buys q ($q \in \mathbf{R}^{n+}$) at prices p ($p \in \mathbf{R}^{n+}$, $p \gg 0$) – is also sensitive to the prestige generated by the level of production Q of his firm ($Q \in \mathbf{R}^+$). He develops professional efforts d ($d \in \mathbf{R}^+$). His salary ρ is a function of the profit b of his firm. He is then interested in maximizing a utility function:

$$U = U(q, Q, d), \tag{5.61}$$

jointly continuous and differentiable in its arguments with $U_q \gg 0$, $U_Q > 0$, $U_d < 0$, under the constraint:

$$pq = \rho(b). \tag{5.62}$$

We now have to express the corporation profit and constraints:

At the production level Q, the firm has an operating margin $m(Q, d)$ – a differentiable function of its arguments. This margin increases with the effort of the managing director ($\partial m/\partial d > 0$), but with respect to Q, it first increases, then passes through a maximum and decreases.

Simultaneously, the firm must cover during the period the amount of investment needed to produce $Q : I(Q)$ – an increasing differentiable function of Q. This can be done through equity capital K or borrowing X at rate i.

Consequently:

$$I(Q) = K + X. \tag{5.63}$$

Profit b is then obviously given by:

$$b = m(Q, d) - iX. \tag{5.64}$$

But the managing director must, at the end of the period, be able to distribute a minimum dividend per franc of equity capital:

$$b \geqslant \beta K, \qquad (0 \leqslant \beta \leqslant 1). \tag{5.65}$$

Finally, he cannot borrow more than a fraction k of equity capital:

$$0 \leqslant X \leqslant hK. \tag{5.66}$$

Any business economist will recognize in relations (5.63) to (5.66) a description of real constraints as satisfactory as the narrow framework of a unique period permits.

The solution of the above problem corresponds to six different regimes, depending on the positions of β and X with respect to the limits in (5.65) and (5.66). In all these regimes for a maximum where $q \geqslant 0$:

$$U_q = \lambda p,$$

λ being the positive Lagrange multiplier associated to (5.62).

First regime: Profit above minimum, no borrowing. The managing director chooses the production and his level of effort in such a way that the marginal value of his additional income is exactly compensated by his marginal utility for prestige or his marginal disutility for effort:

$$U_Q + \lambda \frac{d\rho}{db} \frac{\partial m}{\partial Q} = 0 \tag{5.67}$$

(since $U_Q > 0$, $\partial m/\partial Q < 0$. The production is *greater* than the production for which the profit would be maximum)

$$U_d + \lambda \frac{d\rho}{db} \frac{\partial m}{\partial d} = 0. \tag{5.68}$$

Second regime: Profit equal to minimum, no borrowing. Condition (5.67) and (5.68) are replaced by the following:

$$b = \beta I(Q), \tag{5.69}$$

$$U_d + \mu \frac{\partial m}{\partial d} = 0, \tag{5.70}$$

$$U_Q + \mu \frac{\partial m}{\partial Q} - v \frac{db}{dQ} = 0, \tag{5.71}$$

$$\mu = \lambda \frac{d\rho}{db} + v. \tag{5.72}$$

μ is the marginal value for the individual of an increase in profit, but it is the sum of two terms:

– the value $\lambda(d\rho/db)$ of the induced salary increase,
– the value v due to the fact that the profit constraint is more easily satisfied (v is the Lagrange multiplier attached to (5.65)).

(5.66) is then obvious, while (5.67) means that the additional utility due to prestige is compensated by the loss due to the decrease in margin and by the implicit cost of the variation in profit.

Third regime: Profit above minimum, maximum borrowing. In this regime:

$$X = \frac{k}{1 + k} I(Q), \tag{5.73}$$

$$U_d + \lambda \frac{d\rho}{db} \frac{\partial m}{\partial d} = 0, \tag{5.74}$$

$$U_Q + \lambda \frac{\mathrm{d}\rho}{\mathrm{d}b} \left(\frac{\partial m}{\partial Q} - i \frac{k}{1 + k} \frac{\mathrm{d}I}{\mathrm{d}Q} \right) = 0. \tag{5.75}$$

The amount of borrowing directly results from the level of production. (5.74) is identical to (5.68) and has the same interpretation. On the contrary, in selecting the production level (5.75), the managing director takes into account the additional financial charges which will be deducted from its profit.

Fourth regime: Profit equal to minimum, maximum borrowing. In this regime, relations (5.72), (5.73) and (5.74) remain valid, but a new relation replaces (5.71) and (5.75) of the two preceding regimes:

$$U_Q + \mu \left[\frac{\partial m}{\partial Q} - i \frac{k}{1 + k} \frac{\mathrm{d}I}{\mathrm{d}Q} \right] - \frac{v}{1 + k} \frac{\mathrm{d}b}{\mathrm{d}Q} = 0, \tag{5.76}$$

The first two terms are identical to the left-hand side of (5.75); as for the third, it represents the implicit cost resulting from the need to make profits in order to distribute dividends, the cost being damped by the coefficients $1/(1 + k)$ corresponding to the smaller share of equity capital in financing.

Fifth regime: Profit above minimum, borrowing between minimum and maximum. This regime is never optimal. The director prefers, of course, since he is not limited by the dividend constraint, to finance investment from the firm's own funds, since this does not decrease profit, and, hence, his salary.

Sixth regime: Profit equal to minimum, borrowing between minimum and maximum. This regime is never optimal. According to the sign of $\mu i - v\beta$, the director has an interest in financing totally from equity capital ($\mu i > v\beta$); or totally from borrowing ($\mu i < v\beta$).

Finally, the solution will depend on the director's psychology (utility function), on the productive possibilities of the firm (margin and investment functions), on the financing conditions (represented here by parameters i, β, k). The results are quite in agreement with observed behaviours in business life, at least when one man only plays an essential part in the main decisions.

Perceived in their variety, income constraints are extremely similar to regulation constraints. It would not be incorrect to include them in the general set of social rules. But their historical and practical importance in economics explains why they have been analysed separately.

7. *Regulation constraints*

The constraints already studied do not represent all the limitations society imposes on individual behaviour. It is unnecessary to demonstrate this in our societies, where law is extremely developed at national or organizational levels. Civil law, criminal law, labour law, trade law resulting from Parliament bills or Government decrees, together with instructions, management decisions, internal rules of big organizations, imprison the individual in a very strict network of constraints. Numerous professionals and civil servants earn their living by trying to make more explicit the meaning of the law; by looking for solutions to avoid its consequences; by preparing lawsuits which will decide whether it has been broken or not; by defining penalties to be applied in case of violations.

Of special importance are the constraints related to the *structure of markets* or to the use of *money* for economic exchange. An example of the first category of constraints is to be found in a one-period environment in Benassy (1975), an example of the second in Malinvaud and Younes (1974).

To describe all these constraints here would be an impossible task. It is much more interesting to try to study how they can be introduced for two roles held by most individuals, the family role (father or mother) and the professional role (within a firm or an administrative body).

7.1. *Regulation constraints in a family role*

If the existence of a noncontrolled individual social state is not considered as a constraint – though it directly affects individual utility – regulations can be expressed through the fact that allocations are forbidden, compulsory or compelled to be in a set a priori defined. For instance:

- drug consumption is forbidden,
- parents must send their children to school from 6 to 16,
- in rationing periods, consumption of certain commodities is limited from above.

Mathematically, the corresponding constraints take various shapes:

- a simple equality or inequality involving quantities:

  $q \leqslant \bar{q}$ ($q \in \mathbf{R}^{m+}$ vector of current consumptions, $\bar{q} \in \mathbf{R}^{m+}$ rationing vector);
- a constraint in value:

  $d < \bar{d}$ ($d \in \mathbf{R}$ amount of expenditure in foreign currencies, $\bar{d} \in \mathbf{R}$ maximum authorized amount of expenditure in foreign currencies);
- a transformation of another constraint:

  $pq \leqslant \beta(\rho)\rho$ ($q \in \mathbf{R}^{m+}$ consumption vector, $p \in \mathbf{R}^{m+}$, $p \gg 0$, corresponding price vector, $\rho \in \mathbf{R}^+$ income, $0 \leqslant 1 - \beta(\rho) \leqslant 1$ tax rate on income),

  $T = T_0 - \tau$ (T_0: total time available, τ time compulsorily spent in forced labour in the Middle Ages or in military service in modern societies);
- the adjunction of additional conditions such as the impossibility of obtaining certain information (national defence secrets, examination questions, statistical secrets, health information, . . .).

In each case, the economist has to look for a satisfactory representation of the constraints essential to the understanding of the case and of the related problems of fraud.

Let us take the simple situation of an individual whose consumptions can be broken down into free consumption q_1 with prices p_1 ($q_1 \in \mathbf{R}^{m_1+}$, $p_1 \in \mathbf{R}^{m_1+}$, $p_1 \gg 0$); rationed consumption q_2 with prices p_2 and a maximum allocation $\bar{q}_2$ ($q_2 \in \mathbf{R}^{m_2-}$, $p_2 \in \mathbf{R}^{m_2+}$, $p_2 \gg 0$); foreign consumption q_3 with prices p_3 ($q_3 \in \mathbf{R}^{m_3+}$; $p_3 \gg 0$) and an allocation $\bar{d}$ of foreign currencies ($\bar{d} \in \mathbf{R}^+$). $\rho \in \mathbf{R}^+$ will denote the income. We shall *first neglect the possibility of a fraud and thereafter, introduce it.*

The individual is supposed to maximise a function:

$$U = U[q_1, q_2, q_3], \tag{5.77}$$

strictly concave and jointly differentiable in its arguments, under the constraints:

$$q_2 \leqslant \bar{q}_2, \tag{5.78}$$

$$p_3 q_3 \leqslant \bar{d}, \tag{5.79}$$

$$p_1 q_1 + p_2 q_2 + p_3 q_3 = \rho. \tag{5.80}$$

Associating to the above constraints positive or zero Lagrange multipliers μ, v, λ, $(\lambda \in \mathbf{R}^+, v \in \mathbf{R}^+, \mu \in \mathbf{R}^{m_2 +})$, and assuming that none of the consumptions is zero in the equilibrium situation, the following three relations are valid in the unique maximum of utility:

$$U_{q_1} - \lambda p_1 = 0, \tag{5.81}$$

$$U_{q_2} - \lambda(p_2 + \mu/\lambda) = 0, \tag{5.82}$$

$$U_{q_3} - \lambda(1 + v/\lambda)p_3 = 0, \tag{5.83}$$

which means – as is well-known by all economists – that marginal utility is proportional to the price for free commodities; to the sum of the price and an opportunity rationing cost μ_j/λ $(1 \leqslant j \leqslant m_2)$ for rationed commodities (with $\mu_j = 0$ if $q_{2_j} < \bar{q}_{2_j}$); and to the product of the price and a coefficient greater than one $(1 + v/\lambda)$ for commodities bought in foreign currencies. This coefficient expresses the additional value which the unit of foreign currency has in national currency, with respect to the exchange rate, as a consequence of the constraint in foreign expenditures.

But let us introduce now the possibility of a fraud, though this feature can only be satisfactorily dealt with in a model with uncertain future. Relation (5.78) and (5.79) become:

$$q_2 = \bar{q}_2 + \zeta, \tag{5.84}$$

$$p_3 q_3 = d + \delta, \tag{5.85}$$

denoting by ζ $(\zeta \in \mathbf{R}^{m_2 +})$ and δ $(\delta \in \mathbf{R}^+)$ the quantities of commodities or foreign currencies fraudulently acquired.

$\pi_2(\zeta)a_2(\zeta)$ and $\pi_3(\delta)a_3(\delta)$ will denote the "probable" penalties inflicted upon the individual, these functions taking into account the effective penalties $a_2(\zeta) \in \mathbf{R}^+$ and $a_3(\delta) \in \mathbf{R}^+$ and the probabilities of detection $0 \leqslant \pi_2(\zeta) \leqslant 1, 0 \leqslant \pi_3(\delta) \leqslant 1$.

The individual utility will be assumed to be:

$$U = U[q_1, q_2, q_3, \zeta, \delta, \pi_2, \pi_3], \tag{5.86}$$

a jointly differentiable function of its arguments. Such a formulation expresses the fact that the individual may enjoy breaking the rules ($U_\zeta > 0$, $U_\delta > 0$) or has interiorized them in such a way that fraud displeases him, even without penalties ($U_\zeta < 0$, $U_\delta < 0$). Then there is also the cynical individual interested only in consequences ($U_\zeta = U_\delta = 0$).

On the other hand, the individual cannot be indifferent to the risk of being caught ($U_{\pi_2} < 0$, $U_{\pi_3} < 0$).

As for the income constraint, it becomes:

$$p_1 q_1 + p_2 q_2 + p_3 q_3 = \rho - \pi_2(\zeta)a_2(\zeta) - \pi_3(\delta)a_3(\delta), \qquad (5.87)$$

since we neglect here the probabilistic features of the problem. In this new situation, relations (5.82) and (5.83) become, under normal regularity conditions:

$$U_{q_2} + (U_\zeta + U_{\pi_2}\, d\pi_2/d\zeta) = \lambda(p_2 + d(\pi_2 a_2)/d\zeta), \qquad (5.88)$$

$$U_{q_3} + (U_\delta + U_{\pi_3}p_3\, d\pi_3/d\delta) = \lambda[1 + d(\pi_3 a_3)/d\delta]p_3, \qquad (5.89)$$

these relations being valid only when rationing constraints are effective. They express that the marginal utility of consumption minus the disutility of fraud and its discovery is proportional to the sum of price and "probable" penalty.

When a rationing constraint is not effective:

$$U_\zeta + U_{\pi_2}(d\pi_2/d\zeta) - d(\pi_2 a_2)/d\zeta \leqslant 0. \qquad (5.90)$$

The pleasure of fraud is not great enough to compensage for the risk of penalty. The same analysis can be applied to (5.89).

This simple example shows the possibility of introducing in economics numerous administrative features of social life related to fraud and control (Lesourne, 1972).

7.2. Regulation constraints in a professional role

In spite of its interest, this field seems to have been left almost unexplored by economists, who rely on the dichotomy classifying individuals as workers without initiative and managers maximizing profit...

In the *first case*, if role is represented by an element r of a closed interval I in $\mathbf{R}^+$, if the set of allocations is a finite-dimensional Banach space A, there is a mapping $a(r)$ from I into A which defines the allocations imposed on the holder of role r. We shall assume this mapping to be differentiable. With a utility function: $U[q, r, a]$ jointly differentiable in its arguments, ($q \in \mathbf{R}^{m+}$ is the consumption vector) and with an income constraint $pq = \rho(r)$ (where $\rho(r)$ is the income generated by role r and $p \in \mathbf{R}^{m+}$, $p \gg 0$ the price vector), the job selected by the individual is such that, under normal regularity conditions:

$$\left(U_r + U_a \frac{da}{dr} \right)(-d\rho/dr) = \lambda, \tag{5.91}$$

$$U_q - \lambda p = 0, \tag{5.92}$$

λ being the Lagrange multiplier associated with the constraint, i.e. the individual takes into account the income resulting from the role; the interest of the job itself (for instance, the prestige associated with it); and the dissatisfaction generated by the allocations he is compelled to perform.

In the *second case*, it is necessary to suppose that the individual income ρ is an increasing function of the profit b ($b \in \mathbf{R}$) of the firm and that the utility is independent of the allocations $a \in A$ chosen by the individual as manager. If $b(a)$ is the mapping from A into $\mathbf{R}$ which describes the effect of the manager's decision, it is obvious that the maximization of $U = U(q)$ ($q \in \mathbf{R}^{m+}$ consumption vector) under the constraint:

$$pq = \rho[b(a)], \tag{5.93}$$

($p \in \mathbf{R}^{m+}$, $p \gg 0$ price vector) implies that *the decisions taken by the individual as manager* do maximize profit b. The individual's behaviour is split *between a consumer's and an entrepreneur's behaviour.*

How different from reality! There, workers always have some initiative. As for managers, they scarcely establish a total barrier between their private and their professional life, and they also have to accept rules. Thus, the important case concerns *an individual devoting a part of his time to an organization which requires initiative but imposes constraints.*

To understand the core of the problem, we shall consider the development of a hierarchical structure including, at first, only one decision center and workers performing imposed tasks.

7.2.1. Constraints of a unique decision center

To the demand function for outputs and to the offer functions for inputs have to be added multiple constraints bearing on quantities or values:

- Certain production is forbidden (since it is restricted to State monopolies) or limited in order to avoid a price decrease (sometimes, for instance, agricultural production).
- Certain inputs are rationed (for instance, energy); others cannot decrease (for instance, in some countries, it is impossible to fire staff members).
- Selling prices may have a ceiling or result from an administrative formula, while wages have to be above a minimum and indexed to the cost of living...
- Some production processes are prohibited if certain pollutants are not eliminated.
- Many locations are forbidden; others give rise to advantages.
- Numerous decision procedures are imposed: preliminary announcements, official minutes of Board meetings, ...

All this is linked with a tax system so complex that similar decisions in substance may have totally different fiscal consequences.

Nevertheless, the operation of these constraints is easily understood so long as the decision center is unique. For instance, for a firm producing two commodities 1 and 2 in quantities $(Q_1, Q_2) \in \mathbf{R}^{2+}$, proposing selling prices $(p_1, p_2) \in \mathbf{R}^{2+}$, using inputs j $(1 \leqslant j \leqslant m)$ in quantities $X_j \in \mathbf{R}^+$ and fixing at $F \in \mathbf{R}^+$ the level of its overhead costs, the allocation vector is:

$$a = \{Q_1, Q_2, p_1, p_2, (X_j)_{1 \leqslant j \leqslant m}, F\}, \tag{5.94}$$

an element of $A = \mathbf{R}^{(m+5)+}$. For reasons, which will soon appear, A will be called the *fundamental decision set of the organization*.

The regulation constraints limit a to a subset $A_1 \subset A$.

7.2.2. Hierarchical constraints

Let us suppose now that the unique individual who took all the decisions (whose rank will be labelled 1) creates a new management level and delegates to it certain responsibilities, but without participation.

This means that he has to choose the following allocations:

– If M is the dimension of the fundamental decision set and $I = \{1, 2, \ldots, M\}$, to partition I into $L_1 + 1$ subsets corresponding to the decisions reserved to his deputies or to himself, the corresponding allocations being $a_1, a_{11}, \ldots, a_{1k}, \ldots, a_{1L1}$ in $D_1, D_{11}, \ldots, D_{1L1}$.

– To define rules that must be obeyed by his deputies:
  – *policy rules* limiting the subset A_{1k} where the decisions taken by k must reside. The definition of A_{1k} results from A_1 and from additional constraints (for instance, prohibition on giving salary increases beyond a certain percentage);[8]
  – *information rules* describing the information $j_{1k} \in J_{1k}$ which individual $1k$ must transmit to individual 1 when the state of his environment is $e_{1k} \in E$;
  – *exception rules* ascribing decisions to individual 1 when e_{1k} does not belong to a normal set E_{1k}.

– To appoint the tenants of the L_1 newly created jobs. If n is the total number of individuals available and N the set $\{1, \ldots, n\}$, the associated decision d is represented by an element of the set of all subsets of N having exactly L_1 elements.

Finally, for individual 1, the allocation element is no longer vector a, but an element a' of a set which is no longer a vector space:

$$a' = \{L_1, (D_{1k})_{1 \leqslant k \leqslant L_1}, a_1, (A_{1k})_{1 \leqslant k \leqslant L_1}, (J_{1k})_{1 \leqslant k \leqslant L_1}, (E_{1k})_{1 \leqslant k \leqslant L_1},$$
$$(a'_{1k})_{1 \leqslant k \leqslant m}, d\}, \tag{5.95}$$

where a'_{1k} is the exceptional allocation of individual 1 when an exceptional situation arrives for individual k.

As for the deputy $(1k)$, his allocation vector is in the set:

$D_{1k} \cap A_{1k}$ if $e_{1k} \in E_{1k}$,

0 if $e_{1k} \notin E_{1k}$.

For each individual $(1k)$ of rank 2, the same analysis may be carried out if it is supposed that a part of his responsibility is delegated to individuals of rank 3 and so on.

---

[8] Policy rules may be inserted into *criteria*, which serve to determine the decision expected in a given environment. For instance: "Maximize profit, as defined in the operating accounts."

This short description of a hierarchical organization underlines: the extremely sharp increase of the number of decision *types* when the hierarchy develops, the complexity of the constraints imposed on the tenant of each role. When *participation* is added to decentralization, each individual ($1k$) has, for some types of decision (corresponding to a subset P_{1k} of I), the right to present a vote $v_{1k} \in V_{1k}$. These votes are composed according to a rule f_1, which is a mapping from $\prod_{k \in K} V_{1k}$[9] to $\mathbf{R}^+$ associating an effective decision with the votes.

At this stage of the analysis, it would appear possible to express the existence of a job for an individual by a utility function:

$$U = U[q, r, a, x_r], \tag{5.96}$$

where q, r, a are the same variables as in (5.91), (5.92) and where $x(r) \in X$ is the parameter defining the set $A[x_r]$ in which the individual's allocations have to be if his role is r:

$$a \in A[x_r] \tag{5.97}$$

(naturally, the individual cannot be indifferent to the fact that the constraints are more or less binding; hence the presence of x_r as an argument of U).

But the above analysis forgets two major phenomena:

- *Identification:* If the organization has great prestige, the individual will identify to it and will try to adopt its objectives.
- *Perception filtering:* Through the information it spreads, the organization will influence the perception of reality on which individual decisions are built.

These two phenomena are so important that we must look at them carefully.

7.3. Identification

Let x be a vector ($x \in X$) describing the individual social state of the individual 1 who is the head of the organization. By definition, his utility function is $V(x)$.

When the individual acts alone, x is a function of his decision $d \in D$

---

[9] K is the set of the individuals authorized to vote.

and of the environment $e \in E : x = x(d, e)$. As a result of utility maximization on D, the preferred x is a function $x^*(e)$.

Let us consider now another individual 2 belonging to the organization (for instance, an individual of rank 2) and let us assume that when
he chooses allocation $a \in A$ in the context of an environment $e \in E$, the
result is $x(a, e)$.

Since X is a vector space, one can introduce the distance δ:

$$\delta = \delta[x^*(e), x(a, e)] = \delta(a, e), \tag{5.98}$$

between the answer $x^*(e)$ expected by the organization and the effective
answer $x(a, e)$ of individual 2 when he chooses a.

The identification process means that 2 will be sensitive to δ. For
a given structure of the utility function $U[(S_i)_{1 \leqslant i \leqslant n}]$, identification
increases the satisfaction level of motivations such as prestige and the
gregarious instinct, while it diminishes the satisfaction level of the
desire for independence. The more utility depends on δ, the greater is
identification. *It is not necessary to suppose that identification changes
the psychological factor ω.*

For instance, take an individual with a narcissistic satisfaction S_1
and a prestige satisfaction S_2. His current consumptions q are paid
at prices p ($q \in \mathbf{R}^{m+}$, $p \in \mathbf{R}^{m+}$, $p \gg 0$). For a given environment, the
state of the firm is represented by a vector x chosen by the individual
in X, his resulting income being $\rho(x)$. Individual behaviour will correspond to the maximization of:

$$U = U[S_1(q, x), S_2(x, \delta(x)], \tag{5.99}$$

(where $\delta(x) \in \mathbf{R}^+$ is the distance between x and decision x^*, which is
the best according to the objective of the firm) under the constraint:

$$pq = \rho(x), \tag{5.100}$$

U, S_1, S_2, δ will be assumed to be differentiable in their arguments.

With an obvious notation, the maximum of U is, under normal
conditions of regularity, such that:

$$U_q - \lambda p = 0, \tag{5.101}$$

$$U_{S_1}S_{1x} + U_{S_2}S_{2x} + U_{S_2}S_{2\delta}(\mathrm{d}\delta/\mathrm{d}x) + \lambda(\mathrm{d}\rho/\mathrm{d}x) = 0. \tag{5.102}$$

Let us suppose first $S_{1x} = S_{2x} = 0$. If the compensation is rightly
computed, $\mathrm{d}\rho/\mathrm{d}x$ is equal to zero, when $x = x^*$. As a result of identifi-

cation, U must increase when $\delta(x)$ decreases. Hence: $U_{S_2} S_{2\delta} < 0$.

Since δ is minimum for $x = x^*$, $d\delta/dx = 0$, U is maximum when $x = x^*$. In other words, individual behaviour is compatible with the organization's objectives *under the double influence of compensation scheme and identification*. If, on the contrary, $\rho(x)$ is not properly chosen, there may be a conflict between the compensation scheme and identification. $U_2 S_{2\delta}(d\delta/dx) + \lambda(d\rho/dx)$ is no longer zero for $x = x^*$ especially if the marginal utility of income λ is high or if the "marginal identification" $U_2 S_{2\delta}$ is small.

When S_{1x} and S_{2x} differ from zero, the individual preferences on the state of the organization will intermingle with identification and compensation scheme to generate the final behaviour: the stronger and the more adequate the monetary incentives, the greater the identification, the more similar the individual's and the firm's objectives, the smaller will be the discrepancy between x and x^*.

7.4. Perception filtering

A long presentation is unnecessary. The mechanism has, in fact, been studied in chapter 4 with advertising analysis. Individual of rank 1 sends to the others messages $m \in M$ liable to influence:

- the perception by these individuals of the preferred state in the context of environment e (the image $x'(e, m) \in X$ while reality is $x^*(e)$),
- the perception by these individuals of the effect of their allocations $a \in A$ on the organization (the individuals perceive the answer $x'(a, e, m) \in X$)),
- the perception by these individuals of the distance between the perceived preferred state and the perceived effect of their real behaviour:

$$\delta' = \delta'[x'(e, m), x'(a, e, m), m], \qquad \delta' \in \mathbf{R}^+.$$

The purposes of the messages is, of course, to make the real δ as small as possible, at a reasonable cost.

It seems that, with a proper account of the regulation constraints, the theory presented in this book might be of some help in developing organization theory, that common field of sociology and economics.

8. Technical constraints

We shall make only two remarks about these:

(1) They are not an exclusivity of productive organizations. In every role, an individual finds such constraints. The newly married couple, who cannot buy a piano because their house is too small, experiences such a constraint.

(2) Economists frequently-have a tendency to catalogue as production constraints what are, in fact, complex combinations of technical and regulation constraints:

– When we look at a totally automatic production unit, we know exactly what a production function means, though man always superimposes rules (such as safety and maintenance rules) on physico-chemical relations.
– But when we consider the production function of a firm, we mix the production constraints associated with the elementary production units, and regulation constraints such as the impossibility of going beyond a certain monthly recruitment rate; or increasing the area used; or reducing the number of staff below a given figure. On the other hand, except for the lower jobs in the hierarchy, it is impossible to speak only in terms of labour quantity, since the efficiency of each tenant depends upon specific knowledge and upon relations established with other staff members, with clients, with bankers. Sometimes there are only a few dozen individuals liable to hold the same role after a shorter or longer adaptation period. Then, there is a constant interaction between production possibilities and the satisfactions of the motivations of some individuals. The more important these individuals feel they are, the harder will be the bargaining between them and the head of the organization.

It would be an interesting research field for economists to explore the precise nature of technical constraints within firms and of their relations with other constraints.

We have now at our disposal the two main elements necessary for a theory of the individual, with a given psychology in the context of one period and a certain future. We now have to unite them in a first synthesis, and to show how this can be used to broaden economic theory.

Chapter 6

THE BASIC MODEL

> *L'ère d'une économie liée à la psychologie
> a commencé. Cette économie-là essaie de
> dégager les conséquences des décisions
> économiques individuelles. Les conditions
> de prise de ces décisions incluent à la fois
> des évènements extérieurs et le champ
> psychologique des individus ou des groupes
> décideurs, champ qui englobe aussi bien les
> perceptions des individus que leurs motiva-
> tions, leurs attitudes, leurs prévisions.*
>
> George Katona
> *Analyse psychologique du comportement
> économique*[1]

Introduction

This chapter is devoted to the consistent integration into a unique
model of the concepts introduced in the last two chapters. This model
constitutes the base on which the remaining part of the book is built,
but it does not yet include certain very important elements, since it is
limited by the two essential assumptions of a certain future and a
unique period.

---

[1] Traduction française de: Psychological analysis of economic behaviour, Payot,
Paris, 1969.

To the first part of the chapter, dealing with the presentation of the model itself, is added a second paragraph which explores an important feature of the proposed theory: the existence of *behavioural borders*, separating sets differing by the very nature of the actual behaviour – for instance, beyond certain limits, individuals may revolt, or commit suicide, or prefer emigration. Economics has to take these behavioural discontinuities into account and therefore they must be examined before a general review, in the last three chapters of this book, of possible applications of the model to economic problems.

1. Presentation of the model

First, we have to review the concepts and the variables attached to them; and then the constraints (or the relations) imposed on these variables. The index k defining the individual is dropped when there is no possible ambiguity. Also, to simplify notation, health conditions have not been explicitly introduced.

1.1. The concepts

Table 6.1 can be read almost without additional explanation. To comment on it briefly:

(1) There are n motivations, and each motivation is associated to an index i ($1 \leqslant i \leqslant n$).
(2) The satisfaction S_i of motivation i is an element of $\mathbf{R}$ and the satisfaction vector $S = (S_i)_{1 \leqslant i \leqslant n}$ an element of $\mathbf{R}^n$.
(3) The utility function $U(S)$ is a mapping from $\mathbf{R}^n$ into $\mathbf{R}$. This mapping depends, among other parameters, on a psychological factor $\bar{\omega}$, which is an element of a set π.
(4) Assuming that the social state $E \in \mathscr{E}$ can be described by the position of a countable number of parameters, the following concepts are introduced (see 4.68, 69, 70): the individual social state $e_k \in \mathscr{E}_k$, the complementary social state $e_{-k} \in \mathscr{E}_{-k}$, with:

$$E = \{e_k, e_{-k}\}, \qquad \mathscr{E} = \mathscr{E}_k \times \mathscr{E}_{-k},$$

the controlled individual social state $e_{1k} \in \mathscr{E}_{1k}$ (when are isolated in e_{1k} the efforts d_k, one can write: $e_{1k} = \{e_{1k}^+, d_k\}$), the uncontrolled individual social state $e_{2k} \in \mathscr{E}_{2k}$
with:

$$e_k = \{e_{1k}, e_{2k}\}, \qquad \mathscr{E}_k = \mathscr{E}_{1k} \times \mathscr{E}_{2k},$$

the uncontrolled social state $e_{-k,1} \in \mathscr{E}_{2k} \times \mathscr{E}_{-k}$,
with

$$e_{-k,1} = \{e_{2k}, e_{-k}\}.$$

(5) The individual associates with states e_{1k}, e_{2k} and e_k images $e'_{1k} \in \mathscr{E}'_{1k}$, $e'_{2k} \in \mathscr{E}'_{2k}$ and $e'_k \in \mathscr{E}'_k$, with $\mathscr{E}'_k = \mathscr{E}'_{1k} \times \mathscr{E}'_{2k}$.

(6) A different notion is the forecast image of the effect of the acts: $e'^*_k \in \mathscr{E}'_k$.

(7) There are p roles in the economy, and each role is associated to an index h ($1 \leqslant h \leqslant p$).

(8) The role situation of an individual is totally described by a sequence R of p numbers i_h equal to zero or one.

The intensity of search for information on roles is an element $I \in \mathbf{R}^+$.

The intensity of search for information within role h is an element $J_h \in \mathbf{R}^+$ equal to zero if $i_h = 0$.

The allocations within role h are described by an element $a_h \in A_h$ or $a_h \in \emptyset$ according to whether the individual holds role h or not. Accepting the simplifying assumption of (4.76), individual effort is represented by an element $d \in D$.

Sometimes, we shall find it convenient to introduce an element a describing the individual acts a:

$$a = \{I, R, J_h, a_h, d\}, \qquad a \in A.$$

If P is the set of all possible sequences R, A is a subset of $\mathbf{R}^+ \times P \times \mathbf{R}^{p+} \times \Pi A_h \times D$. This subset is obtained by replacing the hth $\mathbf{R}^+$ in $\mathbf{R}^{p+}$ and the set A_h in ΠA_h by the set $\emptyset$ wherever, in P a sequence with a zero hth component is selected.

(9) There are u capability dimensions, and each dimension is associated to an index j ($1 \leqslant j \leqslant u$).

(10) The capability level c_j of capability dimension j is an element of $\mathbf{R}$, and the capability vector: $c = (c_j)_{1 \leqslant j \leqslant u}$ an element of $\mathbf{R}^u$. c^0, which is the genetic capability, is also an element of $\mathbf{R}^u$.

(11) The effective capability γ is a vector in $\mathbf{R}^u$.

(12) The individual's past is simply represented, at this stage, by an element $t \in T$.

Table 1

Basic model concepts.

Motivations	$1 \leqslant i \leqslant n$
Satisfaction of motivation i	$S_i \in \mathbf{R}$
Satisfaction vector	$S = (S_i)_{1 \leqslant i \leqslant n}, \ S \in \mathbf{R}^n$
Satisfaction vector at the beginning of the period	S^0
Utility function	$U \in \mathbf{R}$
Individual social state	$e_k \in \mathscr{E}_k$
Complementary social state	$e_{-k} \in \mathscr{E}_{-k}$
Controlled individual social state	$e_{1k} \in \mathscr{E}_{1k}$
Part of the controlled individual social state excluding efforts	$e_{1k}^+ \in \mathscr{E}_{1k}^+$
Uncontrolled individual social state	$e_{2k} \in \mathscr{E}_{2k}$
Uncontrolled social state	$e_{-k,1} \in \mathscr{E}_{2k} \times \mathscr{E}_{-k}$
Images of real social states	$e'_{1k} \in \mathscr{E}'_{1k}, \ e'_{2k} \in \mathscr{E}'_{2k}, \ e'_k \in \mathscr{E}'_{1k} \times \mathscr{E}'_{2k}$
Forecast image of the effects of the acts	$e'_k{}^* \in \mathscr{E}'_k$
Roles	$1 \leqslant h \leqslant p$
Individual role structure	$R \in P$
Intensity of search for information on roles	$I \in \mathbf{R}^+$
Intensity of search for information within role h	$J_h \in \mathbf{R}^+$ or $\emptyset$
Allocations within role h	$a_h \in A_h$ or $\emptyset$
Individual efforts	$d \in D$
Individual acts	$a = \{I, R, J_h, a_h, d\}, \ a \in A$
Capability dimensions	$1 \leqslant j \leqslant u$
Capability level in dimension j	$c_j \in \mathbf{R}$
Capability vector	$c = (c_j)_{1 \leqslant j \leqslant u}, \ c \in \mathbf{R}^u$
Genetic capability	c^0
Effective capability	$\gamma \in \mathbf{R}^u$
Individual past	$t \in T$

1.2. The constraints

Contrary to table 6.1, table 6.2 needs some introductory comments:

(1) Since we have introduced simultaneously the forecast image of the effect of the acts $e'_k{}^*$ and the image of the real situation e'_k, it is also necessary to consider: the expected satisfaction vector S^* and the expected corresponding utility U^*. U^* is the function, the individual

will try to maximize; the experienced satisfaction vector S and the experienced corresponding utility U. U will be the effective result of individual acts.

(2) Hence, there is a mapping from $(\mathscr{E}'_k \times \mathscr{E}_{-k,1} \times \pi \times T)$ to $\mathbf{R}^n$, which gives S out of $(e'_k, e_{-k,1}, \bar{\omega}, t)$ and S^* out of $(e'_k{}^*, e_{-k,1}, \bar{\omega}, t)$.

(3) As for the image e'_k, it results from a mapping from $(\mathscr{E}_k \times \mathbf{R}^u \times \mathscr{E}_{-k,1} \times \mathbf{R}^n \times \pi \times T)$ to $\mathscr{E}'_k$ giving e'_k out of $(e_k, \gamma, e_{-k,1}, S^0, \bar{\omega}, t)$. In its turn, e_k is defined by a mapping from $(A \times \mathbf{R}^u \times \mathscr{E}_{-k,1})$ defining e_k out of the individual acts a, effective capability γ and uncontrolled social state (including the actions of others) $e_{-k,1}$.

(4) In chapter 4, two possibilities have been considered for $e'_k{}^*$. One supposes that $e'_k{}^*$ is a function of e_k and γ. The other assumes that $e'_k{}^*$ is the result of a mapping from $(A \times \mathbf{R}^u \times \mathscr{E}_{-k,1} \times \mathbf{R}^n \times \pi \times T)$ and hence depends upon behaviour a, effective capability γ, non-controlled social state $e_{-k,1}$, initial satisfaction vector S^0, psychological factor $\bar{\omega}$ and past learning t.

(5) Effective capability is simply a function of capability c and efforts d. It corresponds to a mapping $\mathbf{R}^u \times D \to \mathbf{R}^u$. Efforts d are a component of e_{1k} (and hence e_k).

As for capability c (see 4.66), it may be considered as a function of $(c^0, S^0_k, \bar{\omega}, t)$, which corresponds to a mapping $(\mathbf{R}^u \times \mathbf{R}^n \times \pi \times T) \to \mathbf{R}^u$.

Let us consider now the constraints:

(1) The time constraints correspond in compact form to a condition: $a \in A_T(c)$.

(2) The condition on individual role structure is obvious, as are the capability and information constraints.

(3) Here we have written the income constraint by expressing the fact that behaviour has to be in a set depending on capability and on uncontrolled individual state. Though perfectly correct, this formulation has the disadvantage of masking the influence of individual behaviour on income.

(4) Regulation constraints were studied at some length in the preceding chapter. They are represented here in a simplified way.

It is pointless to resume here the debate on utility maximization, or even utility aggregation, since we may consider as acceptable any behaviour "a" leading to an expected utility U^* above a certain minimum u, or to a satisfaction vector S^* all of whose components are greater than (or equal to) the components of a vector s.

Table 2

Relations and constraints of the model.

The individual will try to maximize:

$U^* = U(S^*)$	(6.1)	Utility maximization

and will experience utility:

$U = U(S)$	(6.2)	Result of the behaviour
$S^* = \sigma[e_k'^*, e_{-k,1}, \overline{\omega}, t]$	(6.3)	Mapping from the forecast image of the effects of acts to the expected satisfaction
$S = \sigma[e_k', e_{-k,1}, \overline{\omega}, t]$	(6.4)	Mapping from the image of real individual state to experienced satisfaction
$e_k' = \alpha[e_k, \gamma, e_{-k,1}, S^0, \overline{\omega}, t]$	(6.5)	Mapping from the real individual state to its image
$e_k = e[a, \gamma, e_{-k,1}]$	(6.6)	Effect of behaviour on reality
$e_k'^* = e_k'^*[e_k, \gamma]$	(6.7a)	First possibility: the forecast image is defined out of the real individual state
$e_k'^* \triangleq e_k'^*[a, \gamma, e_{-k,1}, S^0, \overline{\omega}, t]$	(6.7b)	Second possibility: the forecast image is defined directly as a consequence of behaviour
$\gamma = \gamma[c, d]$	(6.8)	Definition of effective capability
$c = c[c^0, S^0, \overline{\omega}, t]$	(6.9)	Definition of capability out of genetic capability and initial satisfaction

while choosing:

$a = \{I, R, J_h, a_h, d\}$

within the constraints:

$a \in A_T(c)$	(6.10)	Time constraint
$R \in P$	(6.11)	Constraint on individual role structure
$R \in R_c(\gamma)$	(6.12)	Capability constraint on roles
$a_h \in A_{ch}(\gamma)$	(6.13)	Capability constraint on allocations
$R \in R_I(I, \gamma)$	(6.14)	Information constraint on roles
$a_h \in A_{Ih}(J_h, \gamma)$	(6.15)	Information constraint on allocations
$a \in A_p(c, e_{-k,1})$	(6.16)	Income constraint
$a \in W_h(e_{-k,1})$	(6.17)	Regulation constraints in role h

Technical constraints

1.3. A critical look at the model

By comparison with the analysis of chapter 1, figure 6.1 drawn under the assumption of relation (6.7b) – helps to evaluate the interest of the model.

It shows how the individual looks for information and explores the

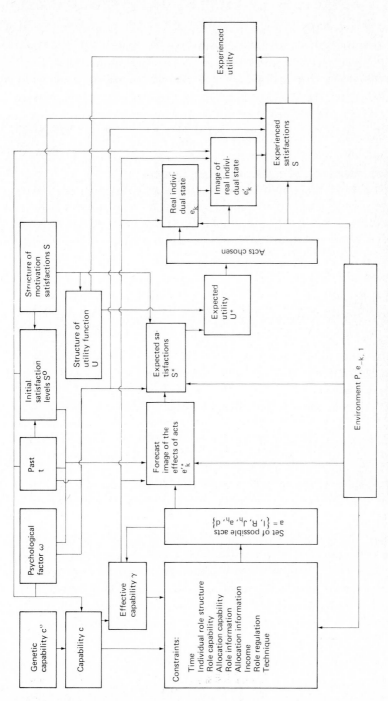

Figure 6.1 (the figure assumes relation (6.7b) for the generation of the forecast image of the effects of acts).

possible acts within the constraints generated by his capability and his environment. He associates with these acts a forecast image of their effects, then expected satisfactions and an expected utility from which he implicitly deduces his behaviour. In conjunction with environment, this behaviour defines the individual social state and its image which, in its turn, defines the experienced satisfactions and utility.

Since the model is limited to one period, it cannot adequately introduce the evolution of behaviour with the passage of time, and the progressive adaptation between forecast image and image of reality, between expected and experienced satisfactions.

But a criticism of another type can be made of the above presentation: the model is far too complex. Economics does not need comprehensive models, but simple models stressing special features of reality and leading to meaningful theorems of general value. To such an objection, two answers can be proposed:

(1) From the "master-model" described here, it is possible to extract a whole range of submodels, emphasizing different aspects and liable to be introduced in models describing an economy as a whole. But the fact that these submodels are derived from a more comprehensive one makes it possible not to underestimate, at any time, the underlying assumptions. As will be outlined in subsequent chapters, these submodels lead to interesting propositions covering practically the whole field of microeconomics.

(2) To prove theorems is an important activity of economic theory, but it is by no means the only one. To build adequate concepts, making it possible to interpret reality, is certainly just as important. To have only mathematical proofs in mind tends to lead to the foundation of elaborate mathematical treatments on narrow and fragile assumptions. The marginal cost of additional research may be greater than the marginal profit for the progress of science.

However, rather than a general discussion, we hope that the last chapters of this part will convince readers that the ideas presented here can be developed in a whole series of directions, according to the purpose and the mentality of the researchers.

Nevertheless, before any overview of these possible applications, we shall examine here a general property of the model, i.e. that it is compatible with the existence of "regions" corresponding to different behaviours.

2. Behavioural borders

In elementary consumer theory, constraints cannot be violated, and consumptions are represented by vectors. Enough assumptions are made to ensure that, when the price vector and the income change in a continuous way, individual behaviour adapts in a continuous way. The only possibility is that, in the course of the process, some consumptions may become equal to zero, or cease to be zero, or reach a level beyond which utility no longer increases or even decreases.

Here nothing of this kind happens, for three reasons:

– One of the essential behavioural choices is to adopt a role structure. There will be a discontinuity in behaviour as soon as this structure changes. The individual may even refuse all roles by committing suicide, or all the roles considered "normal" by taking refuge, from childhood, in psychotic roles.
– Within each role, numerous allocations are also discontinuous. The managing director who decides to close a plant, the citizen whose vote changes from right to left, illustrate such a situation.
– Finally, many constraints can be violated. An individual may steal to increase his income, may refuse to obey the orders of his boss, may prefer revolutionary action to voting...

All these phenomena appear with a *given utility function*. Others will be introduced when the links between utility and individual past history are described in the second volume.

Rather than develop a general theory of behavioural borders, we shall examine these borders in a series of specific cases which will later be included in a synthetic example. Choice of job; acceptance of the regulation constraints imposed by a job; political voting preferences; the decision to join a revolutionary group, will be the subsequent themes illustrated by the cases considered.

2.1. Choice of job

An individual has the possibility of choosing between two jobs, a job $h = 1,2$ generating an income r_h ($r_h \in \mathbf{R}^+$). His utility is a function of two groups of satisfactions S and S', S depending only on the consumption vector $q \in \mathbf{R}^{m+}$ bought at price p ($p \in \mathbf{R}^{m+}$, $p \gg 0$), and S' on the interest of the job and on the prestige attached to it. This prestige is assumed to be a function of the ratio of the income obtained in this job to the income obtained in the other job.

Hence:

$$U = U[S, S'], \tag{6.18}$$

with: $S = S(q)$ and $S' = S'[h, r_h/r_{h'}]$ (h' denoting the other job).

The individual chooses h and q in order to maximize U under the constraint:

$$pq = r_h. \tag{6.19}$$

For h given, this maximization defines a demand correspondence:

$$q_h = q(p, r_h). \tag{6.20}$$

Assume that U is a jointly differentiable, increasing, strictly concave function of S and S', that the same property holds for S with respect to q and for S' with respect to r_h and $r_{h'}$. Then the maximum of U, for h and p given, is a continuous function $V_h(r_h, r_{h'})$. Symmetrically, one can introduce $V_{h'}(r_{h'}, r_h)$ which is the maximum of utility when the individual holds job h'.

In the positive orthant $\mathbf{R}^{2+}$, the points (r_1, r_2) can then be separated into three sets:

– a set in which the individual prefers job 1:

$$V_1(r_1, r_2) > V_2(r_2, r_1);$$

– a set in which the individual prefers job 2:

$$V_1(r_1, r_2) < V_2(r_2, r_1);$$

– a set in which the individual reacts indifferently to the two jobs:

$$V_1(r_1, r_2) = V_2(r_2, r_1).$$

The last set will generally be a curve separating the two zones where jobs 1 and 2 are respectively preferred.

For low incomes, probably only the relative level of income is of importance. For higher incomes, the intrinsic preference for a job should become essential. Figure 6.2 assumes that the individual has an intrinsic preference for job 1.

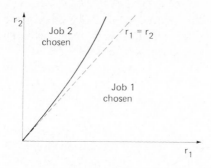

Figure 6.2

2.2. *The acceptance of regulation constraints within a job*

An individual holds a given job, generating an income r. The set of the allocations a feasible in the job is a n-dimensional Banach space A, but the individual is submitted to a regulation constraint:

$$g(a, \mu) \leqslant 0, \tag{6.21}$$

where $\mu \in \mathbf{R}^+$ is a control parameter such that the higher μ, the "smaller" the authorized subset of allocations in A. g is a real-valued function from $A \times \mathbf{R}^+$ on $\mathbf{R}$.

Obviously, g is an increasing function of μ.

Let us call:

$$\varepsilon = g(a, \mu). \tag{6.22}$$

When $\varepsilon > 0$, the constraint is violated. In other words, in Simon's terms (March and Simon (1958)), the individual evokes possibilities, select goals, perceives consequences which do not conform with the demands of the organization.

Naturally, when $\varepsilon > 0$, the individual has to incur a penalty $\pi(\varepsilon)$ (π being an increasing real-valued function of ε) corresponding, for instance, to a decrease in an incentive premium or to a slowdown of his promotion.

But, because of his Superego, the individual generally attaches a certain value to respect of the rules of the organization. His utility, independent from ε for $\varepsilon \leqslant 0$, sharply decreases in a discontinuous way at $\varepsilon = 0$ and is thereafter a decreasing function of ε.

Let us denote by $q(r)$ the optimum commodity bundle for a given price system ($q(r) \in \mathbf{R}^{m+}$). For r and μ given, the individual may choose between two behaviours: (1) to comply with the rules, i.e. to choose a in order to maximize: $U = U[a, q(r), \varepsilon]$ under the constraint $g(a, \mu) \leqslant 0$ which implies that U is independent from ε; (2) to break the rules, i.e. to choose a in order to maximize: $U = U[a, q(r - \pi(\varepsilon)), \varepsilon]$ under the constraint $\varepsilon = g(a, \mu)$, $\varepsilon > 0$.

Consider the orthant (r, μ). The first behaviour leads to a utility $V_1(r, \mu)$ and the second to a utility $V_2(r, \mu)$. Hence, there are three sets in this orthant. In the first, regulation constraints are obeyed, in the second they are violated and in the third, $\varepsilon = 0$ and the utility is not defined.

A possible configuration is shown in figure 6.3.

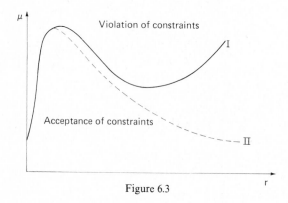

Figure 6.3

For very small r, the individual refuses the constraints, since he has nothing to lose.

For small r, the individual cannot run the risk of the penalty and the rules are accepted up to a high level of control.

For big r, two possibilities seem open, according to the individual psychology: the constraints are accepted, since the high level of income compensates for the burden of control (curve I); the constraints are rejected, since the penalty can be borne (curve II).

Naturally, reality is still more complex, since an individual in a gratifying social situation will interiorize the constraints. The precise picture depends on the individual and on the cultural models he finds in the surrounding environment.

2.3. Political voting preferences

An individual has a job giving him an income r, which he compares to the average income ρ of an individual belonging to a reference social group (for instance, rich people). His consumption vector is a function $q(r) \in \mathbf{R}^{m+}$ for given prices. There are two political parties: a right-wing party (party 0) and a left-wing party (party 1). At a given time, the individual has to vote and must decide whether his vote $\varepsilon = 0,1$ will be for party 0 ($\varepsilon = 0$) or 1 ($\varepsilon = 1$).

His utility takes into account three groups of motivations, the corresponding satisfaction levels being ($S \in \mathbf{R}$, $S' \in \mathbf{R}$, $S'' \in \mathbf{R}$):

- S for utilitarian motivations,
- S' for security motivations,
- S'' for motivations related to self-assertion and altruism.

Through q, S is an increasing function of r. S' certainly increases with income, but also depends on the nature of the party in power. Let us suppose that it is higher when this is the right-wing party. As for S'', this increases with the individual income, but it certainly decreases with the income ρ of the reference group. It is also probably bigger with a vote for the party which is not in power. If μ denotes this party ($\mu = 0$ for party 0, $\mu = 1$ for party 1), the utility of the individual is:

$$U = U\{S[q(r)], S'[r,\mu], S''[r,\rho,\varepsilon]\}. \tag{6.23}$$

Let us start from a situation in which the right-wing party is in power ($\mu = 0$). Elections take place. The individual compares the two possible votes: (1) if he thinks that his vote has no effect on the result (so, μ is not in the controlled individual state), he may vote $\varepsilon = 1$ simply to satisfy his self-assertion need; (2) if he thinks that his vote is decisive ($\mu = \varepsilon$), he will take into account the fact that a victory of the left may change r and ρ into r_1 and ρ_1 and will compare:

$$U_0 = U\{S[q(r)], S'[r,0], S''[r,\rho,0]\}, \tag{6.24}$$

$$U_1 = U\{S[q(r_1)], S'[r_1,1], S''[r_1,\rho_1,1]\}. \tag{6.15}$$

When r is high, and when the individual expects that a victory of the left will decrease his income ($r_1 < r$), the individual will vote for the right-wing party ($\varepsilon = 0$), since he is assured of a higher utilitarian satisfaction and greater security, unless the left is more satisfying for his self-assertion or altruistic needs.

When r is small, and when the individual expects that a victory of the left will increase his income ($r_1 > r$), while decreasing the reference income ($\rho_1 < \rho$), the individual will vote for the left-wing party, unless the right-wing party is considerably better from the point of view of security.

For a given individual, with proper assumptions on the utility and satisfaction functions, the two votes are equivalent in the orthant (r_1, ρ_1) for r and ρ given, when $U_0 = U_1$.

One possibility is that the individual will always vote for the right if r_1 is too small by comparison with r, whatever ρ_1 may be. Figure 6.4 shows the case of an individual who is favourable to the right even if he expects that a change of Government will change neither his income nor the reference income.

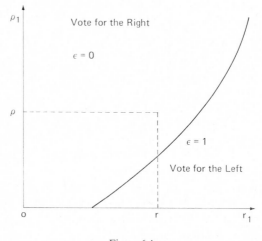

Figure 6.4

Even if this model is too simple, anybody who has taken part in electoral studies during political campaigns will recognize the possibility of improving it and giving it an operational content in a precise socio-cultural context.

2.4. The decision to join a revolutionary group

An individual may find his utility so small when he accepts authorized roles that he accepts forbidden roles. He commits suicide, he performs acts of terrorism... Studies have been made of the principal types of revolutionaries, depending on the relative strength of motivations such as power, protection, exploration... and on the impact of the environment on these satisfactions.[2] We shall only note here that, with the acceptance of forbidden roles, the individual may take into account a new range of allocations. Utility now derives from the satisfactions generated by these allocations. Simultaneously, risks exist and correspond to the probability of being discovered and on the penalties incurred in case of detection.

2.5. A synthetic simple model

Generally, when the environment is represented, for an individual of given psychology, by a point $e_{-k,1}$ in a Euclidian space, it is possible to associate with this point the behaviour selected by the individual. Under appropriate mathematical assumptions, the behavioural borders will correspond to varieties in this space. They separate sets of environment in which behaviour parameters are continuous functions of the environment.

Suppose, for instance, that, for an individual, the environment is reduced to the two incomes r_1 and r_2 he may get in two jobs available to him. It is not impossible to assume that, depending on the values r_1 and r_2, he is liable to adopt seven types of behaviour (figure 6.5).

(1) He votes for the right if his income is high enough, while choosing the job leading to the highest utility and respecting its constraints (areas 1 and 2).

(2) When the income from the two jobs is lower, he votes for the left-wing party, while still choosing the job leading to the higher utility and respecting its constraints (areas 3 and 4).

(3) If income is still lower, he no longer respects the constraints of the chosen job (this, of course, changes the conditions of comparison of the jobs) (areas 5 and 6).

[2] See, for instance, the famous book by Harold Lasswell* (1930).

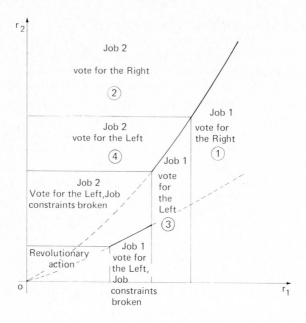

Figure 6.5

(4) In the case of a very low income, he abandons his job and devotes his time to revolutionary action... (area 7).

Of course, things are not so simple: the environment cannot be reduced to potential income. The change of income is probably more important than income itself. Individual psychology modifies the number, the shape and the position of the various areas, etc.; but what is important here is to convince the reader of the interest of behavioural borders for economics.

The preceding examples do not put an end to the study of behavioural borders. To the discontinuities resulting from individual behaviour must be superimposed the discontinuity coming from the environment:

– death by accident or disease (or, on the contrary, discovery of a miracle drug);
– jail if one has broken an important rule and been caught;
– bankruptcy or other types of ruin for the owner of a firm;

- brutal change in information opportunities as the result of a change in the political system;
- discovery of a new means of transport changing time constraints (Concord, etc.);
- availability of computation possibilities making possible a better evaluation of the consequences of a decision.

Some of these discontinuities will be mentioned in the next chapter.

Having progressively built and then presented the basic model in the last three chapters, we now have to answer a major criticism: it is not because a model is consistent and seems to be in agreement with reality that it is necessarily useful for a science. It must also lead to consequences in agreement with the facts and not accounted for by preceding models. This is the challenge to be met in the last chapters of this volume.

Chapter 7

APPLICATIONS OF THE BASIC MODEL
TO PARTIAL FIELDS IN ECONOMICS

> *It is known from the history of science that many theories which at first started from hypotheses quite remote from reality were progressively improved upon by the gradual introduction of new and more suitable hypotheses. There is no reason to suppose that there is any necessary limit to this progressive development.*
>
> G.B. Antonelli
> *Sulla teoria matematica della Economia Politica*

Introduction

This chapter considers several applications of the basic model to various sectors of economic theory. Four main fields have been selected:

(1) demand theory;
(2) labour market;
(3) firms' policies and competition;
(4) organization theory.

Only partial equilibrium situations are examined, the analysis of general equilibrium problems being postponed to the next chapter.

1. Demand theory

After the presentation of the model used (a simplified version of the model in chapter 6), we shall start with the conventional study of consumer equilibrium – here more adequately described as the study of equilibrium of the individual in his role of consumer, his other roles and the other aspects of his behaviour being fixed. We shall then examine the individual's reactions to a change of environment, which will lead us to a theory of advertising and a theory of new product creation. An analysis of the total demand for a commodity will close the section.

1.1. A simplified model

In the economy, m types $(1 \leqslant j \leqslant m)$ of commodities exist; but each commodity can be acquired at different quality levels. I_j is the closed interval of $\mathbf{R}^+$ in which the quality u_j of commodity j can be selected.

$U \in \mathbf{R}$ and $S_i \in \mathbf{R}$ $(1 \leqslant i \leqslant n)$ will denote, respectively, the individual's utility and the level of the ith satisfaction. $q \in \mathbf{R}^{m+}$ will be the vector of quantities consumed, $u \in I$ (with $I = \prod I_j$) the vector of qualities selected, $J \in \mathbf{R}^+$ the time spent in search for information and $L \in \mathbf{R}^+$ the leisure time.

The individual perceives without biases the quantities consumed, but he has a perception u' of the qualities selected which may differ from reality: $u' \in I'$, I' being the product of m closed intervals in $\mathbf{R}^{m+}$. This perception is a function of reality and of external actions transmitting information.

The individual will maximize:

$$U = U\{[S_i(q, u', J, L)]_{1 \leqslant i \leqslant n}\}, \tag{7.1}$$

under income, time and information constraints. The income constraint is written:

$$\delta(J, u)pq \leqslant \rho, \tag{7.2}$$

where $p \in \mathbf{R}^{m+}$ is a reference price vector $(p \gg 0)$ and $\delta(J, u)$ a $(1 \times m)$ matrix of strictly positive price coefficients. These coefficients are supposed bounded upwards and downwards for any value of their arguments. They are a decreasing function of search for information and an increasing function of the quality of the corresponding commodity.

The time constraint can be written:

$$J + tp + L \leqslant T,\qquad(7.3)$$

t being in $\mathbf{R}^{m+}$ the strictly positive vector of the minimum times necessary to consume one unit of each commodity and T the total time available for the role of consumer. Finally, the information constraint is expressed through the inequality:

$$g(J, u) \geqslant 0,\qquad(7.4)$$

g being a function from $\mathbf{R}^+ \times I$ into $\mathbf{R}$.

As for the perceived quality u', it is given by a mapping from I into I', this mapping depending on the value of a parameter $x \in X$ describing individual characteristics as well as exogenous factors:

$$u' = u'(u, x).\qquad(7.5)$$

Relations (7.1), (7.2), (7.3), (7.4), (7.5) completely describe the proposed model.[1]

1.2. The individual equilibrium

Assuming first x given, we shall neglect the difference between u and u'. The set S of admissible strategies $s = (q, u, J, L)$ for the individual is, in $\mathbf{R}^{m+} \times I \times \mathbf{R}^{2+}$ the intersection of: the budget set S_2 defined by (7.2), the time set S_3 defined by (7.3), the information set S_4 defined by (7.4). S_3 is a bounded closed convex set.

As for the information set, we shall make the following assumption:

---

[1] This model contains as a special case a model proposed by H.E. Leland ("Quality choice and competition", a paper presented at the Econometric Congress, Toronto, 1975) with the exception that Leland's model is developed in Lancaster's framework. With our notation, in Leland's model, the quantity of characteristic i that is obtained from a unit quantity of commodity j of quality u_j is $c_i^j(u_j)$ and the total amount of characteristic i available to the individual is:

$$\sum_j c_i^j(u_j) q_j,$$

where c_i^j is a function from I_j into $\mathbf{R}^+$. But Leland assumes that individuals cannot choose u_j, which is selected by the firm producing j and is thus imposed on them.

Assumption 1.   *The function g is a concave function of its arguments.*

In other words:

$$g[\lambda J + (1 - \lambda)J', \lambda u + (1 - \lambda)u'] \geqslant \lambda g(J, u) + (1 - \lambda)g(J', u'),$$
$$\text{for any } J, J' \in \mathbf{R}^+, u, u' \in I. \qquad (7.6)$$

We shall illustrate this assumption in the case $m = 2$. For J given, if u and u' are known, any quality of the segment uu' is also known. Thus the subset $\Sigma(J)$ of qualities known is a convex subset in the plane (u_1, u_2).

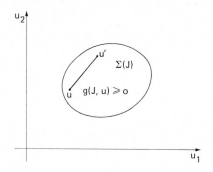

Figure 7.1

When J increases, $\Sigma(J)$ becomes "bigger" and:

$$\Sigma(J) \subset \Sigma(J') \quad \text{if } J < J'$$

But search for information has a decreasing return to scale, so that if u is known for J and u' known for J', $\lambda u + (1 - \lambda)u'$ is certainly known for $\lambda J + (1 - \lambda)J'$ $(0 \leqslant \lambda \leqslant 1)$.

Assumption 1 ensures that S_4 is convex. This set is bounded, since u and J are bounded $(0 \leqslant J \leqslant T)$.

To study the budget set, we shall make the following assumption:

Assumption 2.   *z being a vector in $\mathbf{R}^{m+}$, the set $\delta(J, u)z \leqslant 1$ is a convex set in $\mathbf{R}^+ \times I \times \mathbf{R}^{m+}$.*

Changing the unit of value and the quantity units of commodities, assumption 2 implies that S_2 is a convex set. It is obvious that it is closed and bounded.

Assumption 2 is only a property of the function $\delta(J, u)$. Its meaning is clear: suppose, for instance, that all the components of z are 0 except the first z_1, i.e. the quantity of commodity 1 which can be bought with a unit income:

$$z_1 \leqslant 1/\delta_1(J, u).$$

Convexity implies that:

– for u given, z_1 is a concave function of J. Less and less increased consumption possibility is obtained in exchange for a unit increase in J.

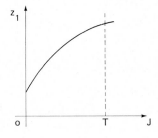

Figure 7.2

– for J given, z_1 is a concave function of u_1. More and more quantities must be renounced in order to increase u by one unit.

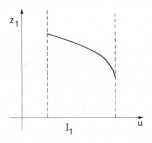

Figure 7.3

A more natural assumption than assumption 2 would have been to suppose that the price coefficients are convex functions of their arguments; but it is easy to verify that this assumption does not imply that S_2 is convex.

As for utility, a natural assumption is:

Assumption 3.   (a) *Utility is a strictly concave increasing function of satisfactions;* (b) *Each satisfaction is a concave function of its arguments.*

3(b) includes three cases:

- a satisfaction is a concave increasing function of an argument: quantity consumed, quality selected, search for information (for instance, if the individual enjoys exercising his curiosity in the whole range of possible search);
- a satisfaction is independent of certain arguments: a consumption may be neutral with respect to a motivation;
- a satisfaction is a concave decreasing or increasing–decreasing function of an argument (for instance, search for information becomes less and less pleasant and more and more tedious).

Given the above assumptions, the strategy set is a bounded closed convex set and the set $U \geqslant U_0$ is for any $U_0 \in \mathbf{R}$ closed and convex, U being a strictly concave function of its arguments. Hence, there is a *unique individual equilibrium,* but this equilibrium results from an active behaviour of the individual to alter environment.

1.3. Individual response to changing environment

Following textbook presentation, a normal question now is to consider how an individual adapts his behaviour to a change in the environment.

From now on, all the functions introduced in the model will be supposed to be jointly differentiable in their arguments. x will be an element of a Banach space X and the function g will also depend on x, i.e. information given from outside.

To avoid the complexity of general treatment, several special cases will be considered.

The change in the environment can be described by a vector $[\mathrm{d}p \ \mathrm{d}t \ \mathrm{d}T \ \mathrm{d}x]$ and the individual response by a vector $[\mathrm{d}q \ \mathrm{d}u \ \mathrm{d}J \ \mathrm{d}L]$.

To relate these two vectors, it is necessary to differentiate the first order equilibrium conditions, the Lagrange multipliers λ, μ, ν being respectively associated to the constraints (2) (3) (4).

1.3.1. The time constraint

If the analysis is restricted to the model:

$$\max U(q, L), \tag{7.7}$$

$$pq \leqslant \rho, \tag{7.8}$$

$$tq + L \leqslant T, \tag{7.9}$$

well-known computations show that, with obvious notation:

$$
\begin{bmatrix}
U_{11} \cdots U_{1m} & U_{1L} & p_1 & t_1 \\
\vdots & & \vdots & \vdots \\
U_{1m} & & p_m & t_m \\
U_{1L} & & 0 & 1 \\
p_1 \cdots p_m & & 0 & 0 \\
t_1 \cdots t_m & & 0 & 0
\end{bmatrix}
\begin{bmatrix}
dq \\
\\
\\
dL \\
-d\lambda \\
-d\mu
\end{bmatrix}
=
\begin{bmatrix}
\lambda\,dp + \mu\,dt \\
\\
\\
0 \\
d\rho - q\,dp \\
dT - q\,dt
\end{bmatrix}
\tag{7.10}
$$

If D is the determinant of the system and D_{ij} the minor of the element of the ith row and jth column:

$$
dq_i = (1/D)\left[\sum_{1}^{m} D_{ij}(\lambda\,dp_j + \mu\,dt_j) + D_{m+2,i}\left(d\rho - \sum_j q_j\,dp_j\right) + \right.
$$

$$
\left. D_{m+3,i}\left(dT - \sum_j q_j\,dt_j\right)\right]. \tag{7.11}
$$

Calling $\sigma = \mu/\lambda$ the marginal value of one unit of time, we can deduce from (7.11) that:

$$(ij)_\rho = \partial q_i/\partial p_j + q_j\partial q_i/\partial p, \qquad i, j = 1, \ldots, m, \tag{7.12}$$

is symmetrical in i and j since $(ij)_\rho = \lambda D_{ij}/D$ and that:

$$(ij)_T = \partial q_i/\partial t_j + q_j\partial q_i/\partial T, \qquad i, j = 1, \ldots, m, \tag{7.13}$$

is also symmetrical in i and j. Furthermore:

$$(ij)_T = \sigma(ij)_\rho. \tag{7.14}$$

(7.13) and (7.14) generalize Slutzky equations when there are time constraints. The interpretation is left to the reader, but he will notice in particular that *an increase in price has the same effect on consumption as an increase in the value of the time spent to buy and consume a unit of product.*

1.3.2. The introduction of satisfactions[2]

The model is then:

$$\max U\{[S_i(q)_{1 \leqslant i \leqslant n}]\}, \tag{7.15}$$

$$pq \leqslant \rho. \tag{7.16}$$

An interesting case is when the number of motivations is equal to the number of commodities ($n = m$) and when the satisfaction levels are, in the neighbourhood of equilibrium, linear functions of the quantities consumed.

In this case:

$$dS = B\,dq \tag{7.17}$$

with $B = [S_{ij}]$ a symmetrical square $n \times n$ matrix

$$dq = B^{-1}\,dS \tag{7.18}$$

with $B^{-1} = [a_{ij}]$ a square $n \times n$ matrix.

Calling:

$$\pi_i = \sum_j a_{ij} p_j, \tag{7.19}$$

the "*local price*" *of satisfaction i*, (which may have any sign), the equilibrium conditions can be written in two equivalent forms:

$$\text{I} \begin{cases} \sum_i U_i S_{ij} - \lambda p_j = 0, & \tag{7.20} \\[2mm] \sum_i p_i q_i = \rho, & \tag{7.21} \end{cases}$$

$$\text{II} \begin{cases} U_i - \lambda \pi_i = 0, & \tag{7.22} \\[2mm] \sum_{ij} q_i S_{ij} \pi_j = \rho. & \tag{7.23} \end{cases}$$

---

[2] For a related paper, see A.C. Koo and V.E. Smith (1975); but in Koo's and Smith's paper, the framework is Lancaster's theory.

(I) corresponds to the commodity space and (II) to the satisfaction space. The study of individual reaction to a change $(dp, d\rho)$ leads to the conventional Slutzky relations in the commodity space. The study of the individual reaction to a change $(d\pi, d\rho)$ leads to the system of equations:

$$\sum_i U_{ii} \, dS_i - \pi_i \, d\lambda = \lambda \, d\pi_i, \tag{7.24}$$

$$\sum_i \pi_i \, dS_i = d\rho - \sum_{ij} q_i S_{ij} \, d\pi_j. \tag{7.25}$$

Calling $-\Delta$, the determinant of this system and Δ_{ij} its minors, it may easily be seen that:

$$\partial S_i / \partial \pi_j = \lambda \Delta_{ij} / \Delta - (\sum_i q_i S_{ij}) \Delta_{n+1,i} / \Delta. \tag{7.26}$$

$\Sigma_i \, q_i S_{ij}$ would be satisfaction S_j if the satisfactions were linear functions of the quantity consumed. If there is only a local linearity, they are what we shall call linear satisfaction levels Σ_j. From (7.26), it is possible to deduce:

$$(ij)_S = \partial S_i / \partial \pi_j |_{U=c^{st}} = \partial S_i / \partial \pi_j + \Sigma_j \, \partial S_i / \partial \rho = \lambda \Delta_{ij} / \Delta. \tag{7.27}$$

$(ij)_S$ is a Slutzky coefficient in the satisfaction space. It is symmetrical. Δ being, under normal assumptions, positive, computation shows that:

$$(ii)_S = -\lambda \pi_i^2 / \Delta, \quad \text{i.e. } (ii)_S < 0,$$
$$(ij)_S = +\lambda \pi_i \pi_j / \Delta, \quad \text{i.e. } (ij)_S \gtrless 0 \quad \text{for } i \neq j.$$

Hence, under common assumptions, *an increase in the local price of satisfaction i, ρ being adjusted to maintain utility constant, decreases the level of this satisfaction, but may have a positive or a negative effect on the other satisfaction levels.*

1.3.3. The introduction of search

We shall examine the very simple model where there is only one commodity:

$$\max U(q_1, J), \tag{7.28}$$

$$\delta_1(J)p_1 q_1 = \rho, \tag{7.29}$$

where $q_1 \in \mathbf{R}^+$ and δ_1 is a decreasing function of J.

The system of equations relating the individual response to change of environment is, with an obvious notation and taking $\delta_1(J) = 1$ at equilibrium without loss of generality:

$$\begin{bmatrix} U_{11} & U_{1J} - \lambda\delta_{1J}p_1 & p_1 \\ U_{1J} - \lambda\delta_{1J}p_1 & U_{J^2} - \lambda p\delta_{1J^2} & \rho\delta_{1J} \\ p_1 & 0 & 0 \end{bmatrix} \begin{bmatrix} \mathrm{d}q_1 \\ \mathrm{d}J \\ -\mathrm{d}\lambda \end{bmatrix} = \begin{bmatrix} \lambda\,\mathrm{d}p_1 \\ \lambda q_1\delta_{1J}\,\mathrm{d}p_1 \\ \mathrm{d}\rho - q_1\,\mathrm{d}p_1 \end{bmatrix}$$
$$\tag{7.30}$$

Normally: $\delta_{1J} < 0$, $U_{J^2} < 0$, $\delta_{1J^2} > 0$. Let us denote:

$$U_{1J} - \lambda\delta_{1J}p_1 = a,$$

$$U_{J^2} - \lambda p_1\delta_{1J^2} = -b, \qquad b > 0.$$

We get:

$$\mathrm{d}q_1 = \left[\lambda p_1(q_1\delta_{1J})^2 - q_1\right] \Big/ \left[\frac{a}{b}\rho\delta_{1J} + p_1\right]\mathrm{d}p_1 + \mathrm{d}\rho \Big/ \left[\frac{a}{b}\rho\delta_{1J} + p_1\right],$$
$$\tag{7.31}$$

and:

$$(a\rho\delta_{1J} + bp_1)\,\mathrm{d}J = (a - U_{11}q_1\delta_{1J})\,\mathrm{d}\rho + q_1(U_{11}\delta_{1J} - a)\,\mathrm{d}p_1 \tag{7.32}$$

while, when no information is possible:

$$\mathrm{d}q_1 = -(q_1/p_1)\,\mathrm{d}p_1 + (1/p_1)\,\mathrm{d}\rho \tag{7.33}$$

The study of the second-order differential of the Lagrangian in the neighbourhood of a maximum of utility shows that $a < 0$ is a condition for a maximum. Hence:

- $\partial J/\partial\rho$ is negative, since normally $U_{11} < 0$ and $U_{1J} < 0$. *The individual feels less compelled to search when his income is higher.*
- $\partial J/\partial p_1$ is positive. *The individual compensates the increased price by a more intensive search.*
- $\partial q_1/\partial\rho$ is smaller when there is a possibility of search, *the individual using his additional income to search less and accepting therefore to pay higher prices.*
- $\partial q_1/\partial p_1$, which is frequently negative, is smaller in absolute value when there is a possibility of search, *the individual increasing his search to obtain better prices and limit his consumption decrease.*

1.3.4. The introduction of quality

We can change J into u and examine the model:

$$\max \ U[u_1, q_1], \tag{7.34}$$

$$\delta_1(u)p_1q_1 = \rho. \tag{7.35}$$

With the same analysis:

$$dq_1 = \left[\lambda p_1(q_1\delta_{1u})^2 - q_1\right]\bigg/\left[\frac{a'}{b'}\rho\delta_{1u} + p_1\right]dp_1 + d\rho\bigg/\left[\frac{a'}{b'}\rho\delta_{1u} + p_1\right], \tag{7.36}$$

$$du = q_1(U_{11}\delta_{1u} - a')\,dp_1/[a'\rho\delta_{1u} + b'p_1] + \\ [a' - U_{11}q_1\delta_{1u}]\,d\rho/[a'\rho\delta_{1u} + b'p_1], \tag{7.37}$$

with:

$$a' = U_{1u} - \lambda\delta_{1u}p_1,$$

$$-b' = U_{u^2} - \lambda p_2\delta_{1u^2}.$$

A condition of maximum is now $a' > 0$, $b' > 0$. Since $\delta_{1u} > 0$:

- $\partial u/\partial\rho$ is positive. *The individual partly uses his additional income to consume a better quality.*
- $\partial u/\partial p_1$ is negative. *The individual decreases the quality consumed when the price increases.*
- $\partial q_1/\partial\rho$ is smaller than when there is no possibility of choosing the quality, *the individual preferring to increase simultaneously the quantity and the quality* when his income increases.
- $\partial q_1/\partial p_1$, which is frequently negative, is smaller in absolute value, *the individual decreasing the quality to maintain a higher quantity consumed.*

Hence, the activity of an individual is a weapon to improve his adaptation to the environment.

The complete study of the response to an external change would be too long for such a volume, but a reasonable conjecture is that it would confirm the model's realism.

1.4. A theory of advertising

Let us consider again the model (7.1) to (7.5) with $x \in \mathbf{R}^{p+}$ denoting the amount of advertising on different messages. Assume that all functions are jointly differentiable in their arguments and that conditions for a unique equilibrium for any x are met.

The first-order conditions of a regular maximum are, with an obvious notation:

$$U_q = \lambda p + \mu t, \tag{7.38}$$

$$U_L = \mu t, \tag{7.39}$$

$$U_{u'} \cdot u_u' = \lambda p q \delta_u + v g_u, \tag{7.40}$$

$$U_J = \lambda p q \delta_J + \mu - v g_J. \tag{7.41}$$

If the information constraint is binding:

$$-g_J \, dJ = g_u \, du. \tag{7.42}$$

Hence: (7.40) means that the marginal utility of the consumption of a better quality is equal to the sum of the marginal increase in expenditure and of the marginal cost of information needed.

(7.41) means that the sum of the marginal utility of search and of the marginal value of the information obtained on *prices* and on *possible qualities* is equal to the marginal cost of the time spent in search.

Such a model sheds a light on the double influence of advertising on behaviour:

– on the one hand, advertising brings the individual information on possible consumptions and on prices and gives him the possibility of improving his consumption while limiting his search effort,
– on the other hand, advertising changes the image of possible consumptions and thus modifies the spectrum of individual consumptions.

To emphasize these two aspects more clearly, we shall examine geometrically a special case: two commodities only, the quantities consumed being imposed, no search for information, no time constraint, the perceptive illusion being due to advertising only and advertising depending uniquely on amount spent. These assumptions correspond to the model:

max $U(u'_1, u'_2)$,   (7.43)

$p_1(u_1)q_1 + p_2(u_2)q_2 = \rho$,   (7.44)

$g(u_1, u_2, x) = 0$,   (7.45)

$u'_1 = u'_1(u_1, x), \qquad u'_2 = u'_2(u_2, x)$.   (7.46a and b)

The income constraint defines, if assumption 2 is satisfied, a closed convex set limited by a curve D.

(1) If there is no advertising, the qualities selected correspond to the point of maximum utility on the curve D inside or on curve G (the equation of which is $g(u_1, u_2, 0) = 0$) i.e. to point M. The information imperfection prevents the individual from choosing the quality N which he would prefer under the income constraint only.

(2) When advertising is x, the image of a quality u becomes $u'(u, x)$. It is then possible to associate to each point P in the plane (q_1, q_2) another point P' which is its image. Reciprocally, if it is a one-to-one transformation, to each P' corresponds a quality P which has P'

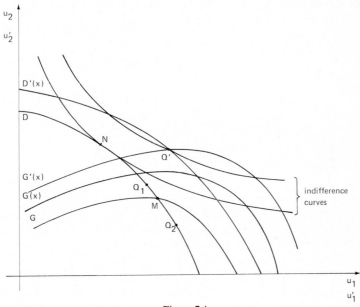

Figure 7.4

as its image: the income constraint implies that the images of possible qualities are on a curve $D'(x)$ which is the transformed of D in $u' = u'(u, x)$; the information constraint is represented by a curve $G(x)$ in the plane (q_1, q_2). This curve also has a transformed $G'(x)$ in $u' = u'(u, x)$.

The new individual equilibrium is obtained in looking, on $D'(x)$, inside $G'(x)$, for the point which gives a maximum utility $U(u')$ with the *same indifference curves*. Let Q' be this point.

Two interpretations are then possible:

(1) To consider that the individual really enjoys the utility corresponding to Q'. Then, advertising increases his utility in a double way, through improvement of information and through transformation of the image.

(2) To suppose that the individual chooses on the basis of the image, but is no longer a victim of perception biasses once the consumption has taken place. He then enjoys, not the consumption corresponding to Q', but the real associated consumption Q. Advertising has a double effect on utility: a positive one related to information improvement, a negative one due to the *distortion of consumption*. Q' can be associated to a utility higher (Q_1) or smaller (Q_2) than utility in M.

Reality should lie in between: Individuals enjoy their illusions but only partially.

As for the firm, it spreads its advertising between information and perception distortion in order to maximize its proceeds for a given advertising expenditure:

(1) For well-known products, the main effort will tend to create a specific image, except if the customers have to be informed of a change in quality or a decrease in price. The image components will be selected after a careful analysis of the motivations that the product may satisfy for different types of customers. With more subtlety, the perception of information constraints may also be modified, the consumer being under the impression that he receives technically important information (see the present advertising campaigns for washing powders).

(2) For new products, advertising will frequently be concentrated on information liable to increase the set of potential customers.

Analytically, the firm's problem could be formulated in the following way: assuming that for each vector $x = (x_k)_{1 \leqslant k \leqslant p}$ defining a possible advertising campaign, the individual chooses $u(x)$ and $q(x)$ in order to maximize:

$$U(u', q), \tag{7.47}$$

subject to:

$$u' = u'(u, x), \tag{7.48}$$

$$p(u)q = \rho, \tag{7.49}$$

$$g(u, x) \geqslant 0. \tag{7.50}$$

find the campaign x which maximizes:

$$b[u(x), q(x)] - d(x),$$

where $b(u, q)$ is the total profit of the firm when it sells quantities q at a quality level u, $d(x)$ is the amount of advertising expenditures.

If x is small, and if the individual wholly regrets his perceptive illusions, the "loss" due to advertising is the difference between the monetary value of $U[u(x), q(x)] - U[u(0), q(0)]$ and the change in the firm's profit (which naturally includes the expenditure cost).

To illustrate the remarks above, consider a naive model where there are only two commodities of a given quality. In this model the individual looks for:

$$\max U\{[S_i(q_1, q_2, x)]_{1 \leqslant i \leqslant n}\}, \tag{7.51}$$

$$p_1 q_1 + p_2 q_2 = \rho, \tag{7.52}$$

x being a vector in $\mathbf{R}^{p+}$ ($1 \leqslant k \leqslant p$). Advertising has only a perception influence.

Computations show that:

$$\partial q_g / \partial x_k = \frac{1}{\lambda} \sum_h U_{kh}(gh), \qquad (g, h = 1, 2) \tag{7.53}$$

where (gh) is the Slutzky coefficient and U_{kh} is the second partial derivative of U with respect to q_h and x_k. Taking into account the well-known identity:

$$p_1(11) + p_2(12) \equiv 0, \tag{7.54}$$

(7.53) can be rewritten:

$$\partial q_1/\partial x_k = \frac{U_1}{\lambda}\,[U_{1k}/U_1 - U_{2k}/U_2]. \tag{7.55}$$

It shows that the effect of the kth's component of advertising on consumption of commodity 1 is the difference between a direct effect and an indirect effect through commodity 2. With an obvious notation:

$$U_{1k} = \sum_i U_i S_{i1(k)} + \sum_{ij} U_{ij} S_{i1} S_{j(k)} \tag{7.56}$$

Hence the *direct* effect of advertising is high when:

(a) Advertising increases especially the marginal desirabilities of the satisfactions marginally important in the individual's utility. (It is exactly in this way that advertising research operates, trying to determine the i's for which U_i is great and looking for messages for which $S_{i1(k)}$ is high.)

(b) Advertising increases especially the levels of the satisfactions which are complementary to the ones for which the marginal satisfaction induced by the product is high (or decreases the levels of the satisfactions which are substitutes of the ones for which the marginal satisfaction induced by the product is high). Example: assume that, for an individual, power and prestige are two complementary satisfactions. The more the man feels powerful, the more he will consume commodities which marginally satisfy his need for prestige.

The above theory could be of some help for a logical analysis of advertising decisions.

1.5. A theory of new product creation

Consider a continuum of consumers defined by three characteristics:

(1) their psychology $\omega \in \pi$, π being assumed to be a finite Banach space,
(2) their income $\rho \in \mathbf{R}^+$,
(3) their access cost to information $c \in \mathbf{R}^+$ (see the definition below),

and introduce, with proper assumptions, the density $n(\omega, \rho, c)$ of consumers in the space $\pi \times \mathbf{R}^{2+}$.

We start from an initial situation in which there are m products, all known to the consumers. Nevertheless, some of them maintain a search activity out of curiosity and in order to be aware of possible innovations.

The behaviour of a (ω, ρ, c) individual results from the solution of:

$$\max U\{[S_i(q, J)_{1 \leqslant i \leqslant n}], \omega\}, \tag{7.57}$$

under the constraint:

$$pq + cJ \leqslant \rho. \tag{7.58}$$

Notation is the usual one, except that c is the unit cost associated to the search for information (it may be, for instance, the value of one unit of time).

Hence, for such an individual:

$$J = J(\omega, \rho, c, p). \tag{7.59}$$

Suppose now that a new product is launched, with a price x. As a consequence of their level of search, a fraction $\alpha[J, \omega, \rho, c]$ of the (ω, ρ, c) individuals will discover the product and a fraction $(1 - \alpha[J, \omega, \rho, c])$ will not discover it.

Those who have discovered the product will adjust their behaviour and demand a quantity y resulting from:

$$\max U\{(S_i(q', y, J')_{1 \leqslant i \leqslant n}, \omega\}, \tag{7.60}$$

under the constraint:

$$xy + pq' + c'J' \leqslant \rho, \tag{7.61}$$

the prime index denoting the new parameter values with c' a function $c'(c)$ of c. Hence, for these individuals, the demand of the new product will be:

$$y = y(x, p, \rho, c', \omega). \tag{7.62}$$

Summing up all consumer demands, the new product demand will be:

$$Y = \int \alpha[J(\omega, \rho, c, p), \omega, \rho, c]y(x, \omega, \rho, c'(c), p)n(\omega, \rho, c)\, d\omega\, d\rho\, dc. \tag{7.63}$$

(7.63) explains the main results of market research:

– The higher an individual's need for curiosity, the greater his search activity and the bigger the probability of his discovering the new product ("explorers" are frequently consumption leaders).

- The smaller the information cost, the greater the search activity and hence the probability of discovering the product. The size of the town in which the individual lives or the amount of advertising tend to decrease the information cost.
- Modernity as such may also be a source of prestige and self-assertion. People who, for this very reason, value nonconventional consumption patterns will tend to have a higher search activity and consequently a bigger probability of discovering the product.
- The higher the income, the smaller the marginal utility of existing products and the more interesting, on the average, the substitution of a new product to old ones.

Hence, the known characteristics of consumption leaders are embedded in the theory: individuals who are fairly young, active, well-informed and who consequently live in big cities, have high incomes and belong to social categories such as "executives and the professions," categories which, incidentally, suppose strong initiative, i.e. high search activity.

Unfortunately, in a one-period model, it is impossible to represent the diffusion and imitation processes which intervene, after the creation period, in the growth of the demand for the new product. Volume 2 will devote a section to this problem.

This example will help us in formulating a theory of the global demand for a commodity.

1.6. The global demand for a commodity

Marris (1964), McNerlove (1974) and many others have contributed in the past to a reformulation of demand theory. Simultaneously, numerous models have been built to answer the needs of market research.

So we shall limit ourselves to an enumeration of the factors included in the basic model and conditioning the demand for a commodity, and to a short analysis of the influence of these factors on global demand.

(i) Since a household is an organization, it is essential to know how *the members of the household allocate the decisions between themselves* when considering buying a given type of products. It is well-known that a woman buying men's shirts does not behave as her husband would, not only because her role in the household generates a more rational study of a product's characteristics, but also because the acquisition is made for somebody else and implies love and self-assertion motivations.

(*ii*) A second essential factor is the *relative importance of the various motivations*, i.e. the psychological factor ω. Numerous market researchers, in recent years, have tried to segment the customers by psychological criteria and to correlate these criteria and behaviour (i.e. reading habits) in order to increase advertising efficiency.

(*iii*) The *role structure* has a huge impact on demand. For instance, in France, blue and white collar workers have for quite a long time had very different consumption patterns, even for identical incomes. Role structure influences identification processes, consumption perceptions, and the association between consumptions and satisfactions. It makes access to information easier or more difficult.

(*iv*) *Capability* is another factor which plays a part in the generation of demand through the facility of access to information, through the perception of the consequences of an act and through the association between consumptions and satisfactions. But it is a slowly-changing factor.

(*v*) Next come all *the supply characteristics which command information*. They are:

- the amount and the content of messages sent by those who already consume the product;
- the amount and the content of advertising directed at potential consumers (including name, packing and other external features);
- the amount and the content of advertising at selling points, the efficiency of which depends on the density of the distribution network;
- the amount and the content of messages retransmitted by retailers as a consequence of the firm's action on its retailers.

(*vi*) The same characteristics will influence the formation of the buyers' *images* of the existing products.

(*vii*) It remains to introduce, as in conventional theory, the *prices* of all known products, the *information cost* and the *time* necessary to buy and consume products or to acquire information about them.

In this respect, the location of the house and the density of the distribution network will be important parameters.

(*viii*) The household *income* will be the last and obvious factor introduced.

This list will help us to present a few remarks on the impact of these factors.

Supply is characterized by: the price vector p $(p \in \mathbf{R}^{m+})$; the distribution density vector δ $(\delta \in \mathbf{R}^+)$, the density being measured, for instance, by the number of selling points, per potential customer; the amount of advertising v $(v \in \mathbf{R}^+)$.

Simultaneously, with each individual will be associated: his psychological factor $\omega \in \pi$ (π a finite-dimensional Banach space); his income $\rho \in \mathbf{R}^+$; his effective capability $\gamma \in \mathbf{R}^{p+}$; his location $u \in \mathbf{R}^{2+}$; the value he attaches to a time unit $\mu \in \mathbf{R}^+$; his role structure $\mathbf{R}$.

We can write: $g = (\bar{\omega}, \rho, \gamma, u, \mu)$ and denote $n(g, R)$ the density of individuals with role structure R at point g in $\pi \times \mathbf{R}^{(p+4)+}$.

Respective adaptation of supply and demand is the result of two *processes:*

– an *information process* which defines the probability α_j that a given individual will know a product j when the distribution density is δ and the advertising volume v:

$$\alpha_j = \alpha_j(g, R, \delta, v). \tag{7.64}$$

– a *buying process* which defines the quantity q_j bought by the same individual if he is informed:

$$q_j = q_j[\bar{\omega}, \rho, \gamma, R, \delta, v, p + \mu t(\delta, u)], \tag{7.65}$$

$t(\delta, u)$ being the sum of the time for access to and consumption of a product when location is u and distribution density δ.

Hence, global demand Q_j:

$$Q_j = \sum_{R \in P} \int \alpha_j(g, R, \delta, v) q_j[g, R, \delta, v, p, t] n(g, R) \, dg. \tag{7.66}$$

It is with this model in mind that marketing managers behave in practice. If we differentiate (7.65) for discrete given classes σ of identified consumers we obtain, with an obvious notation and under the assumption that $\alpha_{j\sigma}$, $Q_{j\sigma}$ and n_σ are differentiable:

$$dQ_{j\sigma}/Q_{j\sigma} = d\alpha_{j\sigma}/\alpha_{j\sigma} + dq_{j\sigma}/q_{j\sigma} + dn_\sigma/n_\sigma. \tag{7.67}$$

In other words, for any infinitesimal variation dy of a factor y influencing demand:

$$dQ_{j\sigma}/Q_{j\sigma} = [e^y_{\alpha j\sigma} + e^y_{q j\sigma} + e^y_{n\sigma}]\,dy/y = E^y_{j\sigma}\,dy/y, \tag{7.68}$$

the e's and the E denoting corresponding elasticities.

So, *the elasticity of demand for a given class of consumers with respect to a parameter is the sum of three elasticities:*

– *the elasticity of the size of the class with respect to this parameter, $e^y_{n\sigma}$,*
– *the elasticity of the information probability of a consumer in the class with respect to this parameter, $e^y_{\alpha j\sigma}$,*
– *the elasticity of the demand of an informed consumer in the class with respect to this parameter, $e^y_{q j\sigma}$.*

Among the influences embedded in (7.66) and (7.67), some are of special interest. In each case, all other parameters are held constant. *As concerns size, the influence of:*

(a) income or role structure on the size of the corresponding consumer classes.

As concerns *information probability*, the influence of:

(b) advertising volume v,
(c) distribution density δ,
(d) income ρ,
(e) capability c,
(f) role structure R.

As concerns *individual consumption*, the influences of:

(g) prices p, unit times t or equivalent costs $p + \mu t$,
(h) distribution density δ or advertising volume v,
(i) income ρ,
(j) role structure R.

Elasticities can be computed for (b) (c) (d) (g) (h) (i). A few remarks will illustrate this analysis:

– For advertising volume v_j, (7.68) gives:

$$dQ_{j\sigma}/Q_{j\sigma} = [e^v_{\alpha j\sigma} + e^v_{q j\sigma}]\,dv_j/v_j. \tag{7.69}$$

The first elasticity measures the effect of *information* and the second the effect of *image distortion*.

- Income ρ and role structure R being correlated, the complexity of the effect on demand of an increase in national income can also be analyzed.
- The distribution density δ clearly has a triple influence: it contributes to *information*, it has an impact on *image formation*, it conditions the level of the *generalized cost* $p + \mu t$.

A complete and rigorous mathematical treatment of a demand theory based on the chapter 6 model could very well be a fruitful research subject for the coming years. This section has shown some directions of interest.

2. Labour market

A ternary division of this section is a logical approach: we shall begin with the individual and the aggregated demand for employment, examine next the employment supply and finally consider the labour market itself. Valuable contributions to this field have been made in the last few years. Phelps (1970, 1972), Holt (1970a, 1970b), Alchian (1970), Mortensen (1970), Becker (1971), Doeringer and Pior (1971), Mackay (1970), Nickell (1976) are, among others, authors of significant papers. Many of their ideas will find a natural place in the applications of the basic model proposed below.

2.1. Individual demand for employment

The parameters of the choice of a job have already been partially mentioned three times in this book. Chapter 2 (§ 3.1) sketches Simon and March's analysis; chapter 4 (§ 3.3) underlines the interaction of the image of the job, the interest of the allocations to which it gives access and the income it generates; chapter 5 (§ 5.1) stresses the special importance of the individual's information and capability. A more integrated model will be proposed here.

For reasons which will soon appear clearly, there is some advantage in considering a two-period economy. Since, in this case, it is a straightforward generalization of chapter 6's model, there is no special difficulty in adopting such a formulation here.

At the beginning of the first period, any individual experiences one of two possible situations: he is unemployed (willingly or not) or he is employed. These two cases will be examined one after the other.

Let us denote:

- $q_1 \in \mathbf{R}^{m+}$, $q_2 \in \mathbf{R}^{m+}$ the current consumptions of the individual in periods 1 and 2 respectively. These consumptions are bought at discounted prices $p_1 \in \mathbf{R}^{m+}$, $p_2 \in \mathbf{R}^{m+}$, $p_1 \gg 0$, $p_2 \gg 0$ and imply a time $t \in \mathbf{R}^{m+}$, $t \gg 0$ for unit consumptions.
- $J_1 \in \mathbf{R}^+$, the time (possibly) spent in looking for a job in period 1. Since it is assumed that a job sought in a period cannot be taken before the beginning of the next period, the time spent in search is obviously zero in the second period.
- $r \in \mathcal{R}$, a vector in a finite-dimensional Banach space $\mathcal{R}$, the types of existing jobs. Dimensions may correspond to the location of the job, to the hierarchical level, to the number of "points" on an evaluation scale, to the budget which is at the disposal of the job-holder. The description should, of course, take into account the *allocations* permitted in the job and the *constraints* imposed on these allocations.
- $c_1 \in \mathbf{R}^{u+}$, $c_2 \in \mathbf{R}^{u+}$, individual capabilities in periods 1 and 2.
- $L_1 \in \mathbf{R}^+$, $L_2 \in \mathbf{R}^+$, leisure times available in periods 1 and 2.
- $x_1 \in X$ the actions taken in the first period by external agents and especially by firms looking for additional staff members to inform individuals and to modify the image of their offer.
- $r'_1 = r'_1(r_1, x_1, c)$, a mapping from $\mathcal{R} \times X \times \mathbf{R}^{u+}$ into $\mathcal{R}$, the image the individual has in period 1 of a job r_1 performed in this period when he is under the influence of external action x_1 and has capability c_1. $r'_2 = r'_2(r_2, x_1, c_1)$ will be the image *in the first period* of job r_2 performed in the second. The image of unemployment will be r'_{10} and r'_{20}.
- $T(r) \in \mathbf{R}^+$, the time at the individual's disposal when he is in job r (total time minus working time and transport time to go to work). $T_0 \in \mathbf{R}^+$ will be the total time available when the individual is unemployed.
- $\rho_1(r, c) \in \mathbf{R}^+$, the individual's discounted net income when he is in period 1 in job r with capability c (transport costs to go to work are assumed deducted). $\rho_2(r, c)$ is introduced similarly, ρ_{10}, ρ_{20} will be

the net discounted incomes of the unemployed individual in periods 1 and 2.

- $f_1 \in \mathbf{R}^+$, $f_2 \in \mathbf{R}^+$, the time spent by the individual in training in period 1 and 2.
- $z_1 = 0$ or 1, $z_2 = 0$ or 1, a variable indicating whether the individual is unemployed (0) or employed (1) in the corresponding period.
- $k \in \mathbf{R}^+$ the cost of changing job, independently of search and unemployment.

2.1.1. The unemployed individual

Under the simplifying assumption that a firm never fires an employee, the strategies available to the individual are:

(i) to remain unemployed during the two periods and not to look for a job;

(ii) not to look for a job and to take immediately the best job available;

(iii) not to look for a job and to take for the next period the best job available;

(iv) to look for a job and to take for the next period the best job available;

(v) to take immediately the best job available, but to look, while working, for a better job for the next period.

(In a world of perfect knowledge, the strategy of looking for a job and not taking any is not optimal, except in a case of sheer curiosity; we shall not consider it.)

(i) The utility experienced by the individual results from:

$$\max U[q_1, q_2, L_1, L_2, f_1, f_2, c_1, c_2, r_{10}, r_{20}, 0, 0],^3 \qquad (7.70)$$

under the constraints:

$$p_1 q_1 + p_2 q_2 = \rho_{10} + \rho_{20}, \qquad (7.71)$$

$$t_1 \dot{q}_i + f_1 + L_1 = T_0, \qquad (7.72)$$

---

[3] The last two zeros are for $z_1 = 0$, $z_2 = 0$.

$$t_2 q_2 + f_2 + L_2 = T_0, \tag{7.73}$$

$$c_2 = c_2(f_1, c_1). \tag{7.74}$$

(7.71) is the income constraint, (7.72) and (7.73) are time constraints, (7.74) expresses change in capability through training. The individual is interested in it independently of the job's opportunities.

It is immediately obvious that: some people may be totally passive: $f_1 = f_2 = 0$; others may accept training to improve their capability and better enjoy some consumptions: $f_1 > 0$, $f_2 = 0$; others may be interested in training as such (eternal students!): $f_1 > 0, f_2 > 0$.

For a given individual, this strategy leads to a utility U_I.

(*ii*) This strategy corresponds to a certain number of subcases for period 2, since the individual may keep his job (A), quit it and prefer unemployment (B), quit his job and take another one without searching (C).

We shall only write the corresponding model for case A:

ii A

$$\max U[q_1, q_2, L_1, L_2, f_1, f_2, c_1, c_2, r'_1, r'_2, 1, 1], \tag{7.75}[4]$$

$$p_1 q_1 + p_2 q_2 = \rho_1(r, c_1) + \rho_2(r, c_2), \tag{7.76}$$

$$t_1 q_1 + f_1 + L_1 = T(r), \tag{7.77}$$

$$t_2 q_2 + f_2 + L_2 = T(r), \tag{7.78}$$

$$c_2 = c_2(f_1, c_1, r), \tag{7.79}$$

$$r'_1 = r'_1(r, x_1, c_1), \tag{7.80}$$

$$r'_2 = r'_2(r, x_2, c_2), \tag{7.81}$$

$$g(r, x_1, c_1) \geq 0, \tag{7.82}$$

$$f(r, c_1) \geq 0. \tag{7.83}$$

We shall notice that: the performance of the job has in itself a training effect, there is an information constraint (7.82), there is a capability constraint (7.83).

This case obviously corresponds to individuals who cannot afford to receive only the income of unemployment and who are passive in

---

[4] The 1's are for: $z_1 = 1, z_2 = 1$.

their job selection. For instance, they may not attach high importance to r'_1 and r'_2. But they may or may not value training and culture.

Case B may describe the behaviour of individuals who dislike working but need some money in order to remain idle. They take the best job available in the first period – probably the one with the highest income – to go back to unemployment in the second.

Case C may correspond to individuals who take advantage of their improved capability or of a change of the information constraint between the first and the second period. A certain type of career-ambitious people may adopt this behaviour.

(*iii*) This strategy is, in some features, symmetrical to (*ii* B) except that here the individual probably has enough money to postpone employment.

(*iv*) This case being an important one, we shall write the corresponding relations:

$$\max U[q_1, q_2, L_1, L_2, J_1, f_1, f_2, c_1, c_2, r'_{10}, r'_2, 0, 1], \tag{7.84}$$

$$p_1 q_1 + p_2 q_2 = \rho_{10} + \rho_2(r_2, c_2), \tag{7.85}$$

$$t_1 q_1 + J_1 + f_1 + L_1 = T_0, \tag{7.86}$$

$$t_2 q_2 + f_2 + L_2 = T(r_2), \tag{7.87}$$

$$c_2 = c_2(f_1, c_1), \tag{7.88}$$

$$g(r_2, x_1, c_2, J_1) \geqslant 0, \tag{7.89}$$

$$f(r_2, c_2) \geqslant 0. \tag{7.90}$$

Here, the information constraint explicitly depends on the amount of search.

An active individual will adopt a high level of search and will probably look for training in order to improve his capability and the set of jobs to which he has access.

(*v*) The individual who cannot wait for an income, but who is ready to make efforts to improve his situation would probably adopt this strategy, which is translated into the following set of relations:

$$\max U[q_1, q_2, L_1, L_2, J_1, f_1, f_2, c_1, c_2, r'_1, r'_2, 1, 1], \tag{7.91}$$

$$p_1 q_1 + p_2 q_2 = \rho_1(r_1, c_1) + \rho_2(r_2, c_2) - k, \tag{7.92}$$

$$t_1 q_1 + J_1 + f_1 + L_1 = T_1(r_1), \tag{7.93}$$

$$t_2 q_2 + f_2 + L_2 = T_2(r_2), \tag{7.94}$$

$$c_2 = c_2[f_1, c_1, r_1], \tag{7.95}$$

$$g(r_2, x_1, c_2, J_1) \geqslant 0, \tag{7.96}$$

$$f(r_2, c_2) \geqslant 0, \tag{7.97}$$

$$r_1' = r_1'(r_1, x_1, c_1), \tag{7.98}$$

$$r_2' = r_2'(r_2, x_1, c_1). \tag{7.99}$$

Notice that J_1 is here much more constrained than in strategy (iv), since obviously $T_1(r_1)$ is considerably smaller than T_0.

For this reason, the set of available jobs for period 2 will be considerably "smaller" than in (iv). *The individual has ̣ ̇hanged a higher immediate income against lower professional expectancies in the future.*

In the line of the research done by Holt and Phelps, the above models give a consistent interpretation of known facts about the demand for labour:

(1) In view of his capability c, the individual only has access to a subset $\mathscr{R}'(c)$ of all possible jobs. Simultaneously, for an amount of search J_1 made with capability c, he only knows the subset $\mathscr{R}''(J_1, c)$ of possible jobs. In other words, he chooses on the intersection of $\mathscr{R}'(c)$ and $\mathscr{R}''(J_1, c)$. Firms may broaden this set by promotional action (use of recruiting consultants, advertising in the press) likely to inform individuals having the required capability.

For each job available, the individual features the allocations which will be at his disposal, taking into account the regulation constraints, and evaluates the two types of consequences which will result from his behaviour in his job: a lower or higher compensation, various satisfaction levels. Hence, the choice of job should normally depend on the image of the different jobs, on the income generated by the job, on the allocations which will be opened to the individuals within the job, and on the behaviour in the job. A firm may influence this choice in a triple way:

– by creating a favourable image of the job itself,
– by promoting a positive perception of the corresponding allocations,

- by developing an identification process which decreases the perception of the regulation constraints in the job.

As for the level of search J_1, it depends heavily on three factors:

- the intensity of the need for exploration, which is a psychological feature, partly conditioned by the surrounding culture;
- the expectancy of an increase in satisfactions as a consequence of the discovery of new jobs through a greater information effort;
- the "cost" of information, which is a function of the actions x of external agents.

Finally, the individual partly controls his future capability through the job performed or through training. He may be interested in a better capability because it increases the satisfactions induced by some consumptions or because it broadens the set of feasible jobs.

(2) The behaviour of the unemployed will depend on the comparison of U_i, U_{iiA}, U_{iiB}, U_{iiC}, U_{iii}, U_{iv}, U_v:

For instance, individuals who, in a certain situation, prefer not to be active (strategy i), may decide to adopt strategy iiA if social values change or if more jobs become available. An example of the first phenomenon is given by the long-term trend in French women's rate of activity; an example of the second by the decrease in the number of people willing to be active when the unemployment rate increases.

Similarly, a restriction on the set of jobs available and known may compel an individual to switch his strategy from iiA to iv. For example, French students having degrees in some disciplines have capabilities and job preferences such that the offer is limited. Consequently, they must spend time in search or recycling, while in the past they would have taken immediately an available job.

A strategy such as iiC has a bad ranking in a society where the cost of change k is high or where a change is considered as a failure... iiB is more probable in our society, where young people do not attach the same value to work, as the preceeding generation did.

A similar analysis has to be made for employed people.

2.1.2. The employed individual

Excepting the case of an individual who refuses internal promotion, and still assuming, for simplicity, that a firm never fires a member of its staff, five main strategies are open to an employed individual:

- to keep his job for two periods (viA)
- to decide to retire from his work at the end of the first period (viB)
- to change job at the beginning of the second period, without search during the first (viC)
- to search for another job while working during the first period and change at the beginning of the second (vii)
- to quit his job immediately and remain unemployed ($viii$)
- to quit his job immediately, remain unemployed for one period and take a new job during the second period, whether after search (ix) or not (x).

There is an obvious correspondence between these strategies and the preceding ones' viA–iiA; viB–iiB; viC–iiC; vii–v; $viii$–i; ix–iv; x–iii, with the difference that at the beginning of the first period, the job is given. Hence, transition costs are different.

A few important factors are implicitly included in the analysis made. When an individual leaves an organization to which he belonged he suffers from a certain number of costs: he loses the part of his capability which was specific to the organization, he has to reconstruct the network of friendly relations developed on the working place, he endures a possible loss of prestige or a feeling of failure.

Of course, these factors do not exist for the individuals to whom a better paid job is proposed, in an organization with a prestigious image, and with a hierarchical promotion.

Hence, *out of a purely theoretical analysis*, we have been able to define the main types of behaviour which are observed in practice. In some countries, the size of the corresponding groups is regularly measured by statistical institutes.

The most important conclusion of these models – obvious for sociologists, more interesting for theoretical economists – is that the demand for a type of job does not depend only on wages offered but also on: *the distribution of capabilities within the population, the image of the different jobs disseminated by the collectivity, the respective impor-*

tance, in individuals, of different motivations strengthened or weakened by the surrounding culture.

Profit possibilities are not sufficient to generate the flow of entrepreneurs assumed by classical economics. Collectivities do exist in which capitalism does not develop and where the most gifted dream of being high civil servants or archbishops.

The analysis of the demand for employment at the individual level can be used to interpret the aggregated demand on a labour market.

2.2. Aggregated demand for employment

Assume that, at the beginning of a period, a firm offers a job r with a compensation $\rho(c)$. What will be the demand for this job? The demand may come from unemployed or from employed people:

If $n(\omega, c)$ is the properly defined density of unemployed individuals on $\pi \times \mathbf{R}^{u+}$, the proportion of these individuals aware of the existence of the job is a function:

$$\alpha[r, \omega, c, x].$$

Among the informed individuals, a certain fraction will be candidates. This fraction is a function:

$$q[r, \omega, c, x, \rho(c), S],$$

S being the set of the other offers known to the informed individuals. Finally, the total demand arising from unemployed people can be expressed as the integral:

$$\int_{\mathscr{C}} \alpha[r, \omega, c, x] q[r, \omega, c, x, \rho(c), S] n(\omega, c) \, d\omega \, dc, \qquad (7.100)$$

computed on the subset $\mathscr{C}$ of individuals having an acceptable capability.

If $n(\omega, c, \rho^*, r^*)$ is the properly defined density of people employed in a job r^* with income ρ^* for a certain standard capability,[5] it is possible to introduce in the same way:

---

[5] It assumes implicitly, for the sake of simplicity, that the compensation function of a firm with a job r^* belongs to a family: $\rho(c) = \rho^*(\lambda(c))$, where $\lambda(c)$ is identical for jobs r^* in any firm.

- the proportion $\alpha[r, r^*, \omega, c, \rho^*, x]$ of these individuals informed of the offer (r, ρ),
- the fraction: $q[r, r^*, \omega, c, \rho^*, x, \rho(c), S^*]$ of them who will be candidates, S^* being the set other offers known to these individuals.

Finally, the total demand arising from employed people is the integral:

$$\int dr^* \, d\rho^* \int_\mathscr{C} \alpha[r, r^*, \omega, c, \rho^*, x] q[r, r^*, \omega, c, \rho^*, x, \rho(c), S^*]$$

$$n(\omega, c, \rho^*, r^*) \, d\omega \, dc. \qquad (7.101)$$

Such a formulation is very similar to the analysis made by Charles Holt (1970a) and, from the demand of a given type of job, it would be possible to construct in the same way the total demand for jobs.

2.3. The firm's supply of employment

As in the third part of this chapter, the firm's management will be represented by a *unique decision center*.

The utility of this decision center will depend on:

- the profit $r \in \mathbf{R}^+$ made by the firm (this profit is a source of prestige or safety, but also conditions the income level of the decision center),
- the quantity $q \in \mathbf{R}^+$ produced by the firm and sold at price $p \gg 0$,
- the "responsibility level" $\pi \in [0, 1]$ chosen by the decision center, parameter which will be more precisely defined below.

In other words:

$$U = U(r, q, \pi). \qquad (7.102)$$

The jobs liable to exist within the firm constitute a sequence $1 \leqslant j \leqslant m$, each job being represented by a responsibility level π_j, for instance a number of points on an evaluation scale. n_j will denote the number of people having a job of level j. The firm can choose its organization: it may have a lot of officers and a few soldiers or many soldiers and a light hierarchical structure. But, whatever its size, the *average* level of responsibility $\bar{\pi}$ of a staff member will be approximately the same. This situation will be represented by the simplest possible relation, a linear one:

$$\bar{\pi} \left(\sum_j n_j + 1 \right) = \sum_j n_j \pi_j + \pi. \qquad (7.103)$$

Of course at a given responsibility level, all the staff members do not necessarily have the same capability and may receive different wages. Assuming the existence of capability classes k ($1 \leqslant k \leqslant p$), n_{kj} will be the number of staff members of responsibility level j in capability class k and w_{kj} the compensation received by any of these staff members:

$$\sum_k n_{kj} = n_j, \quad \forall j. \qquad (7.104)$$

The quantity produced by the firm will, of course, depend not only on the n_j's, but also on the n_{kj}'s: the quality of the staff is as important as the adequacy of the organization. We shall write:

$$q = q\{[n_{kj}]_{1 \leqslant k \leqslant p, 1 \leqslant j \leqslant m}, \pi, y\}, \qquad (7.105)$$

$y \in \mathbf{R}^{m+}$ being the quantity used of other inputs, the prices of which, x, are imposed by the market.

The firm's profit directly results from the above assumptions:

$$r = pq - \sum_{kj} w_{kj} n_{kj} - xy. \qquad (7.106)$$

Two situations will be examined:

– First, it will be supposed that the *wages* w_{kj} *are given by the market*. In other words, the firm has, for each responsibility level and for each capacity, as many candidates as it may dream of, when it pays the market wage. The question, for the firm, is to define its organization and to choose, at each level, the distribution of staff members in capability classes.
– Then, it will be assumed that the number of staff members leaving the firm and the number of candidates asking for jobs depend on the wage structure (w_{kj}) of the firm. The firm then has to determine simultaneously its organization, its capability policy, its wage policy. This second situation is, of course, more realistic and is the strict counterpart of the situation described on the demand side.

2.3.1. Wages given by the market

The problem is to find π, (n_{kj}) and y such that:

$$\max U\left[(pq - \sum_{kj} w_{kj} n_{kj} - xy), q, \pi\right],$$

under the constraints (7.105) and

$$\sum_{jk} \pi_j n_{kj} + \pi - (\sum_{jk} n_{kj} + 1)\bar{\pi} = 0. \tag{7.107}$$

If λU_r and μU_r are Lagrange multipliers associated with the constraints (7.105) and (7.107), the corresponding Lagrangian can be written:

$$U_r[p \, dq - \sum_{kj} w_{kj} \, dn_{kj} - x \, dy] + U_q \, dq + U_\pi \, d\pi -$$

$$- \lambda U_r(dq - \sum_{kj} q_{kj} \, dn_{kj} - q_\pi \, d\pi - q_y \, dy) - \mu U_r(d\pi + \sum_{kj} (\pi_j - \bar{\pi})$$

$$dn_{kj}) = 0, \tag{7.108}$$

with an obvious notation and with adequate differentiability conditions.

In other words, if the maximum is regular:

$$p + U_q/U_r = \lambda, \tag{7.109}$$

$$\lambda q_y = x, \tag{7.110}$$

$$w_{kj} = \lambda q_{kj} + \mu(\pi_j - \bar{\pi}), \tag{7.111}$$

$$U_\pi/U_r + \lambda q_\pi = \mu. \tag{7.112}$$

The meaning of these relations is extremely interesting:

- λ is the marginal value attached to production by the manager. It is obviously equal to p when this manager is only interested in profit ($U_q = 0$);
- the price of the other inputs is equal to their marginal productivity, not expressed in terms of p as in the conventional theory, but in terms of λ,
- the wage of an individual of capability k in a position j is the *sum of two terms:* the first is the usual *marginal productivity of labour* (expressed in terms of λ); the second is a *correction which must be added to this marginal productivity to take into account the influence of the number of staff members (k, j) on the productivity of others.*

When $\mu > 0$, $\mu(\pi_j - \bar{\pi})$ is positive for responsibility levels above the average: to add one man to the hierarchy will not only give the firm the corresponding marginal productivity, but will also improve the efficiency of the work of the other staff members.

When $\mu < 0$, $\mu(\pi_j - \overline{\pi})$ is negative for the same responsibility levels, a heavier hierarchy has a negative impact on the efficiency of the others' work.

Such an analysis shows that, from the firm's point of view, there is not *one marginal productivity attached to a given individual, but a marginal productivity depending on the organizational structure and on the quality distribution of the staff.*

Of course, if relations (7.111) are added, with weighting coefficients n_{kj}, the terms in μ cancel out, the organizational effect disappear and:

$$\lambda \sum_{jk} q_{kj} n_{kj} = \sum_{jk} w_{kj} n_{kj}. \tag{7.113}$$

μ can be interpreted as the marginal productivity of responsibility within the firm.

Depending on his psychology, the boss chooses his responsibility level in such a way that μ is equal to the sum of his marginal utility for responsibility and of the marginal productivity of his level of responsibility. An authoritarian manager will keep for himself a power far beyond the necessary minimum and will, in fact, decrease the number of jobs with high responsibility. For a manager indifferent to the scope of his internal power ($U_\pi = 0$) and only interested in profit ($U_q = 0$, $U_r = 1$), μ is equal to pq_π, i.e. to the value of the production increase induced by a broadening of the number 1's responsibilities.

2.3.2. *Existence of an autonomous wage policy*

In this case, the manager is able to choose the w_{kj}'s and receives in exchange a response from the market, i.e. a set of demands $n'_{k'j}([w_{kj}]_{1 \leqslant k \leqslant p, 1 \leqslant j \leqslant m})$ for $1 \leqslant k' \leqslant p$ and $1 \leqslant j' \leqslant m$. These demands are the difference between the number of external candidates and the number of staff members who leave the firm. Of course, the manager is not compelled to hire all the candidates, so that his problem is well represented in the following way:

$$\max U[(pq - \sum_{kj} w_{kj} n_{kj} - xy), q, \pi], \tag{7.114}$$

under the constraints:

$$q - q\{[n_{kj}]_{1 \leqslant k \leqslant p, 1 \leqslant j \leqslant m}, \pi, y\} = 0, \tag{7.115}$$

$$\sum_{jk} \pi_j n_{kj} + \pi - (\sum_{jk} n_{kj} + 1)\overline{\pi} = 0, \tag{7.116}$$

$$n_{kj} \leqslant n'_{kj}([w_{k'j'}]_{1 \leqslant k' \leqslant p, 1 \leqslant j' \leqslant m}), \tag{7.117}$$

the decision variables being q, (w_{kj}), (n_{kj}), y, π. Introducing Lagrange multipliers λU_r, μU_r and $v_{kj}U_r$, we get, as the first-order conditions of a regular maximum, the two conditions:

$$w_{kj} = \lambda q_{kj} + \mu(\pi_j - \overline{\pi}) - v_{kj}, \tag{7.118}$$

$$n_{kj} = \sum_{k'j'} v_{k'j} n^{kj}_{k'j'}, \tag{7.119}$$

in addition to the three already obtained: (7.109), (7.110), (7.111).

v_{kj} is an opportunity cost equal to zero when the demand constraints are not binding. (7.118) shows that, when the market imposes a limit on recruitment, it prevents the firm from offering a compensation equal to the total marginal productivity (direct and indirect). The meaning of (7.119) is easily understood if $n^{kj}_{k'j'}$ is supposed equal to zero for $k' \neq k, j' \neq j$, since it can be written in this case:

$$n_{kj} = dn'_{kj}/dw_{kj} \cdot v_{kj}, \tag{7.120}$$

or, if the elasticity e_{kj} of demand for employment with respect to compensation is introduced:

$$v_{kj} = (1/e_{kj})w_{kj}, \tag{7.121}$$

which is a very well-known relation of monopsony theory.

Unfortunately, the above analysis neglects a few elements which should be introduced, at least in a multiperiod model:

- the cost of firing staff members and of recruiting and training other people to replace them, a cost more or less compensated by future wage savings,
- the expectation of an increased profit resulting from the hiring of people better adapted to their jobs,
- the psychological cost of a collective dismissal, due to loss of prestige or to a feeling of guilt,
- the psychological cost of the departure of highly esteemed staff members.

Naturally, the balance of costs and benefits will depend to a large extent on the specificity of the situation. Nevertheless, the existence of these "irreversibility" costs justifies a separation of the labour market into two components: the organization's *internal* labour market, and the *external* market where the offers of the different organizations are confronted.

2.4. The labour market

For the *internal market*, certain conjectures seem possible:

- If, from the point of view of employment, the organization is almost completely isolated from the outside world (for instance, if dismissals are practically forbidden), the interest of having a strong union is maximum and the level of wages will result from a bilateral negotiation between the management and the union. The union will have to take into account the relative strength of the various groups of employees. The negotiating power of the management will be greatly influenced by the nature of the constraints imposed on it by the market of its products, the shareholders or the State.
- Within an organization, it is practically impossible to decrease in nominal terms the compensation of an employee through time, since the loss of prestige would be unbearable. Then, probably, the higher the age, the greater the discrepancy between compensation and marginal productivity of labour. The compensation should tend to be above this marginal productivity for elderly people and below for young people. The same remarks can also be made, to a certain extent, for the responsibility level. In both cases, cultural influences are essential, since a society could be conceived, where the prestige of a greater responsibility would be so high that it would make it possible to decrease the compensation.
- In all probability, individual negotiating power is an increasing function of the hierarchical level. On the contrary, variations in the marginal productivities of individuals are probably so high at a given time that other factors tend to reduce the range of compensations (the marginal productivity of one person fluctuates widely during his life time while his compensation is much more stable; the *perceived* wage distribution has to be more or less accepted; interest in others is an element of managers' satisfactions).
- Finally, the more favourable the situation of the firm with respect

to its competitors, the easier it is for the management to accept wage increases without endangering the future. The relative weight of profit with regard to other motivations should be weaker in the managers' utility, while for the staff, the importance of safety should decrease with regard to the interest for higher wages.

At the *level of the whole economy*, the situation is still more complex. Certain features seem to be essential:

- the depth of the divisions between organizations induces a more or less segmented labour market. The borders between job types, with the existence of special categories with closed access, have the same effect (see, for instance, airline pilots);
- cultural norms are of paramount importance: relative prestige of the different jobs, organizational habits, attitudes towards age, responsibility levels. Nothing is more fascinating than a comparison between Japan and the United States in the field of management organizational practice;
- more generally, the external labour market depends on the unions' structure in relation to the socio-political organization of society, and on the competitive structure of the firms.

In consequence, for a study of the labour market of a big city over a period of a few years (five years, for instance) it might be useful to simulate the market, as has been done for the housing market.[6] If the main concern is the adaptation of the demand for employment to supply, we may consider as given:

- at the beginning of year 0, the *number of jobs offered by type* (one type being characterized by economic sector, responsibility level, minimum capability, geographical location), with *wages and working conditions* (number of working hours per day, for instance) *associated with these jobs*,
- for each of the subsequent years, *the number of job creations and suppressions by type* (without any compensation between the two) and the *new wages* and *working conditions* by type.

At the start, the population of individuals is distributed according to: individual characteristics (capability, motivational structure, housing

---

[6] See J. Lesourne, R. Loué (1977), volume II, chapter IX, the description of the SMALA model (Simulation du MArché des Logements dans une Agglomération).

location), the type (salary and working conditions of the job fulfilled), with the possibility of being unemployed, *willingly or not*.

A separate simulation of demographic and educational processes makes it possible to forecast the evolution of the population and to know, year by year, the distribution of individual characteristics (in a first analysis, the influence of the job on housing location may probably be neglected). A special analysis of the alternating or permanent migratory flows has to be added, these flows being supposed either exogenous or depending on the labour market situation in the city.

Surveys may then make it possible to estimate the probability, for a given individual of a given category, to be ready to work if he is unemployed, or to be a candidate for *a change from one organization to another* if he is employed; and thereafter to determine for these two populations of candidates and noncandidates:

- the distribution of preferences (or the preference probabilities) for the jobs liable to interest them within their present organizations, with the corresponding minimum wages;
- the distribution of preferences (or the preference probabilities) for the jobs liable to interest them in other organizations, with the corresponding minimum wages.

At the beginning of a period, before any simulation, individuals who have lost their job as a result of a decrease in the number of jobs within their firm, are added to the population of candidates and non-candidates. It is also assumed:

- that the jobs created by an organization are offered in priority to its own members when considered able (for instance, each individual within an organization will have, depending on his capability, a certain probability of being offered a job by his organization). According to the type of job and the compensation, the individual may accept or refuse. This first allocation being made, a new distribution of jobs offered and of candidates is generated.
- that the candidates and the jobs are put into contact at random, these contact probabilities depending, of course, on the promotional actions of the firms, on individual characteristics and on the types of jobs proposed. For each job proposed, the individual accepts or refuses, according to the wages and the other conditions. If he accepts, he is taken off the list of candidates, while his new job is eliminated from employment offer and his past job added to it.

If he refuses, he is sent back to the population of candidates. The process goes on until there remains no job on offer liable to be taken by an able candidate under the conditions proposed.

This description is a very crude sketch, but the use of simulation methods, with, in the background, the theory presented in this section, would certainly make possible an understanding in depth of how, *through successive adaptations*, the adjustment of employment demand and offer is realized and what are, in the end, the characteristics of those who take advantage of job creations. The link between the theory of the individual and a quantified knowledge of the labour market[7] would become straightforward.

The above process is, of course, totally satisfactory only when each worker tries *individually* to adapt himself to a certain structure of employment offers. Changes have to be made in order to represent adequately the situation – frequent in France – where wage-earners refuse to be fired and struggle collectively, with their unions, to obtain new working conditions.

Nevertheless, as for the theory of demand, the model of chapter 6 appears to lead to interesting developments on the labour market.

It is then an obvious temptation to try to use it to improve the analysis of firms' policies in competitive markets, since the analysis of competition is one of the key fields of classical economics.

3. Firm's policies and competition

According to textbooks, in the absence of any competitive barriers or of any increasing returns to scale, perfect competition tends to generate zero profits for all firms, given equality of price, marginal cost and average cost. But such a result relies on the implicit assumption of the existence of a sufficient number of able and profit-minded potential entrepreneurs.

How much of this conventional analysis is changed when the diversity of policy-makers' personalities is reintroduced?

Tradition suggests a three-step reasoning: first, a reinterpretation of

[7] Such research is at present being carried out at the Econometric Laboratory of the Conservatoire National des Arts et Métiers, Paris, under the responsibility of the author with a grant from the Délégation Générale à la Recherche Scientifique et Technique.

the firm's equilibrium on a market with given prices; second, the study of perfect competition when *the number of firms* is given; third, an examination of *the entry of new firms on the market.*

Throughout this section, it will be assumed that all the firm's decisions are taken by one almighty manager. Hence, organizational features – which will be considered in the last part of the chapter – are neglected here.

3.1. The firm's equilibrium

Let us start from a model where:

- $r \in \mathbf{R}$ is the profit of the firm,
- $J \in \mathbf{R}^+$ and $e \in \mathbf{R}^+$ are respectively the amount of search and the amount of effort by the manager in his professional activity,
- $c \in \mathbf{R}^{u+}$ is the manager's capability and $\gamma \in \mathbf{R}^{u+}$ his effective capability,
- $q \in \mathbf{R}^+$ is the production of the firm, sold on a market on which the price $p \gg 0$ is given,
- $y_j (1 \leqslant j \leqslant p)$ is the quantity of factor j consumed by the firm, bought on a market on which the price $p_j \gg 0$ is given.

The manager looks for:

$$\max\ U[r, J, q, e], \tag{7.122}$$

under the constraints:

$$r = pq - \sum_j p_j y_j, \tag{7.123}$$

$$\gamma = \gamma(c, e), \tag{7.124}$$

$$f[q, y_1, \ldots, y_p, \gamma, J] \gg 0. \tag{7.125}$$

In this model:

- The manager's utility increases with r, because of the consumption possibilities or because of the prestige and power generated by high profits: but it depends also on the size of the firm (source of prestige and power); on the amount of effort needed (which normally has a negative effect on utility); on the intensity of search (which may have a positive or negative effect on utility).

– The production function explicitly depends on the effective capability of the manager and on his search for information. In other words, we *reintroduce ability and imagination.*

A strategy $s = [q, (y_j)_{1 \leqslant j \leqslant p}, J, e]$ of the manager is an element in $\mathbf{R}^{(p+3)+}$. But, to be feasible, such a strategy must be in the set S for which $f \gg 0$.
Three natural assumptions are the following:

Assumption 4. *The set S of strategies for which $f \gg 0$ is a bounded, closed, strictly convex set in $\mathbf{R}^{(p+3)+}$.*

This assumption implies that, for given effort and search for information, the set of feasible production possibilities is strictly convex and that effort and search for information have decreasing returns to scale. It excludes the existence of thresholds of imagination or effort which may be necessary to master new technologies. . .

Assumption 5. $0 \in S$.

Assumption 6. *The manager's utility is a strictly concave function of its arguments r, J, q, e.*

Since r is linear in q and $(y_j)_{1 \leqslant j \leqslant p}$, utility U is also a strictly concave function in $\mathbf{R}^{(p+3)+}$.
As is well-known, under assumptions 4, 5 and 6, there can be for the firm one and only one equilibrium.
The maximum of U is then a well-defined function of $[p, (p_j)_{1 \leqslant j \leqslant p}]$ everywhere differentiable (see K.J. Arrow and F. Hahn (1971, p. 72)).
Assuming, in addition, that U, γ and f are jointly differentiable functions of their arguments, the following conditions are met if the equilibrium is regular:

$$U_r p + U_q - \lambda f_q = 0, \tag{7.126}$$

$$-U_r p_j - \lambda f_j = 0, \tag{7.127}$$

$$U_J - \lambda f_J = 0, \tag{7.128}$$

$$U_e - \lambda f_\gamma \gamma_e = 0, \tag{7.129}$$

the notation being obvious and λ being the positive Lagrange multiplier associated to (7.125). Relations (7.126) to (7.129) can be rewritten:

$$p = -U_q/U_r + d, \tag{7.130}$$

$$d = p_j f_q/f_j = -(U_J/U_r)f_q/f_J = -(U_e/U_r)f_q/f_\gamma \gamma_e, \tag{7.131}$$

d is *a marginal cost of production.* Contrary to the usual interpretation, it does not correspond to the marginal change of the *absolute minimum* of expenditures, but to the marginal change of the minimum of expenditures attainable in view of the manager's ability and information.

For the manager, the marginal cost of production is the same, whether the production is obtained through increased consumption of a production factor, through increased information or through increased effort. $(-U_J/U_r)$ and $(-U_e/U_r)$ can be considered as implicit prices for information and effort. It implies that J is developed to a level at which $U_J < 0$.

How will the manager react to a change in the surrounding market prices? By differentiating the relation (7.123) and (7.126) to (7.129), it is possible to show, that when p increases, the p_j's being kept constant:

– $\partial r/\partial p$ is positive, but smaller than in the traditional situation: the manager takes advantage of the improvement in the market situation to *increase his power* (increase in q), *to moderate his efforts or his search for information.*
– $\partial J/\partial p$ is negative: the manager is *less creative* when the pressure of necessity decreases.
– $\partial e/\partial p$ is negative: the manager transforms the increase in price, *partly into higher profits and partly into an easier life...*
– $\partial q/\partial p$ is positive, but higher than in the traditional situation: the price increase makes higher production profitable, but it also gives the manager a *better opportunity to look for power* (and hence to increase production for that very reason).

On the contrary, when the selling price drops, managers attach higher importance to profit, tend to abandon other objectives, increase search for new solutions and accept a very high level of efforts. This is especially true when a high penalty cost is incurred for $r < 0$.

Many authors, such as Baumol (1959), Penrose (1959), Williamson (1963), Cyert and March (1963), Marris (1964) and Lesourne (1973), have stressed the importance of such behaviour, commonly observed in practice. Cyert and March, for instance, have introduced the concept of "slack," the "slack" resulting from the difference between the parameters' real values and the values which would maximize profit.

The above model could be improved in different ways. If the manager is sensitive to comfort, the level of comfort may be a function of profit (which smoothes relations with shareholders) and of wages (which smoothes relations with the staff). Hence, an increase in the selling price will result in an increase of internal wages in the firm. This is one of the reasons why the higher wages tend to be, the greater is a firm's rate of profit.

If the manager's psychological factor ω is introduced, the utility function becomes a function $V[r, J, q, e, \omega]$ which is the same for all managers and the profit can be written as a result of V's maximization for q, c and ω given:

$$r = pq' - D[q, c, \omega]. \tag{7.132}$$

The expenditures D are a function of the production level, but also of the manager's ability and psychology.

Then, (7.130) can be expressed under the equivalent form:

$$p = \partial D(q, c, \omega)/\partial q - U_q/U_r. \tag{7.133}$$

We shall assume that, for p given, this equation in q has only one root $q(p, c, \omega)$. The firm will effectively produce this amount on a perfectly competitive market if:

$$pq(p, c, \omega) - D[q(p, c, \omega), c, \omega] \geq 0, \tag{7.134}$$

since a positive or zero profit is a condition of existence.

3.2. Perfect competition with a given number of firms

Let us consider now an economic sector with m firms $(1 \leq k \leq m)$ producing the same commodity from production factors with *given prices*.

To simplify the discussion, we shall assume that:

- for a given production, the level of expenditure of a firm k only depends on the manager's capability (c_k being now in $\mathbf{R}^+$),
- the marginal utility of production with respect to profit is, for each manager, a constant ϕ_k.

Equation (7.133) can then be written:

$$p = \partial D[q_k, c_k]/\partial q_k - \phi_k. \tag{7.135}$$

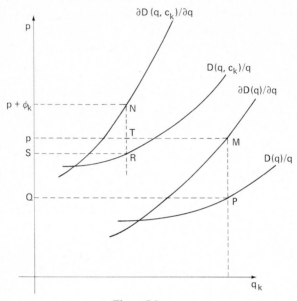

Figure 7.5

In figure 7.5, are pictured:

- the average and marginal cost curves $D(q)/q$ and $\partial D/\partial q$ corresponding to the manager with the highest possible capability,
- the average and marginal cost curves $D(q, c_k)/q$ and $\partial D(q, c_k)/\partial q_k$ corresponding to the manager of capability c_k,
- the horizontal line p defining the point of operation M chosen by a perfectly able manager interested only in profit,
- the horizontal line $p + \phi_k$ defining the point of operation N chosen by a manager of capacity c_k and of "psychology" ϕ_k.

The profit of the "perfectly managed firm" is represented by the area $pMPQ$, while the profit of the firm (c_k, ϕ_k) is the area $pTRS$, which is necessarily smaller. In case of figure 5, the increase in marginal cost reduces the production level, while the manager's psychology increases it.

For a given selling price, it is then possible to draw in the plane (c_k, ϕ_k) of managers' characteristics, the curve $g[c_k, \phi_k, p] = 0$ which separates the managers who will operate their firm at a positive profit from those which will make a loss and will be eliminated (figure 7.6).

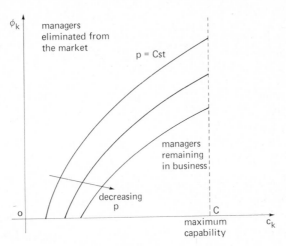

Figure 7.6

Point C represents the perfect manager of traditional theory. When p decreases, the surface of the characteristics of the managers remaining in business shrinks progressively.

(In the model of section 1, the managers would use effort e and search for information J to avoid being eliminated from the market.)

Figure 7.7 represents the offer $q[p, c_k, \phi_k]$ of a firm managed by an individual (c_k, ϕ_k) when the price is p. This offer is zero when the price p is smaller than the price p_k for which:

$$p_k q[p_k, c_k, \phi_k] - D[q(p_k, c_k, \phi_k), c_k] = 0, \tag{7.136}$$

p_k is the minimum price for which the manager can stay in business.

For $p > p_k$, $q[p, c_k, \phi_k]$ is an increasing function of p.

In other words, if M denotes the set of the m existing firms, to each value of p can be associated: a subset $K(p) \subset M$ of viable firms, a production $\sum_{k \in K(p)} q_k[p, c_k, \phi_k]$ of these firms.

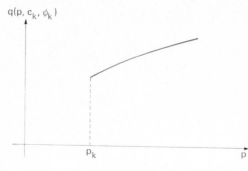

Figure 7.7

If a demand curve is defined separately it is possible to determine the market equilibrium corresponding to the highest number m' of firms so that $m' \leqslant m$.

What happens if one manager is replaced by another, more able and more search and effort-minded?

- If the new manager has the same ϕ_k, he will sell a higher production, since he is able to produce at a lower average and marginal cost. The total offer increasing, the price will drop. *The new manager will compel his competitors to increased search and additional efforts.*
- If the new manager has a higher ϕ_k, he will be able to use his efficiency to increase his production more than the maximization of profit would command. We interpret a well-known fact: managers who are at the same time efficient and interested in power impose very high pressure on their competitors.
- If the new manager has a lower ϕ_k, the production of the firm may not change and may even decrease. The price on the market may not decrease and may even become higher. The firm with a new manager will make higher profits, taking full advantage of the inefficiency of its competitors, but these will not suffer. Here again, the situation predicted by the model corresponds to observed facts.

Obviously, reality is more complex. Among other things, shareholders' decisions and takeovers play their part in eliminating incapable or insufficiently profit-minded managers. Nevertheless, it is true that, *for a given number of firms, differences between managers' characteristics do generate a dispersion in profits and sizes.*

3.3. Entrance of new firms on the market

Assume that the situation which has just been described prevails on the various markets: a potential manager of capability c_k considers the subset $H_k \in \mathscr{P}$ of professional roles he is informed about and among which he may select a possible activity.

Some of these roles $(h \in H_k^1)$ correspond to non-managerial positions which may be characterized by the wages, the prestige, the power, the comfort, etc., they generate. The individual appreciates the utility U_h he may get from such a choice.

Other roles $(h \in H_k^2)$ correspond to managerial position in the various sectors of the economy. Taking into account the prices p_h existing on the associated markets, the individual tries to estimate the profit r_{hk} and the production q_{hk} he would be able to get with an adapted behaviour, and hence the utility $U_h = U_h[h_1, r_{hk}, q_{hk}]$ he could enjoy as manager in an activity open to him.

Finally, the individual selects the h which maximizes U_h on H_k.

In such a model, the behaviour of the potential manager depends: on his information on the various activities and on the intensity of his creative search for possible roles, and on his specific interest for the various activities, this interest being partly conditioned by the prestige and power to which these activities give access in society.

To each price level p, it is then possible to associate, *other things being equal*, a subset $K'(p)$ of managers k of capability c_k and "psychology" ϕ_k who enter the market and offer a production $q_k'[p, c_k, \phi_k]$. Their supply function may be different, since they may, for instance. have access to new technologies.

If the demand curve is $q(p)$, the market equilibrium will be such that:

$$q(p) = \sum_{k \in K(p)} q_k[p, c_k, \phi_k] + \sum_{k \in K'(p)} q_k'[p, c_k, \phi_k]. \tag{7.137}$$

The model explains many essential features of real competition:

– If an activity h arouses great interest among individuals (for instance, if this activity makes it possible to be independent, free, powerful, ...), the flow of candidates may be high, even if prospects of profit are poor. A regular stream of bankruptcies will not prevent the continuous entry of new firms. In France, road transport, which does not seem to need very high capabilities, which offers personal liberty, and where entry does not imply high investment, has been a perfect example of such a situation for quite a long time.

– If an activity is prestigious, managers' selection will be severe and only very good managers will be able to stay in business. So the sector's efficiency will be high with respect to purely economic criteria. On the contrary, the existence of activities where management is chronically deficient should also be observed.

– Because of cultural norms, the able individuals of a society may despise productive activities and prefer to be bishops or civil servants. Commodity prices will tend to be high, the scarce competent managers enjoying exceptional competitive advantages. The standard of living of the greatest part of the population may be seriously damaged. It is a kind of "trahison des clercs," as Julien Benda would have said: the freedom of the more gifted in role-choices compels the others to suffer smaller consumptions. It is not surprising, then, that through the political system, a "coalition of individuals" will demand the creation of national firms by the State, with the double purpose: (1) of attracting or appointing (willingly or not) competent managers who will find in their jobs the satisfaction of motivations different from those enjoyed in the management of private firms, (2) of reducing the inequality of income distribution due to the high rents generated by the dispersion of managers' characteristics.

The efficiency of the economy appears, then, to depend greatly on social values, on individual attitudes, on levels of education, and not to be only the result of the nature of market organization.

Hence, the proposed model might be useful to help understand the coexistence in the same country of advanced and backward sectors; to compare the operation of decentralized and centrally-planned economies; to analyze the differences between developed and developing economies. Important topics in international trade could receive a precise theoretical treatment.

But this analysis is not the end of the story, for two reasons:

(1) Some managers may imagine solutions that change the nature of competition, thus transforming perfect competition into monopoly or some kind of oligopoly.

(2) Some managers may invent new products and thus create new activities.

Thus, the theory developed here seems necessary to be able to consider the change in the *structure* of the economic system induced by the behaviour of individuals.

Nevertheless, it has the defect of forgetting that a firm is an organization and not a one-man show. It is then important to consider whether the basic model can be used for organization theory.

4. Organization theory

As was stressed in chapter 3, an adequate theory of organization is as critical for economics as a theory of the individual, and obviously any improvement in the theory of the individual broadens the basis of organization theory.

The modest purpose of this section is to sketch some of the possibilities which could be explored, but obviously, the assumptions of period unicity and perfectly-known environment are not the most convenient for such an objective. The framework chosen by J. Marschak and R. Radner (1972) is far more suitable, but will be used only in the second volume of this book.

The present developments will heavily rely on J. Marschak's and R. Radner's pioneering work and on papers by A. Cotta (1974a, b, 1975), T. Marschak (1959), D. Soulié (1974), C. Carpentier (1974) and E. Ames (1971, 1974).

Starting from the simplest model and progressively broadening the hypothesis, we shall consider several kinds of teams: teams of geniuses, teams of n-tuples, teams of musketeers; and then two types of conflicting organizations: organizations of roundheaded Britons and organizations of influenceable fellows. The precise meaning of these words will be given below.

4.1. Teams of geniuses

As is well known, an organization is a team if all its members have the same utility function. These members are *geniuses* if they are not liable to perceptive biases and if their capability is infinite, so that they can forecast perfectly the consequences of their acts.

Consider a team of *two executives* who have to take n decisions d_i ($1 \leqslant i \leqslant n$), each d_i being, for instance, a vector in $\mathbf{R}^{m_i+}$. They can split the decisions between themselves in many different ways, each decision-structure corresponding to a given sequence π of n 0's and 1's.

(0 if a decision is taken by executive no. 2, 1 if it is taken by executive no. 1.) But before choosing, each executive may select:

- the amount $J_1 \in \mathbf{R}^+$ $(J_2 \in \mathbf{R}^+)$ of information of unit cost c_1 (c_2) he will buy,
- whether he will or will not transfer to his partner his knowledge of the information constraint, c being the cost of this transfer (in other words, he chooses a variable ε_{12} (resp. ε_{21}) equal to 1 if there is a transfer and 0 if there is no transfer).

Assume first that the context is *separable*, i.e.: (*i*) that the utility U is equal to the difference between a sum of partial payoffs r_i attributable to the various decisions and the information costs:

$$U = \sum r_i(d_i) - c_1 J_1 - c_2 J_2 - \varepsilon_{12} c - \varepsilon_{21} c; \qquad (7.138)$$

(*ii*) that, for each manager, there is an information constraint on each partial decision:

$$f_i[d_i, J_1] \geqslant 0, \quad 1 \leqslant i \leqslant n \quad \text{for manager 1,} \qquad (7.139)$$

$$g_i[d_i, J_2] \geqslant 0, \quad 1 \leqslant i \leqslant n \quad \text{for manager 2.} \qquad (7.140)$$

Three situations may be imagined, where each manager always has a perfect knowledge of U:

(a) Each manager ignores the other's information constraints and, in the absence of a message, does not take them into account. No message can be sent by a team-member before the selection of his information level.
(b) Each manager ignores the other's information constraints, but can make *guesses* (which he will take as certain) about them. No message can be sent by a team-member before the selection of his information level.
(c) A manager may transmit his information constraints to his colleague before any information search, according to a cost K.

Let us take *situation* (a). The problem is then well posed and for *each decision structure* π, four *information policies* can be studied:

(*i*) *No communication* $\varepsilon_{12} = \varepsilon_{21} = 0$. Each manager maximizes the payoff on the subset A_1 or A_2 of the decision types attributed to him. For instance, for manager 1 the behaviour $[(d_i)_{i \in A_1}, J_1]$ corresponds to:

$$\max \sum_{i \in A_1} r_i(d_i) - c_1 J_1, \tag{7.141}$$

subject to:

$$f_i[d_i, J_1] \geqslant 0, \qquad i \in A_1. \tag{7.142}$$

The resulting utility of the team can be written $V(\pi, 0, 0) = V_1(\pi, 0) + V_2(\pi, 0)$ where 0 stands for ε_{12} and ε_{21} in V, for ε_{21} in V_1 and for ε_{12} in V_2, and where V_1 and V_2 are the respective values of (7.141) for the two managers.

(ii) (iii) *One-way communication* $(\varepsilon_{12} = 1, \varepsilon_{21} = 0,$ or vice-versa). Assume $\varepsilon_{12} = 1$, $\varepsilon_{21} = 0$. The second manager will know now that d_i $(i \in A_2)$ has to be *either* in the set defined by:

$$g_i[d_i, J_2] \geqslant 0, \qquad i \in A_2, \tag{7.143}$$

or in the set defined by:

$$f_i[d_i, J_1] \geqslant 0, \qquad i \in A_2. \tag{7.144}$$

The first manager has the same behaviour as in (i), selecting J_1 only on the basis of his own needs. J_1 being given, he transfers the information (7.144). Thus, the second manager maximizes:

$$\sum_{i \in A_2} r_i(d_i) - c_2 J_2, \tag{7.145}$$

subject to:

$$f_i[d_i, J_1] \quad or \quad g_i[d_i, J_2] \geqslant 0, \qquad i \in A_2, \tag{7.146}$$

The resulting utility of the team can be written:

$$V(\pi, 1, 0) = V_1(\pi, 0) + [V_2(\pi, 1) - c]. \tag{7.147}$$

For π given, this strategy is preferable to the absence of communication if:

$$V_2(\pi, 1) - c > V_2(\pi, 0). \tag{7.148}$$

The case $(\varepsilon_{21} = 1, \varepsilon_{12} = 0)$ is dealt with in the same way.

(iv) *Two-way communication* $(\varepsilon_{12} = \varepsilon_{21} = 1)$. We may suppose that each manager will begin by choosing the information level on the basis of his own needs, finding the J_1 (resp. J_2) maximizing (7.141) under

(7.142). But after the exchange of information, each one will determine the d_i's such that, for instance, for the first:

$$\max_{i \in A_1} \sum r_i(d_i), \tag{7.149}$$

subject to:

$$f_i[d_i, J_1] \quad \text{or} \quad g_i[d_i, J_2] \geqslant 0, \qquad (i \in A_1), \tag{7.150}$$

the information levels being *given*.

The resulting utility of the team can be written:

$$V(\pi, 1, 1) = V_1(\pi, 1) + V_2(\pi, 1) - 2c. \tag{7.151}$$

Then, for each π, there is one or, exceptionally, several optimal information structures and a maximum utility $W(\pi)$. The best decision structure results from the solution of:

$$\max_{\pi} W(\pi). \tag{7.152}$$

Of course, the picture would be different with *situation* (b) where each manager is entitled to make a *guess* at the other's information constraints. For instance, in the case of one-way communication, the first manager would look for the d_i's $(i \in A_1 \cup A_2)$ and for the levels of information J_1 and J_2 such that:

$$\max_{i \in A_1 \cup A_2} \sum r_i(d_i) - c_1 J_1 - c_2 J_2 - c, \tag{7.153}$$

subject to:

$$f_i[d_i, J_1] \geqslant 0, \qquad i \in A_1, \tag{7.154}$$

$$f_i[d_i, J_1] \quad \text{or} \quad g_i^*[d_i, J_2] \geqslant 0, \qquad i \in A_2, \tag{7.155}$$

the asterisk recalling that a guess has been substituted to the real constraint. He would find decisions $(d_i^*)_{i \in A_1}$, $(d_i^*)_{i \in A_2}$, J_1^*, J_2^* but would, of course, put into operation only $(d_i^*)_{i \in A_2}$ and J_1^*.

The landscape is similar when the context is *not separable in terms of utility*, i.e.:

$$U = r[(d_i)_{1 \leqslant i \leqslant n}] - c_1 J_1 - c_2 J_2 - \varepsilon_{12} c - \varepsilon_{21} c. \tag{7.156}$$

Thus, *even in the no-communication case*, each manager has to make a guess about the other's information constraints. Having solved the problem in this way, he puts into operation the decisions under his control. When there is *one-way communication*, only the first manager has to make guesses if he communicates to the second *not only* the information constraints, but also the d_i's he has selected $(i \in A_1)$. The second can then behave optimally for the d_i's $(i \in A_1)$ and J_1 given. In *two-way communication*, J_1 and J_2 are chosen on the basis of guesses at information constraints, but the d_i's are selected optimally.

Situation (c) is easier. With an information cost K, either of the two managers may have knowledge of the total structure of the problem and take directly all decisions on information search and actions.

Obviously, if K is sufficiently small, situation (c) is optimal. The team is reduced to a one-man show, but it does not matter who decides.

In situation (a), the level of information costs is crucial for the information structure but for the decision structure, *the differences in environment are also crucial*. The man with the "looser" information constraints and the lower information costs should obviously carry great weight in the partitioning of decisions. "Trust the man on the spot," as elementary business wisdom recommends.

For teams of geniuses, the only interest of hierarchies is to save information costs, while leaving to the people with the best information the decisions which have the greatest impact on utility. (The cases (*ii*) (*iii*) of one-way communication above may be considered as a kind of hierarchy.)

But geniuses are not human. If we suppose the team members to be real people, while neglecting the differences between them, we are confronted with the interesting case of teams of *n*-tuples.

4.2. Teams of n-tuples

Two identical twins jointly manage a firm in a separable context. In comparison with the preceding case, they have the same limited capability $c \in \mathbf{R}^{u+}$ and must divide their time between the search for information $(J_1, J_2) \in \mathbf{R}^+$ and the effort to carry out adequately the decisions taken, $(e_1, e_2) \in \mathbf{R}^+$.

If manager 1 takes the decisions $i \in A_1$ and associates effort e_{1i} to each of them, he is able to obtain the payoff:

$$\sum_{i \in A_1} r_i(d_i)\delta(\gamma_{i1}), \tag{7.157}$$

where:

$$\gamma_{i1} = \gamma_i(c, e_{i1}), \qquad \gamma_{i1} \in \mathbf{R}^{u+}, \tag{7.158}$$

is the effective capability and $\delta(\gamma_{i1})$ *an efficiency coefficient*, which is positive, smaller than 1 and tending to 1 for an "infinite" capability. Simultaneously:

$$J_1 + \sum_{i \in A_1} e_{i1} \leqslant T,$$

is the time constraint, while (7.139) still represents the information constraint.

For geniuses, if the information constraints and the cost of information had been similar for the two executives, all decisions would have been taken by one. But this is no longer the case here. If an executive takes too many decisions, he has not enough time to get information or to carry out the decisions adequately. Hence, *his efficiency decreases.* This different type of decreasing returns generates a division of labour independent of information constraints and costs of information.

Assume, for instance, that the transmission cost between the managers is 0 and give the information constraints the expressions:

$$f_i[d_i, J_1 + J_2] \geqslant 0, \tag{7.160}$$

so that the team has information resulting from its joint efforts. For a partitioning π of the decisions, each manager will maximize (7.157) subject to (7.158), (7.159) and (7.160) and the utility will become a function of π; but there is no point in concentrating the information search and decision-making on one person, since his marginal efficiency would then be lower than that of his colleague.

Two main types of division of labour are conceivable, depending on the functions involved: a kind of horizontal specialization, each manager being in charge of some decisions and some information search; a vertical specialization, one of the managers being essentially an "information officer" and the other a policy-maker.

When the information costs and the differences in environment are reintroduced, a new insight into hierarchies is gained: *not only are the decisions with the greatest impact on utility left to the people with the best information, but these people are freed from making less important decisions in order to protect their efficiency.*

Hence, teams of n-tuples constitute an important step in any organization theory.

But since it is difficult to conceive General Motors managed by the Dionne quints, we have to introduce differences between people.

4.3. Teams of musketeers

Alexandre Dumas' musketeers had one motto: "Tous pour un, un pour tous." So they were a team. But they were very different indeed. They were different in capability, which restricted what they could do, and led them to forecast differently the consequences of the same decision in the same context.

Let us try to formulate this situation with two managers only, c_1 and c_2 being their respective capabilities in $\mathbf{R}^{u+}$. Manager 1 will try to maximize:

$$\sum_{i \in A_1} [r_i(d_i) + \varepsilon_i(d_i, \gamma_{i1})] \delta(\gamma_{i1}), \tag{7.161}$$

under the information constraints (7.139) and under the conditions:

$$\gamma_{i1} = \gamma_{i1}(c_1, e_{i1}), \tag{7.162}$$

$$J_1 + \sum_{i \in A_1} e_{i1} \leqslant T, \qquad i \leqslant I(c_1), \tag{7.163} \, (7.164)$$

where $\varepsilon_i(d_i, \gamma_{i1})$ is *a perception and forecasting error* which decreases with effective capability and $I(c_1)$ the subset in $\{1, \ldots, n\}$ of decisions liable to be taken by a manager with ability c_1.

The study of this case shows that additional reasons are found for a division of labour:

- their limited capability may prevent team-members from performing certain tasks;
- the differences in ability induce differences in the efficiency ratio. It is then logical to entrust to the most gifted the tasks having the greatest impact on utility;
- the perception and forecasting error introduces a bias depending on effective capability. This is an essential feature, since it implies that *two managers in the same informational context will take different decisions. One consequence is that a manager may find it convenient*

to transmit false information to his colleagues in order to correct his evaluation error.

For the first time, then, we come across this problem of cheating, which is so crucial in organization theory. To understand it, assume two decisions only, each being taken by one manager, and suppose a one-way communication from 1 to 2.

The payoff is:

$$U = [r_1(d_1) + \varepsilon_1(d_1, \gamma_{11})]\delta(\gamma_{11}) + [r_2(d_2) + \varepsilon_2(d_2, \gamma_{22})]\delta(\gamma_{22}) - c, \tag{7.165}$$

with:

$$\gamma_{11} = \gamma_{11}(c_1, e_{11}), \qquad \gamma_{22} = \gamma_{22}(c_2, e_{22}), \tag{7.166}$$

$$J_1 + e_{11} = T, \qquad J_2 + e_{22} = T, \tag{7.167}$$

$$f_1[d_1, J_1] \geqslant 0, \qquad f_2[d_2, J_2] \geqslant 0 \quad \text{or} \quad f_1[d_2, J_1'] \geqslant 0. \tag{7.168}$$

$f_1[d_2, J_1'] \geqslant 0$ being the information transmitted by 1 (with $J_1' \leqslant J_1$), which is "false" or incomplete, if $J_1' < J_1$. The team's payoff may be increased by choosing $J_1' \neq J_1$, i.e. by restriction in information which will limit the decision possibilities of the second manager. In other words, the first manager tries to prevent the consequences of his colleague's incapacity. However, the second manager, confident in his own judgement, might suspect his colleague's behaviour and take it into account, thus beginning a chain well known to psychiatrists.[8]

In practice, organizations are not teams. Each of their members has his own utility function, but the study of regulation constraints leads us to consider two situations: a situation in which the members are not sensitive to identification processes (the organization of round-headed Britons), a situation in which identification processes do exist (the organization of influencable fellows).

4.4. Organizations of round-headed Britons

Let us consider an organization composed of two individuals, a boss (Number 1) and a dependent (Number 2). Number 1 can fire his

[8] See for instance: R.D. Laing* (1961).

employee or behave in such a way that the employee will leave, and knows that in this case he gets a utility U_{10}. The employee can leave the organization or behave in such a way that he will be fired, and knows that in this case he gets a utility U_{20}.

Thus, a condition of existence of the organization is:

$$U_1 \geqslant U_{10}, \qquad U_2 \geqslant U_{20}. \tag{7.169}$$

Assume first that there is *no information problem.* The boss has only to decide on a partition π and a reward $\rho[(d_i)_{i \in A_2}] \in \mathbf{R}^+$ such that, in a separable context the boss utility will be:

$$\sum_{i \in A_1} r_{1i}(d_i)\delta(\gamma_{i1}) + \sum_{i \in A_2} r_{1i}(d_i)\delta(\gamma_{i2}) - \rho[(d_i)_{i \in A_2}]. \tag{7.170}$$

For $i \in A_1$, (d_i) and (e_{i1}) will maximize:

$$\sum_{i \in A_1} r_{1i}(d_i)\delta(\gamma_{i1}), \tag{7.171}$$

under the constraints:

$$\sum_{i \in A_1} e_{i1} \leqslant T. \tag{7.172}$$

For $i \in A_2$, (d_i) and (e_{i2}) will maximize:

$$\sum_{i \in A_2} r_{2i}(d_i)\delta(\gamma_{i2}) + \rho[(d_i)_{i \in A_2}], \tag{7.173}$$

under the constraints:

$$\sum_{i \in A_2} e_{2i} \leqslant T. \tag{7.147}$$

The payoff r_{2i} resulting from decision d_i is assumed to be different for individuals 2 and 1.

Knowing the "answer" $\{d_i[\rho]\}_{i \in A_2}$, $\{e_{i2}[\rho]\}$ of individual 2 to a reward function ρ, individual 1 will choose this function so as to maximize:

$$\sum_{i \in A_2} r_1(d_i)\delta(\gamma_{i2}) - \rho[(d_i)_{i \in A_2}]. \tag{7.175}$$

Of course, the above process takes into account conditions (7.169) which restrict the decision sets of the two organization members.

A few conclusions are immediately obvious in this example:

– *Rewards are used by the boss to distort the difference in utilities.*
– The boss accepts a dependent with a different utility function *because*

the increase in efficiency may more than offset the differences in objectives.

- In choosing the partitioning π, *the boss will keep for himself the decisions with a very high influence on his utility.*
- Of course, *the boss could also impose constraints on his subordinate's choices* of the type:

$$[d_i]_{i \in A_2} \in D, \tag{7.176}$$

D being a subset of a certain Euclidian orthant.
- *The behaviours of the boss and the employee will depend on the external conditions* defining U_{10} and U_{20}. For instance, the lower U_{20} and the higher U_{10}, the more freedom number 1 will have to obtain the desired behaviour from his employee.

Let us now *reintroduce the information constraints and transmissions:* we shall again find that the boss may consider his interest to send false messages in order to induce the required behaviour in his subordinate; while the employee may give wrong information in order to decrease pressure on himself.

With an organization of more than two members, other phenomena would appear, since coalitions may be created between subordinates to extract bigger advantages from the boss.

4.5. Organizations of influenceable fellows

Such organizations exhibit all the features previously described; but, in addition, the conditions prevailing in the organization and the various messages sent by its members may favour the development of an identification process which decreases the gap between the goals of Number 1 and the goals of the other members.

Imagine, for instance, the following situation: Number 1 has two subordinates, 2 and 3, who are the heads of two separate divisions of the organization. Number 1 divides the possible amount of investment $I \in \mathbf{R}^+$ into: I_1, which he keeps for himself (for instance, to build impressive headquarters); I_2 and I_3, which he attributes to his subordinates.

The boss is interested in the profit levels ρ_2 and ρ_3 reached by the two divisions. He sends the other members two kinds of messages: a precise message giving the profit targets of the divisions $m_2 \in \mathbf{R}^+$ and

$m_3 \in \mathbf{R}^+$, a general message m with the purpose of reinforcing the identification.

The utilities of the subordinates may be of the type:

$$U_2 = U_2[I_1, I_2, I_3, \rho_2, \rho_3, \delta(\rho_2, m_2, m), m_3, e_2], \qquad (7.174)$$

$$U_3 = U_3[I_1, I_2, I_3, \rho_2, \rho_3, \delta(\rho_3, m_3, m), m_2, e_3], \qquad (7.175)$$

and are supposed to show the following properties with respect to their arguments:

Beyond a certain level, an increase in I_1, is considered unjustified and decreases the subordinate's utility.

A subordinate's utility increases with the authorized amount of investment, but decreases when the amount given to the other subordinate becomes too important.

A subordinate's utility is maximal for a certain profit level of the division, since the subordinate may consider greater profit to be unjust. We shall assume that it is, on the contrary, a decreasing function of the other division's profit.

δ is the distance between the profit-target and the profit achieved. The bigger this distance, the smaller the utility, so that the individual will try, other things being equal, to decrease δ, unless the target is considered unrealistic. To a certain extent, δ is an increasing function of m; but if m is too big, the boss is not credible, the subordinate no longer believes in his propaganda and δ decreases with m.

The utility is an increasing function of the target given to the other. Finally, the utility is a decreasing function of effort $(e_2, e_3) \in \mathbf{R}^+$.

Now, for each subordinate, the production function can be written:

$$\rho_2 = \rho_2(e_2, I_2), \qquad \rho_3 = \rho_3(e_3, I_3). \qquad (7.179)$$

As for the boss, his utility is:

$$U_1 = U_1[I_1, \rho_2, \rho_3, m_2, m_3, m], \qquad (7.180)$$

if he is sensitive to the messages given.

The managers have to respect the investment constraint:

$$I_1 + I_2 + I_3 = I. \qquad (7.181)$$

For a given behaviour by the chief $(I_1, I_2, I_3, m_2, m_3, m)$, each subordinate has an answer function:

$$\rho_2 = \rho_2[\rho_3, I_1, I_2, I_3, m_2, m_3, m], \qquad (7.182)$$

$$\rho_3 = \rho_3[\rho_2, I_1, I_2, I_3, m_2, m_3, m]. \tag{7.183}$$

If the system (7.182)–(7.183) has only one solution in profit levels, then profit levels can be introduced in (7.180), leading to an expression of the boss's utility with respect to the arguments $I_1, I_2, I_3, m_2, m_3, m$:

$$U_1 = V[I_1, I_2, I_3, m_2, m_3, m]. \tag{7.184}$$

The maximization of V under the constraint (7.182) defines the chief's policy.

The important thing in this model is that the chief has *limited power* over the other members of the organization:

– He will decrease the efficiency of the organization if he keeps too much discretionary investment for himself, or if he distributes scarce resources unjustly between the members.

– He can induce the required behaviour by choosing the profit targets, but these targets have to be credible, otherwise they have a negative effect on real behaviour. Efficiency may also be undermined by inacceptable differences in the targets demanded of the various members.

– Finally, he may succeed, through his messages, in developing a feeling of identification with the organization; but extreme messages may have an adverse effect.

In his turn, subordinate 2, for instance, may claim that his production function is different:

$$\rho_2 = \rho_2^*(e_2, I_2), \tag{7.185}$$

or disguise his real level of effort in order to obtain a lower m_2. He may also join forces with subordinate 3 in order to obtain a reduction in targets for them both.

Of course, with more than two hierarchical levels or more than three organization members, it would be possible to discuss additional features of organizational life; but the important thing is to understand that *the main properties of any organization can be explained by suitable models of individual behaviour.*

4.6. Organization theory and the theory of the individual

This section has not really proposed an organization theory since it has not gone beyond a crude description of elementary models without even defining all the assumptions precisely. However, we hope it has established a few key conclusions:

- The basic model of chapter 1 is necessary to construct a formal organization theory; this model seems to comprise the main elements which have to be taken into account.
- The elaboration of a formal organization theory is indeed feasible, as we already knew from Marschak's and Radner's work; but it must be done by steps, each additional possibility in individual behaviour enlarging the spectrum of phenomena appearing in organizational life.
- The theory will, for two different reasons, be highly complex: first, because of the great number of cases and subcases to be considered; second, because of the nature of the mathematical structures involved.
- Nevertheless, even at the elementary level of our models, the conclusions reached are fully in agreement with the facts observed and this should strongly encourage research in this field. To replace purely empirical knowledge by a formal theory would probably help train managers and improve organizational procedures and structures; but it would also make it possible to replace the abstract firm of economic theory by more realistic models of organizations.

5. *Conclusions*

As many recent and independent papers have implicitly shown, a broader theory of the individual can contribute to significant improvements in many partial fields of economic theory.

Although, in each case, only some of the new features are introduced, the interest of a central model is that it shows how the new developments are interrelated. Hence, it may be a modest contribution to a broader general and comprehensive theoretical framework.

Nevertheless, the approach by topics is obviously not the only one. The introduction into economics of the model of the individual presented in this book may also be attempted through the leading theory of present-day economic science: the much criticized but inevitable general equilibrium theory.

Chapter 8

THE BASIC MODEL AND GENERAL EQUILIBRIUM THEORY

> *One of the major triumphs of mathematical economics during the past quarter of a century has been the proof of the existence of a solution for the neoclassical model of economic equilibrium.*
>
> H. Scarf
> *The computation of economic equilibria*

> *Le spécialiste le sait bien: sous quelque forme que ce soit, l'équilibre général n'a pas encore été construit de façon pleinement satisfaisante. Et, le plus souvent, il tend à minimiser (pour dire le moins) l'activité des agents économiques, comprise comme leur capacité de changer leur environnement.*
>
> F. Perroux
> *Unités actives et mathématiques nouvelles*

Introduction

General equilibrium theory plays a central part in economics, for reasons which are naturally obscure to the layman and are not even totally clear to many professional economists. These reasons seem to be the following:

- In any science, the analysis of dynamics encounters much greater difficulties than the study of statics. Frequently, evolutions through time are only understood by reference to equilibrium situations, whatever may be the stability areas of these situations. For instance, Keynes, after a sharp criticism of the economic science of his time, proposes a new equilibrium theory, though his thinking is dominated by the observation of short-term economic fluctuations.
- Since the dawn of their science, economists have been haunted by the very fact of the simultaneous determination of all the economic parameters, as a consequence of the independent actions of these agents, whatever the power relations between them may be. Hence the importance of any theory which, like the equilibrium theory, introduces simultaneously the behaviour of all the agents and all the flows of production and exchange.
- But if the equilibrium theory has taken the shape almost codified by A. Arrow and G. Debreu – the agents receiving only price messages which they cannot influence – the cause is a double one: on the one hand, this theory is the last stage of a long historical process which, since the "invisible hand" of the past, is the product of the dominant ideology of Western societies; on the other hand, this theory is the simplest possible with regard to the constraints imposed on behaviours, to the nature of information procedures and to the treatment of time.

For these three reasons, general economic theory, in spite of the oversimplified character of its assumptions and the poor adaptation of its conclusions to reality, still compels economists to define themselves with respect to it as classicists, iconoclasts or reformers.

Starting from an internal analysis of the postulates of the theory, these reformers realize that the insufficiencies are due less to the equilibrium notion itself than to the constraints imposed on it. Like Arrow, they reintroduce monopolistic firms. Like Benassy and Dreze, they accept rationing messages. Like Grandmont, they take money into account, they take two periods and consider in temporary equilibria the plans built by agents confronted with an uncertain future. Like F. Perroux, they try a still more ambitious synthesis. In short, they contribute to the transformation of equilibrium theory into one of the most potentially fruitful fields of economics.

This chapter is similarly inspired. It explores, very imperfectly, some of the consequences, in terms of general equilibrium theory, of the replacement of the conventional model of the individual by the basic model presented in chapter 6. Since our central purpose is to examine the usefulness of this model, and not to develop equilibrium theory in all its aspects, many sections present only the skeleton of global equilibrium models which could be fruitfully studied in depth. Hence, in view of the immensity of the field, the chapter must be considered as the definition of a research program rather than the final product of such an enterprise.

A normal order of presentation is to consider the successive stages usually covered in the writings on equilibrium theory:

- One section will deal with an *exchange economy*, in which the only problem is the allocation of resources among the various individuals. We shall have to study the consequences of the introduction of both satisfactions and individual social states; to examine the implications of perceptive illusions; to analyze the impact on general equilibrium of the rich network of constraints limiting individual behaviours, with greater or smaller capabilities.

- With the introduction of a *productive sector* generating private commodities, the following section will first explore the changes generated by the alteration of the model of the individual, when firms still maximize profits. It will then examine the consequences of the new policies of firms resulting from the abilities or the psychological traits of their managers. This analysis will lead directly to general equilibrium models where the social and economic aspects are closely entangled.

- The introduction of the *State* as an economic agent will be the "raison d'être" of the last section, which will not only take into account the public sector, but will also raise important problems of interactions between the economic and political spheres.

But, before this rather classical tour, we shall present some introductory comments on economies considered as noncooperative games. Such an analysis does not present much interest when the utility of each individual depends only on his own consumptions. But the picture changes radically when, *as in real life, no individual can really control his individual social state.*

1. Economies as noncooperative games

The structure of noncopperative games is in some ways richer, in others poorer, than the usual microeconomic models of an economy. But we may refer to it in order to understand some aspects of social interactions. Because of the differences from the usual models, the definition of an economy, of an equilibrium and of a Pareto optimal state is a prerequisite to the study of the conditions of equivalence between equilibria and optimal states.

1.1. Definition of an economy

The *social state* defining the situation of the society will be described by an n-dimensional vector of a subset X of $\mathbf{R}^{n+}$:

$$x = (x_i)_{1 \leqslant i \leqslant n}, \qquad x \in X, \quad X \subset \mathbf{R}^{n+}, \tag{8.1}$$

each x_i being called a *state variable*. The society is composed of m individuals, whose preferences on X are represented by independent utility functions $U_k(x)$ (with $1 \leqslant k \leqslant m$). Each individual has at his disposal an *action vector* a_k, an element of a subset A_k of $\mathbf{R}^{p_k+}$,

$$a_k = (a_{kh})_{1 \leqslant h \leqslant p_k}, \qquad a_k \in A_k, \quad A_k \subset \mathbf{R}^{p_k+}, \tag{8.2}$$

each a_{kh} being called an *action variable*.

At the society level, the set of individual actions corresponds to a *collective action* a:

$$a = (a_k)_{1 \leqslant k \leqslant m}, \qquad a \in A, \quad A = A_1 \times \ldots \times A_m. \tag{8.3}$$

The operation of the society, taking into account physical possibilities, technical knowledge, social organization, transforms any collective action into a social state:

$$x = x(a), \tag{8.4}$$

through an *operational relation* which is a mapping from A into X.

We shall assume that the various individuals choose their action variables independently and cannot cooperate. In other words, in this first part, *an economy is an m-person noncooperative game in which individual utility functions depend on a social state generated by the action variables chosen by all the individuals.*

Example: two individuals 1 and 2 have resources in amount A and B respectively $(A \in \mathbf{R}^+, B \in \mathbf{R}^+)$. They can consume them directly or use them to maintain a certain level of national defence.

The state variables are the consumptions Q_1, Q_2 and the national defence level D. The action variables are the contributions I_1 and I_2 to national defence. Hence:

$$x = (Q_1, Q_2, D), \qquad a = (I_1, I_2),$$

$x(a)$ being the set of relations:

$$Q_1 = A - I_1; \qquad Q_2 = B - I_2; \qquad D = D(I_1 + I_2). \tag{8.5}$$

The above formulation is *quite general.* An individual may act not only through the level of his exchanges, but also by imposing regulations, by restricting or diffusing information, by strengthening perceptive illusions, by giving commodities freely.

The *limitation* lies in the fact that he chooses, once and for all, an *action vector.* In an ordinary exchange economy, for instance, each individual k chooses *a vector-valued function* $\zeta_k(p)$ defining the levels $\zeta_{ik}(p)$ he is willing to buy when the price vector is p. The state variables are then: the price vector p defined by:

$$\sum_k \zeta_k(p) = 0, \tag{8.6a}$$

and the individual consumptions given by:

$$x_k = w_k + \zeta_k(p), \quad \forall k, \tag{8.6b}$$

where w_k is the vector of commodity quantities possessed initially by individual k. But, in the usual exchange model, the utility of individual k depends only on the consumption vector x_k.

1.2. Definition of an equilibrium and of a Pareto optimal state

A social state will be an equilibrium iff it is a Nash-equilibrium for the corresponding m-person noncooperative game.

Let us break down a into the action vector a_k of individual k and the set $\bar{a}_k$ of the action vectors of all the other individuals. By definition, a collective action a^* is an equilibrium action iff:

$$U_k[x(a^*)] = \max_{a_k \in A_k} U_k[x(a_k, \bar{a}_k^*)] \quad \forall k. \tag{8.7}$$

In an equilibrium, no individual has any advantage in modifying his action, since this never brings a utility increase.

A theorem due to Nash (Nash (1951), Berge (1957)) enables us to assert:

An economy has an equilibrium if: the sets A_k are convex; the mappings $x(a) (A \to X)$ and $U_k(x) (X \to \mathbf{R})$ are continuous and differentiable in their arguments $(\forall k, \forall x \in X, \forall a \in A)$; for any $\bar{a}_k$ and for every k, the maximum with respect to a_k of $U_k(x)$ is reached for one and only one vector a_k.

In the following, the conditions of this theorem will be assumed met.

A social state will be a relative Pareto optimum iff there are number $\lambda_k \in \mathbf{R}^+$ for every k, not all zeros such that $\sum_k \lambda_k U_k(x)$ is maximum with respect to $a \in A$.[1]

On the contrary:

A social state will be an absolute Pareto optimum iff there exist numbers $\lambda_k \in \mathbf{R}^+$ for every k, not all zeros such that $\sum_k \lambda_k U_k(x)$ be maximum with respect to $x \in X$.

Obviously any absolute optimum is a relative one, but the contrary is not true: the distribution of decisions between individuals, defined by the sets A_k, may be such that it prevents the group from reaching an absolute optimum.

Examples: (i) In the example of section 1, the economy, under rather general and well-known assumptions, has an equilibrium such that, with an obvious notation:

$$-U_{1A} + U_{1D}D_I = 0, \tag{8.8}$$

$$-U_{2B} + U_{2D}D_I = 0. \tag{8.9}$$

On the other hand, for a relative Pareto optimum, there exists λ_1 and λ_2 such that:

$$-\lambda_1 U_{1A} + \lambda_1 U_{1D}D_I + \lambda_2 U_{2D}D_I = 0, \tag{8.10}$$

and then an equilibrium state is not a relative optimum and a relative optimum is not an equilibrium state.

(ii) In an economy, there are only two collective goods consumed in quantities x and y. There are only two individuals, the first one

---

[1] A relative optimum is obviously a second-best optimum.

choosing the level of the first commodity, and the second one the level of the second: $a_1 = x$, $a_2 = y$ $(x \in \mathbf{R}^+, y \in \mathbf{R}^+)$.

Under well-known conditions, to any relative optimum may be associated numbers λ_1 and λ_2 not all zeros such that:

$$\lambda_1 U_{1x} + \lambda_2 U_{2x} = 0, \tag{8.12}$$

$$\lambda_1 U_{1y} + \lambda_2 U_{2y} = 0, \tag{8.13}$$

which defines a curve (c) of relative optima: $x = x[\lambda_2/\lambda_1]$, $y = y[\lambda_2/\lambda_1]$ in the plane (x, y) (figure 8.1). These relative optima are obviously also absolute optima.

But if there are social rules such that x is chosen first and:

$$x \leqslant \bar{x}, \tag{8.14}$$

$$y \leqslant \alpha x, \tag{8.15}$$

the only possible set in the plane (x, y) is the triangle OPM. P is a relative optimum which is not absolute if $\bar{x} < x_0$, x_0 corresponding to the absolute optimum Q.

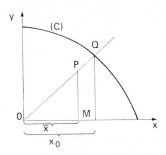

Figure 8.1

All these definitions are standard.

1.3. Properties of equilibrium states

With an obvious notation, if a set of actions a^* corresponds to an equilibrium, any small move of an individual around this equilibrium is such that:

$$dU_k \leqslant 0 \quad \text{or} \quad \sum_{ik} U_{ki}^* x_{ikh}^* \, da_{kh} \leqslant 0 \quad \text{for } \forall k. \tag{8.16}$$

Many economists, political scientists and sociologists[2] define the *power* of an individual with respect to another as the ability of the individual to influence the other's utility. (8.16) means that, *in an equilibrium state, no individual has any power over his own situation.*

More generaly, in a context $\bar{a}_k$, any small change in behaviour da_k of individual k, can be written:

$$da_k = u_k \, dl_k, \tag{8.17}$$

where u_k is the vector of norm one having the direction of da_k and dl_k is the norm of da_k. Hence, the change in utility of an individual k' as a consequence of the change in behaviour da_k of individual k is:

$$dU_{k'} = \sum_h (\sum_i U_{k'i} x_{ikh} u_{kh}) \, dl_k. \tag{8.18}$$

Let us denote:

$$f_{kk'} = (\sum_i U_{k'i} x_{ikh})_{1 \leqslant h \leqslant p_k}, \tag{8.18}$$

the vector of *marginal effects of the acts of individual k on the utility of individual k'*. (8.16) can be written:

$$dU_{k'} = (f_{kk'} \cdot u_k) \, dl_k, \tag{8.19}$$

or:

$$dU_{k'} = \pi_{kk'} \, dl_k; \tag{8.20}$$

$\pi_{kk'}$ will be called *the marginal power of individual k over individual k' in the behavioural situation a, in the direction u_k.*

Obviously, *in an equilibrium situation:*

– *For any possible direction of action, an individual has a negative or zero marginal power over his own situation.*
– On the contrary, *the marginal power of any individual over the others is, for almost every possible direction of action, different from zero.* In equilibrium, each individual would like to obtain a change in others' behaviour in a direction increasing his utility, but he is unable to obtain it since it is not compatible with the interests of others.

---

[2] See, for instance, A. Dahl* (1963–1970), M. Crozier* (1970) and F. Perroux (1975).

In a nonequilibrium situation, a set $u = (u_k)_{1 \leqslant k \leqslant m}$ of directions will be called *a path* and a path will be considered *feaisble* if, for every k, $\pi_{kk} \geqslant 0$, not all π_{kk}'s being zero. With each feasible path u, can be associated the $m \times m$ matrix:

$$M(a, u) = [\pi_{kk'}], \tag{8.21}$$

of the corresponding marginal powers. We shall call it the *power-structure of the path*. The sign-structure of this matrix is illustrative. For example:

– a matrix with only + signs corresponds to a path of *local solidarity*.
– a matrix with + signs in the first diagonal and − signs everywhere else corresponds to a path of local *antogonism*.
– a matrix with + signs in the first diagonal and 0's elsewhere corresponds to a path of *local independence*.
– a matrix like the following:

$$\begin{bmatrix} + & + & - & - & - \\ + & + & - & - & - \\ - & - & + & + & + \\ - & - & + & + & + \\ - & - & + & + & + \end{bmatrix}$$

features a *society divided locally into two classes*. Individuals 1 and 2 on one side, 3, 4 and 5 on the other side, exhibit solidarity, but these two groups have antoginistic interests.

In an equilibrium situation, to any feasible path corresponds a matrix with only negative or zero elements in the first diagonal.

The matrix $M(a, u)$ is a valuable source of information to understand the situation of each individual of the society and to identify the pressures he is under and the influences he exerts (see, for instance, Cotta (1974)).

It can be used to analyze the relations between equilibrium and relative optimum states.

1.4. Relations between equilibrium and relative optimum states

In a relative optimum, characterized by a vector $\lambda = (\lambda_k)_{1 \leqslant k \leqslant m}$

$$\sum_k \lambda_k \, dU_k \leqslant 0, \tag{8.22}$$

for all possible marginal changes in behaviour. In other words, for any path $u = (u_k)_{1 \leqslant k \leqslant m}$ such that u_k is, for every k, compatible with the constraints, in the state considered:

$$\sum_{k'} \lambda_{k'} \pi_{kk'}(u_k) = 0, \tag{8.23}$$

$\sum_k \lambda_k U_k$ may be viewed as a local collective utility, λ_k being the weight attributed to individual k. Hence, (8.23) means that, in a relative optimum, *no individual has the power to improve the collective situation.*

A relative optimum of the economy $\{(U_k)_{1 \leqslant k \leqslant m}, x(a)\}$ *is then an equilibrium for the economy composed of the same number of individuals k, taking the same decisions a_k but having all the utility $\sum_k \lambda_k U_k$ of a team.*

But under what conditions is an equilibrium state a relative optimum?

Consider an equilibrium state a^*. In such a state, the directions u_k compatible with the constraints for individual k are in a set v_k^*,

$$u_k \in v_k^*. \tag{8.24}$$

For a^* to be a relative optimum, it is necessary that, for any path u^* around a^*, compatible with (8.24):

$$\sum_{k'} \lambda_{k'} \pi_{kk'}^*(u_k) = 0, \tag{8.25}$$

for numbers $\lambda_{k'}$ positive or zero, but not all zeros. We shall call (8.25) *condition (D)*. Condition (D) is very special, but it is possible to find more meaningful conditions which imply it.

One obvious possibility is to assume that, in the equilibrium situation, the vector of marginal effects of the behaviour of k on the utility of k', is, for all k and k' colinear to the vector of marginal effects of the behaviour of k on his own utility. In other words, a set of numbers $\alpha_{kk'}^*$ is supposed to exist with:

$$f_{kk'} = \alpha_{kk'}^* \cdot f_{kk}, \tag{8.26}$$

which implies:

$$\pi_{kk'} = \alpha_{kk'}^*(f_{kk} \cdot u_k) = \alpha_{kk'}^* \cdot \pi_{kk}. \tag{8.27}$$

Then, the fact that each individual is in a local maximum of utility has for consequence that (8.25) is verified.

We shall call this condition (α):

If $\alpha_{kk'}^* > 0$ individual k is locally *in total agreement* with k',

$\alpha^*_{kk'} < 0$ individual k is locally *in total disagreement* with k',
$\alpha^*_{kk'} = 0$ individual k is locally *independent* from k'.

Conditions more specific than (α) are the following:

- *Condition of independence* (I) with $\alpha^*_{kk'} = 0$ for k, k' with $k \neq k'$;
- *Condition of local unanimity* (U) with $\alpha^*_{kk'} > 0$ for k, k' with $k \neq k'$;
- *Condition of local antagonism* (A) with $\alpha^*_{kk'} < 0$ for k, k' with $k \neq k'$;
- *Condition of class breakdown* (C) with $\alpha^*_{kk'} > 0$ when the two individuals belong to the same class and $\alpha^*_{kk'} < 0$ when they belong to different classes.

Unanimity corresponds to one class only, antagonism to m classes. The various conditions introduced are linked as shown in figure 8.2.

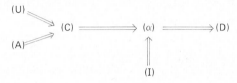

Figure 8.2

The reader should note that condition (D) is necessary but by no means sufficient for the equilibrium to be a relative optimum.

This analysis suggests that it would be useful to build a general theory of social interactions based on noncooperative game theory and to search for the conditions under which equivalences between Pareto optima and equilibria would exist.

But it would be necessary, as we have seen for exchange economies, to replace by function spaces the euclidian spaces of the action vectors.

2. *Exchange economies*

The purpose of this section is clear: what can be said about general equilibrium theory in exchange economies, when the model describing individual behaviour and constraints is enriched? Research along these lines has been conducted by many authors, in particular F. Hahn (1971), M. Kurz (1974a), (1974b), Drèze (1975), Younès (1975), Benassy (1975),

Dupuy (1974), Becker (1974). The plan will be the one announced above, which means that we shall examine:

(1) the social interactions resulting from the generalization of the individual social states,
(2) the consequences of the existence of perceptive illusions,
(3) the influence of the behavioral constraints,
(4) the effects due to differences between individual capabilities.

2.1. Social interactions through individual social states

Two rather different situations have to be looked at: in the first we exclude *cumulative effects* due to the fact that the utility of an individual depends on the utility of another *and reciprocally*. In the second, we explicitly take into account these interactions.

Let us consider first an exchange economy where these are only purely private consumptions, composed of m individuals $(1 \leqslant k \leqslant m)$ and p resources $(1 \leqslant j \leqslant p)$, $q_{jk} \in \mathbf{R}^+$ denoting the quantity of resource j enjoyed by individual k. The total quantities available b_j are given. Hence:

$$\sum_k q_{jk} = b_j, \qquad q_{jk} \geqslant 0. \tag{8.28}$$

Let us assume that the state of the economy may be represented by the suite:

$$E = (q_{jk})_{\substack{1 \leqslant k \leqslant m, \\ 1 \leqslant j \leqslant p}} \tag{8.29}$$

and that the kth individual's social state e_k is a suite extracted from E:

$$e_k = (q_{jk'})_{(j,k') \in I_k}, \tag{8.30}$$

where $I_k \subset M \times P$ with $M = \{1, \ldots, m\}$, $P = \{1, \ldots, p\}$. Consequently, k's utility is a function of e_k, which means that *the utility U_k of each individual may depend on the consumptions of the other individuals*.

To characterize e_k, coefficients $\delta_{jkk'}$, will be introduced with:

$$\delta_{jkk'} = 1 \Leftrightarrow (j, k') \in I_k, \qquad \delta_{jkk'} = 0 \Leftrightarrow (j, k') \notin I_k. \tag{8.31}$$

Simultaneously, since participation procedures are excluded in order to simplify the exposé, a consumption q_{jk}, can be controlled only by one individual k. It is then possible to introduce: the social state f_k individually controlled by k:

$$f_k = (q_{jk'})_{(j,k')\in J_k}, \quad \text{with } J_k \subset M \times P; \tag{8.32}$$

coefficients $\varepsilon_{jkk'}$ such that:

$$\varepsilon_{jkk'} = 1 \Leftrightarrow (j,k') \in J_k, \quad \varepsilon_{jkk'} = 0 \Leftrightarrow (j,k') \notin J_k, \tag{8.33}$$

but contrary to $\delta_{jkk'}$, $\varepsilon_{jkk'}$ is equal to 1 for one k only.[3]

In such an economy, we may consider *several types of states*:

(i) *A state E will be Pareto optimal iff there are m numbers $s_k > 0$ such that the linear form $\sum_k s_k U_k$ is maximum under the constraints (28).*

Associating with the constraints positive or zero Lagrange multipliers μ_j and λ_{jk} and a slack variable u_{jk}, we shall consider the function H:

$$H = \sum_k s_k U_k - \sum_j \mu_j (\sum_k q_{jk} - b_j) + \sum_{jk} \lambda_{jk}(q_{jk} - u_{jk}^2),$$

which gives the conditions:

$$\lambda_{jk} u_{jk} = 0, \quad \forall k \in M, \ j \in P, \tag{8.34}$$

$$\sum s_k \delta_{jkk'} U_{jkk'} - \mu_j + \lambda_{jk} = 0, \quad \forall j \in P, \tag{8.35}$$

and, as is well-known, either $u_{jk} = 0$, $q_{jk} \geqslant 0$ and $\lambda_{jk} = 0$ or $u_{jk} > 0$, $q_{jk} = 0$ and $\lambda_{jk} > 0$.

(ii) *A state E will be called a market state iff there are prices $p_j \geqslant 0$, such that the utility of each individual is maximum under the budget constraint when he chooses the part of the social state he controls, and the quantity constraints are satisfied for the whole economy.*

Let us introduce coefficients $o_{jkk'}$ equal to 1 or 0 according to the fact that individual k has to pay out of his income the consumption (j, k'). In the usual case:

$$o_{jkk'} = 1 \quad \text{if } k' = k; \qquad o_{jkk'} = 0 \quad \text{if } k' \neq k.$$

Hence, individual k maximizes:

$$U_k\{(q_{jk'})_{(j,k')\in Ik}\}, \tag{8.36}$$

---

[3] As in chapter 4, a more general hypothesis would be to assume that k can choose only $q_{jk'}$, in a subset of $\mathbf{R}^+$, or f_k in a subset of $\mathbf{R}^{|J_k|+}$.

under the constraints:

$$\sum_j p_j o_{jkk'} q_{jk'} = \rho_k, \qquad q_{jk'} \geq 0, \tag{8.37}$$

ρ_k being the income of individual k.

Associating to the income constraint a positive Lagrange multiplier $1/\sigma_k$, and to the inequality constraints positive Lagrange multipliers $v_{jk'}$, the following conditions prevail in a market state:

$$\sigma_k \varepsilon_{jkk'} \delta_{jkk'} U_{jkk'} - o_{jkk'} \varepsilon_{jkk'} p_j + \sigma_k \varepsilon_{jkk'} v_{jk'} = 0, \forall j \in P, \forall k, k' \in M, \tag{8.38}$$

with:

$$v_{jk'} > 0 \text{ implying } q_{jk'} = 0, \qquad v_{jk'} = 0 \text{ implying } q_{jk'} \geq 0.$$

We shall interpret these relations, first, for an individual k who has control. If *individual k has control of $q_{jkk'}$*:

$k \neq k'$: (a) $\delta_{jkk'} = 0$. The individual is not concerned by $q_{jk'}$.
- Generally $o_{jkk'} = 0$ and relation (8.31) reduces to an identity $0 = 0$. The individual has no basis whatsoever for any action.
- If, exceptionally $o_{jkk'} = 1$ (he has to pay), he will choose $q_{jkk'} = 0$. This would be the case for a gift to a person to whom you are indifferent.

(b) $\delta_{jkk'} = 1$. The individual is concerned by $q_{jk'}$.
- If he has not to pay for it, $o_{jkk'} = 0$ and he will choose the preferred value of the parameter:

$$U_{jkk'} = 0. \tag{8.39}$$

- If he has to pay, $o_{jkk'} = 1$ and the individual determines the consumption $q_{jk'}$ (which may very well not be for himself) in such a way that:

$$\sigma_k U_{jkk'} = p_j \qquad (\text{if } v_{jk'} = 0).$$

$k = k'$: (a) $\delta_{jkk} = 0$. The individual is not concerned by q_{jk}.
- Since generally $o_{jkk} = 1$, the individual will take $q_{jk} = 0$.
- If, exceptionally, $o_{jkk} = 0$, any action is indifferent.

(b) $\delta_{jkk} = 1$. The individual is concerned by consumption q_{jk}.

- Usually $o_{jkk} = 1$ and the individual will select a value q_{jk} such that:

$$\sigma_k U_{jkk} = p_j \qquad (\text{if } v_{jk} = 0). \tag{8.41}$$

- If, exceptionally, $o_{jkk} = 0$, he will select the bliss consumption:

$$U_{jkk} = 0. \tag{8.42}$$

When an individual k has no control of $q_{jkk'}$, ($\varepsilon_{jkk'} = 0$), he has to accept passively the consumptions he is concerned with ($\delta_{jkk'} = 1$), whether they are his own or not.

This formulation makes it possible to reinterpret one of the basic problems of economics: *the equivalence of market states and of Pareto optimal states.*

This equivalence is obtained, for instance, in two cases:

(a) The first is a case of *separability:*

- Any individual is concerned by the consumptions he controls:

$$\delta_{jkk'} = 1 \quad \text{if } \varepsilon_{jkk'} = 1.$$

- Any individual is concerned only by the consumptions he controls:

$$\delta_{jkk'} = 0 \quad \text{if } \varepsilon_{jkk'} = 0.$$

- Any individual pays for the consumptions he controls and for these only:

$$o_{jkk'} = 0 \quad \text{if } \varepsilon_{jkk'} = 0.$$

$$o_{jkk'} = 1 \quad \text{if } \varepsilon_{jkk'} = 1.$$

Since it may be supposed that $\delta_{jkk} = 1$ ($\forall j \in P$), this case corresponds to the elementary result of economic theory:

There is an identity between optimal states and market states if: For each individual, there is an identity between the consumptions he is concerned with and the consumptions he controls, In the market states, an individual controls only the consumptions he pays.

The very special nature of the situation usually considered becomes cristal clear, since it supposes that the three notions of *concern, control* and *payment* are identical. In other words, if an index x is introduced to replace $(j, k') : 1 \leqslant x \leqslant |M \times P|$, three matrices $m \times |M \times P|$ may be considered:

- A *matrix of concern* C, the element c_{kx} of which is equal to 1 or 0, according to whether individual k is or is not concerned by q_x.
- A *matrix of control* T, the element γ_{kx} of which is equal to 1 or 0, according to whether individual k controls or does not control q_x. This matrix has, per column, one and only one element equal to 1.
- A *matrix of payment* D, the element d_{kx} of which is equal to 1 or 0, according to whether individual k pays or does not pay for q_x. This matrix exists only in a market state and contains, per column, one and only one element equal to 1.

The condition $C = T = D$ ensures the identity of optimal and market states.

In such a case, it can be said that *the preferences and market structures are such that no individual exerts power over any other.*

(b) The second case is the case of *the family*. The individuals are divided into two classes: the *children* and the *fathers*, each child having one and only one father.

The children have no income. Each father is concerned by his own consumptions and by the consumptions of his child(ren). He pays for both of them.

A market state is optimal iff, for any couple of a father k and a child k':

$$U_{jkk'} = \alpha_{kk'} U_{jkk'}, \qquad \alpha_{kk'} > 0. \tag{8.43}$$

In other words *the father accepts the child's preferences*, which means that his utility can be considered as a function of the child's utility. The situation is equivalent to a situation in which *the father would transfer to the child a part of his income*, this part depending on the level of $\alpha_{kk'}$.

The market situation is no longer optimum if the children have an income of their own and if the fathers control only some of their children's consumptions. Denote, for instance, j_1 the child's consumptions selected by the father and j_2 the ones selected by the child himself. The child looks for:

$$\max_{q_{j_2 k'}} U_{k'}[q_{j_1 k'}, q_{j_2 k'}] \quad \text{with} \sum_{j_2} p_{j_2} q_{j_2 k'} = \rho_{k'}, \tag{8.44}$$

while the father determines, *for $q_{j_2k'}$ given:*

$$\max_{q_{jk}, q_{j_1k'}} U_k\{q_{jk}, U_{k'}(q_{j_1k'}, q_{j_2k'})\} \quad \text{with} \quad \sum_j p_j q_{jk} + \sum_{j_1} p_j q_{j_1k'} = \rho_k.$$

(8.45)

The child would increase his utility if he received from the father, instead of $(q_{j_1k'})$, the income transfer:

$$\rho_{kk'} = \sum_{j_1} p_{j_1} q_{j_1k'},$$

(8.46)

since he would choose differently his consumptions $q_{j_2k'}$; but *the decision structure prevents the father from making a transfer.*

Such a possibility is explicitly available in the *market states with transfers.*

(c) *A state E will be called a market state with transfers if it is a market state and if each individual may transfer parts of his income to other individuals.*

Consider, for instance, a child (utility U') who controls all his consumptions q' and has an income ρ'. His father, who has an income ρ, controls only his consumptions q and accepts the child's preferences (utility $U(q, U')$) will normally transfer to his child an income t. From

$$\max U'(q'),$$

(8.47)

$$pq' = \rho' + t, \quad t \geqslant 0,$$

(8.48)

the father deduces U' as a function of t and then looks for:

$$\max U[q, U'(t)],$$

(8.49)

$$pq = \rho - t, \quad t \geqslant 0.$$

(8.50)

If ρ' is small and if the father cares about his child, t will be positive.

Such a situation has been explicitly studied by Becker in his "Theory of social interactions" (1974):

"The head maximizes a utility function that depends on the consumption of all family members subject to a budget constraint determined by family income and family consumption. In this sense, then, a family with a head can be said to maximize "its" consistent and transitive utility function of the consumption of different members subject to a budget constraint defined on family variables. The family's utility function is identical with that of one member, the head, because his concern for the welfare of other members, so to speak, integrates all the members' utility function into one consistent "family" function. That is, a "family's" utility function is the same as that of one of its members not because this member has dictatorial power over other members, but because he (or she!) cares sufficiently about all other members to transfer resources voluntarily to them."

Obviously, a market state with transfer is optimal when the only interactions are within families, each person controlling his consumptions and paying for them, each father (or mother) being sufficiently concerned by his (or her) children's consumptions and accepting their preferences.

This analysis shows how important it would be to *study systematically the impact on the economy of the structures of the matrices of concern and control*, since the very strong assumptions usually made on these structures have prevented the introduction into economics of extremely important cases of social interactions.

Till now, *the feedback effects* of interactions between individuals have been excluded. In the preceding paragraph, *fathers did care about children, but children did not bother about their father's situation.*

Here, on the contrary, will be examined the cases of *mutual love* or *mutual hatred*.

2.2. Mutual love

Two individuals (1 and 2) have to divide between them two commodities (1 and 2) available in quantities q_1 and q_2. With an obvious notation, their utilities U_1 and U_2 are:

$$U_1 = F[U_2, q_{11}, q_{12}], \qquad (8.51)$$

$$U_2 = G[U_1, q_{21}, q_{22}], \qquad (8.52)$$

with:

$$q_{11} + q_{12} = q_1, \quad q_{21} + q_{22} = q_2, \quad q_{11}, q_{12}, q_{21}, q_{22} \geqslant 0. \quad (8.53)$$

F and G being differentiable increasing functions of their arguments. In such a situation, the happiness of 1 strengthens the happiness of 2, which in its turn increases the happiness of 1. "Ils vivent d'amour et d'eau fraîche" says a popular expression.

Take, for instance, the two functions:

$$U_1 = U_2 q_{11} q_{12}, \tag{8.54}$$

$$U_2 = U_1 + q_{21} q_{22}, \tag{8.55}$$

which exhibit the required properties.

Resolving (8.54) and (8.55) in U_1 and U_2, we get:

$$U_1 = q_{11} q_{12} (q_1 - q_{11})(q_2 - q_{12})/(1 - q_{11} q_{12}), \tag{8.56}$$

$$U_2 = q_{21} q_{22}/(1 - q_{11} q_{12}). \tag{8.57}$$

The shape of the indifference curves in the Edgeworth's box is of the utmost interest (figure 8.3):

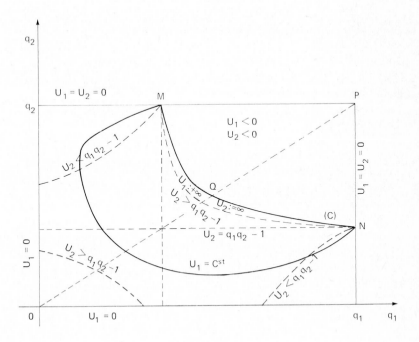

Figure 8.3

Both utilities are infinite positive near the curve (C):

$$q_{11}q_{12} = 1, \qquad\qquad\qquad\qquad (8.58)$$

for $1 - q_{11}q_{12} > 0$.

The curve (C) crosses the sides of the box at points M and N such that:

$$q_{11} = 1/q_2, \qquad q_{12} = 1/q_1.$$

The utility of the *first* individual is zero as soon as one of the *four* consumptions is zero, i.e. on the four sides of the box. All the indifference curves of this individual pass through M and N where the utility U_1 is not defined. They have, for $U_1 > 0$, the shape indicated on figure 8.3 which results from a progressive alteration of the polygonal line Mq_2Oq_1N.

The utility of the *second* individual is zero when one of his consumptions is zero, i.e. on two sides of the box only. All the indifference curves pass through M and N where U_2 is not defined.

For $U_2 = q_1q_2 - 1$, the indifference curve is composed of the vertical of M and the horizontal of N. If $U_2 < q_1q_2 - 1$, the indifference curve is decomposed into two parts going southwestwards from M and N. If $U_2 > q_1q_2 - 1$, one part of the indifference curve joins M to N (part I), while the other has the usual shape around the origin (part II). In this case, two positions are equivalent for the individual: high personal consumptions with low consumptions for the other (part I), lower personal consumptions with greater consumptions for the other (part II).

The equilibrium position of the couple should be on (C), but where on this curve? If we admit that it is also on the *contract curve*, locus of the points of tangency between the indifference curves of the two individuals, it will be in Q, since here the contract curve is the first diagonal of the box. *The utilities of both individuals are infinite.*

Many readers may think that this example is a mathematical curiosity. I am not so sure and I suspect that, as sociologists would recognize, strong interactions between individuals' preferences lead to consequences which may be observed in practice, but have been, until now, excluded from economics, because of simplifying assumptions.

Is hatred or jealousy more compatible than love with conventional economic theory?

2.3. Mutual hatred or jealousy

In the case of the Edgeworth's box, the result is obvious: the utility of consumptions q_{11} and q_{12} is increased by the fact that these consumptions decrease the amounts available to individual 2 and hence his utility. The situation is similar for individual 2 with respect to 1. If the system of utility functions is written:

$$U_1 = F[U_2, q_{11}, q_{12}], \tag{8.59}$$

$$U_2 = G[U_1, q_{21}, q_{22}], \tag{8.60}$$

each function being decreasing in its utility variable and increasing in its consumptions, this system can be solved in terms of utilities:

$$U_1 = U_1[q_{11}, q_{12}], \tag{8.61}$$

$$U_2 = U_2[q_{21}, q_{22}], \tag{8.62}$$

and the indifference curves in the Edgeworth's box exhibit the *usual shape*, though they are, of course, like the contract curve, altered by jealousy or hatred.

But the influence of this factor is more disturbing in the case of three individuals, two of them being jealous of each other, but having to enjoy jointly a quantity q_0 of a commodity given by the third one. With an obvious notation, the system is such that:

$$U_1 = U_1[U_2, q_0], \tag{8.63}$$

$$U_2 = U_2[U_1, q_0], \tag{8.64}$$

$$U_3 = U_3[q_3], \tag{8.65}$$

$$q_0 + q_3 = q, \tag{8.66}$$

q_3 being given and all the q's being positive or zero. An example of this situation is given by the functions:

$$U_1 = q_0^\alpha - k_1 U_1, \qquad 0 < \alpha < \beta < 1, \tag{8.67}$$

$$U_2 = q_0^\beta - k_2 U_2, \qquad 0 < \gamma < 1, \tag{8.68}$$

$$U_3 = q_3^\gamma, \qquad k_1 \geqslant 0, \ k_2 \geqslant 0. \tag{8.69}$$

If the individuals are *pure egoists* ($k_1 = k_2 = 0$), they are willing to consume as much of the commodity as possible.

If they are jealous $(k_1 > 0, k_2 > 0)$, an easy computation shows that:

$$dU_1/dq_0 = \alpha q_0^{\beta-1}[1/(q_0)^{\beta-\alpha} - k_1\beta/\alpha]/(1 - k_1k_2), \tag{8.70}$$

$$dU_2/dq_0 = aq_0^{\beta-1}[\beta/\alpha - k_2/(q_0)^{\beta-\alpha}]/(1 - k_1k_2). \tag{8.71}$$

When $k_1k_2 < 1$, i.e. when *mutual dislike is moderate*, dU_1/dq_0 is positive for $0 < q_0 < q_{01}$, with:

$$q_{01} = [\alpha/k_1\beta]^{1/(\beta-\alpha)}, \tag{8.72}$$

and negative afterwards, while dU_2/dq_0 is negative for $0 < q_0 < q_{02}$, with,

$$q_{02} = [\alpha k_2/\beta]^{1/(\beta-\alpha)}, \tag{8.73}$$

and positive afterwards. Since $q_{02} < q_{01}$, the situation is the following:

q_0	0		q_{02}		q_{01}	
dU_1/dq_0		+		+	0	−
dU_2/dq_0		−	0	+		+

The first individual, because of jealousy, does not want to go beyond a certain level of consumption to limit the utility of his enemy. The second, on the contrary, prefers to be totally deprived, being dominated by jealousy; or to enjoy a very high consumption, being dominated by narcissism.

When $k_1k_2 > 1$, i.e. when *mutual dislike is high*, the situation is reversed $(q_{01} < q_{02})$ and the above table becomes:

q_0q_0	0		q_{01}		q_{02}	
dU_1/dq_0		−	0	+		+
dU_1/dq_0		+		+	0	−

Hence, we have to accept the conclusion that *to explore interactions between utilities is an important task for economic theory*. It should lead to the interpretation of a certain number of facts which are not accounted for by the usual independence assumptions.

The existence of perceptive illusions opens another set of possibilities to individuals who are willing to influence the utilities of their colleagues.

2.4. The manipulation of perceptive illusions

A special way of exerting power over other economic agents is partially to control their perceptions. This goes far beyond advertising, to include: the actions of university alumni to create a good image of their past institution; the moves of political parties seeking to be favourably perceived (for instance, the operation "Open doors" of the French Communist Party); the messages included by firms in their reports to shareholders; the military parades organised by the French Government on the 14th of July; the frescoes representing Hell painted by monks in the Middle Ages to freighten the faithful. Of course, counter-measures are possible and collective decision theory has studied occasions when cheating is advantageous for an individual.

To try to understand the effect on economic equilibrium of the manipulation of perceptive illusions, we shall examine three different situations:

(i) *A market economy where each individual controls his own consumptions and pays for them, but where only one individual is allowed to send messages* (notation is the same as in section 2.1).

From elementary economics, it is well-known that, in the absence of actions on perceptive illusions, the equilibrium price-vector p is given by the p equations:

$$\sum_k q_{jk}(p, b^k) = b_j, \tag{8.74}$$

where b^k is the vector of initial resources for individual k ($\sum_k b_k^j = b_j, \forall j$) and $q_{jk}(p, b^k)$ the demand of commodity j by individual k when he has initial resources b^k and is confronted with a price-system p. These equations verify the relation:

$$\sum_j p_j \sum_k q_{j,k}(p, b^k) = \sum_j p_j b_j. \tag{8.75}$$

The price vector is defined up to a scalar.

Imagine now that one individual (individual 1) has the power to use, out of his resources b^1, an amount a^1 ($a^1 \in \mathbf{R}^{p+}$) to send a message $x \in \mathbf{R}^+$ in order to alter others' utilities and hence others' demands.

The demands become a set of functions $q_{jk}[p, b^k, x]$, for $\forall j$ and $k = 2, \ldots, m$ and the new equilibrium price-vector $p(a^1)$ is given by the equations:

$$a_j^1 + q_{j1}(p, b^1 - a^1) + \sum_{2 \leqslant k \leqslant m} q_{jk}[p, b^k, x] =: b_j, \tag{8.76}$$

where $q_{j1}(p, b^1 - a^1)$ is the demand of individual 1, when his vector of initial resources is $b^1 - a^1$, and the price-system p. Naturally:

$$x = x(a^1), \tag{8.77}$$

will denote the relation between the resources consumed for "information" and the level of the message (a mapping from $\mathbf{R}^{p+}$ into $\mathbf{R}^+$). Consequently, individual 1's utility is a function:

$$U_1\{q_1[p(a^1), b^1 - a^1)]\}, \tag{8.78}$$

and the individual should choose a^1 in order to maximize this utility.

The meaning of this operation is clear. Through his propagand, the individual tries to modify others' utility to change the price-system in his favour, making the goods he wants to sell more expensive and the goods he wants to buy cheaper.

In other words, individual 1 looks for

$$\max U\{[q_{j1}]_{1 \leqslant j \leqslant p}\}, \tag{8.79}$$

under the condition:

$$\sum_j p_j(a^1)q_{j1} = \sum_j p_j(a^1)(b_j^1 - a_j^1). \tag{8.80}$$

Assuming that U is jointly differentiable in its arguments and that the functions $p_j(a^1)$, solution of the system (8.76) are differentiable functions of a^1, the following relations are met in a regular maximum:

$$U_{j1} = \lambda p_j(a_1), \quad \forall 1 \leqslant j \leqslant p, \tag{b.81}$$

$$\sum_{1 \leqslant i \leqslant p} [q_{i1} - b_i^1 - a_i^1] \partial p_i / \partial a_j^1 = p_j(a_1), \quad \forall 1 \leqslant i \leqslant p. \tag{8.82}$$

Relation (8.82) expresses the fact that, *for each commodity, the amount used to manipulate others' utilities is such that the price is equal to the marginal income obtained as a result of the changes in prices.*

(ii) *A market economy with the same characteristics as before, but where the individual allowed to send messages also has the possibility of fixing the prices.*

In this situation, individual 1 chooses his consumptions q_{j1}, the message-inputs a_j^1 and the prices p_j such that:

$$\max U\{[q_{j1}]_{1 \leq j \leq p}\},\tag{8.83}$$

under the constraints:

$$\sum_j p_j q_{j1} - \sum_j p_j(b_j^1 - a_j^1) = 0,\tag{8.84}$$

$$q_{j1} + a_j^1 + \sum_{2 \leq k \leq m} q_{jk}(p, b^k, x) - b_j = 0.\tag{8.85}$$

Associating with (8.83) and (8.84), Lagrange multipliers λ and μ_j, the following relations are met in a regular maximum:

$$U_{j1} - \lambda p_j = \mu_j,\tag{8.86}$$

$$U_{j1} = -\sum_{\substack{2 \leq k \leq m \\ i}} \mu_i(\partial q_{ik}/\partial x)x_j,\tag{8.87}$$

$$-\lambda(q_{j1} - b_j^1 + a_j^1) = \sum_{\substack{2 \leq k \leq m \\ i}} \mu_i \partial q_{ik}/\partial p_j.\tag{8.88}$$

with $x_j = \partial x/\partial a_j^1$.

μ_j *is the rent that the individual is able to get on commodity j* as a result of his behaviour.

If we notice that:

$$\sum_{2 \leq k \leq m} dq_{jk} = -(dq_{j1} + da_j^1).\tag{8.89}$$

(8.87) means that, for each commodity, the marginal loss of utility, U_{j1} due to renunciation of a message-input is equal to the sum of the increased availabilities of commodities induced, weighted by the corresponding rents. The same relation has already been found in advertising theory.

(8.88) means that, for each commodity, the marginal income obtained through a small change in price is equal to the sum of the increased availabilities induced, weighted by the corresponding rents.

In this model, *individual 1 simultaneously uses the price and the "psychological action" to change others' demands in his favour.*

(iii) *A market economy with the same characteristics as in (i), but where every individual is allowed to send messages, while considering others' messages as given.*

In this model, the equilibrium price-vector is a function $p(a_1, \ldots, a_m)$. Each individual k tries to maximize:

$$U_k\{[q_{jk}]_{1 \leqslant j \leqslant p}, \bar{a}_k\}, \tag{8.90}$$

under the constraint:

$$\sum_j p_j(a_k, \bar{a}_k)q_{jk} = \sum_j p_j(a_k, \bar{a}_k)(b_j^k - a_j^k), \tag{8.91}$$

for $\bar{a}_k = (a_1, \ldots, a_{k-1}, a_{k+1}, \ldots, a_m)$ given.

It would be interesting to search for the assumptions under which this game has a Nash-equilibrium, i.e. under which there exists a suite of messages a^*, such that *no individual is willing to alter his psychological action for given messages issued by the others.*

Remarks: (1) In the analysis of perfect competition, it is generally assumed that no individual can influence prices through his purchases. If the assumption is enlarged to include any type of behaviour, the price-vector becomes independent from any a_k and *nobody has an interest in spoiling resources in order to try, in vain, to influence others.* But economists have long known that perfect competition is an extreme situation. (2) Independently of others' actions, individuals do attempt to modify their perceptions; they consume drugs to escape reality... but in such a case, they themselves manipulate the relation between the real consumption vector q_k and its perception q'_k.

2.5. Individual constraints and equilibrium in exchange economies

We shall first introduce only time constraints and regulations, then transaction costs and search for information, and finally monetary constraints.

2.5.1. Introduction of time and regulation constraints

For each individual, the utility depends on the consumption vector $q_k \in \mathbf{R}^{n+}$:

$$U_k = U_k(q_k). \tag{8.92}$$

We shall assume:

D1. For each individual, the consumption set is $\mathbf{R}^{n+}$. The preference ordering $\lesssim_k$ corresponding to U_k is continuous on $\mathbf{R}^{n+}$.

D2.   The preference ordering $\lesssim_k$ is convex, i.e. if q_k and q'_k are in $\mathbf{R}^{n+}$ and $q_k \gtrsim_k q'_k$ then $\lambda q_k + (1 - \lambda)q'_k \gtrsim_k q'_k$ for $\lambda \in [0, 1]$.

Now, w_k will denote the initial endowment of individual k. We shall suppose:

E1. $w_k \gg 0, \quad \forall k,$ (8.93)

which means that any individual has some positive initial endowment of any commodity.

Because of time constraints and regulations, the consumption vector has to be in a set T_k. In other words, when p is the price vector with which individual k is confronted, the budget correspondence is defined by:

$$B_k(p) = \left\{ q_k \in \mathbf{R}^{n+} \left| \begin{array}{l} \text{(a)} \ \ pq_k \leq pw_k \\ \text{(b)} \ \ q_k \in T_k \\ \text{(c)} \ \ q_k \geq 0 \end{array} \right. \right\}. \tag{8.94}$$

We shall assume that:

T1.   The set T_k is a closed convex set. This is a reasonable assumption, since regulations generally put upper limits on some consumptions and since time constraints are frequently expressed by linear inequalities.

T2.   If $q_k \in T_k$, then $q'_k \leq q_k$ implies $q'_k \in T_k$. A consumption "smaller" than a feasible one is always feasible.

T3. $(0) \in T_k$. It is possible, technically, to consume nothing.

T4.   There exists $\hat{q}_k \geq 0$ such that $\hat{q}_k \in T_k$. In other words, the constraints do not prohibit any positive consumption.

It is then possible to apply the proof given by M. Kurz in his theorem 1 (M. Kurz (1974, pp. 702–707)) and to show that:[4]

---

[4] It is, of course, well known that it derives directly from the proof of the existence of an economic equilibrium, since such a proof is always made on the assumption that the consumption sets of the individuals are closed and convex.

The economy with time and regulation constraints satisfying D1, D2, E1, T1, T2, T3, T4 has a competitive equilibrium, i.e. a pair $\{p, (q_k)_{1 \leqslant k \leqslant m}\}$ such that: (a) $\sum_k q_k \leqq \sum_k w_k$; (b) *for all* $k, q_k \in B_k(p)$ *and* $q_k \gtrsim_k q_k'$ *for any* $q_k' \in B_k(p)$.

To understand exactly what this means, we shall consider the Edgeworth box of an economy limited to two individuals. With an obvious notation, the consumptions are q_{11}, q_{12} for the first individual q_{21}, q_{22} for the second. The time constraints will be:

$$t_{11}q_{11} + t_{12}q_{12} \leqslant T_1, \tag{8.95}$$

$$t_{21}q_{21} + t_{22}q_{22} \leqslant T_2. \tag{8.96}$$

The situation is depicted in figure 8.4, where M is the point of initial endowments. From M, it is possible to draw 0, 1 or 2 tangents to each of the indifference curves of any individual. The tangency points generate the curves (C_1) and (C_2).[5]

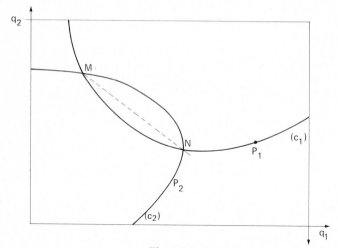

Figure 8.4

C_1 (resp. (C_2)) is the locus of the situations P_1 (resp. P_2) of maximum utility of individual 1 (resp. 2), when the unique constraint is the income constraint, and when the price ratio is the slope of MP_1 (resp. MP_2).

[5] As an example of fruitful research in this field, see Y. Balasko (1976).

In addition to M, (C_1) and (C_2) cross at a point N, which is the point of the contract curve at which the common tangent to the individuals' indifference curves passes through M. It is the competitive equilibrium in absence of time constraints.

For each individual, the time constraint is represented by a straight line $(L_1$ or $L_2)$ sloping down southeastwards.

Let us take individual 1 (figure 8.5a): when L_1 is above AB, it never crosses (C_1) and the time constraint is so loose that nothing is changed for individual 1.

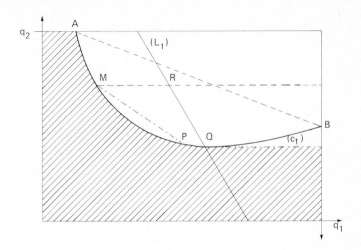

Figure 8.5a

When L_1 is in the shaded area, it never crosses (C_1), but the time constraint is so strict that time is always the limiting factor. When L_1 cuts (C_1), it may be: in one point between A and M, in one point between M and B, in two points.

Assume, for instance, that L_1 crosses C_1 in Q. Let us explore the equilibrium of individual 1 when the price ratio p progressively decreases from the slope of the vertical to the slope of the horizontal.

As long as p is greater than the slope of MQ, individual 1's equilibrium is given by the intersection P with (C_1). When p still decrease, the equilibrium point describes the segment QR on (L_1).

Consider now (figure 8.5b) a situation in which L_1 crosses (C_1) in Q and Q'. When p is greater than the slope MQ, the time constraint is binding and the equilibrium position describes the segment RQ on (L_1). When p is between the slope of MQ and MQ', the income constraint is binding and the curve (C_1) between Q and Q' is the locus of equilibrium points. When p is smaller than the slope MQ', the equilibrium point describes $Q'R'$.

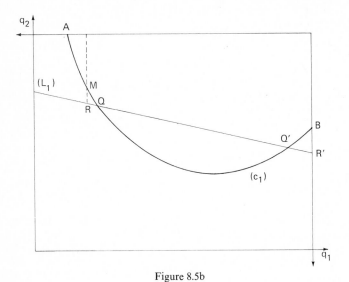

Figure 8.5b

Thus, when there is a time constraint, the equivalent of curves (C_1) and (C_2) are broken lines. The structure of equilibria is greatly affected by this situation: figure 8.6a shows a situation where the time constraint is binding only for individual 1 and where the old unique equilibrium N is replaced by a new unique equilibrium N', where both individuals may be in a worse situation. Figure 8.6b shows a situation where the time constraint is still only binding for individual 1, but where there are *three equilibria:* The old one, N, which is still feasible and two new ones, N' and N''. Figure 8.6c shows a case where the time constraints may be binding for the two individuals, with three equilibriums N', N'' and N'''. In N', the time constraints are binding for the two individuals, in N'' and N''' the time constraint is binding for one individual only. Figure 8.6d shows a situation where the time constraints are especially strong. Any price ratio between the slope of MR_1 and MR_2 is an equilibrium price ratio and the quantity $R_1 R_2$ of commodity 2 is left unconsumed.

Hence, the proof of *the existence of a competitive equilibrium hides a great variety of situations in the number of equilibria as soon as the time or regulation constraints become important, even in a simple case where, in their absence, there is a unique equilibrium.*

2.5.2. Introduction of transaction costs and search for information

As a first model, assume that, to enlarge his information, individual k can buy an input vector $g_k \in \mathbf{R}^{n+}$, so that his consumption vector q_k is constrained by:

$$(q_k, g_k) \in T_k, \qquad T_k \subset \mathbf{R}^{2n+}. \tag{8.97}$$

Keep hypothesis D1, D2, E1, T1, T3 and replace T2 and T4 by:

T2. If $(q_k, g_k) \in T_k$ then $q'_k \leqq q_k$ and $g'_k \geqq g_k$ imply $(q'_k, g'_k) \in T_k$.

In other words, if g_k are resources sufficient to make available q_k, any $g'_k \geqq g_k$ is sufficient to make possible a consumption of smaller or equal volume.

T4. There are $\hat{q}_k > 0$ and $\hat{g}_k$ such that $(\hat{q}_k, \hat{g}_k) \in T_k$.

Then, when p is the price vector with which individual k is confronted, the budget correspondence is defined by:

$$B_k(p) = \left\{ (q_k, g_k) \in \mathbf{R}^{2n+} \;\middle|\; \begin{array}{l} \text{(a) } (q_k, g_k) \in T_k \\ \text{(b) } pq_k \leqq pw_k - pg_k \\ \text{(c) } q_k \geqq 0 \end{array} \right\}. \tag{8.98}$$

With a proof similar to the one given by M. Kurz, the economy with the information constraints defined by (8.97) and satisfying D1, D2, E1, T1, T2, T3, T4 has a competitive equilibrium, i.e. a triple $\{p, (q_k)_{1 \leqslant k \leqslant m}, (g_k)_{1 \leqslant k \leqslant m}\}$ such that: (a) $\sum_k q_k \leqq \sum_k w_k - \sum_k g_k$, (b) for all k, $(q_k, g_k) \in B_k(p)$ and $q_k \gtrsim_k q'_k$ for any $(q'_k, g'_k) \in B_k(p)$.

It would be interesting to extend the proof to the following more general model:

For each individual, the utility depends on the consumption vector

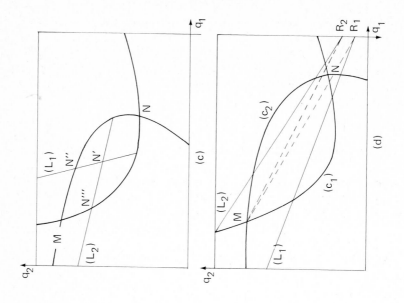

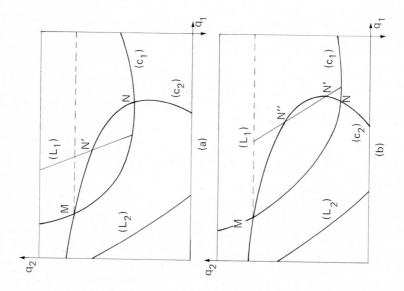

Figure 8.6

$q_k \in \mathbf{R}^{n+}$, on leisure time $L_k \in \mathbf{R}^+$ and on information search $J_k \in \mathbf{R}^+$:

$$U_k = U_k[q_k, L_k, J_k].\tag{8.99}$$

U_k is an increasing function of q_k and L_k, but a decreasing function of J_k. w_k still denotes the initial endowment of individual k, x_k is the amount bought and y_k the amount sold. Consequently:

$$q_k = w_k + x_k - y_k.\tag{8.100}$$

The individual behaviour is submitted to a certain number of constraints:

(i) *a budget constraint:*

$$px_k \leqq py_k - pg_k,\tag{8.101}$$

where $g_k \in \mathbf{R}^{n+}$ is the vector of inputs consumed for the transactions.

(ii) *a transaction constraint:*

$$(x_k, y_k, g_k) \in C_k,\tag{8.102}$$

where C_k is the transaction set.

(iii) *a time constraint:* which can be written

$$\alpha_k q_k + \beta_k x_k + \gamma_k y_k + J_k + L_k \leqslant T_{0k},\tag{8.103}$$

where α_k, β_k and γ_k are vectors, the components of which are the times necessary for unit consumptions, unit buyings and unit sales. Replacing q_k by its value (8.100), the above constraint is transformed into:

$$\delta_k x_k + \varepsilon_k y_k + J_k + L_k \leqslant T_k,$$

where δ_k and ε_k are easily computed out of $\alpha_k, \beta_k, \gamma_k$ and $T_k = T_{0k} - \alpha_k w_k$.

(iv) *an information constraint:* which expresses that the available purchases and sales are in a set depending on J_k:

$$(x_k, y_k, J_k) \in D_k.\tag{8.104}$$

Following the lines of M. Kurz's theorem 2 (M. Kurz (1974, p. 708–716)) it is probable that, with adequate assumptions, the above economy has a competitive equilibrium.

But here, too, the existence of a competitive equilibrium hides some complexity. In figure 8.7, it is assumed that individual 1 can enlarge his information set while abandoning increasing amounts of commodity 2.

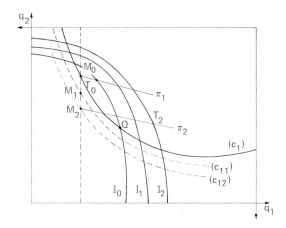

Figure 8.7

To M_0, M_1, M_2 correspond information borders I_0, I_1, I_2 and through M_1, M_2 pass curves (C_{11}), (C_{12}) similar to (C_1).

An equilibrium locus may be associated with each M. Depending on the price ratio p, the individual will choose the amount of initial resources he is ready to lose to improve his overall possibilities. For instance, in figure 8.7, the best solution when the price ratio is steeper than M_0Q is not to search for information; but when the price ratio is low (for instance, represented by the straight line π_1), to sacrifice M_0M_2 makes it possible to consume T_2 on π_2 instead of T_0 on π_1.

2.5.3. Introduction of monetary constraints

Fascinating progress has been made in recent years on monetary economies. Drèze (1975), Benassy (1975), Younès (1975), Grandmont, Laroque and Younès (1975), Malinvaud and Younès (1974) have, among others, made distinguished contributions.

As another example of regulation constraints, a brief summary of Malinvaud and Younès's formulation will be presented here.

In this exchange economy, with m individuals $(1 \leqslant k \leqslant m)$ and n commodities $(1 \leqslant i \leqslant n)$, a *transaction type* is a direction in $\mathbf{R}^n$ characterized by a vector $t = (t_i)_{1 \leqslant i \leqslant n}$. $t \in \mathbf{R}^n$, the components of t being the amounts of the various commodities exchanged one for the other.

If transaction t is feasible, it is assumed that, for any real α, transaction αt is also feasible.

But in any real situation, not all t's are feasible. Their feasibility depends on the structure of institutions – for instance markets. Hence, it is necessary to introduce *the set T of admissible t's*. For instance:

– a *Walrasian economy* is one in which T is identical to $\mathbf{R}^n$ and in which each individual can freely combine any type of transactions.

– a *pure monetary economy* is one where commodity n is money and in which any transaction involves money and another commodity. Hence, the condition $t_r = 1$ can be imposed:

$$T = \{t \in \mathbf{R}^n \,|\, \exists\, i : t_i > 0, t_n = -1; t_j = 0 \text{ for } 1 \leqslant j \leqslant n, j \neq i, n\}.$$
(8.105)

– a *pure Keynesian economy* would be one where the price vector $p = (p_i)_{1 \leqslant i \leqslant n}$ is fixed, in which commodity n is money ($p_n > 0$) and in which any transaction involves money. Then T is given by:

$$T = \{t \in \mathbf{R}^n \,|\, pt = 0; t_n = 1\}.$$
(8.106)

To characterize the *behaviour of individual k*, it is natural to introduce numbers $a_k(t) \in \mathbf{R}$ which define the intensity with which individual k uses transaction type t. The vector $a_k(t)t \in \mathbf{R}^n$ will then define the corresponding exchanges of individual k. According to $a_k(t) \gtrless 0$, k will be a seller, or a buyer, or will abstain. Formally, the introduction of the $a_i(t)$'s implies the definition of a σ-algebra on T so that $a_i = (a_i(t))$, $t \in T$, is introduced as a measure on T.

The result of the *plan $a_k(t) \in \mathbf{R}$* is an exchange vector: $z_k \in \mathbf{R}^n$ $(z_k = (z_{ki})_{1 \leqslant i \leqslant n})$:

$$z_k = \int_T t \, da_k(t) \quad \text{or} \quad z_{ki} = \int_T t_i \, da_k(t),$$
(8.107)

or, more briefly:

$$z_k = La_k,$$
(8.108)

L being the operator associating with the plan a_k its transactional results.

For a plan to be accessible to individual k, physical conditions of the type:

$$w_k + La_k \in X_k,$$
(8.109)

must be satisfied, where $w_k \in \mathbf{R}^{n+}$ is the vector of initial endowments of individual k and $X_k \subset \mathbf{R}^n$. If the last commodity is money, (8.109) must imply:

$$w_{kn} + z_{in} \geqq 0 \tag{8.110}$$

which imposes a special structure on X_k.

But in addition to the physical constraints, the individual's behaviour is limited by *institutional constraints* specifying the transaction types to which he has access as a "seller" or a "buyer":

$$a_k \in A_k, \tag{8.111}$$

A_k being a subset of all the measures on T corresponding to the σ-algebra chosen. Individual k's consumption vector is naturally:

$$q_k = w_k + z_k, \qquad q_k \in \mathbf{R}^n. \tag{8.112}$$

This individual has preferences which can be represented by a utility function U_k, concave and nondecreasing in each of its arguments, and even strictly increasing in the quantity of money.

In this economy, *a strong noncooperative equilibrium (SNCE) E^* is defined by plans a_k^* and consumptions q_k^* (for all $1 \leqslant k \leqslant m$) fulfilling the three following conditions:*

(I) *On each market, offers and demands are in equilibrium:* $\sum_k a_k(H) = 0$ for all set H of the σ-algebra introduced on T. (8.113)

(II) *For each individual (a_k^*, q_k^*) maximizes $U_k(q_k)$ under the constraints*

$$q_k = w_k + La_k \in X_k \cap [\{w_k\} + LA_k], \tag{8.114}$$

$$a_k(t) \in I[a_k^*(t)] \quad \text{for all} \quad t \in T, \tag{8.115}$$

(8.115) expressing that, if individual k has decided to use a transaction of type t at level $a_k^*(t)$, he could have chosen to use it at any level $a_k(t)$ *with the same sign, but lower in absolute value.*

(III) *There do not exist $\hat{t} \in T$, a couple of individuals (k, l), plans a_k and a_l both satisfying (II) and a number ε such that the plans $a_k + \varepsilon\hat{\delta}$ and $a_l - \varepsilon\hat{\delta}$ are possible for k and l and considered by these individuals as preferable to a_k^* and a_l^*.* ($\hat{\delta}$ being the measure which give the value 1 to $\hat{t}$ and 0 to the complement of $\hat{t}$ in T.)

In other words, in an equilibrium, two individuals cannot find a transaction such that by making an exchange between them they can both improve their situation.

Within this framework, the authors have been able to prove certain interesting proposition:

Proposition 1. *In a walrasian economy, any competitive equilibrium may be obtained as a SNCE.*

Proposition 2. *In an exchange economy, in which the utility functions U_k are quasi concave and differentiable (with $U_{kn} > 0$), if the SNCE E^* corresponds to consumption vectors q_k^* interior to the sets $X_k \cap [\{w_k\} + LA_k]$, it is a competitive equilibrium.*

Proposition 3. *Assume the following definition: in a SNCE E^*, transactions of type $\hat{t}$ are rationed for individual k if there is a number ε_k and a plan $a_k \in I(a_k^*)$ such that $a_k + \varepsilon_k \hat{\delta}$ is possible for k and preferred by him to a_k^*. Then, if transactions of a type $\hat{t}$ are simultaneously rationed for individuals (k, l) having convex sets X_k, X_l, A_k, A_l and convex preferences, then:*

$$a_k^*(\hat{t}) \cdot a_l^*(\hat{t}) \geqq 0. \tag{8.116}$$

In other words, the transactions effectively used in equilibrium belong to three categories only: those for which nobody is rationed, those for which rationing concerns individuals acting as "buyers" ($a_k^*(t) > 0$), those for which rationing concerns individuals acting as "sellers" ($a_k^*(t) < 0$).

Proposition 4. *Assume the following definition: a restricted monetary economy is a pure monetary economy (8.105) where the constraints (8.111) are dropped. Then, for any T, if X_k coincides with $\mathbf{R}^{n+}$ for $\forall k$, there exists a SNCE for a restricted monetary economy.*

Proposition 5. *Assume the following definition: a monetary economy with rigidities is a restricted monetary economy in which, for $\forall i \neq n$:*

$$1/t_i \in C_i = \{p_i \,|\, 0 < \underline{p_i} \leqq p_i \leqq \overline{p_i}\} \tag{8.117}$$

(in other words, for any commodity other than money, the price has to be between a minimum and a maximum). Then, in a SNCE of a monetary economy with rigidities, the transactions on a given commodity are all made at the same price. If the functions U_k are continuous and if the q_k^*

are interior to the X_k's, all the transactions on a commodity i such that some buyers are rationed are at price $\bar{p}_i$.

This summary of Malinvaud and Younès's paper proves how far-reaching it may be, for the realism of economic models, to introduce a more adequate description of the constraints limiting individual behaviour.

Since behavioural constraints are so important in exchange econo-mies, a natural course of action is to examine the influence of individual capabilities on equilibrium states.

2.6. Individual capabilities and exchange economies

Even in exchange economies, the levels of individual capabilities are essential in many respects: they partly determine the utilities; they condition the efficiency of information search or the amount of inputs necessary for transactions; they alter sensibility to the messages sent by others; they influence the adequacy of psychological messages sent to others.

But the effect, on an individual, of an increase in capability of another individual is far from obvious. Take, for instance, the two individuals of the Edgeworth box:

If the capability of individual 1 is high enough, N is the equilibrium state (figure 8.8). If the capability of individual 1 limits the maximal consumptions to the curve (L_1), the equilibrium state is N' at the crossing of (C_2) and (L_1) where both individuals have lower utilities. When individual 1's capability increases, N' describes the curve (C_2) towards N and the two utility increase.

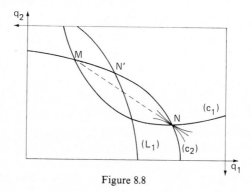

Figure 8.8

In this case, the inability of individual 1 adequately to combine his consumptions compels individual 2 to consume more of commodity 1 and less of commodity 2 than he would like. Obviously, it is easy to draw cases in which the opposite effect appears.

But an increase in capability of individual 1 alters his tastes and hence his indifference curves. The effect on the level of utility of individual 2 may be positive or negative. Simultaneously, the facts: that individual 1 is less sensitive to the messages sent by 2 and aims at a change of his perceptions favourable to 2; that individual 1 more adequately directs his psychological messages towards 2 is normally favourable to individual 1 and unfavourable to individual 2.

Hence, though individual capabilities have an important impact on the characteristics of equilibria, the only possible assertion is that an increase in the capability level of an individual has a positive impact on the utility of this individual. Nothing can be said about the utilities of others.

Obviously, the enrichment of the basic model of the individual opens the possibility of studying many interesting problems even in the simple-framework of exchange economies. *Jealousy and love, perceptive illusions, psychological actions, regulation and time constraints, information search, capabilities, monetary constraints greatly modify the conventional picture.* While equilibrium states still exist, under the usual cohort of necessary assumptions, two major changes seem to occur:

(I) The first – which is only a conjecture – is that the conditions of unicity of equilibrium are radically altered. A systematic study of this fact in simple cases would be highly interesting.
(II) The second is that in most situations Pareto optimum states and equilibrium states no longer coïncide. This very important conclusion is also found in economies with a productive sector, so that it will appear as an essential result of the chapter.

3. Economies with production

In which fields can we expect the basic model to induce fruitful developments in general equilibrium theory of economies with production?

The introduction of satisfactions should, as in chapter 7, facilitate the analysis of quality choices for the various commodities. It is also a useful tool to examine externalities in consumptions (cf. chapter 4, section 1.4).

The recognition of perceptive biases makes it possible to take into account all the actions performed by firms to modify the images of their products; but for sake of brevity, this point, already examined in exchange economies, will be omitted here.

The division of acts into role choices and allocations should play a vital part as soon as capabilities are introduced.

Among the constraints, the most important with respect to our topic are certainly the information, role and capability constraints and also the regulation constraints within firms.

Consequently, the first two sections, dealing with quality choices and externalities in consumption, will still accept profit maximization by firms, while the subsequent sections will introduce managers' preferences and individual capabilities. This will lead naturally to models where the social aspects are dominant.

3.1. Quality choices

We shall follow here a presentation by H.E. Leland. The economy is composed of m individuals k ($1 \leqslant k \leqslant m$), n commodities i ($1 \leqslant i \leqslant n$) and n firms, commodity i being produced by the ith firm.

Each firm is characterized by an implicit production function:

$$f_i[x_i, q_i, y_i] = 0, \tag{8.118}$$

where:

$$x_i \in \mathbf{R}^+$$

is the *quality* chosen for the production,

$$q_i \in \mathbf{R}^+$$

is the *quantity* produced, and

$$y_i \in \mathbf{R}^{n+}$$

is the vector of input quantities. f_i will be assumed to exhibit the usual concavity properties with respect to x_i, as well as with respect to q_i and y_i.

[6] H.E. Leland (1975).

Firms will choose the combination (x_i, q_i, y_i) in order to maximize their profit π_i. They consider that the output price p_i is a function of the quality and the quantity produced, while the input prices vector $r = (r_i)_{1 \leqslant i \leqslant n}$ is constant:

$$\pi_i = p_i(x_i, q_i)q_i - ry_i. \tag{8.119}$$

The first order necessary conditions are, in the case of a regular maximum, and with an obvious notation:

$$q_i \partial p_i / \partial x_i + \phi_i f_{ix} = 0, \tag{8.120}$$

$$p_i + q_i \partial p_i / \partial q_i + \phi_i f_{iq} = 0, \tag{8.121}$$

$$-r_i + \phi_i f_{iy} = 0, \tag{8.122}$$

where ϕ_i is a Lagrange multiplier associated to (8.118).

Each consumer will have a utility function depending on p different satisfaction levels:

$$U_k = U_k \{ (S_{jk})_{1 \leqslant j \leqslant p} \}, \tag{8.123}$$

where the satisfaction levels depend simultaneously on quantity and quality consumed:

$$S_{jk} = S_{jk} [(x_i)_{1 \leqslant i \leqslant n}, (q_{ik})_{1 \leqslant i \leqslant n}]. \tag{8.124}$$

Consumer k is a price-taker. If he possesses a quantity $\bar{y}_{ki}$ of primary commodity i and a fraction $\mathcal{O}_{ki}$ of the ith firm, he will select $(q_{ik})_{1 \leqslant i \leqslant n}$, so as to maximize (8.125) under the constraint:

$$\sum_i p_i q_{ik} = \sum_i p_i \bar{y}_{ki} + \sum_i \mathcal{O}_{ki} \pi_i. \tag{8.125}$$

The first-order necessary conditions are, in the case of a regular maximum, and with an obvious notation:

$$\sum_j U_{kj} S_{jkqi} + \lambda_k p_i = 0. \tag{8.126}$$

The final link to close the equilibrium model is the set of market equilibrium conditions:

$$\sum_k q_{ik} = q_i, \tag{8.127}$$

$$\sum_k \bar{y}_{ki} = \sum_{i'} y_{ii'}, \tag{8.128}$$

where $y_{ii'}$ is the ith component of y_i.

Naturally, $\partial p_i/\partial x_i$ and $\partial p_i/\partial q_i$ in (8.120) and (8.121) are *perceived* price changes (see, for instance, K. Arrow and F. Hahn (1971, p. 152)). In a case of perfect competition, there would be $\partial p_i/\partial q_i = 0$, but naturally $\partial p_i/\partial x_i \neq 0$.

An interesting question is *whether an equilibrium fulfilling conditions* (8.118)–(8.128) *is a Pareto optimum.* Such an optimum would satisfy:

$$\max \sum_k \lambda_k U_k\{[S_{jk}((x_i)_{1 \leqslant i \leqslant n}, (q_{ik})_{1 \leqslant i \leqslant n})]_{1 \leqslant j \leqslant p}\}, \tag{8.129}$$

under the constraints:

$$f_i(x_i, q_i, y_i) = 0, \quad \forall i, \tag{8.130}$$

$$\sum_i q_{ik} - q_i = 0, \quad \forall k, \tag{8.131}$$

$$\bar{y}_i - \sum_i y_{ii'} = 0, \quad \forall i, \tag{8.132}$$

where λ_k are positive or zero numbers, not all zeros. Associating Lagrange multipliers $(-\mu_i)$, $(-v_i)$ and $(-\sigma_i)$ with constraints (8.130) (8.131), (8.132), we get the necessary conditions:

$$\sum_j \lambda_k U_{kj} S_{kjxi} - \mu_i f_{ix} = 0, \tag{8.133}$$

$$\sum_j \lambda_k U_{kj} S_{kjqi} - v_i = 0, \tag{8.134}$$

$$v_i - \mu_i f_{iq} = 0, \tag{8.135}$$

$$\sigma_i - \mu_i f_{iyi'} = 0. \tag{8.136}$$

These conditions (added to (8.130), (8.131), (8.132) will be sufficient as well as necessary (assuming an equilibrium exists) if utility functions are jointly quasi-concave in x_i and q_{ik}. But as Leland points out, the structure of the utility functions, with arguments of the form $S_j(x_i, q_{ik}, \ldots)$ does not make this certain.

If the competition is perfect $(\partial p/\partial q_i = 0)$ relation (8.134) is equivalent to (8.126), relation (8.135) to (8.121) and relation (8.136) to (8.122), but *relations* (8.120) *and* (8.133) *are different.* In other words, the existence of quality prevents the competitive equilibrium from existing.

Leland has studied the slightly more restricted case where:

$$S_{jk} = \sum_i c_{ij}(x_i) q_{ik}. \tag{8.137}$$

In this case, every commodity has p *characteristics* and a unit of commodity i gives rise to a quantity $c_{ij}(x_i)$ of the jth characteristic which depends on the quality x_i. The total quantity available of the jth characteristic is the sum of the quantities generated by the various consumptions.

With assumption (8.137), relation (8.133) may be written:

$$q_{ik} \sum_j \lambda_k U_{kj} \frac{\partial c_{ij}}{\partial x_i} - \mu_i f_{ix} = 0, \tag{8.138}$$

while (8.120) has the form:

$$q_i \frac{\partial p_i}{\partial x_i} - \mu_i f_{ix} = 0. \tag{8.139}$$

For these relations to be equivalent, Leland has shown that two conditions were sufficient:

(i) *Consumer unanimity with respect to the trade-off between price and quality*, which assures a single "willingness to pay" per unit consumption for a small change in quality.

(ii) *An implicit competitive market for characteristics*, "presumed invariant to firms' quality and quantity decisions which guarantees that profit maximizing firms in equilibrium will have the same trade-off between price and quality change as the consumers have."

Under these conditions, the prices π_j of the characteristics are such that:

$$p_i = \sum_j \pi_j c_{ij}, \tag{8.140}$$

with:

$$\lambda_k U_{kj} = \pi_j, \quad \forall k, \tag{8.141}$$

and:

$$\partial p_i / \partial x_i = \sum_j \pi_j \partial c_{ij} / \partial x_i, \tag{8.142}$$

so that (8.139) is easily deduced from (8.138), and reciprocally.

Naturally, the discrepancy between optimum and equilibrium here has a rather superficial cause: *the absence of markets on which several qualities may be traded,* since this prevents each individual from selecting the quality he prefers.

This section shows, nevertheless, how useful *the satisfaction concept* may be in the study of certain problems of general equilibrium. The next section will provide a second example.

3.2. *Externalities in consumption*

A short summary of J.P. Dupuy's (1974) paper: "Innovation et obsolescence psychologique" will be sufficient to underline the most important features. Notation has been adapted.

m individuals *k* $(1 \leqslant h \leqslant m)$ compose the economy in which two commodities only are produced and consumed.

- The *first commodity* is produced in a variety of different qualities represented by a number x in the closed interval $[0, \bar{x}]$ of the positive real line. $\bar{x}$ is the best quality available.
- The *second commodity*, available in the economy in quantity $y_0 \in \mathbf{R}^+$, is partly used as an input for the production of the first commodity (quantity $y_e \in \mathbf{R}^+$) and partly consumed, $y_k \in \mathbf{R}^+$ being the consumption of individual k. Hence:

$$\sum_k y_k + y_e \leqslant y_0. \tag{8.143}$$

$Q(x)$ will denote the total quantity of the first commodity consumed in the economy with a quality smaller than or equal to x. The production function of the first commodity is, for simplicity, given the form:

$$\int_0^{\bar{x}} f(x)\,\mathrm{d}Q(x) + \int_0^{\bar{x}} c(x)\,\mathrm{d}x \leqslant y_e, \tag{8.144}$$

where "$c(\bar{x})$ is the expenditure in research and development necessary to pass from a maximum quality $\bar{x}$ to a maximum quality $\bar{x} + \mathrm{d}\bar{x} : f(x)$ is the marginal cost, assumed constant, of production of a unit of commodity 1 in quality x (c and f being expressed in units consumed of commodity 2)." [7]

Individual k's utility will be given the special expression:

$$U_k = y_k [\int_0^{\bar{x}} s(x, \bar{x})\,\mathrm{d}Q_k(x)], \tag{8.145}$$

[7] J.P. Dupuy (1974).

where the function $Q_k(x)$ is the total amount of the first commodity consumed by individual k in the quality interval $[0, x]$ and $s(x, \bar{x})$ the marginal utility obtained from the consumption of one unit of commodity 1 at quality x, $\bar{x}$ being given. Generally:

$$\partial s(x, \bar{x})/\partial x > 0, \tag{8.146}$$

$$\partial s(x, \bar{x})/\partial \bar{x} < 0. \tag{8.147}$$

This assumes that *two motivations are implied in the consumption of the first commodity:*

- a prestige satisfaction: for x given, its level decreases when the maximum quality available increases, because the discrepancy between the quality x consumed and the most prestigious quality widens,
- a utilitarian satisfaction: an increase in the consumption of the first commodity is desirable per se.

Obviously:

$$\left. \begin{array}{l} \sum_k dQ_k(x) \leqslant dQ(x) \\[2mm] dQ_k(x) \geqslant 0 \quad \forall k \end{array} \right\} \quad \forall x \leqslant \bar{x}, \quad dx > 0. \tag{8.148}$$

In such an economy, *what are the conditions for a competitive equilibrium and for a Pareto optimum, when $\bar{x}$ is treated as a given parameter or as a variable chosen by the producers?*

3.3. $\bar{x}$ given

Equilibrium: Denote by r_k the income of individual k, by p the price of the second commodity and by $p(x)$ the price of the quality x of the first commodity. The individual maximizes (8.145) under the constraints:

$$py_k + \int_0^{\bar{x}} p(x) \, dQ_k(x) \leqslant r_k, \tag{8.149}$$

$$dQ_k(x) \geqslant 0 \quad \forall x \leqslant \bar{x}, \quad dx > 0. \tag{8.150}$$

Associating with these constraints positive or zero Lagrange multipliers λ_k and $\eta_k(x)$, the following necessary condition is obtained:

$$y_k \partial s(x, \bar{x})/\partial x - \lambda_k p'(x) + \eta_k'(x) = 0. \tag{8.151}$$

It is possible to show that, under reasonable assumptions, *only one* quality will be consumed by consumer k in equilibrium.[8] For this quality $\hat{x}_k$:

$$\frac{\partial s(\hat{x}_k, \bar{x})}{\partial x} = \frac{\lambda_k p'(\hat{x}_k)}{y_k} \tag{8.152}$$

If the production is carried out by one firm, this firm will try to maximize:

$$\pi = \int_0^{\bar{x}} p(x)\, dQ(x) - p\bar{y}_e, \tag{8.153}$$

where $\bar{y}_e$ is the available quantity, once the expenditures needed to ensure the existence of $\bar{x}$ have been made:

$$\bar{y}_e = y_e - \int_0^{\bar{x}} c(x)\, dx, \tag{8.154}$$

under the constraint:

$$\bar{y}_e \geqslant \int_0^{\bar{x}} f(x)\, dq(x). \tag{8.155}$$

The production function being linear, it is well known that in equilibrium, π will be equal to zero and:

$$p(x) = pf(x). \tag{8.156}$$

Optimum: Necessary conditions for a Pareto optimum are obtained, under usual assumptions, through the maximization of $\sum_k \lambda_k U_k$ under the constraints (8.143), (8.144), (8.148), the λ_k's being positive or zero, but not all zeros.

An easy computation, left to the reader, shows that *an optimum state is a competitive equilibrium* with the prices p for commodity 2, and $pf(x)$ for quality x of commodity 1.

But the situation is totally different when $\bar{x}$ is chosen by the producers.

---

[8] If $Q(x)$ is strictly increasing on a finite interval, $\eta(x) = \eta'(x) = 0$. Since $p'(x)$ is not proportional to $\partial s/\partial x$, (151) cannot be verified. Hence $Q(x)$ increases by steps. For a quality x_i consumed, $\eta(x_i) = 0$, since $dQ(x_i) > 0$. But $\eta(x_i) \geqslant 0$, and then $\eta'(x) = 0$. For $x_i : [\partial s(x_i, \bar{x})/\partial x]/p'(x_i) = \lambda_k/y_k$. But the left-hand side of this relation is obviously a decreasing function of x_i. Thus, the relation cannot be satisfied for more than one value of x.

3.4. $\bar{x}$ variable

Since each consumer consumes only the quality $\hat{x}_k$ in an optimum (or equilibrium) situation for any $\bar{x}$, we can introduce the total quantity q_k of commodity 1 consumed by k.

An optimum program is such that:

$$\max \sum_k \lambda_k y_k q_k s(\hat{x}_k, \bar{x}), \tag{8.157}$$

for λ_k's positive or zero but not all zero, with:

$$\sum_k y_k + \sum_k f(\hat{x}_k)q_k + \int_0^{\bar{x}} c(x)\,\mathrm{d}x \leqslant y_0, \quad \hat{x}_k \leqslant \bar{x}, \quad \forall k. \tag{8.158}{(8.159)}$$

Associating with (8.158) and (8.159), Lagrange multipliers p and v_k, we can form the Lagrangian. It leads to the conditions for an optimum for $\bar{x}$ given *and to the additional relation:*

$$pc(\bar{x}) - \sum_k \left[\lambda_k y_k q_k \frac{\partial s_k}{\partial x}(\hat{x}_k, \bar{x}) \right] = \sum_k v_k. \tag{8.160}$$

This condition is easily interpretable. It means that the sum of *the marginal increase in research and development costs* $pc(\bar{x})$ *and of the decrease in utility for all the individuals consuming qualities below the maximum, is equal to the marginal value of the increase to the individuals consuming the best quality (for whom* $v_k \neq 0$).

A competitive equilibrium is, on the contrary, such that:

$$pc(\bar{x}) = \sum_k v_k. \tag{8.161}$$

The marginal cost to the producer of the increase of the best quality available is equal to the sum of the marginal values to the individuals who will consume it.

The result is clear: the market does not take into account the "*psychological obsolescence*" *of all the consumptions* $x < \bar{x}$ *which is created by the increase in* $\bar{x}$.

This is certainly one of the best and most profound criticism ever made of the consumer society. It is *a direct consequence of the assumptions made on individual utilities.*

3.5. Capability

Two models will illustrate the importance of capability for equilibrium theory: the first is concerned with *taxation* and is directly inspired by the work of Atkinson (1970), Mirrlees (1971), Phelps (1973), Kolm (1974), Sadka (1976), the second with *education* and starts from analysis made by Lesourne (1972) and Mourre (1973).

3.5.1. Capability and taxation

In the *original model* (Mirrlees (1971)) there are only two commodities – consumption (denoted by x) and labour services (denotes by y) – and a continuum of individuals.

Each individual is identified by his capability represented by a real number c in a closed and bounded interval $[c_1, c_2]$, with $c_1 \geqslant 0$. $F(c)$ is the number of persons with capability c or less. F is continuous and strictly increasing on $[c_1, c_2]$. All individuals have the same utility function $u(x, y)$ and the same endowment of leisure T.

$u(x, y)$ is strictly quasi-concave, twice continuously differentiable, strictly increasing in x, strictly decreasing in y. Both commodities have diminishing marginal utilities and $u_{xy} > 0$.

An individual with capability c who works y hours earns a gross income $\rho = cy$ and a net income

$$r = cy - t(\rho),$$
(8.162)

where $t(\rho)$ is the tax functions. The individual chooses y and x so as to maximize $u(x, y)$ under the constraint:

$$x = cy - t(cy),$$
(8.163)

the income being measured in terms of consumption goods.

The criterion of social ordering is, for instance, an additive social welfare function:

$$W = \int_{[c_1, c_2]} u[x(c), y(c)] \, dF(c),$$
(8.164)

where $x(c)$ and $y(c)$ denote the bundle maximizing individuals' utilities.

The government aim is to choose $t(cy)$ so as to maximize W subject to the budget constraint:

$$\int\limits_{[c_1,c_2]} t(cy)\,dF(c) \geqslant B. \tag{8.165}$$

A *more general model* like the following, would still more emphasize the *central part of capability*:

- In addition to the consumption good, there exists a public good z.
- The utility of an individual of capability c is:

$$u = u(x, y, z, c). \tag{8.166}$$

- The marginal weight attached by the government to the individuals of capability c is $\lambda(c) > 0$.
- $L_1(c)$ and $L_2(c)$ will denote the total amount of labour of capability c effectively used for the production of the two goods. If:

$$Y_1 = \int\limits_{[c_1,c_2]} cL_1(c)\,dc, \tag{8.168}$$

$$Y_2 = \int\limits_{[c_1,c_2]} cL_2(c)\,dc, \tag{8.168}$$

are the amounts of *efficient labour* used for the production of x and y, the quantities produced of these two commodities are given by the production function:

$$X = X(Y_1), \tag{8.169}$$

$$z = z(Y_2). \tag{8.170}$$

- An individual of capability c is assumed to possess the fraction $\beta(c) \geqslant 0$ of the private productive sector.

Assume the fiscal system given. For an individual of capability c, the salary per hour is $s(c)$ and the profit of the private sector is π, both in terms of the consumption good and given. The individual chooses x and y so as to maximize $u(x, y, z, c)$ for z given, under the constraints:

$$\rho(c) = s(c) + \beta(c)\pi, \tag{8.171}$$

where ρ is the gross income and:

$$x = \{1 - t[\rho(c)]\}\rho(c), \tag{8.172}$$

where $t(\cdot)$ is the taxation function.

The private sector maximizes its profit, i.e. determines its production X and $L_1(c)$ such that:

$$\pi = X - \int_{[c_1,c_2]} s(c)L_1(c)\,dc, \tag{8.173}$$

is a maximum under the constraints (8.167) and (8.169).

As for the public sector, it maximizes the production z of the public good under the constraints (8.168) and (8.170) and under the budgetary equilibrium condition:

$$\int_{[c_1,c_2]} t[\rho(c)]\rho(c)\,dF(c) = \int_{[c_1,c_2]} s(c)L_2(c)\,dc. \tag{8.174}$$

The salary levels must be such that the markets are cleared:

$$\int_{[c_1,c_2]} x\,dF(c) = X, \tag{8.175}$$

$$L_1(c) + L_2(c) = y(c)\,dF(c)/dc \quad \text{(for all } c). \tag{8.176}$$

As a result, the individuals' utilities depend on the function $t(\rho)$ only. The problem of the community is to choose this function so as to maximize a collective welfare function:

$$W = \int_{[c_1,c_2]} \lambda(c)u[x, y, z, c]\,dF(c). \tag{8.177}$$

Economic theory is obviously just at the beginning of the exploration of the consequences of the introduction of the capability concept, especially since the capabilities may be transformed through education.

3.5.2. Capability and education

Though a one-period framework is not ideal for such an analysis, we shall examine here some aspects of education and training.

Individual k's utility will depend on his consumption $q_k \in \mathbf{R}^{n+}$, on his capability $c_k \in \mathbf{R}^{u+}$ and on his leisure time $L_k \in \mathbf{R}^+$:

$$U_k = U_k[q_k, c_k, L_k], \tag{8.178}$$

but the capability itself will depend on consumption (assuming that there is a relation between consumption and health and between health and effective capability); on time spent on education T_{ek}; and on time spent in labour T_{lk} (because of the implicit training given by performance of a job):

$$c_k = c_k[q_k, T_{ek}, T_{lk}], \tag{8.179}$$

$$T_{ek} + T_{lk} + T_k = T. \tag{8.180}$$

The individual income will depend on capability and labour time:

$$pq_k = s(c_k)T_{lk} + pw_k + \mathcal{O}_k\pi, \tag{8.181}$$

where $p \in \mathbf{R}^{n+}$ is the price vector; $s(c_k) \in \mathbf{R}^+$ is the salary paid to an individual with capability c_k, w_k is the vector of initial endowment of individual k: $w_k \in \mathbf{R}^{n+}$ and $\mathcal{O}_k$ is the share of the profits π of the productive sector given to individual k.

The productive sector has a production function:

$$f[q_h, (T_{lk})_{1 \leqslant k \leqslant m}, (c_k)_{1 \leqslant k \leqslant m}] = 0, \tag{8.182}$$

where $q_h \in \mathbf{R}^n$ is the vector of commodity quantities put into operations, $q_{hi} \geqq 0$ for a production and $q_{hi} \leqq 0$ for an input ($1 \leqslant i \leqslant n$).

The education sector has a simple production function, since labour is not introduced as a production factor and since production is measured by the total number of hours of education produced (which implicitly assumes a given quality of education):

$$g[\sum_k T_{ek}, q_e] = 0, \tag{8.183}$$

where $q_e \in \mathbf{R}^{n+}$ is the vector of inputs.

The equilibrium of consumptions and resources is expressed by the equality:

$$\sum_k q_k + q_e = q_h + \sum_k w_k. \tag{8.184}$$

Let us study first *the general equilibrium* of this system:

Associating with the constraints (8.179), (8.180) and (8.181), Lagrange multipliers μ_k, v_k and λ_k we find the necessary conditions for *the equilibrium of individual k* for p, $s(c_k)$ and π given under the assumptions suitable for a regular equilibrium. With an obvious notation, after the elimination of μ_k and v_k:

$$U_{ki}/\lambda_k = p_i - c_{ki}s(c_k)/(c_{ke} - c_{kl}), \tag{8.185}$$

$$U_{kc}/\lambda_k + T_{lk}\,\mathrm{d}s/\mathrm{d}c_k = s(c_k)/(c_{ke} - c_{kl}), \tag{8.168}$$

$$U_{kL}/\lambda_k = -c_{ke} \cdot s(\dot{c}_k)/(c_{ke} - c_{kl}). \tag{8.187}$$

The term:

$$\mu_k = s(c_k)/(c_{ke} - c_{kl}), \tag{8.188}$$

is obviously of great importance. Since $(c_{ke} - c_{kl})$ is the marginal difference in efficiency of education and training on the job, $s(c_k)/(c_{ke} - c_{kl})$ is *the cost to the individual of a marginal increase of capability through substitution of education to labour.*

The first relation (8.185) means that the marginal value of an increased consumption of i is equal to the price minus the effect induced on capability.

The second (8.186) expresses that the sum of the direct marginal value of capability and of the marginal increase in salary is equal to the cost of a marginal increase of capability through substitution of education to labour.

The third (8.187) results directly from the arbitrage between leisure and education and is easily interpreted.

The equilibrium of the productive sector corresponds to:

$$\max \pi = pq_h - \sum_k s(c_k)T_{lk}, \tag{8.189}$$

under the constraints (8.182) and (8.179), *which implies that the productive sector takes into account the training it gives to its staff members.*

With an obvious notation, the necessary conditions for a regular equilibrium are under, suitable conditions:

$$\mu f_{hi} = p_i, \quad \forall i, \tag{8.190}$$

$$\mu[f_{ck}c_{kl} + f_{Tk}] = s(c_k) + T_{lk} \cdot \frac{ds}{dc_k} \cdot c_{kl}, \tag{8.191}$$

μ being a Lagrange multiplier attached to (8.182).

(8.190) is ovious. (8.191) means that the marginal value of an increase in labour time (including the induced effect of increased capability) is equal to the sum of the wages paid and of the increase in wages implied by the increment in capability.

Finally, the *education sector* takes $\sum_k T_{ek}$ as given and minimizes its expenditure:

$$\sigma g_{li} = p_i, \quad \forall i, \tag{8.192}$$

σ being a Lagrange multiplier attached to (8.183).

It is easy to verify that the equilibrium defined above would be Pareto-optimum *if the individuals had to pay for the marginal cost of education.* But, in reality, other causes than the pricing policy of education also generate discrepancies:

(a) *The individuals may make a poor evaluation of the relation defining capability out of individual behaviour* (8.180).
(b) *The firms may find it difficult to estimage the impact of labour on individual capability and cannot really take this impact into account in their wages policy.*

Hence, it is not surprising if, as has been stressed by Mourre (1973), the State is led to put many correcting devices into operation in the field of education.

3.6. A society with various groups

To illustrate some of the consequences of the basic model, let us consider a society divided into three social groups: proletarians, managers and capitalists. Of course, we do not pretend that this model is a realistic picture of an existing society, but we believe it will shed some light on the possibility of building models representing certain economies more adequately.

– *A proletarian* k ($1 \leqslant k \leqslant m$) consumes a commodity vector $q_k \in \mathbf{R}^{p+}$ and provides $\sigma_k \in \mathbf{R}^+$ units of non-skilled labour. He has a utility function: $U_k[q_k, \sigma_k]$ which decreases with the amount of work provided. In strict accordance with the definition, the proletarians have just but their children, which means here that they have no initial endowment of resources.
– A *manager* h ($1 \leqslant h \leqslant n$) consumes a commodity vector $q_h \in \mathbf{R}^{p+}$ and shares his time among various firms, taking into account his preferences about activities. He has a utility function $U_h[q_h, \sigma_h, \alpha_h]$ where $\sigma_h \in \mathbf{R}^+$ is the total number of units of labour he performs and $\alpha_h \in \mathbf{R}^{p+}$ is a vector whose components are the number of labour units spent at the service of the different firms. The change of U_h as a consequence of a change of α_h for σ_h given, represents the effect of a modification of the distribution of labour time among the various jobs, the total number of hours σ_h remaining constant. The manager's capability is represented by $c_h \in \mathbf{R}^{u+}$, a vector of a nonnegative orthant of a Euclidian space. Like the proletarians the managers possess no initial endowment of resources.
– A *capitalist* l ($1 \leqslant l \leqslant p$) consumes a commodity vector $q_l \in \mathbf{R}^{p+}$. But the essential difference is that he possesses, not only a vector

$w_l \in \mathbf{R}^{p+}$ of initial endowments, but also the firm producing the lth commodity. His utility function $U_l[q_l, q_l']$ depends explicitly on the total production $q_l' \in \mathbf{R}^+$ of commodity l within the economy, since the capitalist is sensitive to the prestige of a big firm. Another important feature is that the capitalist does not work.

We shall assume that for each firm, the total management capability is a weighted sum of the times spent by the various managers. Hence for firm l:

$$\gamma_l = \sum \alpha_{hl} c_h, \qquad \gamma_l \in \mathbf{R}^{u+}. \tag{8.193}$$

Each firm is characterized by a production function which will be written:

$$f_l[q_l', q_l'', \sigma_l, \gamma_l] = 0, \tag{8.194}$$

where $q_l'' \in \mathbf{R}^{p+}$ is the input vector, $\sigma_l \in \mathbf{R}^+$ the total amount of unskilled labour used and $\gamma_l \in \mathbf{R}^{u+}$ the total management capability. σ_{kl} being the number of labour units provided by proletarian k to firm 1, the following equalities result from definitions:

$$\sum_k \sigma_{kl} = \sigma_l, \tag{8.195}$$

$$\sum_l \sigma_{kl} = \sigma_k. \tag{8.196}$$

We are now in a position to define *an equilibrium*.

In the above economy, an allocation $(q_k^*, q_h^*, q_l^*, \alpha_h^*, q_l'^*, q_l''^*, \sigma_{kl}^*, \sigma_h^*)$ *is a competitive equilibrium allocation if there are a price vector* $p^* \in \mathbf{R}^{p+}$, *a salary* $s^* \in \mathbf{R}^+$ *for nonskilled labour and a compensation vector* $s_h^* \in \mathbf{R}^{p+}$ *representing the compensations offered to manager h in the various activities, such that:*

– $U_l[q_l^*, q_l'^*]$ is maximum under the constraints:

$$p^* q_l^* = [p_l^* q_l'^* - p^* q_l''^* - s^* \sigma_l^* - \sum_h s_{hl}^* \alpha_{hl}^*] + p^* w_l, \tag{8.197}$$

$$f_l[q_l'^*, q_l''^*, \sigma_l^*, \sum_h \alpha_{hl}^* c_l] = 0. \tag{8.198}$$

– $U_h[q_h^*, \alpha_h^*, \sigma_h^*]$ is maximum under the constraints:

$$p^* q_h^* = \sum_l s_{hl}^* \alpha_{hl}^*, \tag{8.199}$$

$$\sigma_h^* = \sum_l \alpha_{hl}^*. \tag{8.200}$$

- $U_k[q_k^*, \sigma_k^*]$ is maximum under the constraint:

$$p^* q_k^* = s^* \sigma_k^*, \tag{8.201}$$

and with:

$$q_l'^* + \sum_l w_{ll} = \sum_l q_i^* + \sum_h q_h^* + \sum_k q_k^* + \sum_l q_l''^*, \tag{8.202}$$

$$\sum_k \sigma_k^* = \sum_l \sigma_l^*. \tag{8.203}$$

This model may be considered as a special case of a general microeconomic model and it is known that an equilibrium exists, given suitable assumptions on utility and production functions.

Let us study the properties of this equilibrium:

If we associate with (8.197) and (8.198) the Lagrange multipliers λ_1 and μ_1, we obtain, denoting by i or j ($1 \leqslant i, j \leqslant p$) the various commodities and introducing an obvious notation:

$$U_{li} - \lambda_l p_i = 0, \qquad \forall i, \tag{8.204}$$

$$U_{ll}' + \lambda_l p_l - \mu_l f_{ll}' = 0, \quad (U_{ll}' = \partial U/\partial q_l'; \ f_{ll}' = \partial f_l/\partial q_l'), \tag{8.205}$$

$$-\lambda_l p_j + \mu_l f_{lj} = 0, \qquad \forall j, \tag{8.206}$$

$$-\lambda_l s + \mu_l f_{l\sigma} = 0, \tag{8.207}$$

$$-\lambda_l s_{hl} + \mu_l f_{l\gamma} c_h = 0, \qquad \forall h, \quad (f_{l\gamma} = \partial f_l/\partial \gamma_l), \tag{8.208}$$

when the conditions for a regular equilibrium of capitalist l are met. Relations (8.204) to (8.208) can also be written:

$$U_{li}/p_i = \lambda_l, \tag{8.209}$$

$$p_l = -U_{ll}'/\lambda_l + (\mu_l/\lambda_l) f_{ll}, \tag{8.210}$$

$$p_j = (\mu_l/\lambda_l) f_{lj}, \tag{8.211}$$

$$s = (\mu_l/\lambda_l) f_{l\sigma}, \tag{8.212}$$

$$s_{hl} = (\mu_l/\lambda_l) f_{l\gamma} c_h, \tag{8.213}$$

Notice that $d = (\mu_l/\lambda_l) f_{ll}$ is easily interpreted as the *marginal cost of production*. Hence:

– The selling price of a commodity is equal to the marginal cost minus the marginal value of the production for the capitalist (relation already found in chapter 7).
– For the various inputs, the prices are equal to the marginal productivities:

$$p_j = d(f_{1j}/f_{ll}), \quad s = d(f_{l\sigma}/f_{ll}), \quad s_{hl} = d(f_{l\gamma}c_h/f_{ll}). \tag{8.214}$$

If we associate with (8.199) and (8.200) the Lagrange multipliers λ_h and μ_h, we get, with an obvious notation:

$$U_{hi} - \lambda_h p_i = 0 \quad \forall i, \tag{8.215}$$

$$U_{hl} + \lambda_h s_{hl} + \mu_h = 0, \tag{8.216}$$

$$U_{h\sigma} - \mu_h = 0, \tag{8.217}$$

when the conditions for a regular equilibrium of manager h are met. Relations (8.215) to (8.217) can also be written:

$$U_{hi}/p_i = \lambda_h, \tag{8.218}$$

$$(U_{hl} + U_{h\sigma})/s_{hl} = -\lambda_h. \tag{8.219}$$

Each manager distributes his time in such a way that, for each activity, his salary is proportional to his marginal disutility for this type of labour. This marginal disutility is the sum of the *general marginal disutility for labour* $(-U_{h\sigma})$ and of the *specific marginal disutility* for labour in a given activity $(-U_{hl})$. While $U_{h\sigma}$ is negative, U_{hl} may very well be positive.

(8.219) may be written:

$$s_{hl} = -\frac{U_{hl}}{\lambda_h} + s_h, \tag{8.220}$$

s_h being the "normal" wage accepted by h and U_{hl}/λ_h *the positive or negative premium he asks for working in activity h.*

Of course, for many managers, the assumption of a regular equilibrium is unacceptable for some activities. For these activities $\alpha_{hl} = 0$ and:

$$U_{hl} + U_{h\sigma} < -\lambda_h s_{hl}.$$

Introducing the value of s_{hl} into (8.214), we obtain:

$$d = \frac{s_h}{f_{l\gamma}c_h/f_{ll}} - \frac{U_{hl}/\lambda_h}{f_{l\gamma}c_h/f_{ll}}, \quad \forall h. \qquad (8.221)$$

The first term of the right-hand side would be *the expression of the marginal cost d_0 if the managers were sensitive only to consumption*. The second term represents *the discrepancy due to the managers' preferences about activities*. But, of course, each of these terms depends on the values of all the parameters.

The price of commodity 1 can be written:

$$p_l = -U'_{ll}/\lambda_l - \frac{U_{hl}/\lambda_h}{f_{l\gamma}c_h/f_{ll}} + d_0. \qquad (8.222)$$

Finally, if we associate with (8.201) a Lagrange multiplier λ_k, we obtain with an obvious notation:

$$U_{ki}/p_i = \lambda_k, \quad \forall i, \qquad (8.223)$$

$$U_{k\sigma}/s = -\lambda_k, \qquad (8.224)$$

when the conditions for a regular equilibrium of proletarian k are met.

A few *important conclusions* can be drawn from this model:

In an equilibrium where capitalists only maximized profits and managers were indifferent to the type of jobs, perfect competition would lead, under usual assumptions, to a situation in which: it would be impossible to increase an individual's utility without decreasing that of another individual; it would be impossible to increase the total consumption of a final commodity without decreasing that of another good.

Here, *the capitalists are not only able to take advantage of all the monopoly situations in their pricing policies, but they impose their management criteria, their interest in power, in prestige, in comfort...* As a consequence, two discrepancies appear with the optimal price and production policy: a discrepancy due to *monopoly profits*, a discrepancy due to the *differences between capitalists' objectives and effective profit-maximization*.

As for the managers, they use their capability, which is a scarce resource, to choose the activities they like. In modern, fashionable, pleasant activities, the offer of able managers will be abundant and the compensation moderate (for *given levels of capability*). Consequently, production will be efficiently organized; costs will be low and the equilibrium of supply and demand of the product will correspond to a higher quantity produced. On the contrary, in sectors without prestige or with traditional production techniques, the supply of able managers will be low, in spite of fairly high compensations. The costs of production will be high and the market equilibrium will be reached at lower levels of production.

In other words, production is not orientated only by consumers' tastes, but also by the preferences of the owners of scarce resources: the owners of firms, i.e. capitalists; and highly skilled workers, i.e. in this model, managers.

As a result, *the optimum such as that it is impossible to increase the total consumption of a final commodity without decreasing the consumption of another one, is no longer identical with the optimum where it is impossible to increase an individual's utility without decreasing that of another individual.*

A set of values which induces the capitalist to maximize profits and the workers to be interested only in income is then necessary for the identity of these two concepts of optimality.

In other words, *to be efficient – in terms of the bundle of commodities available – competition does not only imply some technical conditions* (lack of externalities), *some kind of market organization* (absence of monopoly), but also a *suitable set of values.* It is not efficient per se, but efficient in some types of societies where the individuals' objectives are adequate.

To submit these questions to a precise mathematical analysis is obviously of great importance to economics. One of the contributions of chapter 6's model may be to make such analysis easier.

A second model will illustrate other aspects of similar problems.

In this model, the manager will become the central figure:

The submodel of the proletarian is unchanged.

Capitalist l $(1 \leqslant l \leqslant p)$ consumes the vector $q_l \in \mathbf{R}^{n+}$ and obtains his income from the payments made to him for the services of the capital goods vector $w_l \in \mathbf{R}^{v+}$ which he possesses.

Manager h $(1 \leqslant h \leqslant n)$ consumes the vector $q_h \in \mathbf{R}^{n+}$, produces an amount of effort $e_h \in \mathbf{R}^+$, keeps for himself the extra income, once the capitalist has been paid. He has his own objectives, represented by the introduction in his utility function of the production q_h' of his firm. He is endowed with a capability $c_h \in \mathbf{R}^{u+}$.

In such an economy, an allocation $(q_k^*, q_h^*, q_l^*, e_h^*, q_h'^*, q_h''^*, \sigma_{kh}^*, w_{hl}^*)$ *is a* *competitive equilibrium allocation if there are a price vector* $p \in \mathbf{R}^{n+}$, *a salary* $s^* \in \mathbf{R}^+$ *for nonskilled labour, and a price vector* $\pi^* \in \mathbf{R}^{v+}$ *for capital goods, such that:*

– $U_l[q_l^*]$ is maximum under the constraint:

$$p^* q_l^* = \pi^* w_l. \tag{8.225}$$

– $U_h[q_h^*, q_h'^*, e_h^*]$ is maximum under the constraints:

$$f_h[q_h'^*, q_h''^*, \sigma_h^*, e_h^*, \sum_l w_{hl}^*, c_h] = 0, \tag{8.226^z}$$

$$p^* q_h^* = p_h^* q_h'^* - p^* q_h''^* - s^* \sigma_h^* - \sum_l \pi^* w_{hl}^*. \tag{8.227}$$

– $U_k[q_k^*, \sigma_k^*]$ is maximum under the constraint:

$$p^* q_k^* = s^* \sigma_k^*, \tag{8.228}$$

and with:

$$q_h'^* = \sum_l q_l^* + \sum_h q_h^* + \sum_k q_k^* + \sum_h q_h''^*, \tag{8.229}$$

$$\sum_k \sigma_{kh}^* = \sigma_h^*, \tag{8.230}$$

$$\sum_h \sigma_{kh}^* = \sigma_k^*, \tag{8.231}$$

$$\sum_h w_{hl}^* = w_l. \tag{8.232}$$

Here, the situation of the management of the firm is practically the one described in chapter 7.

We can enunciate directly the equilibrium conditions under suitable assumptions and with an obvious notation:

$$U_{li}/p_i = \lambda_l, \tag{8.233}$$

$$U_{ki}/p_i = -U_{k\sigma}/s = \lambda_k, \tag{8.234}$$

$$U_{hi}/p_i = \lambda_h, \tag{8.235}$$

$$p_h = -(U_{hh}'/\lambda_h) + (\mu_h/\lambda_h) f_{hh}, \tag{8.236}$$

$$U_{he} - \mu_h f_{he} = 0, \tag{8.237}$$

$$p_j = (\mu_h/\lambda_h) f_{hj}, \tag{8.238}$$

$$s = (\mu_h/\lambda_h) f_{h\sigma}, \tag{8.239}$$

$$\pi_l = (\mu_h/\lambda_h) f_{hl}, \tag{8.240}$$

λ_h, μ_h, λ_l, λ_k being respectively associated with constraints (8.226), (8.227), (8.225), (8.228).

The relations are apparently the same, but the sociological content is totally different. Here J.K. Galbraith's technostructures impose their objectives and make their own arbitrages between: (i) power and prestige, (ii) profitability, (iii) efforts for innovation, information, managerial improvements, etc. Their constraints result, of course, from the competition between them and from the prices they have to pay the workers for their services and the capitalists for the use of capital.

In some ways, these two models describe extreme situations:

- In the first, the capitalists prevent the managers from having any freedom in the choice of business objectives. Hence the only possibility for the latter is *to select the roles they like.*
- In the second, *the managers have total freedom in their objectives* and hence in their *selection of allocations*, the capitalists being able only to get the market prices. In this case, the better the manager, the more resources he can extract to develop his business, to hit his competitors, to earn a high income, or to live lazily.

The managers are not the only group who may experience these situations. We could, in a similar way, introduce various types of relations between managers and "proletarians." To go further along these lines, it would be necessary to utilize simultaneously the theory of the individual developed in this book and the theory of organization announced in chapter 3 and sketched in the preceding chapter.

In another direction, the above considerations could be used for a theory of long-term structural changes in economies if two other kinds of elements were added:

- a link between the present state or the past evolution of an economy and the transformation of individual utilities;
- a theory of the mechanisms through which the decisions left to the various types of individuals are progressively changed.

Then a real bridge could be established between contemporary economic science and some of the key aspects of Marx's thinking.

In such research, it may be important to look at the connections between the economic and political spheres. Hence, obviously, a preliminary step is to examine some of the consequences of chapter 6's model for economies with a State.

4. Economies with a state

Though the model presented in chapter 6 may be the starting point for fruitful research in political science, only a politico-economic model will be discussed here. It is an extension of a model developed by Saposnik (1974).[9]

Saposnik considers a society composed of m individuals k having a utility $U_k(e)$, e denoting the state of the economy in the set E of feasible states. Each individual has a power index $K_k(e)$ *depending on the state of the economy*, which measures the ability of the individual to influence social choices.

A *power relation* $\geqslant_e$ on E is introduced with $e_1 \geqslant_e e_2$ for $e_1 \in E$, $e_2 \in E$ if, in state e, the sum of the power indices of individuals preferring e_1 to e_2 is greater than that of individuals preferring e_2 to e_1. Arrow's paradox is avoided by an assumption insuring a certain coherence of individual preferences. The power relation is then transitive on E.

A state of the economy e is chosen by society if $e \in E$ and $\{e \geqslant_e e'$; $\forall e' \in E\}$.

With some assumptions, the author shows the existence of such an equilibrium state.

Let us now describe the economy itself:

The vector $g \in \mathbf{R}^{u+}$ will represent the production of collective goods, these goods being at the disposal of the individuals without payment. These collective goods include, of course, elements such as national defence highways, police, education, health services.

To obtain g, it is necessary to use as inputs goods produced by the private sector. The vector $q_p \in \mathbf{R}^{n+}$ will represent these inputs. The production function of the public sector may be represented either by:

$$(g, q_p) \in Y_p, \tag{8.241}$$

where Y_p is a subset of $\mathbf{R}^{(u+n)+}$ or by:

$$f[g, q_p] = 0, \tag{8.242}$$

where f is a mapping from $\mathbf{R}^{(u+n)+}$ into $\mathbf{R}$.

[9] For research stemming from the same philosophy, see, for instance, Pething M. Mannheim, "Environmental management in general equilibrium: a new incentive compatible approach," paper presented at the Econometric Society's European Meeting, Helsinki, August 1976.

The vector $q_h \in \mathbf{R}^n$ will represent the quantities of private goods on which the private sector operates. If $1 \leqslant i \leqslant n, q_{hi} \geqslant 0$ for a production, $q_{hi} \leqslant 0$ for an input.

The production function of the private sector may be represented either by:

$$q_h \in Y_h, \tag{8.243}$$

where Y_h is a subset of $\mathbf{R}^n$ or by:

$$f_h[q_h] = 0, \tag{8.244}$$

where f_h is a mapping from $\mathbf{R}^n$ into $\mathbf{R}$. For the sake of simplicity, *this production function is assumed to be independent from the production of collective goods.*

Each individual k has a utility function $U_k(q_k, g)$ where $q_k \in \mathbf{R}^{n+}$ denotes the consumption of private goods. He has an initial endowment $w_k \in \mathbf{R}^{n+}$ of private goods and possesses the fraction $\mathcal{O}_k$ of the private sector. We denote $w = (w_k)_{1 \leqslant k \leqslant m}$ and $\mathcal{O} = (\mathcal{O}_k)_{1 \leqslant k \leqslant m}$.

We assume that *commodity n is taken as the numeraire* and denote by $p \in \mathbf{R}^{n+}$ the price vector for private commodities. The public sector covers its expenditures without making any profit, through a lump-sum tax t_h levied on the private sector and through lump-sum taxes t_k levied on the various individuals: $t_h \in \mathbf{R}^+, (t_k) \in \mathbf{R}^{m+}$.

A state e of the economy $\{(U_k)_{1 \leqslant h \leqslant m}, Y_h, Y_p, (w_k)_{1 \leqslant k \leqslant m}, (\mathcal{O}_k)_{1 \leqslant k \leqslant m}\}$ is a suite:

$$e = \{(q_k)_{1 \leqslant k \leqslant m}, g, q_p, q_h, p, (t_k)_{1 \leqslant k \leqslant m}, t_h\},$$

i.e. an element of $\mathbf{R}^{mn+} \times \mathbf{R}^{u+} \times \mathbf{R}^{n+} \times \mathbf{R}^n \times \mathbf{R}^{n+} \times \mathbf{R}^{m+} \times \mathbf{R}^+$.

By definition, *a state e^* will be an equilibrium if:*

(i) It is a *competitive equilibrium* of the economy for $g^*, q_p^*, t_h^*, (t_k)_1^*{}_{\leqslant k \leqslant m}$ given, which means that:

(ia) *The utility of each individual k is maximum on the set of the private consumptions available under the income constraint:*

$$U_k(q_k^*, g^*) = \max_{q_k \in B_k(p^*)} U_k(q_k, g^*), \tag{8.245}$$

with:

$$B_k(p^*) = \{q_k \mid p^* q_k \leqq q^* w_k + \mathcal{O}_k r^* - t_k^*\}. \tag{8.246}$$

(ib) *The profit of the private sector is maximum on the set of possible productions:*

$$r^* = \max_{q_h \in Y_h} [p^* q_h - t_h^*].$$ (8.247)

(ic) *Offers and demands are equal on the market of private goods*

$$\sum_k q_k^* = q_h^* - q_p^*.$$ (8.248)

(ii) The *public sector* is such that:

(iia) *Its expenditures are minimum for g* and p* given*

$$d^* = \min_{(q_p, g^*) \in Y_p} p^* q_p.$$ (8.249)

(iib) *The public sector is in equilibrium:*

$$t_h^* + \sum_k t_k^* = d^*.$$ (8.250)

(iii) A *transitive power relation* being assumed, the production of collective goods and the taxes g^*, t_h^*, $(t_k)_{1 \leqslant k \leqslant m}^*$ is such that:

$$e^* \succsim_{e^*} e' \quad \text{for} \quad \forall e' \in E_0,$$

E_0 being the set of competitive equilibria generated by all feasible $\{g, t_h, (t_k)_{1 \leqslant k \leqslant m}\}$'s.

Let us sketch the way in which the existence of such an equilibrium could be analyzed:

– For $g, q_p, t_h, (t_k)_{1 \leqslant k \leqslant m}$ given, it is easy to enumerate the conditions under which a competitive equilibrium exists. For this equilibrium or one of these:

$$q_k = q_k[g, q_p, t_h, t, w, \mathcal{O}],^{10}$$ (8.251)

$$p = p[g, q_p, t_h, t, w, \mathcal{O}],$$ (8.252)

assuming Y_p and Y_h given.
– The public sector takes the price vector as given and determines q_p as a function of g and p, so that:

$$q_k = q_k[g, q_p(g, p), t_h, t, w, \mathcal{O}],$$ (8.253)

---

[10] To simplify notation: $t = (t_k)_{1 \leqslant h \leqslant m}$.

$$p = p[g, q_p(g, p), t_h, t, w, \mathcal{O}].$$ (8.354)

Under conditions to be studied, (8.254) defines a price vector p (with $p_n = 1$):

$$p = \pi[g, t_h, t, w, \mathcal{O}],$$ (8.255)

and a consumption vector q_k:

$$q_k = \gamma_k[g, t_h, t, w, \mathcal{O}].$$ (8.256)

t_h and t must satisfy the constraints resulting from (8.249) and (8.250):

$$t_h + \sum_k t_k = d(g, p),$$ (8.257)

and replacing p by its value (8.253):

$$t_h + \sum_k t_k = d(g, t_h, t, w, \mathcal{O}).$$ (8.258)

Out of (8.254), the utility of individual k is easily computed:

$$U_k = U_k[q_k, g] = V_k[g, t_h, t, w, \mathcal{O}].$$ (8.259)

For w and $\mathcal{O}$ given, denote by S the set of (g, t_h, t) satisfying (8.258). Each individual has preferences on S which correspond to the weak order generated by (8.259). This individual is able to compare any pair $(s, s') \in S \times S$.

If we assume that each individual possesses a *power index* K_{ks} in state s, and if we admit Saposnik's hypothesis, there are a transitive power relation on S and an equilibrium $s^* = (g^*, t_h^*, t^*)$ such that:

$$s^* \gtrsim_{s^*} s' \quad \text{for} \quad \forall s' \in S.$$

Several assumptions may be made about the power indices:

(1) *The power index is the same for all individuals* and it is independent of s. In other words:

$$K_{ks} = K.$$ (8.260)

All the individuals have an equal weight in the political decisions, but their preferences differ, for several reasons: they have different utilities and their arbitrages between the consumption of private or public goods are not the same; they have different shares in the society's resources; their initial endowment and their share of the private sector are not identical; they are hit in an asymmetric way by the tax structure (t_h, t).

(2) *The power index of an individual depends on his net income:*

$$K_{ks} = K\{p(s)w_k + \mathcal{O}_k[p(s)q_h(s) - t_h(s)] - t_k(s)\}, \qquad (8.261)$$

and obviously also depends on s.

This assumption corresponds to a rather naive interpretation of political life, but it is mentioned here because it will sound familiar to many socialist ears.

(3) *The power index of an individual depends on the role structure of each individual* and is independent of s.

In the present framework of the model, we can only write:

$$K_{ks} = K_k. \qquad (8.262)$$

A few conjectures could be made on the function V_k:

- Probably the higher $\mathcal{O}_k$, the more unfavourable to business tax t_h and the less interested in collective goods production g is individual k.
- In spite of the fact that an increase in tax enables an increase in collective goods production g, every individual k is unfavourable to an increase in the tax t_k paid by himself.
- Every individual k is favourable to an increase in the tax $t_{k'}$ ($k' \neq k$) paid by other individuals, since it makes it possible to increase the production of collective goods.

Naturally, a lump-sum tax structure is only one of the many possible structures. Another simple structure would be an income-tax structure of rate τ for individuals and τ_h for private firms.

To go further, changes in the model would be necessary. It could be done in two directions:

- A first idea would be to introduce a time-constraint. Any individual k could split his time T between time spent in working T_{1k} and time spent in political action T_{2k}. His utility would become:

$$U_k = U_k[g, q_k, T_{1k}, T_{2k}], \qquad (8.263)$$

and the constraints limiting his actions:

$$T_{1k} + T_{2k} = T, \qquad (8.264)$$

$$pq_k = sT_{1k} + pw_k + \mathcal{O}_k\tau - t_k. \qquad (8.265)$$

But in exchange, his power index would be a function of T_{2k}:

$$K_{ks} = K[T_{2k}]. \qquad (8.266)$$

An individual may prefer to increase his income directly, or to fight for a greater weight in political decisions through political action.
– A second idea would be to consider explicitly the economic *and political* roles available to an individual of a given capacity. If (ρ_{1k}, ρ_{2k}) denotes a pair of economic (ρ_{1k}) and political (ρ_{2k}) roles chosen by k (capability $c_k \in \mathbf{R}^{u+}$) in the set $R(c_k)$ available to him, the power index would be defined by a mapping from $R(c_k)$ into $\mathbf{R}^+$:

$$K_{ks} = K[\rho_{1k}, \rho_{2k}]. \tag{8.267}$$

Simultaneously, the utility function and the income would depend on the role structure chosen and the description of the two production sectors would be adapted accordingly.

What is important here is *the possibility of a breakthrough into the politico-economic field.* Because of the broader representation of individual behaviours, it becomes feasible to link two types of decision processes: a competitive decision process operating in the private sector, a political decision process operating in the public sector-though this second sector has to take into account, as in reality, the market prices for its expenditures. With the development of such models, *general equilibrium theory* would no longer be limited to strict economic considerations but *would be open to the analysis of interactions between the economic and political aspects of the life of a society.* An ocean for research!

5. Conclusion

In many respects, this chapter is tentative. Some of the proofs are only sketched, others are not even developed. More important: only a few of the possibilities implicitly contained in the basic model are explored.[11]

But essential results for the orientation of economic research have been obtained:

(1) The broadening of the model of individual behaviour generates a host of new and meaningful problems in equilibrium theory. Some of

[11] As an example, we could have examined a society in which individuals attach a utility to their liberty to take business decisions and compared, from the point of view of efficiency, a decentralized organization with perfect competition and a centralized one in the case of a production sector with increasing returns to scale.

these problems remain in the classical field of theoretical economics (for instance, the manipulation of perceptions in exchange economies); but others are on the borders between sociology and economics or between political science and economics.

(2) The assumptions behind the conventional equilibrium models, which frequently lack realism, can be replaced by much more acceptable assumptions describing a variety of social situations. The equilibrium analysis appears as having a much broader scope than is ordinarily thought by iconoclasts, who assimilate the whole concept of equilibrium to the use made of it by Arrow and Debreu in their classical papers.

(3) In as much as they are reflected in the utility functions of "complete" individuals choosing and performing various roles in society, *the social values are crucial for the nature and the properties of equilibrium*. Hence, the interest, for *economics*, of a theory describing the evolution of these values as a consequence of the evolution of the social system.

(4) The equilibrium is not passively experienced by inactive individuals, but it is the result of the conflicting behaviours of creative individuals looking for information, inventing solutions, stimulated by power and prestige.[12]

(5) As a consequence of the diversity in individuals' objectives, of the abundance of constraints and of the existence of perceptive biases, the equivalence between equilibrium states and Pareto optimal states frequently collapses. But – and this may be just as important – a discrepancy appears between an optimum defined in terms of a utility frontier and an optimum defined in terms of a production frontier; and both optima may present characteristics which make them ethically debatable, though logically consistent.

Our dearest wish, in concluding this chapter, is that it may give rise to additional research in the various fields mentioned.

---

[12] With all the limitations resulting from the certain environment hypothesis.

CONCLUSION

Les premières causes nous seront à jamais
cachées, ... les résultats généraux de ces
causes nous seront aussi difficiles à con-
naître que les causes mêmes; tout ce qui
nous est possible est d'apercevoir quelques
effets particuliers... Mais, puisque c'est la
seule voie qui nous soit ouverte, puisque
nous n'avons pas d'autres moyens pour aller
à la connaissance des choses naturelles, il
faut aller jusqu'où cette route peut nous
conduire...

Buffon
Histoire Naturelle

If a broader economic theory can be built around the five concepts: resources, individuals, organizations, processes and constraints, this book appears as a first step in this direction. Centered on the individual, it tries to enlarge the representation of individual behaviour in such a way that a whole range of observed facts – in economic reality or in other human sciences – can be incorporated in theoretical models.

It introduces important notions such as motivations and satisfactions; individual states – perceived or real, controlled or not; roles and allocations; capabilities. It shows the variety of constraints limiting individual behaviour: time constraints, health constraints, capability constraints; constraints on role structure, on information; regulation constraints, etc. It molds notions and constraints into a basic model, able to accept discontinuities in behaviour.

Then the book tries to apply this model to special fields of economics: demand theory with considerations on quality choice, on advertising, on new products; the labour market, with an analysis of employment demand and supply; competition, with special emphasis on managers' psychology and capabilities; organization theory, with a description of various models stressing different aspects of the operation of an organization. The last chapter examines some consequences of the basic model in the field of general equilibrium theory for economies described as noncooperative games, for exchange economies, for economies with production and for economies with a State.

Clearly, the result is full of imperfections, but the analysis of the causes of this situation shows that some of these defects may be progressively removed:

(I) Frequently, in order to be able to cover a field as broad as possible, the preference has been given to shortened mathematical treatments. This may sometimes have led to a certain lack of rigour which, on the whole, does not impair the conclusions; or it points to the need for additional research when totally new topics are suggested, as in the last chapter.

(II) In spite of this broad coverage, the possibilities opened up by richer models of individual behaviour are so huge that the impression remains, especially after chapters 7 and 8, that the applications developed have been chosen partly at random, and are far from constituting a coherent picture of all the analysis made feasible by the concepts of chapters 5 and 6.

(III) The assumptions of one-period and a certain environment, though necessary in a first step, strictly delineate the domain which may be considered and exclude a proper treatment of a whole list of essential features: creativity and information search are no longer random processes; forecasts made by the individual for the next periods cease to be important determinants of present behaviour; learning mechanisms of any kind cannot be represented; the progressive change of utility functions under the influence of the individual past and of the surrounding economy cannot be introduced, and the resulting similarities of attitude among the members of the same social group cannot be adequately dealt with; questions related to life cycles, pensions, retirement, inheritance are eliminated, etc. and this enumeration is far from complete. Only a second volume would offer enough space for a reasonable extension of the basic ideas to an uncertain environment and to a multiplicity of periods.

(IV) A theory of the individual is only a stone in any economic construction. Obviously, if the organization with several decision-centers must replace the firm with one-decision center as a key economic agent, a tremendous research effort, partly based on models of the individual, is needed in this field. As only one example of possible types of interactions between organizations or individuals, the market must also be the basis for a broadened theory of exchange processes.

In parallel with these efforts, which could give rise to a renewed analysis of synchronic equilibria, where economic, social and political elements would be mixed, it would be vital to examine how an equilibrium state generates forces which will transform it. Some of these forces – like the impact on utilities – are relevant to a theory of the individual; but others, like the incentive to the creation of coalitions of economic agents, or the influence on the structure of exchange processes, or the pressure of the political on the economic system, go far beyond such a theory.[1] The result would be a theory of diachronic evolutions of economic systems.

But Science does not like to be pushed. Long-term visions may be useful as a guide for research. They do not replace modest, profound, precise and limited pieces of work. It will take a long time before this last gap will be greatly reduced.

Our only wish, in writing this last line, will be fulfilled if the book generates creative and serious research on economic individual behaviour.

---

[1] For a development of these ideas, see J. Lesourne (1975, 1976).

BIBLIOGRAPHY

The bibliography is separated into two parts, the first one devoted to articles and books from the field of economics, the second one to publications from other human sciences.[1] None of these parts is exhaustive, but the first is rather comprehensive while the second is voluntarily limited to a small number of important texts.

Bibliography from economics

Adar, Z. and Edelson, N.M., Gambling behavior and lottery prize structures, School of Public and Urban Policy and Department of Economics, Fells Center of Government, University of Pennsylvania, Philadelphia, 1975.

Alchian, A.A., Information costs, pricing and reserve unemployment, Phelps et al. (eds.), 1970.

Allais, M., Traité d'économie pure, Sirey, Paris, 1953. New edition of: A la recherche d'une discipline économique, Paris, 1943.

Allais, M., Economie et intérêt, Présentation nouvelles des problèmes fondamentaux relatifs au rôle économique du taux de l'intérêt et de leurs solutions, Paris, Imprimerie Nationale, 1947.

Allais, M., Le comportement de l'homme rationnel devant le risque: Critique des postulats et axiomes de l'école américaine, Econometrica, 21, 1953.

Allais, M., The foundations of a positive theory of choice involving risk and a criticism of the postulates and axioms of the american school, Centre d'Analyse Economique, no. 2824, 1972.

Allingham, M.G. and Sandmo, A., Income tax evasion: A theoretical analysis, Journal of Public Economics, 1, 1972.

Ames, E., A priceless planned economy, Economic research bureau, working paper no. 38, Stony Brook, New York, 1971.

Ames, E., Théorie de la planification économique, Revue d'Economie Politique, 1974.

Anastasopoulos and Kounias, S., Optimal consumption over time when prices and interest rates follow a markovian process, Econometrica, 1975.

Anscombe, F.J. and Aumann, R.J., A definition of subjective probability, Annals of Mathematical Statistics, 34, 1963.

Antonelli, G.B., Sulla teoria matematico della economia politica, Tipografia del Folchetto, Pisa, 1886. Translation in J.S. Chipman, L. Hurwicz, M.K. Richter, H.F. Sounenschein, Preference, utility and demand, Harcourt Brace Jovanovich, 1975.

Arrow, K.J., Utilities, attitudes, choices: A review note, Econometrica, 1958.

---

[1] A few papers from economists, only quoted in chapter 2 are included in the second list.

Arrow, K.J., Rational choice functions and orderings, Economica, 1959.

Arrow, K.J. and Kurz, M., Optimal consumer allocation over an infinite horizon, Journal of Economic Theory, 1969.

Arrow, K.J., Essays in theory of risk bearing, North-Holland, Amsterdam, 1971.

Arrow, K.J. and Hahn, F.M., General competitive analysis, Holden Day, San Francisco, Oliver and Boyd, Edinburgh, 1971.

Aumann, R.J., Utility theory without the completeness axiom, Econometrica, 30, 1964.

Aumann, R.J., Utility theory without the completeness axiom: A correction, Econometrica, 32, 1964.

Atkinson, A.B. and Stiglitz, J.E., The design of tax structure: Direct versus indirect taxation, Journal of Public Economics, 6, 1976.

de Backer, P., Négociation et conflit dans l'entreprise, Quelques indications d'application de la psychologie des conflits, Metra, vol. XI, no. 1, 1972.

Balasko, Y., Equilibrium analysis and envelope theory, Paper presented at the Econometric Society European Meeting, Helsinki, August 1976.

Barten, A.P., The systems of consumer demand function approach: A review, Third World Congress of the Econometric Society, Toronto, August 1975.

Bartoszynski, A metric structure derived from subjective judgments: Scaling under perfect and imperfect discrimination, Econometrica, 42, 1974.

Baumol, W., Business behavior, value and growth, MacMillan, New York, 1959.

Becker, G.S., Human Capital, Columbia University Press, 1964, 1975.

Becker, G.S., A theory of the allocation of time, The Economic Journal, no. 299, 1965.

Becker, G.S., The economics of discrimination, University of Chicago Press, Chicago, 1971.

Becker, G.S., A theory of social interactions, Journal of Political Economy, 1974.

Becker, G.S., Crime and punishment: An economic approach, Journal of Political Economy, 76, 1968.

Becker, G.S. (ed.), Essays in labor economics, Journal of Political Economy, 84, 1976.

Bell, D.E., A utility function for time streams having inter period dependencies, IIASA, Laxenburg, 1975.

Bellman, R.E. and Zadeh, L.A., Decision making in a fuzzy environment, Management Science, vol. 17, no. 4, 1970.

Benassy, J.P., Neokeynesian disequilibrium theory in a monetary economy, Review of Economic Studies, 1975.

Benassy, J.P., Théorie neokeynésienne du déséquilibre dans une économie monétaire, Cahiers du Séminaire d'Econométrie, 17, C.N.R.S., Paris, 1976.

Berge, C., Théorie générale des jeux à n personnes, Mémorial des Sciences Mathématiques, Fasc., 138, 1957.

Bernard, G. and Besson, M.L., Douze méthodes d'analyse multicritère, Revue d'Informatique et de Recherche Opérationnelle, 1971.

Bernard, G., On utility functions, Theory and Decision, 5, 1974.

Blinder, A.S. and Weiss, Y., Human capital and labor supply: A synthesis, Journal of Political Economy, 84, 1976.

Brown, C., A model of optimal human capital accumulation and the wages of young high school graduates, Journal of Political Economy, 84, 1976.

Brown, M. and Heien, D., The S-branch utility tree: A generalization of the linear expenditure system, Econometrica, vol. 40, no. 4, 1972.

Burness, H.S., On the role of separability assumptions in determining impatience implications, Econometrica, 44, 1976.

Bush, R.R. and Mosteller, F., Stochastic models of learning, Wiley, New York, 1955.

Carpentier, C., Structure administrative et délégation du pouvoir, Revue d'Economie Politique, 1974.

Cherry, C., On human communication: A review, a survey and a criticism, The Techno-
logy Press of Massachusetts Institute of Technology and John Wiley, 1957.
Cherry, C. (ed.), Pragmatic aspects of human communication, D. Reidel Publishing
Company, Dordrecht, Holland, 1975.
Chipman, J.S., The foundations of utility, Econometrica, 28, 1960.
Chipman, J.S., Hurwicz, L., Richter, M.K., Sonnenschein, H.F., Preferences, utility and
demand, Harcourt Brace Jovanovich, New York, 1975.
Chite, V., Wealth effect on the demand for money, Journal of Political Economy, 83,
1975.
Cochrane, J.L. and Zeleny, M. (ed.), Multiple criteria decision making, University of
South Carolina Press, 1973.
Cohen, K.J. and Cyert, R.M., Theory of the firm: Resource allocation in a market
economy, Prentice Hall, Englewood Cliffs, New Jersey, 1965.
Cotta, A., La structure du pouvoir dans les organisations, Théorie Economique et
Croissance des Organisations, June 1972.
Cotta, A., Pouvoir et optimum, Revue d'Economie Politique, 1974.
Cotta, A., Le pouvoir et la stratégie du chef dans un système décentralisé, Revue d'Eco-
nomie Politique, 1974.
Cotta, A., Analyse des processus de pouvoir dans les organisations, Université Paris
Dauphine, Sciences des Organisations, 1975.
Cotta, A., Eléments pour une théorie des conflits: La diversité des objectifs dans une
organisation, CREPA, 1975.
Cyert, R.M. and March, J.G., A behavioral theory of the firm, Prentice Hall, Englewood
Cliffs, New Jersey, 1963.
Day, R.H., Rational choice and economic behavior, Theory and Decision, 1, 1973.
Debreu, G., Representation of a preference ordering by a numerical function, in R.M.
Thrall, C.H. Coombs, R.L. Davis (eds.), Decision Processes, 1954.
Debreu, G., Stochastic choice and cardinal utility, Econometrica, vol. 26, no. 3, 1958.
Debreu, G., Theory of value, Wiley, New York, 1959.
Debreu, G., Topological methods in cardinal utility theory, in K.J. Arrow, S. Karlin and
P. Suppes (eds.), Mathematical methods in the social sciences, 1959, Stanford University
Press, 1960.
Debreu, G., Smooth preferences, Econometrica, 40, 1972.
Deschamps, R., Risk aversion and demand functions, Econometrica, 41, 1973.
Diamond, P.A., The evaluation of infinite utility streams, Econometrica, 33, no. 1,
1965.
Diewert, W.E., Intertemporal consumer theory and the demand for durables, Econo-
metrica, 42, 1974.
Doeringer, P. and Piorer, M., Internal labor markets and manpower analysis, Heath,
Lexington, MA, 1971.
de Donnea, F.W., Consumer behaviour, transport mode choice and value of time: Some
microeconomic models, Regional and Urban Economics, vol. 1, 1972.
Dornbusch, R. and Mussa, M., Consumption real balance and the hoarding function,
International Economic Review, 16, 1975.
Dreze, J.H., Existence of an exchange equilibrium under price rigidities, International
Economic Review, 16, 1975.
Dupuy, J.P., Encombrement et valeur sociale du temps, CEREBE, Paris, 1973.
Dupuy, J.P., Les aspects psychologiques de la croissance des dépenses de médicaments,
CEREBE, Economie de la Santé, 1973.
Dupuy, J.P., Innovation et obsolescence psychologique: Essai de formalisation dans le
cadre d'une économie de marché, Cahiers du Séminaire d'Econométrie, no. 15,
C.N.R.S., Paris, 1974.

Dupuy, J.P., Rationalité sociale des politiques de santé, Revue d'Economie Politique, 1974.

Dupuy, J.P., L'espace-temps distordu, Pour une théorie des dommages causés à l'environnement symbolique, CEREBE, Paris, 1975.

Dupuy, J.P., Valeur sociale et encombrement du temps, Monographies du Séminaire d'Econométrie XI, C.N.R.S., Paris, 1975.

Epstein, L., A disaggregate analysis of consumer choice under uncertainty, Econometrica, 43, 1975.

Fair, R.C., On controlling the economy to win elections, Cowles Foundation for Research in Economics at Yale University, 1975.

Findlay, R., Slavery, incentives and manumission: A theoretical model, Journal of Political Economy, 83, 1975.

Fischer, S., Assets, contingency commodities and the Slutsky equations, Econometrica, 40, 1972.

Fishburn, P.C., Decision and value theory, Wiley, New York, 1964.

Fishburn, P.C., Methods of estimating additive utilities, Management Science, 13, 1967.

Fishburn, P.C., Semi-orders and risky choices, Journal of Mathematical Psychology, 5, 1968.

Fishburn, P.C., Utility theory, Management Science, 14, 1968.

Fishburn, P.C., A general theory of subjective probabilities and expected utilities, Annals of mathematical statistics, 40, 1969.

Fishburn, P.C., A study of independence in multivariate utility theory, Econometrica, 37, no. 1, 1969.

Fishburn, P.C., Utility theory for decision making, Wilry, New York, 1970.

Fishburn, P.C., Intransitive indifference with unequal indifference intervals, Journal of Mathematical Psychology, 7, 1970.

Fishburn, P.C., Utility theory with inexact preferences and degrees of preference, in Synthese, D. Reidel Publishing Co., Dordrecht, Holland, 1970.

Fishburn, P.C., A mixture set axiomatization of conditional subjective expected utility, Econometrica, 41, no. 1, 1973.

Fishburn, P.C., Choice functions of finite sets, International Economic Review, 15, 1974.

Fishburn, P.C., Axioms for lexicographic preferences, Review of Economic Studies, 1975.

Fishburn, P.C., On the nature of expected utility, Theory and decision supplementary volume on rational decisions under uncertainty, 1975.

Fishburn, P.C., Semi-orders and choice functions, Econometrica, 43, 1975.

Fishburn, P.C., Bounded one-way expected utilities, Econometrica, 43, 1975.

Fishburn, P.C., Representable choice functions, Econometrica, 44, 1976.

Fishburn, P.C. and Porter, R.B., Optimal portfolios with one safe and one risky asset: Effects of changes in rate of return and risk, vol. 22, 1976.

Friedman, M. and Savage, L.J., The utility analysis of choices involving risk, Journal of Political Economy, 56, 1948.

Friedman, M. and Savage, L.J., The expected utility hypothesis and the measurability of utility, Journal of Political Economy, 60, 1952.

Frish, R., Dynamic utility, Econometrica, vol. 32, no. 3, 1964.

Galbraith, J.F.K., The new industrial state. Traduction française: Le nouvel état industriel, Gallimard, Paris.

Georgescu-Roegen, N., The pure theory of consumer's behavior, Quarterly Journal of Economics, vol. 50, 1936.

Georgescu-Roegen, N., Threshold in choice and the theory of demand, Econometrica, vol. 26, 1958.

Ghez, G. and Becker, G., The allocation of time and goods over the life cycle, National Bureau for Economics Research, New York, 1975.

Gintis, M., Welfare criteria with endogenous preferences: The economics of education, International Economic Review, 15, 1974.

Gorman, W.M., Separable utility and aggregation, Econometrica, 27, 1959.

Gorman, W.M., Tastes, habits and choices, International Economic Review, 8, 1967.

Gorman, W.M., The structure of utility functions, Review of Economic Studies, 1968.

Grandmont, J.M. and Younes, Y., On the role of money and the existence of a monetary equilibrium, Review of Economic Studies, 1972.

Grandmont, J.M., Short-run equilibrium analysis in a monetary economy, in J. Dreze (ed.), Allocation under uncertainty, equilibrium and optimality, Macmillan, 1973.

Grandmont, J.M., Laroque, G., Equilibres temporaires keynesiens, Séminaire d'Econométrie, C.N.R.S., 1973.

Grandmont, J.M., Laroque, G., On money and banking, Review of Economic Studies, 1975.

Grandmont, J.M., Laroque, G., Younes, Y., Disequilibrium allocations and recontracting, Technical Report, no. 186, 1975.

Grandmont, J.M., Laroque, G., Younes, Y., Equilibres avec rationnement et théorie des jeux, Séminaire d'Econométrie, C.N.R.S., 1976.

Grandmont, J.M., Laroque, G., On temporary keynesian equilibria, Review of Economic Studies, 1976.

Green, J.R., Temporary general equilibrium in a sequential trading model with spot and future transactions, Econometrica, 41, 1973.

Groves, T., Incentives in teams. Econometrica, 41, 1973.

Hahn, F., Savings under uncertainty, Review of Economic Studies, 1970.

Hahn, F., Equilibrium with transactions costs, Econometrica, 39, 1971.

Hakanson, N., Optimal investment and consumption strategies for a class of utility functions, Econometrica, 1970.

Hammond, P.J., Changing tastes and coherent dynamic choice, Review of Economic Studies, 1976.

Haque, W., Samuelson's self-dual preferences, Econometrica, 43, 1975.

Hartley, R., Aspects of partial decision making, Kernels of quasi-ordered sets, Econometrica, 44, 1976.

Hausner, M., Multidimensional utilities, in R.M. Thrall, C.M. Coombs and R.L. Davies (eds.), Decision processes, Wiley, New York, 1954.

Heller, W.P. and Starr, R.M., Equilibrium with on-convex transactions costs: Monetary and nonmonetary economics, Review of Economic Studies, 1976.

Herstein, I.N., Milnor, J., An axiomatic approach to measurable utility, Econometrica, 21, 1953.

Herzberger, H.G., Ordinal preference and rational choice, Econometrica, 41, 1973.

Holt, C.C., Job search, Phillips' wage relation and unions influence: Theory and evidence, in Phelps et al. (eds.), Microeconomic foundations of employment and inflation theory, W.W. Norton and Company, New York, 1970.

Holt, C.C., How can the Phillips curve be moved to reduce both inflation and unemployment?, in Phelps et al. (eds.), Microeconomic foundations of employment and inflation theory, W.W. Norton and Company, New York, 1970.

Houthakker, M.S., The present state of consumption theory, Econometrica, 29, no. 4, 1961.

Hurwicz, L., Radner, R., Reiter, S., A stochastic decentralized resource allocation process, Part I and II, Econometrica, vol. 43, no. 2 and no. 3, 1975.

d'Iribarne, P., Consommation, prestige et efficacité économique, Revue d'Economie Politique, Paris, 1969.

d'Iribarne, P., La consommation et le bien-être, Approche psychosocio-économique, Revue d'Economie Politique, Paris, 1972.

d'Iribarne, P., La politique du bonheur, Le Seuil, Paris, 1973.

Ishikawa, T., Family structures and family values in the theory of income distribution. Journal of Political Economy, 83, 1975.

Jacquet-Lagreze, E., How can we use the notion of semi-orders to build outranking relations in multicriteria decision making? Metra, Direction Scientifique, note no. 189, 1973.

Jaffray, J.Y., Existence of a continuous utility function: An elementary proof, Econometrica, 43, 1975.

Jamison, D.T., Lau, L.J., Semi-orders and the theory of choice, Econometrica, 41, no. 5, 1973.

Jones-Lee, Price-influenced utility functions: a note, Econometrica, 39, 1971.

Kalman, P.J., Dusansky, R., Wickström, B.A., On the major Slutsky properties when money is the sole medium of exchange, International Economic Review, 15, 1974.

Kalman, P.J., Theory of consumer behavior when prices enter the utility function, Econometrica, 36, no. 3–4, 1968.

Katona, G., Psychological analysis of economic behavior, MacGraw-Hill, New York, 1951.

Katona, G., Consumer behavior: Theory and findings on expectations and aspirations, American Economic Review, 58, 1968.

Katona, G., Theory of expectations, in B. Strumpel, J.N. Morgan and E. Zahn (eds.), Human behavior in economic affairs, Elsevier, Amsterdam, 1972.

Katona, G., The human factor in economic affairs, in A. Campbell and P.E. Converse (eds.), The human meaning of social change, Russell Sage Foundation, New York, 1972.

Katona, G., Psychological economics, Elsevier, New York, 1975.

Keeney, R.L., Utility functions for multiattributed consequences, Management Science, vol. 18, no. 5, Part I, 1972.

Keeney, R.L., Decomposition of multiattribute utility functions, Research Seminar on Decision Theory, Beaulieu Sainte-Assise, 1973.

Keeney, R.L., Concepts of independence in multiattribute utility theory, in Cochrane and Zeleny, 1973.

Keeney, R.L., Risk independence and multiattributed utility functions, Econometrica, 41, 1973.

Klein, L.R., Rubin, H., A constant utility index of the cost of living, The Review of Economic Studies, 1948.

Klevmarken, A., Quigley, J.M., Age, experience, earnings and investment in human capital, Journal of Political Economy, 84, 1976.

Kolm, S.Ch., L'état et le système des prix, Dunod, Paris, 1970.

Kolm, S.Ch., Le service des masses, Dunod, Paris, 1971.

Kolm, S.Ch., Justice et équité, Monographies du Séminaire d'Econométrie, C.N.R.S., Paris, 1972.

Koo, Y.C., Smith, V.E., Consumer decision rules in new demand theory, Paper presented at the World Econometric Congress, Toronto, August 1975.

Koopmans, T.C., Stationary ordinal utility and impatience, Econometrica, 28, 1960.

Koopmans, T.C., Diamond, P.A., Williamson, R.E., Stationary utility and time perspective, Econometrica, 32, 1964.

Kraft, A., Kraft, J., V-Branch: A generalized utility function, Third World Congress of the Econometric Society, Toronto, August 1975.

Krelle, W., Präferenz- und Entscheidungstheorie, J.C.B. Mohr, Tübingen, 1968.

Krelle, W., Production, demande, prix (Vol. I), Gauthier-Villars, 1970.

Krelle, W., Dynamics of the utility function, in J.R. Hides and W. Weber, Carl Menger and the Austrian School of Economics, 1973.

Kroeber-Riel, W., Constructs and empirical basis in theories of economic behavior, Theory and Decision, 1, 1971.

Kurz, M., Arrow-Debreu equilibrium of an exchange economy with transaction cost, International Economic Review, 15, 1974.

Kurz, M., Equilibrium in a finite sequence of markets with transaction cost, Econometrica, 42, 1974.

Lancaster, K., A new approach to consumer theory. Journal of Political Economy, vol 76,.1966.

Lancaster, K., Consumer demand, A new approach, Columbia University Press, New York, 1971.

Leland, H.E., Optimal growth in a stochastic environment, Review of Economic Studies, 1974.

Leland, H.E., Quality choice and competition, Third World Congress of the Econometric Society, Toronto, 1975.

Lesourne, J., A mi-chemin entre la micro et la macroéconomie, Les Cahiers Economiques, 1954.

Lesourne, J., Recherche sur les critères de rentabilité des investissements routiers, Metra, 1963.

Lesourne, J., Le calcul économique, Dunod, Paris, 1964.

Lesourne, J., Les critères de choix en avenir aléatoire, Metra, VII, 1968.

Lesourne, J., Modèles de croissance des entreprises, Dunod, Paris, 1973.

Lesourne, J., Un programme pour la science économique, La Revue Economique, Paris, September 1975.

Lesourne, J., Esquisse d'une théorie de l'individu, Revue d'Economie Politique, 1975.

Lesourne, J., Au-delà de l'équilibre général de concurrence parfaite, Economie Appliquée, 1976.

Lesourne, J., Loue, R., Etudes de planification régionales et urbaines (3 vol.), Dunod, Paris, 1977 (forthcoming).

Levhari, D., Srinivasan, T., Optimal savings under uncertainty, Review of Economic Studies, 1969.

Linder, S.B., The harried leisure class, Columbia University Press, New York, 1970.

Lluch, C., Expenditure, savings and habit formation, International Economic Review, 15, 1974.

Luce, R.D., Semi-orders and a theory of utility discrimination, Econometrica, 24, no. 2, 1956.

Luce, R.D., Two extensions of conjoint measurement, Journal of Mathematical Psychology, no. 3, 1966.

Lusky, R., Consumers' preferences and ecological consciousness, International Economic Review, 16, 1975.

McGuire, J.W., Theories of business behavior, Prentice Hall, Englewood Cliffs, New Jersey, 1964.

Mackay, D.I., Wages and labor turnover, in D. Robinson (ed.), Local labor markets and wage structures, Gower Press, London, 1970.

McNerlove, Household and economy: Toward a new theory of population and economic growth, Journal of Political Economy, 1974.

Malinvaud, E., Younes, Y., Une nouvelle formulation générale pour l'étude des fondements microéconomiques de la macroéconomie, CEPREMAP, INSEE, 1974.

Marris, R., The economic theory of managerial capitalism, Macmillan, London, 1964.

Marschak, J., Rational behavior, uncertain prospects and measurable utility, Econometrica, 1950.

Marschak, J., Elements for a theory of teams, Management Science, 1955.

Marschak, J., Efficient and viable organizational forms, Modern Organisation Theory (Mason Haire Ed.), Wiley, New York, 1959.

Marschak, J., Radner, R., Economic theory of teams, Yale University Press, New Haven, CT, 1972.

Marschak, J., Economic information, Decision and prediction, Selected Essays (3 volumes), D. Reidel Publishing Company, Dordrecht, Holland, 1974.

Marschak, J., Guided soul-searching for multicriterion decisions, Multiple criteria decision making, Kyoto, M. Zeleny (ed.), Springer Verlag, 1975.

Marschak, J., Utilities, psychological values and the training of decision makers, Western Management Science Institute, University of California, Los Angeles, 1975.

Marschak, J., Economics of organizational systems, in man and computers, Marois (ed.), North-Holland, Amsterdam, 1975.

May, O., Intransitivity, utility and the aggregation of preference patterns, Econometrica, vol. 22, 1954.

Meginniss, J.R., Alternatives to the expected utility rule, Unpublished doctoral dissertation in progress at Graduate School of Business, University of Chicago, completion expected, 1976.

Meginniss, J.R., A new class of symmetric utility rules for gambles, subjective marginal probability functions, and a generalized Bayes' rule, Research Paper, 118, Graduate School of Business, New York, 1976.

Menuet, J., Quasi-ordres et modélisation des préférences, METRA, Direction Scientifique, note no. 197, 1974.

Miller, B.L., Optimal consumption with a stochastic income stream, Econometrica, 1974.

Mirrlees, J.A., An exploration in the theory of optimum income taxation, Review of Economic Studies, 1971.

Mirrlees, J.A., Population policy and the taxation of family size, Journal of Public Economics, 1, 1972.

Mirrlees, J.A., Optimal commodity taxation in a two-class economy, Journal of Public Economics, 4, 1975.

de Montbrial, T., Une nouvelle formalisation de l'utilité de la monnaie, Séminaire d'Econométrie du C.N.R.S., Séance du lundi 22 janvier 1973.

de Montgolfier, J., Tergny, J., Les décisions partiellement rationnalisables, METRA, vol. X, no. 2, 1971.

Mortensen, D.T., A theory of wage and employment dynamics, in Phelps et al. (eds.), 1970.

Mourre, B., Redistribution, biens tutélaires et capital humain, Aspects théoriques, C.N.R.S., Séminaire d'Econométrie de R. Roy et E. Malinvaud, Séance du 29 janvier 1973.

Murphy, R.E. Jr., Adaptive processes in economic systems, Academic Press, New York, 1965.

Nash, J.F., Noncooperative games, Annals of Mathematics, 1951.

Nickell, S.J., Wage structures and quit rates, International Economic Review, 17, 1976.

Ordover, J.A., Distributive justice and optimal taxation of wages and interest in a growing economy, Journal of Public Economics, 5, 1976.

Pazner, E.A., Scheidler, D., Competitive analysis under complete ignorance, International Economic Review, 16, 1975.

Peleg, B., Utility functions for partially ordered topological spaces, Econometrica, 38, no. 1, 1970.

Penrose, E., The theory of the growth of the firm, Wiley, New York, 1959.

Perroux, F., Unités actives et mathématiques nouvelles. Dunod, Paris, 1975.

Pething, R.M., Environmental management in general equilibrium: a new incentive compatible approach. Paper presented at the Econometric Meeting of the Econometric Society, Helsinki, August 1976.

Phelps, E.S., The accumulation of risky capital: A sequential analysis, Econometrica, 30, 1962.

Phelps, E.S., et al. (eds.), Microeconomic foundations of employment and inflation theory, W.W. Norton, New York, 1970.

Phelps, E.S., Inflation policy and unemployment theory: The cost benefit approach to monetary planning, McMillan, New York, 1972.

Plott, C.R., Little, J.T., Parks, R.P., Individual choice when objects have "ordinal" properties, Review of Economic Studies, 1975.

Pollak, R.A., Consistent Planning, Review of Economic Studies, 1968.

Pollak, R.A., Habit formation and dynamic demand functions, Journal of Political Economy, 78, 1970.

Pollak, R.A., Generalized separability, Econometrica, 40, 1973.

Pollak, R.A., The risk independence axiom, Econometrica, 41, 1973.

Pollak, R.A., Wachter, M.L., The relevance of the threshold production function and its implications for the allocation of time, Journal of Political Economy, 83, 1975.

Radner, R.A., A behavioral model of cost reduction. The Bell Journal of Economics, vol. 6, no. 1, 1975.

Radner, R.A., Rothschild, M., On the allocation of effort, Journal of Economic Theory, vol. 10, no. 3, 1975.

Ramsey, J.B., Limiting functional forms for market demand curves, Econometrica, 40, 1972.

Robbins, L., Essai sur la nature et la signification de la science économique (French translation: 1947).

Roy, B., Classement et choix en présence de points de vue multiples, Revue d'Informatique et de Recherche Opérationnelle, no. 8, 1968.

Roy, B., Décisions avec critères multiples: Problèmes et méthodes, METRA, vol. XI, no. 1, 1972.

Roy, B., How outranking relations helps multiple criteria decision making. Selected proceedings of a seminar on multicriteria decision making, University of South Carolina Press, Columbia, SC, 1973.

Roy, B., Critères multiples et modélisation des préférences. L'apport des relations de surclassement, METRA, Note de la Direction Scientifique, no. 74, 1973.

Roy, B., La modélisation des préférences: Un aspect crucial de l'aide à la décision, METRA, XIII, 1974.

Ryder, Jr., H.E., Optimal accumulation under intertemporally dependent utility, Institute for Mathematical Studies in the Social Sciences, 1971.

Sadka, E., On income distribution, incentive effects and optimal income taxation, Review of Economic Studies, 1976.

Samuelson, P.A., Foundations of economic analysis, Harvard University Press, Cambridge, MA, 1948.

Samuelson, P.A., Using full duality to show that simultaneously additive direct and indirect utilities imply unitary price elasticity of demand, Econometrica, 33, 1965.

Sandmo, A., Public good and the technology of consumption, Review of Economic Studies, 1973.

Sandmo, A., Public goods and the technology of consumption: A correction, Review of Economic Studies, 1975.

Sandmo, A., Portfolio theory – Asset demand and taxation: Comparative statics with many assets. European Meeting of Econometric Society, Helsinki, August 1976.

Saposnik, R., Power, the economic environment and social choice, Econometrica, 42, 1974.

Sato, E., Self dual preferences, Econometrica, 44, 1976.
Savage, L.J., The foundations of statistics, Wiley, New York, 1954.
Scarf, H., The computation of economic equilibria, Yale University Press, New Haven, CT, 1973.
Schelling (ed.), Symposium: Time in economic life, The Quarterly Journal of Economics, vol. 87, 1973.
Scott, D., Suppes, P., Foundational aspects of theories of measurement, Journal of Symbolic Logic, 23, 1958.
Selected proceedings of a seminar on multicriteria decision making, Columbia, University of South Carolina Press, Columbia, SC, 1973.
de Serpa, A.C., A theory of the economics of time, The Economic Journal, no. 324, 1971.
Shafer, W.J., The non transitive consumer, Econometrica, 42, 1974.
Shakun, M.F. (ed.), Game theory and gaming, Management Science, 18, 1972.
Shubik, M., Games for society, Business and war, Elsevier, 1975.
Sonnenschein, H.F., Demand theory without transitive preferences, with applications to the theory of competitive equilibrium, in J.S. Chipman, L. Hurwicz, M.K. Richter, H.H. Sonnenschein, Preferences, utility and demand, Harcourt Brace Jovanovich, New York, 1975.
Soulie, D., Pouvoir et théorie des alliances, Revue d'Economie Politique, 1974.
Stigum, B.P., Finite state space and expected utility maximization, Econometrica, vol. 40, no. 2, 1972.
Strotz, R.H., The empirical implications of a utility tree, Econometrica, 25, 1957.
Strotz, R.H., The utility tree, A correction and further appraisal, Econometrica, 27, no. 3, 1959.
Suppes, P. and Winet, M., An axiomatization of utility based on the notion of utility differences, Management Science, 1, 1955.
Suppes, P., Behavioristic foundations of utility, Econometrica, vol. 29, no. 2, 1961.
Suppes, P., Zinnes, L.J., Basic measurement theory, in R.D. Luce, R.R. Bush and E. Galanter (eds.), Handbook of mathematical psychology, Wiley, New York, 1963.
Sweeney, J.L., Quality, commodity hierarchies and housing markets, Econometrica, 42, 1974.
Taylor, C.A., The precautionary demand for money: A utility maximization approach.
Theil, H., Theory and measurement of consumer demand (2 vols.), North-Holland, Amsterdam, 1975.
Thom, R., Stabilité structurelle et morphogénèse, W.A. Benjamin, Reading, MA, 1972.
Thrall, R.M., Coombs, C.H., Davis, R.L., Decision Processes, John Wiley, New York, 1960.
Tintner, G., La théorie des choix dans le cas des utilités interdépendantes, C.N.R.S., Séminaire d'Econométrie, Paris, mai 1957.
Tversky, A., On the elicitation of preferences: Descriptive and prescriptive considerations, Workshop on decision making with multiple conflicting objectives, IIASA, Laxenburg, 1975.
Uzawa, H., Preference and rational choice in the theory of consumption, in K.J. Arrow, S. Kaplin, P. Suppes (eds.), Mathematical methods in the social sciences. Stanford University Press, 1959.
Von Neumann, J. and Morgenstern, O., Theory of games and economic behavior, Princeton University Press, Princeton, NJ, 1947.
Von Weizsäcker, C.C., Notes on endogenous changes in tastes, Journal of Economic Theory, 1971.
Wagstaff, P., A benthamite wages policy, Review of Economic Studies, 1975.
Wallace, T.D., Ihnen, L.A., Full-time schooling in life-cycle models of human capital

accumulation, Journal of political Economy, 83, 1975.

Waud, R.N., Asymmetric policy maker utility functions and optimal policy under uncertainty, Econometrica, vol. 44, 1976.

Weiss, Y., The wealth effect in occupational choice, International Economic Review, 17, 1976.

Wendt, D., Vlek, C. (eds.), Utility, probability and human decision making. D. Reidel Publishing Company, Dordrecht, Holland, 1975.

Williamson, O.E., A model of rational managerial behavior, in R.M. Cyert, J.G. March, A behavioral theory of the firm, Prentice Hall, Englewood Cliffs, NJ, 1963.

Yew-Kwang Ng, Bentham or Bergson? Finite sensibility, utility functions and social welfare, Review of Economic studies, 1975.

Younes, Y., On the role of money in the process of exchange and the existence of a nonwalrasian equilibrium, Review of Economic Studies, 1975.

Zabel, E., Consumer choice, portfolio decisions and transaction costs.

Zusman, P., The incorporation and measurement of social power in economic models, International Economic Review, 17.

Bibliography from other human sciences

Albou, P., Besoins et motivations économiques, Presses Universitaires de France, Paris, 1976.

Almond, G.A. and Powell, G., Comparative politics, A developmental approach, Little, Brown, Boston, 1966.

de Backer, P., Description d'un modèle de diagnostic des ressources humaines, METRA XII, 1973.

de Backer, P., Analyse des conflits dans les organisations, METRA, 1974.

Bastide, R.G., Sociologie et psychanalyse. Presses Universitaires de France, Paris, 1972.

Bazykin, A.D., Structural and dynamic stability of models of predator–prey systems, IIASA, Laxenburg, 1976.

Benedict, R., The patterns of culture, Boston, 1934.

Bhattacharya, R.N. and Majumdar, M., Random exchange economies, Journal of economic theory, 6, 1973.

Block, M.D. and Marschak, J., Random orderings and stochastic theories of responses, in I. Olkin et al. (eds.), Contributions to probability and statistics, Stanford University Press, Stanford, CA, 1960.

Bock, R.D. and Jones, L.V., The measurement and prediction of judgment and choice, Holden-Day, San Francisco, 1968.

Boulding, K.E., L'économie et les sciences du comportement: Une frontière déserte?, Diogène, July, 1965.

Bowlby, J., Attachment and loss (3 volumes), The Hogarth Press and the Institute of Psychoanalysis, 1970.

Buckley, W., Sociology and modern systems theory, Prentice Hall, Englewood Cliffs, NJ, 1967.

Buckley, W. (ed.), Modern systems research for the behavioral scientist, Aldine Publishing Company, Chicago, 1968.

Buser, P., Fonctions nerveuses, in: Physiologie, Encyclopédie de la Pléïade, Gallimard, Paris, 1969.

Bush, R.R. and Mosteller, F., Stochastic models of learning, Wiley, New York, 1955.

Cattell, R.B., Description and measurement of personality, Harper and Company, London, 1946.

Cattell, R.B., Personality, motivation structure and measurement, World Book Company, New York, 1957.

Centre de Royaumont, L'unité de l'homme, Le Seuil, Paris, 1974.

Chauvin, R., Psychophysiologie, Volume II, Le comportement animal, Masson, Paris, 1969.

Cooper, W.W., Leavitt, H.J., Shelly, M.W., New Perspectives in organisation research, J. Wiley, New York, 1964.

Crozier, M., La Société bloquée, Le Seuil, Paris, 1970.

Dahl, R.A., Modern political analysis, Prentice Hall, Englewood Cliffs, NJ, 1963-1970.

Delmas, A., Voies et centres nerveux, Masson, Paris, 1970.

Deutsch, E., L'étude psychosociologique du distributeur, METRA, vol. 2, 1963.

Devereux, G., Essais d'ethnopsychiatrie générale, Gallimard, Paris, 1970.

Eccles, J.C., Brain and conscious experience, Springer Verlag, 1966.

Eibl-Eibesfeldt, Ethologie, Biologie du comportement, Naturalia et biologa, Editions scientifiques, Paris, 1972.

Eysenck, H.J., Dimensions of personality, Kegan Paul, London, 1947.

Eysenck, H.J., The structure of human personality, Methuen and Company, London, 1960.

Faverge, J.M., Recherche et traitement des informations dans l'étude de motivation, METRA, vol. 2, no. 2, 1963.

Fayol, H., Industrial and general administration, London, 1930.

Fisk, G., The psychology of management decision, The second symposium of the college on management psychology of the Institute of management sciences, Philadelphia and Vienna, Sept. 1965, Gleerup Publishers, Sweden, 1967.

Fortet, R. and Le Boulanger, H., Eléments pour une synthèse sur les systèmes à auto-organisation, METRA, 12, 1967.

Fraisse, P. and Piaget, J., Traité de psychologie expérimentale (9 volumes) Presses Universitaires de France, Paris, 1963: (1) Histoire et méthode, (2) Sensation et motricité, (3) Psychophysiologie du comportement, (4) Apprentissage et mémoire, (5) Motivation, émotion et personnalité, (6) La perception, (7) L'intelligence, (8) Langage, communication et décision, (9) Psychologie sociale.

Freud, A., Le moi et les mécanismes de défense, Paris, 1949.

Freud, S., Complete works, 24 volumes, The Hogarth press and the Institute of Psycho-analysis, London, 1955.

Freud, S., Malaise dans la civilisation, Presses Universitaires de France, Paris, 1971.

Freud, S., Totem et tabou, Payot, Paris.

Fromm, E., The anatomy of human destructiveness, Holt, Rinehart and Winston, New York, 1973.

Georgescu-Roegen, N., The pure theory of consumer's behavior, The quarterly journal of Economics, 50, 1936.

Gouldner, A.W., Patterns of industrial bureaucracy, Glencoe, 3, 1954.

Guilford, J.P., Personality, McGraw-Hill, New York, 1959.

Hall, C.S. and Lindzey, G., Theories of personality, Wiley, New York, 1957.

Harary, F. and Norman, R.Z., Graph theory as a mathematical model in social science, Institute for social research, Ann Arbor, MI, 1953.

Herzberg, F., Mausner, B., Snydermann, B., The motivation to work, Wiley, New York, 1959.

Hildenbrand, W., Random preferences and equilibrium analysis, Journal of Economic theory, 3, 1971.

Joannis, P., De l'étude de motivation à la création publicitaire, Dunod, Paris, 1965.

Kardiner, A., The psychological frontiers of society, New York, 1945.

Kardiner, A., The individual and his society, New York, 1969.

Kayser, C., Physiologie: Système nerveux, muscle, Flammarion, Paris, 1969.

Klein, M., Essais de psychanalyse, Payot, Paris, 1972.

Koestler, A., Le cri d'Archimède, Calmann-Lévy, Paris, 1964.

Koestler, A., Le cheval dans la locomotive, Calmann-Lévy, Paris, 1967.

Kotler, Ph., Marketing management, Prentice-Hall, Englewood Cliffs, NJ, 1967.

Krantz, D.H., Luce, R.D., Suppes, P., Tversky, A., Foundations of measurement, vol. I, Additive and polynomial representations, Academic Press, New York, 1971.

Krantz, D.H., Luce, R.D., Atkinson, R.C., Suppes, P., Contemporary developments in mathematical psychology, Measurement, psychophysics and neural information processing, W.H. Freeman and company, San Francisco, 1974.

Laborit, H., Physiologie humaine cellulaire et organique, Masson, Paris, 1961.

Laborit, H., L'aggressivité détournée, Introduction à une biologie du comportement social, Union générale d'éditions, Paris, 1970.

Laborit, H., L'homme et la ville, Flammarion, Paris, 1971.

Laing, R.D., The self and others, Further studies in sanity and madness, 1961.

Laplanche, J. and Pontalis, J.B., Vocabulaire de la psychanalyse, Presses Universitaires de France, Paris, 1967.

Lasswell, H.D., Psychopathology and politics, Chicago, 1930.

Lazorthes, G., Le système nerveux central, Masson, Paris, 1967.

Lesourne, J., Les systèmes du destin, Dalloz, Paris, 1976.

Lewin, K., Psychologie dynamique, recueil publié par C. Faucheux, Presses Universitaires de France, Paris, 1967.

Lorenz, K., Evolution et modification du comportement, L'inné et l'acquis, Payot, Paris, 1967.

Lorenz, K., L'agression, Une histoire naturelle du mal, Flammarion, Paris, 1969.

Lorenz, K., Essais sur le comportement animal et humain. Les leçons de l'évolution de la théorie du comportement, Le Seuil, Paris, 1970.

Luce, R.D. and Raiffa, H., Games and decisions, Wiley, New York, 1957.

Luce, R.D., Individual choice behavior, A theoretical analysis, Wiley, New York, 1959.

Luce, R.D., Bush, R.R., Galanter, E., Handbook of mathematical psychology (3 volumes), Wiley, New York, 1963–1965.

Luce, R.D., Bush, R.R., Galanter, E. (eds.), Readings in mathematical psychology (2 volumes), Wiley, New York, 1963.

Luce, R.D., Suppes, P., Preference, utility and subjective probability, in R.D. Luce, R.R. Bush, E. Galanter (eds.), Handbook of mathematical Psychology, Wiley, New York, 1965.

Manski, C.P., The structure of random utility models, Third World Congress of the Econometric society, Toronto, August 1975.

March, J.G. and Simon, H.A., Organizations, Wiley, New York, 1958.

Marcus-Steiff, J., Les études de motivation, Hermann, Paris, 1960.

Marschak, J., Binary choice constraints and random utility indicators in K. Arrow, S. Karlin and P. Suppes (eds.), Mathematical methods in the social sciences, 1959, Stanford University Press, Stanford, CA, 1960.

Maslow, A., Motivation and personality, Harper and Row, New York, 1954.

McFadden, D., Economic applications of psychological choice models, Third World Congress of the Econometric society, Toronto, August 1975.

Mendel, G., La révolte contre le père, Payot, Paris, 1968.

Mendel, G., La crise de générations, Payot, Paris, 1969.

Mendel, G., Anthropologie différentielle, Payot, Paris.

Meili, R., La structure de la personnalité, in Fraisse P., Piaget J., Traité de psychologie expériementale, Presses Universitaires de France, Paris, 1968.

Merton, R.K., Social theory and social structure, Glencoe, Illinois, 1957.

Morin, P., Organisation du changement et changement de l'organisation, METRA, XII, 1973.

Morin, E., Le paradigme perdu: La nature humaine, Le Seuil, Paris, 1973.

Moscovici, S., La Société contre nature, Union Générale d'éditions, Paris, 1972.

Mossin, A., Elements of a stochastic theory of consumption, The Swedish Journal of Economics, 70, 1968.

Nacht, S., La théorie psychanalytique, Presses Universitaires de France, Paris, 1969.

Newcomb, T., An Approach to the study of communicative acts, Psychological Review, 60, 1953.

Newcomb, T., The prediction of interpersonal attraction, American Psychologist, 11, 1956.

Nuttin, J., La motivation, in: Fraisse P., Piaget J., Traité de Psychologie expérimentale, Presses Universitaires de France, Paris, 1968.

Palmade, G. (ed.), L'économique et les sciences humaines (2 volumes), Dunod, Paris, 1967.

Parsons, T., An outline of the social system, in: T. Parsons, E. Shils, K. Naegele, J.R. Pitts (eds.), Theories of society, The Free Press, New York, 1961.

Piaget, J., La formation du symbôle chez l'enfant, Delachaux et Niestlé, Neuchâtel, 1945.

Piaget, J., La construction du réel chez l'enfant, Delachaux et Niestlé, Neuchâtel, 1945.

Piaget, J., Psychologie de l'intelligence, Armand Colin, Paris, 1949.

Piaget, J. (ed.), Logique et connaissance scientifique, Encyclopédie de la Pléïade, Paris, 1967.

Piaget, J. (with Inhelder, B.), La genèse des structures logiques élémentaires, Delachaux et Niestlé, Neuchâtel, 1968.

Piaget, J., La naissance de l'intelligence chez l'enfant, Delachaux et Niestlé, Neuchâtel, 1968.

Quandt, R.E., A probabilistic theory of consumers behavior, The Quarterly Journal of Economics, 70, 1956.

Rapoport, A., Mathematical models of social interactions, in: Luce R.D., Bush R.R., Galanter E., Handbook of mathematical psychology, Wiley, New York, 1963.

Reynaud, P.L., Précis de psychologie économique, Presses Universitaires de France, Paris, 1974.

Ribeill, G., Modèles et sciences humaines, METRA 12, 1973.

Rohein, G., Psychanalyse et anthropologie, Gallimard, Paris, 1962.

Sattah, S. and Tversky, A., Unite and conquer: A multiplicative inequality for choice probabilities, Econometrica, 44, 1976.

Segal, H., Introduction to the work of Melanie Klein, William Heinemann, Medical Books, London, 1964.

Selznick, P., Foundations of the theory of organization, American Sociological Review, 1948.

Simon, H.A., Models of man, Wiley, New York, 1957.

Simon, H.A., Administrative behavior, Macmillan, Cambridge, MA, New York, 1958.

Simon, H.A., The science of the artificial, MIT Press, 1969.

Simon, H.A., Theories of bounded rationality, in: C.B. McGuire and R. Radner (eds.), Decision and organization, North-Holland, Amsterdam, 1972.

Spitz, R.A., De la naissance à la parole, la première année de la vie, Presses Universitaires de France, Paris, 1968.

Spitz, R.A., Le non et le oui, Presses Universitaires de France, Paris.

Suppes, P. and Atkinson, R.C., Markov learning models for multiperson interactions, Stanford University Press, Stanford, CA, 1960.

Tversky, A., Elimination by aspects: A theory of choice, Psychological review, 79, 1972.

Tversky, A., Choice by elimination, Journal of mathematical psychology, 9, 1972.

UNESCO, Tendances principales de la recherche dans les sciences sociales et humaines,

Partie I: Sciences sociales, Chapitre III: La psychologie by Jean Piaget, Mouton, Paris, 1970.

Urwick, L., The elements of administration, New York, 1963.

Vroom, V.H., Work and motivation, Wiley, New York, 1964.

Watzlawick, P., Helmick-Beavin, J., Jackson, D., Pragmatics of human communication. A study of interactional patterns, pathologies and paradoxes, W.W. Norton, New York, 1962.

Zazzo, R. (ed.), L'attachement, Delachaux et Niestlé, Neuchâtel, 1974.

AUTHOR INDEX

SUBJECT INDEX